PETER FLE...

A Biography

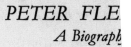

DUFF HART-DAVIS

PETER FLEMING
A Biography

Oxford   New York
OXFORD UNIVERSITY PRESS
1987

Oxford University Press, Walton Street, Oxford OX2 6DP

Oxford New York Toronto
Delhi Bombay Calcutta Madras Karachi
Petaling Jaya Singapore Hong Kong Tokyo
Nairobi Dar es Salaam Cape Town
Melbourne Auckland
and associated companies in
Beirut Berlin Ibadan Nicosia

Oxford is a trade mark of Oxford University Press

First published 1974 by Jonathan Cape Ltd.
First issued as an Oxford University Press paperback 1987

British Library Cataloguing in Publication Data
Hart-Davis, Duff
Peter Fleming: a biography.—(Oxford lives).
1. Fleming, Peter—Biography 2. Authors,
English—20th century—Biography
I. Title
910'.92'4 PR6011.L47Z/
ISBN 0–19–282034–6

Printed in Great Britain by
Richard Clay Ltd.
Bungay, Suffolk

*For Peter's
family*

Contents

Illustrations

Maps

I

In Those Days

'With the possible exception of the Equator,' wrote Peter Fleming in a typical throw-away line at the start of his book *One's Company*, 'everything begins somewhere'; and his own life began at ten minutes to midnight on May 31st, 1907, when he was born at 27 Green Street, off Park Lane, the first child of Valentine Fleming and his strikingly beautiful wife Eve. He was christened Robert Peter, the first name being that of his grandfather.

The family, though recently established, was rich and powerful. Val, then twenty-eight, was working in the City (which he hated) but his salary was relatively unimportant, for when he was twenty-one he had been given a quarter of a million pounds by his father. Besides the house in London he owned a modest estate in Oxfordshire, and his parents had a much larger estate near by. Peter was thus born into a solid, spacious world, and from his first conscious moments he must have been aware of big houses full of servants—maids, butlers, nannies and governesses, and, outside, gardeners, chauffeurs, grooms and gamekeepers: whole private kingdoms in which life seemed immutably secure.

And yet, in spite of all this material comfort and solidity, most of his early childhood was dominated by a strange illness which persistently defied diagnosis and cure. From the age of a year he was plagued by some form of colitis which produced violent sickness and pains in the stomach. On one occasion, according to later legend, he vomited continuously for fourteen hours. As the months dragged by, one doctor after another retired baffled, and his young parents became increasingly afraid that their son was doomed to be a chronic invalid.

In a fragment of autobiography entitled *In Those Days*, written and

13

left unpublished more than half a century later, Peter recalled some of the highlights of his malady:

> At one stage my grandmother, a lady of strong will, got it into her head that all would be well if my appendix were removed, and a quorum of medical advisers, who were by now very numerous, were badgered into recommending this experiment. The operation, which was carried out in a London nursing-home during a heat-wave, disclosed that, whatever was wrong with the rest of me, my appendix was in tip-top condition; and the episode, of which I have nightmare memories, for some reason left me with an uncontrollable stammer ...
>
> It was the good Doctor Comma (if that is how he spelt his name) who finally put an end to my intermittent visits to death's door. A small man, fairly closely resembling a marmoset, he practised in Lausanne, and to the Hotel Beaurivage in that city my mother took me for four spells of treatment, each lasting almost a month. To begin with my stomach was X-rayed every day, its owner standing on a contraption rather like a railway station weighing-machine while lights mysteriously flashed; later a sort of geological map of the stomach's contents was produced ...
>
> On the second or third visit to Lausanne I was put on a series of diets so rigorous that there can have been little or nothing for the X-ray to record, but at the end of the fourth I was encouraged to eat anything—absolutely *anything*—I wanted, and as much of it as I liked. No ill effects ensuing, I was adjudged to have been cured; and funnily enough I had been ...
>
> I was still under the stigma of being 'delicate', and for some time had to undergo the monthly ordeal of *désinfection*. This consisted of being required, first thing in the morning, to swallow a dessert-spoonful of viscous red medicine with an unimaginably loathsome taste, after which I had to drink a cup of tea ... For the rest of the day until tea-time nothing—not even water—was allowed to pass my lips, and, in summer especially, I learnt in a very mild form one of the harsh lessons in stoicism which are part of the curriculum for small children who live in drought-prone parts of the world.

Peter himself believed that his long illness had permanent effects on him, both physical and mental. The stammer soon wore off, but as a child he was always small for his age, and he grew up shorter than any of his three younger brothers, the only one under six foot. Another curious result was that he emerged with very little sense of taste and absolutely none of smell (once, years later, while he was flighting duck, his pipe set fire to the rubber lining of his jacket-pocket, and he remained unaware of the devastating stench that seriously disconcerted the gun in the next hide a hundred yards away). To his sickly childhood, also, many of his friends later ascribed his phenomenal appetite for exercise: in persistently driving himself to the limit, they believed, he was subconsciously compensating for the weakness of his boyhood.

The mental effects, he considered, were equally long-lasting:

> I suspect that my childhood ailments, and the semi-convalescence that followed them, helped to make me rather a solitary person and to immunize me—partially, at any rate—against the devastating pangs of loneliness. A chronically sick child spends of necessity a long time by himself; and the road to recovery is milestoned—at least it was in my case—by embargoes on and warnings against gregarious activity. One did not go to children's parties because one was on a diet, one might get over-tired or over-excited; one had a *tête-à-tête* (and at Christmas-time a box of crackers) with Nanny.

Solitary Peter certainly was: throughout his life he remained intensely individualistic, a tightly enclosed person, a loner. It seems certain that the privations of his first six or seven years strongly reinforced his most deep-rooted natural characteristic—shyness—and encouraged him always to conceal his emotions behind a façade of imperturbability.

Miraculously, however, his wretched start never stunted, let alone broke, his ebullient sense of humour. As a child he was constantly laughing, constantly making jokes. At first the imp in him expressed itself in normal small-boy ways (such as the laying of ambushes for the terrified French governess), but as he grew older his humour became increasingly verbal: cracking jokes, and later writing them, became his chief delight.

The quality which enabled him to survive so buoyantly was simply determination. Later in life many people supposed that his success as traveller and author came without any effort on his part, the result of his great natural gifts. Far from it: he achieved what he did by means of steely will-power and extraordinary self-control. His modesty led him always to conceal the effort he was making; yet his affected nonchalance could never quite contain the exceptional force of his personality. Even while he was a boy this was apparent: not merely grown-ups, but other children too, involuntarily felt the power that emanated from him.

The origins of this power are not hard to discern, for both his parents were strong characters.

His father Val was a tall man of enormous energy, but as gentle as he was robust. His strong sense of duty was never offensive, for he had the great gift of attracting friendship from every class of people among whom he moved. Farmers and stalkers liked and admired him, but so did senior statesmen. Among the friends who rejoiced in his company was Winston Churchill: to him Val was 'always a gay and gallant companion'. Another close comrade was Geoffrey Lawrence (later Lord Oaksey), whom Val made his executor. A third was F. E. Smith; but he, though he knew Val well, used to remark on the reserve within which he (like Peter after him) always kept his inner self hidden.

At Eton Val rowed in the Eight, and he would have rowed for Oxford too, had he not been smitten by a boil at the critical moment. His passion for physical exercise found many outlets: a keen deer-stalker, game-shot and fisherman, and a first-class rider to hounds, he also kept his own pack of Beagles, and then one of Bassets, and played tennis and squash whenever he could devise no other way of stretching his muscles. Though never by any means an intellectual, he wrote amusingly with a spirited turn of phrase.

At Oxford Val read law, but he never practised at the Bar, and he was working in his father's merchant bank when Peter was born. That same year, however, he was adopted as the Conservative and Unionist parliamentary candidate for the Liberal stronghold of Henley and South Oxfordshire, and in 1910 he was elected to Westminster with a record majority. Cynics remarked that the main reason for his success at the polls was his popularity with the local farmers, and the dashing manner in which he jumped the gates out hunting. Whatever the truth, his victory so incensed Lady Ottoline Morrell, the wife of the defeated Liberal candidate, that she rushed up to Eve Fleming in public and shook her by the lapels of her coat.

Lady Ottoline was by no means the only woman who felt like shaking the former Evelyn Ste Croix Rose. Many more were jealous of her classical good looks—her slender figure, her long, strong face with its wide cheek-bones, huge dark eyes and appropriately roseate complexion.

Her background was relatively sedate. Her father was a solicitor, and *his* father had been solicitor to Disraeli. Her other grandfather was the leading surgeon Sir Richard Quain, and perhaps it was from him that the strange elements in her character came; for in the portrait of him, painted by Millais for the Royal College of Surgeons, there is a hint of devilry, of pent-up exuberance, behind the tightly shut mouth. In any

case, her own generation of the family earned itself such a raffish reputation that her brothers were known as 'the wild Roses', and were for
years carefully kept away from their Fleming nephews in case they
eroded their moral fibre. Eve herself was a startling figure, for she
emphasized her high natural colouring by wearing clothes which would
have been garish even by today's standards, but by those of sixty years
ago were positively staggering. Her rivals and enemies were greatly disconcerted by the violent contradictions in her character: at one moment
she could be tremendously selfish, but at another she would take immense
trouble on her children's behalf. At times rather shrewd, she could also
be exceedingly silly; moreover, she was a snob, and liked to surround
herself with politicians, artists and intellectuals, even though she had no
real interest in the lives which these people lived. Yet, although she
may have looked a fragile, hothouse bloom, she was in fact highly
practical. Like Val, she had immense energy, and she could do almost
anything with her hands—cooking, carpentry, decorating and gardening,
besides the gentler skills of sewing and playing the violin.

Once they had started a family, they added to it steadily: Peter was
followed a year later by Ian, and then, at two-year intervals, by Richard
and Michael. Eve made an excellent mother, for she gave the children
far more time and attention than did most upper-class parents of the
day, the majority of whom were all too glad to leave their offspring to
the mercy of nannies. From an early age Peter was embarrassed by her
eccentricities, and although, as he grew older, he learnt to laugh at them,
he spent much of his school career in dread of the nervous discomfort her
behaviour might create. And yet, in spite of the strain she caused him, he
loved her devotedly.

There already existed in the family a strong tradition of nicknames.
His grandfather Robert was known as 'Pupsie', and Peter unconsciously
maintained the custom by calling his father 'Mokie' (a nursery reference
to the fact that he smoked a pipe) and his mother 'Mie'.

One of Eve's quirks was a penchant for moving house, and when Val
was elected to Parliament she persuaded him to sell 27 Green Street and
buy Pitt House, the white Georgian mansion overlooking Hampstead
Heath in which the Elder Pitt had immured himself when overcome by
melancholia during the 1770s. In the country the Flemings already had a
substantial home in the form of Braziers Park, near the Oxfordshire
village of Ipsden, only four miles from where Val's parents had settled
at Nettlebed.

Braziers nestles in a hollow of the Chilterns where the hills fall
gently towards the Oxford plain. A chunky, Strawberry Hill Gothic,

17

mock-castle of a building, it ought to be ridiculous, so obviously is it not what it pretends to be, so patently fake are its narrow, arched windows and its crenellations. Yet somehow it escapes absurdity—perhaps by virtue of its saucy charm.

The original house, built in 1688, was of straightforward Jacobean design. But at the end of the eighteenth century the whole thing was heavily Gothicized, and by the time Val and Eve bought it another wing had been added. As usual, Eve set to work to remodel the inside, moving the stairs to the other end of the hall and importing fine oak panelling from a church in France for the dining-room and study. As usual, she painted several of the rooms gold. And yet, in spite of her sophisticated aims, she made the house perfect for children: its rooms, especially those upstairs, were pleasantly proportioned, not too big; and the multiplicity of cupboards, staircases, passages, cellars and attics seemed made for games like hide-and-seek. The boys' day- and night-nurseries were on the front of the house, whose windows looked out over the distant plain, and a large playroom at the back housed, among other toys and creatures, Peter's rocking-horse Mushki. Outside, Val had stables for his horses and kennels for his Bassets.

Like his father, Peter proved a real country boy. As soon as his legs were long and strong enough to carry him, he began to explore the beech-woods and the fields, bird-nesting and hunting for snakes, of which he soon became an ardent fancier. If ever Braziers' own land became too familiar, he could resort to the two thousand acres owned by his grandfather at Nettlebed, across the hill to the east.

By the time Peter knew his grandfather, Robert Fleming was already sixty, and in this tall, taciturn figure, with full, white moustache, there can have been little obvious trace of the fact that his had been one of the outstanding financial brains of his generation. Yet some of his forceful-ness and tenacity is plainly apparent in a photograph taken of him in his thirties (see between pages 80–81).

It was entirely to Robert that the Flemings owed their wealth and position. The son of a Scottish farmer who had moved into Dundee and lost his money in the collapse of the jute industry, he left school at fourteen and started work as an accountant; but by his industry, financial flair and sheer persistence he flourished in the north, moved south to London, made a fortune in the City, bought a 2,000-acre estate in Oxfordshire, built a colossal house on it, sent his sons to Eton, and generally, in only one generation, grafted the Flemings firmly on to the establishment of Edwardian England.

The Nettlebed estate, when he bought it, was in a state of some neglect. The land had originally belonged to the Camoys family, and had been part of the Stonor estate until the great sale of 1896. In that year it had been sold, without any house, to H. H. Gardiner, who is said to have been an army-clothing contractor; but he, although he planted a great many trees, went bankrupt before he could buy or build a home, and the land was sold again—to Robert Fleming—in 1903.

In that same year the Flemings bought Joyce Grove, a pleasant 17th-century house on the outskirts of the village of Nettlebed, which had belonged to the Havers family. Local legend connected the house with Cornet Joyce, the regicide, who was alleged—in the teeth of historical evidence to the contrary—to have been hanged from the branch of a tree in the garden. Had the old house been preserved, the subsequent history of the estate might have been very different; as it was, Robert's wife Kate, who came from Fife and was fired by social ambition, persuaded her husband to demolish the old building and to erect in its place a terrific pile of red brick and liverish yellow stone. *Let the deed shaw*, proclaimed the family motto from a plaque on the outside wall—and by God (a cynical observer might be forgiven for remarking), it does.

Vaguely French, decidedly Gothic and totally hideous, the new Joyce Grove was a monster even when it was built. In 1913 it was struck by lightning, and after advantage had been taken of the accident to extend the house by adding a new wing, it had forty-four bedrooms, besides a dozen bathrooms, where, from every tap (as Peter once lugubriously remarked) there emerged a different kind of soup. Yet this great hulk, solid as a rock, suited the Flemings of that generation exactly, for it was extremely comfortable and had plenty of room for entertaining. The fact that it was of devastating ugliness did not worry them at all.

Thus, by the time Peter was a child, his grandparents were firmly established as the squire and first lady of Nettlebed. In order to extend his own garden, Robert had taken in part of the old recreation ground (an exceedingly unpopular move) and had made the village a new one, which was hewn out of the hillside by hand. He had also built a new club and recreation hall, and on days of national celebration such as jubilees and coronations he and Kate would entertain the entire population of the village to lunch and tea. It was the old Flemings' presence at Nettlebed that brought Val to Braziers, near by, for the family retained a strong Scottish sense of the importance of the clan, and their instinct was to herd together in a large tribal group.

In Nettlebed also lived Peter's great childhood friend Sybil Mayor, a red-headed French girl who had been taken in, though never formally adopted, by the Barrys, another family in the village (Mabel Barry, her foster-mother, was Kate Fleming's sister). 'Wizzel', as Peter called her, was as much a country child as he, and together they incessantly quartered not only the Braziers and Nettlebed estates, but also the neighbouring ground of Soundess, which the Barrys owned. At first Peter's only weapon was a catapult or bow and arrow, but at the earliest possible moment he armed himself with an air-rifle, and then with a single-barrel 28-bore shotgun. The result of all these forays was that he drove roots deep into the chalky, flinty soil; for that whole stretch of country, with its great beech-woods crowning the hills, he conceived a love that lasted throughout his life.

Had the choice been his, he would doubtless have spent all day and every day in the open air; yet he had also to learn, and his intellectual precocity was soon apparent. At the age of five he earned the first money of his life—one penny paid him by his governess for learning and reciting correctly the names of the English counties. At first, because of his delicate state of health, his education was entirely home-based; both Pitt House and Braziers had school-rooms, and the first formal establishment to which he went—a school for difficult children in Hampstead— proved such a failure that he was withdrawn.

By then the First World War had begun to change Peter's life more profoundly than he could possibly appreciate, for at the outbreak of hostilities in August 1914 his father had ridden off to France as a Captain in the Queen's Own Oxfordshire Hussars, and from the age of seven Peter scarcely saw him again. To the four boys (Peter wrote in his autobiographical fragment) their father became a kind of demi-god:

> Not remote, but temporarily removed: his image, insecurely based on the warm but fragile memories of early childhood, was preserved solid and upstanding in the minds of his sons by our mother's strong love for him, reinforced by a sense of duty—to him and to us— which impelled her to keep him always in our minds. Sometimes she invoked him *in absentia*, as an agent of discipline, as a deterrent ... but mostly she invoked him as an example, as an ideal to live up to. Before and for long after he was killed, we always ended our prayers: 'And please God make me grow up like Mokie.'

Although Peter was too young to be aware of it, the war brought out the best in his father, who proved an exceptionally efficient and inspiring officer. An affectionate record kept by Val's younger brother

Phil, who was with him for most of the time in France, shows clearly how invaluable he became to his cavalry regiment.

Always he would do the proper thing, even if it meant taking the most strenuous and dangerous course: 'Just typical of Val was that,' wrote Phil. 'Duty first.' He was for ever keeping his men 'bright and cheery'. While they were in reserve, he would run every morning to keep himself fit; he organized the first games of polo ever seen in France, held sandbag-filling competitions, started football, and brought over some of his Bassets to see how they would tackle the French hares. His little white Cairn-cross terrier Cluanie (which accompanied him everywhere and even went 'over the top' with him during attacks) became such a popular regimental mascot that when it was kidnapped by the Canadian unit next along the line, the Oxfordshire Yeomanry refused to fight any more until it was returned.

In billets Val was always the best turned-out officer, and 'up the line' the most practically equipped. He was also outstandingly brave. Once his pipe was broken in his mouth by a fragment of shell as he walked along a trench during a bombardment to see that all his men were under cover, and on another occasion, when a man had been wounded, he carried him back, helped by a sergeant, in full view of the Germans. Yet when a senior officer wanted to put him in for a D.S.O. he would not hear of it, thinking he had not done enough.

At first the war was relatively civilized. Between spells of front-line duty, the regiment returned to Dunkirk and Mâlo-les-Bains, where most of the officers took to the hotels, but Val and his friend Arthur Villiers lived in tents near the horse lines, their idea, as Phil wrote, 'being to harden off and get fitter for campaigning'. While they were there, in the late autumn of 1914, Eve came over and had dinner with them at the Hôtel des Arcades. A few months later Winston Churchill came out to St Omer, and Val dined with him twice.

But then, as the war grew grimmer, the opportunities for such pleasant meetings dwindled. In December 1914 Val was promoted to major and took over C Squadron, with Phil as his second-in-command. Thereafter, though he bombarded the boys intermittently with coloured picture postcards, his only direct contact with the family at home came during his brief spells of leave, and it was left to Eve to direct the upbringing of her sons.

One of her most urgent tasks was to find a suitable boarding school. It is no longer clear how or why she hit upon Durnford, near Swanage in Dorset, but her choice, so far as Peter was concerned, could hardly have been happier.

Of that outlandish establishment, and its headmaster Tom Pellatt, Laurence Irving has written a glowingly nostalgic account in his autobiographical volume *The Precarious Crust*. Unorthodox, amateurish, unruly, barbaric—the place was all these; yet Pellatt himself had a flair amounting to genius for spotting and fostering talent, and the school's results were outstanding.

T P, as the boys invariably called him, was short and stout, with, according to Irving, 'the rolling gait of a sailor ashore', and the face of a comedian which he could put to good and varied use:

> He could assume a look of bovine innocence, but in a rage (usually feigned) he took on the colour and appearance of a lacquered mask of a Chinese war demon, his features contorted, his full moustache a-bristle, his teeth bared and gnashed in menacing grimace. Such miming delighted all his boys but the hapless victims of his stage thunderbolts.

T. P. might *play* the buffoon, yet in fact he was anything but one. At Oxford he got a First in history; he was immensely well-read, and under the name of Wilfred T. Coleby wrote a number of plays, several of which were successfully performed in London. The secret of his behaviour (and of his success as a pedagogue) was that he never grew up: at heart he remained a boy, and so could communicate perfectly with others.

The manner in which he ran Durnford was uninhibitedly eccentric. In the main T-shaped school-room he and three other masters contended simultaneously for the attention of their pupils. If reprimands were needed, he would administer them in front of the whole school while he carved the lunch-time joint. At Dancing Ledge, the bathing-pool he had blasted out of the rocks on the edge of the sea, he would dive and swim stark naked, and every boy present would cry 'Tidal wave, T. P.!' in a chorus of derision as his gross, Silenus-like figure hit the water.

On Sunday evenings the entire school would crowd into the great hall for their favourite treat—T. P.'s wife Nell reading aloud some stirring adventure story such as *The Prisoner of Zenda*, *Moonfleet*, or *Bulldog Drummond*. Laurence Irving sketches the scene vividly:

> She lay on the sofa in the soft folds of an elegant teagown. To divert her, privileged pages stroked her neck and tickled her silk-stockinged feet. Not one of her successive audiences would ever read again those books she brought to life without recalling the tone

and inflexion of her voice, the thrill of her delivery of the last line that preluded a week's suspense. These enthralling interludes were often brought to a close by the appearance upon the gallery of a figure robed in towelling, and crimson in the face, that bellowed: 'Time, Nell ... TIME!' and so gave the signal for the chorus of traditional boos from the throats of sixty protesting boys.

Something in all this inspired chaos appealed strongly to Eve Fleming. Perhaps it was Tom Pellatt himself, with his vigour and old-fashioned courtesy. Certainly she appealed strongly to him, for he wrote in his book *Boys in the Making*:

> The striking beauty of Peter's mother ... has been immortalized by Augustus John; though could I have conjured them back to their easels and had my way with them, Reynolds, Romney, Raeburn, Lawrence and Gainsborough would have been set down round her and given *carte blanche* in order to see which could provide for us a more *spiritual* reflection of that lovely face.

And so, in the autumn of 1916 at the age of nine, to Durnford Peter went—a small, dark, good-looking child, full of fun, yet deeply shy and endowed by his illness with a gravity beyond his years. Had he been more robust, he would probably have gone earlier; as it was, his mother kept him back until Ian (a year younger but considerably larger) was also ready to go.

At home the boys fought verbally and physically; but now they needed every available ounce of mutual support, for the environment into which they were plunged was strange and Spartan in the extreme. One of the chief horrors was a ritual which Peter afterwards described:

> We were awakened by a loud, horrible bell at 7 o'clock. Discarding our pyjamas, we raced, naked, along the corridors to the Plunge, queued up, sprang into a large vat—a sort of mini-swimming pool— of cold water, dried ourselves on damp towels, returned to our dormitories, dressed and then assembled for the first lesson of the day before wolfing down what we regarded as a totally inadequate breakfast.

It was not only the boys, but many of their parents too, who regarded the food as inadequate. By then the blockade by German U-boats of the sea-routes leading to the British Isles was becoming dangerously effective, and no doubt it was the war, rather than meanness on the part of the Pellatts, that rendered the Durnford fare so revolting.

'The tongue, still faintly tinged with green from the rabbit's last meal, was the best part if your helping consisted of the head only,' wrote Peter later, and he is reputed once to have told his mother that for lunch they had had rabbit's entrails and some not precisely identifiable remains of T. P.'s pedigree goat Bolo which had died of influenza.

Nor were gastronomic privations the only ones with which the young Flemings had to contend. To help them learn quickly, boys were hoisted by their hair to the tips of their toes, and newcomers soon found that, in the free-for-all atmosphere deliberately fostered by Pellatt, bullying was rife, and the atmosphere in the dank corridors of the old stone house was almost Dickensian in its cheerlessness. Peter's first letter home, written on October 1st, 1916, betrayed a certain nervousness, in spite of its nonchalant tone:

Dear Mum and Mokie,
Thanks awfully for the knife, it's a stunner. I like school, only not very much. Most of the chaps hate us, and there's one beast that always says something beastly to us when he passes us. This letter must do for both of you. I know the Norris chap you mean, his name's Nibby; he talks to us often, I don't like him much. Yesterday we all went out blackberrying yesterday and had rather a dull time. I shall have to finish here.

Love from PETER

It was not long, however, before Peter settled down. T. P. felt intuitively that he would distinguish himself early in life. 'He was a brilliantly clever child,' he wrote in his book, and his own far-ranging intelligence proved ideal for guiding and stimulating that of his new pupil.

On the physical front Peter did not progress so fast. Still delicate, he was forced to eat a prodigious number of milk-puddings in an attempt to make him gain strength—a fate which earned him the nickname 'Pudding'. Yet what he lacked in muscle and inches, he made up in spirit. 'I've had a little adventure,' he wrote to his mother:

It was like this, we were having drill for the whole afternoon, which was very dull, and when we were standing easy Shaw-Stewart (he's the beastly chap I told you about) started calling you an ass woman and lots of other beastly names, so after drill I went and gave him a few punches in the chest 'cos I couldn't get at his head. Well, he said I'd jolly well better stop, but I didn't, and just as he was getting ready to give me one, one of the chaps (who's going to act the

Demon of the Forest at half-term) came up and said the same as Shaw-Stewart, but I told him about it and he went away and presently S. S. came and apologised, and has been decent to me ever since then ... Only 25 days till half-term! I LOVE SCHOOL.

Love from PETER

He further insured himself against the possibility of being bullied by teaming up with 'Nig'—Nigel Birch, a large, tough boy who led one of the main factions and was described by another contemporary as 'the school Flashman'. As one of his trusty lieutenants, Peter enjoyed a measure of protection—and he himself was by no means averse from a little gang-warfare, as another letter home shows:

The last two nights it's been awfully exciting—there's going to be a rebellion under Nig. It's coming off tonight, I think. On Friday night I was told to go and knock at the door of the Pink and I did; nothing happened, though. Last night there was to be a raid by the Sick Room. They wanted to do something to Nig. But when their scout found Nig and Dringo ... armed with knotted towels, belts (Nig had a short curtain pole) and all sorts of things, the raid didn't come off.

Love from PETER

P.S. I was in the fighting lot.

For Peter, however, the chief attractions of Durnford lay in its surrounding country. Pellatt himself was a keen countryman, and at all seasons of the year he would loose the boys for the afternoon into the undulating woods and fields that surrounded the school. Sometimes in winter he would impress a few of his pupils as beaters, and once a fox that he had shot was laid out in triumph on the dining-room table; on other days he would form the boys into lines and march them systematically across the fields, turning the cowpats so that each did a double stint of manuring.

But the boys' main resort was a valley cloaked with oak, ash and hazel, through which ran a stream. Here the engineers would build dams and the architects huts, while the more bellicose spirits simply marauded, attacking whatever targets took their fancy. To the south lay the wild, steep coast, with its limestone cliffs and caves. On half-holidays organized expeditions were held, with Nell Pellatt bringing out tea in the panniers of a donkey; and still farther afield there lay many delights, not least Corfe Castle—a ruin magically enhanced by its reputation as a former haunt of smugglers.

Dear Mokie, [wrote Peter to his father in France]
We had a ripping time yesterday when Mum came down. We took lunch and tea to Corfe, and we climbed over the railings and explored the Castle ... You must have had a ripping time in Paris, and I wish I'd been there. Do you remember the battles we used to have at Lausanne, and how I would never shoot at my cavalry?

In Durnford's sylvan surroundings Peter's bent as a naturalist was strongly encouraged. Almost always, it seemed, he had a grass-snake or a slow-worm in his pocket, and frequently during lessons he was convulsed by the need to deny a serpent egress from the sleeves of his jersey. He became a celebrated adder-basher, and Pellatt would pay him for every corpse brought home.

Thus, in spite of his physical handicap, Peter made an excellent start at school. But he had been there only two terms when tragedy struck his family.

At the end of the Easter holidays in 1917 he had his tonsils out, and Ian went back to Durnford alone.

For Peter, one compensation was that the operation was carried out at Pitt House, and he had the double pleasures of recuperating at home and of not being at school. Fifty years later he recalled some of the events that followed with the precision of an awful dream:

To these pleasures were unexpectedly added the excitement and joy of seeing my father, who had come home on special parliamentary leave to attend a secret session at the beginning of May. Alas, all I can remember about what was to prove our last meeting was the screech of delight which I uttered when his tall, khaki-clad figure appeared suddenly at my bedside; I remember it because it hurt my throat extremely.

The regimental history records that he went back to France on May 13th; I was taken down to Joyce Grove to convalesce for ten blissful days. They were blissful chiefly because I had my mother to myself, which is what all children who belong to an even-aged litter either consciously or sub-consciously desire. Loving her dearly, I basked in a sense of privilege at finding the field, for once, clear of competitors and myself the sole beneficiary of all the gifts she had to give. Perhaps I enjoyed this exclusive relationship the more highly because I had enjoyed it before, in the endless sickrooms of early childhood, and unwittingly had missed it since those days.

The sun shone; in the tall beech-trees level with my window at the top of the enormous house the rooks were feeding their young, and

I roamed the Nettlebed woods and hedgerows, firing indiscriminately but mercifully (as I now think) with scant success at small birds which should have been left in peace to rear their broods.

At length the idyll came to an end. In the train going up to London, whence next day I would travel desolate to Dorset, we had a compartment to ourselves and my mother read aloud to me from a book which we had been reading together and wanted to finish. It had some such title as *Down in the Forest* and was a romantic tale about trappers in Canada. In the last chapter misfortune overtook one of the characters, or perhaps one of their dogs, and when, coming to the end, my mother closed the book, she said: 'I'm afraid that was rather a sad story.' She looked away from me, and sorrow seemed suddenly to fill the compartment.

I remember nothing about the drive from Paddington out to Hampstead, but I do remember very clearly walking with my mother through the hall at Pitt House—it was a long room—and my aunt Kathleen, my mother's younger sister, coming suddenly, as though from an ambush, out of the dining-room door on our right. She had a paper in her hand.

'Eve,' she said. 'A telegram has come about Val.'

Somebody grabbed me and bustled me away upstairs. Behind me in the hall were the terrible sounds of grief. I knew that my father had been killed.

For some reason I was put to bed on a sofa in the school-room. Later, as I lay there engulfed in misery, I heard the French governess talking to somebody—or perhaps to herself—outside the door, which had been left ajar so that grown-ups could peer in and see that I was all right without making a noise.

'*Le pauvre petit,*' the French governess was saying, '*tout d'un coup il se trouve orphelin. C'est vraiment ...*' Her voice died away as she moved farther from the door.

I did not like the French governess, and felt suddenly and deeply offended by her use of the word *orphelin*. This was partly because it had not until then occurred to me that I was an orphan, a word which for me, probably because of its biblical associations, connoted a certain lowering of one's status, relegation to the world of the unfortunate and disaster-prone, to the tail of the queue. But the main reason for my annoyance was that I conceived that the French governess had been talking her own language to hide from me the import of her words, and I took umbrage at her assumption that I would not know the meaning of the word *orphelin*.

27

Then a feeling of guilt overcame me. How could I allow my mind to dwell on such small things when it ought to be engrossed in grief? Worse still, how much of my unhappiness, which was indeed acute, was caused not by my father's death, but by the fact that tomorrow I must go back to school? Tormented by—on top of everything else—a feeling of disloyalty and unworthiness, I fell asleep. Before I did so, I heard from somewhere in the house the sound of a man crying, loudly and uncontrollably. I assumed it was my grandfather. It was a sort of bellowing noise. Life had become a nightmare. I was completely out of my depth.

Next morning some quirk of eccentricity led me to put on my new cricket-boots, a form of footwear I had never seen before; I thought them extremely smart, and, thus inappropriately shod, I clumped round the four-acre garden with my airgun, hitting nothing but for an hour or so keeping sorrow and bewilderment at bay. Soon ... it was time to leave for the station. Before I went I was taken to see my mother. They said she was not very well, and I could be with her only for a moment.

She was lying in bed. Her face was white. She looked a different, a frighteningly different person from my idolized companion of the last fortnight. I felt lost. The bottom had fallen out of my world, and I had landed overnight in another world, where everything was strange, harsh, incomprehensible, and much too big for a boy of nine to cope with.

My mother said something to me in a low, weak voice. I cannot remember what it was, or whether I replied. I stood for a moment in the doorway, and then was led away, secretly relieved that I had not been allowed to go to her bedside to be kissed goodbye by a stranger.

I have forgotten who, or of what sex, my escorting grown-up was; but I remember very clearly what was said to me outside my mother's bedroom door. 'You must be very good and brave, Peter, and always help your mother: *because now you must take your father's place.*'

For me, whose tenth birthday was still a week or so distant, this was a momentous occasion. I could not, save in a petty way, share the loss or feel the wound which had suddenly been inflicted on my mother. I was, as I have said, out of my depth among grown-up emotions; children always are. But I could, and I think that in a sort of muddled, tribal, instinctive way, I did, acknowledge the responsibility thrust upon me by the words: '*Now you must take your father's place.*'

In the next few days a flurry of letters from France brought details of what had happened.

On the night of May 17th Val's squadron took over an advanced post in the front line called Guillemont Farm, opposite the Hindenburg Line, north of St Quentin. It was clear that a major German attack was imminent, and Val organized his defence with typical care and thoroughness. The night of the 18th was relatively quiet, but in the early hours of Sunday, May 20th, as a prelude to their assault, the Germans opened up a heavy bombardment. It seems that Val and another officer, Lt. Silvertop, were taking a short cut between two trenches when both were hit and killed instantly by big pieces of shell.

The doctor who saw Val afterwards said that he could have felt nothing, and that his face bore an extraordinarily peaceful expression. His body was taken back behind the line, and the next day he was buried at a place called St Émilie. Besides the two officers, four men were killed in the action, but the defence held out against a determined attack, and it was thought that the seventy Oxfordshire Hussars had beaten off some two hundred Germans.

The news reached his brother Phil at breakfast that morning, and he passed it on in a heartbroken note to his mother:

My Darling Mum ... I couldn't realize it first of all, but now, after an hour, oh, it is too awful. But it's fine, too ... what held that position against the Germans, who tried to attack after, was Val's absolutely extraordinary example of sticking to duty. It was outstanding and held the men—this influence of Val's. It was a hero's death he died. Dear Mum and Pupsie, help yourselves by knowing that Val could not have died a more noble death. It does make it easier. I will write again to you and to poor Evelyn.

From your loving

PHIL

Letters from brother-officers bore out every word Phil wrote. 'We, all of us, were devoted to him,' said one. 'The loss to the Regiment is indescribable. He was, as you know, absolutely our best officer, utterly fearless, full of resource, and perfectly magnificent with his men.'

'He was beloved and looked up to by everyone,' wrote the Brigade Chaplain. In a private note to Eve, General Thomas Pitman wrote: 'I don't think in all my thirty years' experience in the army I have known a finer character.'

Winston Churchill, deeply moved, contributed to *The Times*—under the initials 'W.S.C.'—a tribute full of love and admiration which ended with the sentence:

> As the war lengthens and intensifies and the extending lists appear, it seems as if one watched at night a well-loved city whose lights, which burn so bright, which burn so true, are extinguished in the distance in the darkness one by one.

In London Eve lay prostrated by grief; and at Durnford Peter and Ian were left to carry on as best they could, dimly aware that their father had died a hero, but without any inkling of the effect his death would have upon their lives.

2

The Scholar

Val was awarded a posthumous D.S.O., and a memorial service for him was held in the Henley parish church on June 12th 1917. His will proved a strange and awkward document: he left Eve Pitt House, together with all 'his carriages, motors, horses, harness and stable furniture'; but the bulk of his estate—some £265,000—he put into a trust fund, directing the trustees to pay the income to Eve so long as she remained a widow, but laying down that her share would be only £3000 a year if she married again. Another clause gave her the power of discriminating financially between her sons (and grandchildren), so that she could, if she wished, disinherit any of the four boys—a weapon with which she threatened them from time to time but to which she never in fact resorted.

Eve afterwards felt certain that Val had never looked at the will, but had merely signed a stereotyped document in the rush of going off to war. 'It is a bad will,' she wrote in a letter to Peter nearly twenty years later, 'and I am sure that Mokie never even read it. It was drawn up the day war was declared, and I know its wishes were the very last things he would have wanted.' Even so, the result of it was to leave Eve, at thirty-two, with a strong incentive to remain single.

For months after Val's death she went about in deepest mourning, deliberately (it seemed) attracting attention by the histrionic extravagance of her clothes and behaviour. Nigel Birch remembered her arriving at Durnford in a great whirl of black, enveloped in clouds of some fearsomely sharp, exotic scent—the most beautiful woman, he thought, that he had ever seen.

Never again was her behaviour entirely predictable. There is no doubt that she and Val had been wonderfully in love (he had written to her on almost every day of the war), and she never recovered fully from the shock of his death. Evidently there was some truth in the remark made by the family's old Scottish maid Joan Campbell, who said that Val was the only person who understood how to keep Eve under control.

On Peter the effect of the tragedy was equally striking. At first his distress was so severe that he could not hide it; and even when the initial shock wore off, his friends noticed that he had become extraordinarily mature. To say that he was grown-up by the time he was ten or eleven must sound ridiculous; yet in many respects he was. His self-control and sense of responsibility were out of all proportion to his age, and he had already cultivated to a high degree the habit of playing things down, to which he became uniquely addicted in later life.

To Dido and Primrose Harley, daughters of a friend of Eve's, he became a childhood hero. Primrose could never forget how *good* a boy he was: how he would sit there at nursery meals eating (because of his colitis) his gruel, pretending he did not mind missing the treats that the others were enjoying. 'You don't know how nice this is,' he would say— with such conviction that the others almost believed him.

In three consecutive summers the Harleys and the Flemings went together to Salcombe in Devon for their holidays, and there Peter had always to be the bravest and the toughest (even though he was by no means physically the strongest) of all the children. His favourite sport was gulls'-egging, and he would lead the others on expeditions. He would pin up his jersey to make a pouch, or hold it in his teeth, and ascend sheer cliffs to collect the eggs, which they would take back and cook for tea in their lodgings. When they went for walks, he would insist on going farther than anyone else, no matter how tired he might be. And always he had to make everything into a joke, to reduce whatever happened to absurdity. Once Dido—a hefty girl—rushed down a steep slope towards a cliff-top, lost control of her limbs, and seemed certain to hurtle over the brink. As she passed Peter he simply murmured, 'Good old Dido—over you go'; and over she might well have gone, had not her mother screamed at her to throw herself to the ground, which she managed to do at the last possible moment.

And yet, joke as he might, Peter also harboured an almost puritanical streak of righteousness. Coming upon Primrose and Ian disembowelling limpets for use as fishing bait, he exclaimed, 'You cruel brutes! How could you do such a thing?' and rushed out of the room, reducing them both to tears. Such was the force of his ten-year-old character.

He himself could be cruel enough, for he was already fired by the hunting instinct. At the age of ten he was caught and severely reprimanded for shooting frogs at the bottom of a dried-up tank with his air-gun. Writing to his mother from Durnford in the summer of 1918, he gave a graphic description of the kind of nature-ramble he liked best—the highlight of this one being the capture of a fledgling owl:

It was a sweet little thing; the mother was out hunting when we went up to it, and we brought it down in a haversack. Then we wished we'd got something for it to eat. So as we were going adder-hunting we were going to give it adders' inside, if we got one. We went to that very good place where we got two the Sunday before last, and I saw one coiled up asleep in some bushes, and picked it up by the tail (I had an old pair of wicketing gloves on) and we took it into the open and sloshed it. But before it was dead, when it was wriggling about in the grass, I photoed it.

The owl in the haversack was snapping its beak all the time. Then we went along to a farm where you get swallows' eggs but aren't allowed to, to try and kill some mice. There we found KG [another of the boys] ... We showed the owl to KG and he said we'd never be able to feed it, and the mother would probably desert ... so we had to go and put it back. Before we did I photoed it. When we got up to the nest we tied one of its wings rather clumsily so that it shouldn't fly away when it could feed itself. We also tied a tie-clip to its leg as a souvenir ...

Going through the marsh we caught a huge marsh-lizard and put it in a box. We christened it Tchaka, after that great king you know him. We've still got him and he's just shedding his skin. He *is* pretty. I'm rather bucked. I submarined the length of the bath, which is quite hot stuff.

In his school-work, as in his letters, Peter's verbal facility developed fast, and Pellatt was soon sending particularly good exercises home with appreciative notes scrawled on them. 'I know you will like to see this,' he scribbled to Eve on a Latin exercise which Peter had got entirely right. Six months later Peter won first prize of three bits of chocolate—well worth having, considering the rations on which the boys normally had to subsist—in a competition for the best poem completed within an hour.

His high spirits proved a sore trial for Durnford's matron, known as 'Mas'. He led her a 'weird and hectic dance', according to Pellatt, who added naively: 'I do not believe he liked her very much, but let me now tell him that the term after he left, her hair recovered from its premature greyness, and she soon married most happily.'

Peter certainly did not like her; along with most of the other boys he hated her, for to them she seemed a tall, dour wardress, and to be left in her care was an experience to be avoided at all costs. 'It's a beastly swizz about my mouth,' Peter wrote to his mother one summer term while incarcerated in the sick bay:

> My food consists of calvesfoot jelly and custard pudding and milk ditto and junket and rusk and milk. Mas was beastly at the beginning but she's getting a little better. I dunno what I should have done without Maniac [Basil Maine, one of the masters]. He's been up here every minute he can spare reading to me and jawing and telling ghost stories, and he lent me stacks of books.
>
> Thanks awfully for your ripping long letter. Parts did amuse me so ... Last Sunday I went down to the woods and went to sleep.

This last sentence was his typically off-hand way of describing an event that became celebrated in the annals of the school. He went down to the woods, as he said, but there he fainted, was found lying unconscious with a high fever, and had to be carried back. The trouble seems to have been a recurrence of his earlier colitis; and its persistence, combined with a lack of natural aptitude for games, ensured that he never shone on the playing-fields.

However, he more than made up for this by his intellectual achievements, prominent among which were the writing and acting of plays. His interest in the theatre delighted Pellatt—himself a playwright—and master and boy seem to have combined their talents in several of the school productions. It is no longer possible to ascertain who was the author of *Beppo the Boplet* or *The Liquid Corkscrew*, a fairy melodrama with music, set in Sloppitania, in which Peter played the part of Mr Tonks. Probably Pellatt wrote it himself, with or without help from his pupils; but it is certain that Peter himself was writing plays, and he used to draw recruits aside into a school-room called the Loose Box and frog-march the wretched conscripts through their parts.

He also read enthusiastically—Henty, Sapper and Buchan were favourites—and he invented at least one word of his own, *chumish*, which was perhaps derived from the name of the boys' magazine *Chums* and served as a term of complete dismissal for anything such as a book which was patently ridiculous and impossible.

By the time Peter was twelve he was an accomplished scholar with a real feeling for language. Some verses on Humpty Dumpty in the style of Marlowe (frivolous though they are) show the excellence of his ear and pen:

> Like to a thunder-cloud upon some Alpine peak,
> Sombrely menacing the inferior plain,
> Vast, awe-inspiring Humptio made his seat.

Pellatt marked this exercise with an alpha and wrote on it: 'This has got excellent points and the right *tone*.' Peter, he had no doubt, would win a high place in the Eton scholarship list, and he coached him intensively towards this end. Eve, equally ambitious on her son's behalf, arranged for Basil Maine to give him extra tutoring in the holidays. Eventually, however, all their efforts were frustrated, for on the day before the scholarship exam—to Pellatt's intense chagrin—Peter went down with measles.

He thus left Durnford in less than the blaze of distinction which he might otherwise have enjoyed. But no one was happier to see him go than the matron, Mas. 'I know Peter breaks all the dormitory rules every night,' she had once sobbed to Pellatt, 'but I can never catch him. And you mark my words, when that boy grows up he will either do something very good or very bad.'

The Flemings' home life, meanwhile, was based on London and Nettlebed. Val had sold Braziers at the start of the war and Eve had since lived at Pitt House, whence, from a relatively safe distance, the children enjoyed the excitement of the Zeppelin air raids on London. It was then that Peter first exhibited what he himself called his 'prowess' as a sleeper. Whenever the alarm sounded, the household would retire to the cellar, but since it proved virtually impossible to wake Peter up, and no one fancied the task of carrying him down the five flights of stairs from his bedroom, he was generally left alone. The house was never damaged, but great was the children's delight one morning when they discovered a tiny piece of shrapnel on the doorstep.

During the holidays they stayed regularly at Joyce Grove, and there Peter made a new friend—Bill Barry, son of Sybil Mayor's foster-parents, who, though seven years older than Peter, was delighted to have such a fanatical recruit for his own favourite pastime—shooting. The close sporting partnership which they formed lasted for years; Peter called Bill 'Captain', and they shot together constantly both in Oxfordshire and in Scotland. At Nettlebed the devoted Sybil acted as loader, beater, stop and carrier of game; she also rode with him as a second hare in pony-powered paper-chases. Gradually the childish affection between her and Peter began to evolve into something far more serious.

By the age of twelve or thirteen Peter could not help being aware of the fact that he had been born into an intensely energetic family. His father had been perhaps the most prodigious exercise-taker of the lot, but, even with him gone, there remained some terrific walkers in and around the family circle. Peter's grandfather Robert was still deer-stalking at seventy; his grandmother also stalked, and at Joyce Grove she was happier if she could fit two rounds of golf into a day than if she had to make do with one. Never one to economize, she would have her chauffeur drive her to the course at Huntercombe, some two miles away, soon after breakfast. The man would then wait until she had finished her round: almost always she would decide to walk home, but there was just a chance that she might not want to, and even if she did walk, the car was needed to take back her clubs. Very often the entire performance would be repeated in the afternoon.

It was in Scotland, however, during their annual autumn holidays, that the family's passion for exercise found its real outlet. Every year from 1892 the Flemings rented some Scottish estate; at first they took modest grouse moors, but after shooting four stags at Lude in Perthshire in 1901 they acquired a taste for deer-stalking that never left them. Next year they took Rannoch Lodge, also in Perthshire, and shot thirty-three stags and 2,315 grouse. So much did they enjoy the place that they returned to it for the next seven years. Then, for one season, they went to Loch Choire, in the far north of Sutherland, where their bag of 130 stags and 1,814 grouse beat all previous records by such a margin that the owner, the Duke of Sutherland, was said to have been severely shaken.

Except in 1918, they went north every season—to Glenborrodale, to Kinloch, to Braemore, to Rannoch again, to the neighbouring Corrour, and then in 1924 to Black Mount, a magnificent deer-forest whose 90,000 acres include some of the wildest and grandest hill country in Argyllshire. There they settled, first renting the estate from the impoverished Breadalbane family but eventually buying it.

Thus the family established themselves as Highland lairds, and Robert enjoyed the Scottish holidays immensely, for he was an enthusiastic stalker and a first-class rifle shot, having been trained as a young man in the local militia near Dundee. During their Highland gatherings the Flemings reverted to their natural state of Scottishness; the men wore kilts, and stalked, shot and fished expertly. But a strange feature of the family was that the women were scarcely less energetic and sporting. The first time that Eve went north with them (to Rannoch) she was greeted by Peter's aunts Dorothy and Kathleen with the news that they were about to walk round the loch, and that she had better go with them. Thinking that this was a normal Sunday excursion (which for them indeed it was), and not wanting to appear churlish, Eve went— only to find that the circuit was one of more than twenty miles. It says much for her determination that she survived such a fearful initiation unscathed.

The Flemings' obsession with exercise was nicely sent up in a family poem based unashamedly on Kipling's 'If' ('Mum' is Granny Katie):

> If you can stalk with Mum and not grow weary,
> If you are only moist while others drip,
> If with a self-control unequalled,
> You pass cold springs and never crave one sip—
>
> If you can crawl or worm upon your belly,
> If you can fall on rocks and never squeal,
> Although your limbs are battered to a jelly,
> And there's a 'normous blister on your heel—
>
> If you can force your breathing apparatus
> To function when its breathing power has gone,
> You struggle on, because you have no flatus
> With which to gasp 'Hold on a bit, I'm done!'—
>
> If, when twelve miles from home, you'd give a fiver
> To motor back, and you're too tired to talk,
> You falter with parched lips—you've no saliva—
> 'Yes, Mum, I'd *rather* walk'—
>
> If, when you swim with Mum, you hear her mutter
> 'How mild the sea, so balmy, is it not?'
> You force your frigid, lying lips to stutter
> 'Why Mum, it's almost hot!' ...
>
> In short, if you are strong enough to beat creation,
> If you can smile when frozen in a wave,
> You will have earned the Flemings' approbation,
> Or else—they'll write 'Hic Jacet' on your grave!

An atmosphere so highly charged with competition could have only one effect on a boy as determined as Peter: it simply ensured that he outdid everyone else. In spite of the fact that his illness had left him small and slight, he grew up the most formidable walker of them all. Before long his name was closely associated with a Scottish word for which the family had a special predilection—*stravaig*, which they adapted from its dictionary definition ('to wander about idly') to mean instead, to walk frightful distances at superhuman speed, if possible in filthy weather. The hand filling up the game-book had only to write, 'Peter his usual stravaig' to indicate that he had undertaken some awful march of fifteen or twenty miles over the roughest terrain available.

Stravaiging in Scotland brought on apace Peter's passion for shooting. The first day which he himself recorded in his own game-book (given him by his mother) was August 10th, 1918, when he shot seven rabbits with his 28-bore at Glenborrodale. 'Got seven with eight shots, all sitting!' he reported. 'Fearfully bucked.' A week later, out with Bill Barry, he got his first grouse and wrote: 'Shot really well for first and last time. A lovely day.' Later his comments became more and more self-deprecating: 'A good deal of honest fluking,' he wrote when he shot his first snipe and his first teal at the age of twelve; and a year later, when he got his first woodcock: 'A tremendous surprise to both of us.'

Peter's six years at Eton (autumn 1920 – summer 1926) were probably the happiest of his life. His school career was a brilliant success; all his closest friends were made at Eton, and the atmosphere of the whole place, with its emphasis on reticence and understatement, suited his temperament perfectly. Throughout his life he continued to use Etonian expressions—'rears' for lavatory, 'mobbing up' for ragging, 'socking' for standing someone something—and his affection for the school never faded.

He achieved his success in spite of the fact that he never got on well with his house-master, E. V. Slater, who was then occupying the Timbralls, a Victorian house which overlooks the Slough road at one end and the School Field along its main front. 'Sam' Slater was a bachelor, short of temper and red of face, for whom Peter had no great liking; the two, however, established a good enough working relationship, but Slater, for his part, was by no means unaware of Peter's gifts. Once, after dinner, he took a visitor with him on his evening round, expressly to introduce him to Fleming Major—'one of the most interesting and remarkable boys I have ever had in my house.'

Having missed the scholarship exam, Peter was put in Lower Remove, the highest division (or form) open to him, and on the strength of his performance during his first year was awarded an Oppidan Scholarship. Rupert Hart-Davis, who arrived two halves (or terms) later and also took Lower Remove, remembers him sitting at the right-hand end of the front row of desks (the top position) up to the Lower Master, A. B. Ramsay, looking very small and neat with his Eton collar (which his shortness obliged him to wear for several halves, until he was tall enough for tails) and his smooth black hair.

His scholastic record was outstanding. In trials (the end-of-term exams) he won one distinction after another, and he carried off several of the school prizes. Specializing in languages, he won the Head Master's French Prize at fifteen, the King's French Prize at seventeen (after coming second the year before), and the Duke of Newcastle's Spanish Prize at eighteen. He finished by winning a scholarship to Christ Church, Oxford, and by becoming Captain of the Oppidans—the senior boy apart from the seventy-odd Collegers, or full-blooded scholars, and in effect the head of the school.

In spite of his intellectual precocity, he was never damned with the label 'sap'—the term used by Etonians to disparage anyone offensively studious or clever. He easily escaped any such opprobrium—first, because he had extraordinary powers of concentration that enabled him to learn fast and so not spend too much time working; and second, because his own character anyway led him to conceal the amount of work he was doing and made him a natural practitioner of the quintessentially Etonian habit of appearing not to try.

While Peter flourished as an intellectual, Ian was achieving equal distinction as an athlete. At first he had been overshadowed by the brilliance of his elder brother, with whom he could not compete at work. But in 1924 he won seven out of ten events in the junior sports—a record unparalleled before or since—and in the following two years he was Victor Ludorum in the school sports—again, a feat not since surpassed.

On the playing-fields Peter's guts and exceptional coolness compensated to some degree for his lack of strength. At the Field Game—Eton's unique combination of soccer and rugger—he played behind, or back. 'Can be relied on not to lose his head in a crisis,' said the house games book of 1922, about his performance as a junior. A year later he played goals (full-back) for Slater's house side, but did not win his colours. 'He had the distinction of being the only behind who played for my tutor's in two ties with impunity and without showing any signs of funking,' wrote Harold Caccia, who by then was captain of games and afterwards became Peter's lifelong friend.

In 1924 Peter did win his house colours and was involved in some desperate battles in the knock-out house ties. Of Slater's 7–0 victory over Brinton's in the second round, Harold wrote:

Fleming ma by now had torn all his muscles, but as he was playing short, he found it difficult to stop playing, which he did excellently, falling down oftener than anything seen before.

Slater's reached the semi-final, but they were beaten 1–0 by Sheep-shanks'. When Harold blamed himself for the defeat and wrote: 'We reached the line hundreds of times but never scored, which was entirely Caccia's fault, as he was always given it and should have gone for goal,' Peter added in the margin of the book: 'ROT, to put it politely.' Later he took up the Wall Game and was awarded his Oppidan Wall, again as a behind.

At cricket he achieved modest success. He captained his junior house side admirably, doing most of the bowling and a good deal of the batting, and eventually became Keeper (or Captain) of Second Upper Club, a team generally known (because of its red-and-white cap) as 'Strawberry Mess', in which the cricket, though not too serious, was by no means entirely farcical.

His manifold achievements made him an obvious candidate for Pop, the self-electing oligarchy which forms the nearest equivalent at Eton to a corps of school prefects. He was a member of the Society for five halves—an exceptionally long time—and ended by being its Auditor.

All these successes enormously gratified his mother, who smouldered with ambition on his behalf. But his own blind childhood love for her was slowly being tempered by an increasingly uncomfortable awareness of her eccentricities—most obviously apparent in her clothes and appearance. Almost always, it seemed, she was in fancy dress, her colours so violent that they invariably provoked comment. At parties in London she would drape herself on a chair or sofa at the edge of the room and strike fantastic attitudes, as though posing for a photograph; and when she descended on Eton in huge yellow feathered hats and orange dresses, the boys of Slater's would line the windows of the house to witness her arrival. Peter's embarrassment was dreadfully intense, yet never did he say a word against her or falter in his loyalty.

In 1923 she sold Pitt House and moved to the Chelsea Embankment, where she had three houses knocked together. One was nondescript, the second was a pub, and the third was Turner's house, after which she ren med the whole. She had the artist's studio made into a huge sitting-room which she lined with gold wall-paper and filled with piles of tomato and magenta velvet cushions; there she played her violin and entertained a more and more artistic circle of friends. Among them was Augustus John, who painted her portrait repeatedly, although (curiously enough) always from exactly the same angle. In every picture that he did of her (as in all her photographs), the eyes have a most disconcerting look of calculation.

Though stunningly decorated and full of comforts, Turner's House never made much of a family home, especially for Peter, who would far rather have lived in the country. His lack of a rural base was probably a greater deprivation to him than his mother realized, for it meant, among other things, that he could not keep a dog, which he would dearly have liked. Chelsea made a far better home for Ian, who, though he was frequently in trouble for bribing the servants to bring him breakfast in bed, fully appreciated its metropolitan advantages.

Within the family Eve relied heavily on the memory of their father to keep the boys in order. 'Mokie wouldn't have liked that,' she would say if one of them swore, was late or told a lie. 'Mokie would never have done that.' One of the prohibitions which she sought to enforce in his name was a ban on cigarette-smoking, and in this case she reinforced the veto with a bribe: any of the boys who reached twenty-one without smoking would be able to claim a considerable reward (Peter got his in due course). Eve was uneasily fascinated to find that her eldest son had unconsciously inherited one of his father's tricks—a habit of sitting with his elbows on the arms of his chair and his hands raised together in front of him, tapping his left-hand knuckles quite loudly with his right-hand fingers.

Her great mistake lay in failing to realize that her sons' credulity was bound to decrease in inverse proportion to their age: by the time Peter was fifteen, it occasioned only secret derision in him to be told that a spiritual message had been received from his father during the night which forbade him to do the particular thing on which he had set his heart.

The lack of a father—and the age of their grandfather—left all four boys very much subject to the whims of their mother, and, to a lesser extent, of Grannie Katie, both of whom, though fired by the best intentions, were capable of great foolishness. Except that both were snobs, and on occasion silly, Eve and her mother-in-law had little in common. Kate was exceptionally naive, cared nothing about her appearance, and was incapable of guile. To her grandsons she appeared agreeably eccentric and was the object of enormous affection; to outsiders she seemed impossibly ridiculous. She would take her guests round

Joyce Grove proudly telling them in her shrill voice how much every
hideous room had cost, and then disappear, wearing boots and a diamond
ring, for a couple of rounds of golf. At dinner she would whisper loudly
down the table at Robert, telling him (often in French) to wipe his
mouth or sit up—for he was already a little senile—and chatter non-stop
about the achievements of her grandsons, often in front of the boys
themselves, so that all they could do was to sit and writhe. Another
family poem neatly caught her chronically confused ebullience:

Overheard at the Flemings' Dinner Table

A Monologue by Our Hostess

> How clever of your son, Lord Shaw!
> But I must really tell you more
> Of how *my* grandsons do excel
> In all they do—they work so well.
>
> All four of them got into Pop—
> Peter was Master of the *Opp*.
> (Make conversation, Robert, dear!
> It helps to keep the larynx clear.)
>
> Dear Ian won a steeplechase:
> He won it third—three in the race.
> (Now really, Kathleen, you must take
> Another trout, for goodness sake!!)
>
> Yes, Richard bowled the Eton crew,
> Was captain of the beagles, too;
> And Michael now will try his best
> To do as well as all the rest.
>
> And those dear girls, Lord Shaw, you know,
> Just look at them all in a row.
> Such jolly, big, strong, hearty things!
> (*Essuyez*, Robert! Something clings!)

The boys teased her mercilessly, telling her that, among numerous
other fictitious achievements, Richard had won the Eton knitting prize.
But this did nothing to stop her: indeed, she knew she was being teased,
enjoyed it and played up to it, creating still greater confusion in the
minds of her visitors.

'I am at the moment being harrowed,' Peter wrote to Rupert in 1926:

by the pitiable spectacle of a Peer of the Realm gradually realizing that my grandmother has asked him to stay the weekend without asking anyone else: a wire has just come to say that Ian won the hurdles at Stamford Bridge [in the Public Schools' Athletics], and I think that sheer force of grandmaternal rhetoric has scored the fact so deeply on My Lord of Bective's brain that whatever else he forgets he will never forget that.

The essential point of all this raillery, however, was its good nature. The boys loved being at Joyce Grove, and they were by no means unaware of their grandmother's kindness, for she invited them all to stay for weeks every school holidays, and had they not been given the run of the Nettlebed estate, their lives would have been a great deal less amusing.

It was the outdoor life—the shooting and the riding—that most appealed to Peter, for the house was one of the few buildings that positively oppressed him. As a rule he was untouched by—or even unaware of—his surroundings; but at Joyce Grove the size and weight of the house and its furnishings actively lowered his spirits. Although the amenities included a formal library, there was scarcely a readable book in sight, and the only remotely congenial place he could find in which to write was a gun-room bristling with trophies, among them the head of a rhinoceros shot by one of his aunts.

'I must now creep up to the Peruvian lavatory—or whatever they call the place I sleep in,' he wrote to Sybil once while she was away in Canada; and his letters to Rupert Hart-Davis often cynically extolled the house's portentous gloom. It was, he said, like an American film set, on which you could see people coming over polished floors from miles away; and one evening he wrote, 'There is no one else in this house; at least I haven't found anyone. My room is three and a quarter miles from here, but I must go to bed as there is a rhinoceros over the mantelpiece.'

In May 1926 the family was unexpectedly increased by the arrival of a baby girl called Amaryllis, whom Eve said she had adopted. 'It seems quite a humorous brat,' Peter wrote to Rupert from Eton, and in due course he became extremely fond of the girl, who, he later realised, was in fact his half-sister, and the daughter of Augustus John.

At Eton it was in two extra-mural activities that he showed the greatest originality. The first was the theatre, for which he further enlarged the appetite acquired at Durnford. Until he himself took an interest, theatre at Eton had been almost unknown, but in 1924 he founded the Symposium Club, whose original object—to read plays on

Sundays—was soon superseded by an ambition to perform them as well. It was through the Symposium Club that Peter got to know Rupert Hart-Davis, and so laid the basis of another lifelong friendship.

The club was greatly helped by Miss Oughterson, the Dame (or Matron) in College, who shared Peter's enthusiasm and herself directed the two productions put on in his time. The first, in December 1925, was of Shaw's *Androcles and the Lion* and achieved considerable success, in spite of the fact that it was given in the cavernous School Hall, where the acoustics were terrible and the absence of a raised stage ensured that anyone farther back than the first two or three rows of the audience could see nothing except the tops of the taller actors' heads.

Peter apart, the prime movers of the enterprise were Quintin Hogg and Jack Donaldson, and in a programme note all three craved the indulgence of the audience for the fact that the production had, for reasons of economy, to be given in modern dress. Peter played two parts—Spintho and the Lion—and George Lyttelton, one of the masters, adroitly praised both roles in a single sentence when he reviewed the play anonymously in the *Eton College Chronicle:*

> Fleming, as Spintho, with a face of parchment, proceeded terribly on his course of progressive mental derangement not only ... was Fleming's acting real enough to make us chary of seeing him mad on stage, but his success as the lion, whether roaring in chase or lying meekly on his back having his tummy scratched, deserved to be rewarded by a meal.

Fired by the good reception accorded this first attempt, Peter arranged another Shaw production for the following half, and *The Devil's Disciple* was given two performances on March 19th and 20th, 1926. Peter played the leading role, Dick Dudgeon, but because Ralph Jarvis, another of the actors, persisted in calling Dudgeon 'Hodgson', the play was soon known to the entire cast as *Hodgson's Disciple*.

By the date of the production School Hall had been furnished with a stage—entirely through Peter's efforts—and the audience certainly had a better view. The first night was enough of an event to attract the attention of *The Times*, but its critic took a rather stern view of the proceedings. Although he praised the members of the Symposium Club for their initiative, he concluded that in staging *The Devil's Disciple* their 'zeal has a little outrun their discretion ... in the earlier part of the play only R. C. Hart-Davis as the parson, and R. P. Fleming as Dick Dudgeon, showed much ease of manner.'

The *Eton College Chronicle* was also uncomfortable, but singled Peter out for praise: although (it said) 'there were moments when he seemed to lose his grip a little ... he did, on the whole, get the part across the footlights, and that was an achievement.' Besides providing valuable experience for the players, the production was a financial success, raising more than fifty pounds for one of the school's own charities, the Eton Mission.

The second extra-mural activity at which Peter excelled was the editing of the *Eton College Chronicle*. Before he took the job over he was already known as a witty and accomplished writer (once, up to George Lyttelton for Extra Studies, he had won a competition for the 'best first and last sentences of a brilliant essay on hats' with the concluding phrase: 'That swart and ignominious bulb of discomfort that men call bowler'). But as soon as he became Editor in the summer of 1925 his brilliantly facetious leaders transformed what until then had been a journal of leaden dullness.

Earnest social comment was unknown in the *Chronicle* of those days. Wit (if anyone could produce it) was all—and in the fourth issue which he edited Peter wrote a leader which is still, fifty years later, remembered by his contemporaries with delight. Entitled 'Fons et Origo', it purported to describe an expedition to find the source of Jordan—the stream that runs through Eton to join the Thames. His account of the expedition's departure, 'accompanied by four Siberian newt-hounds,' was full of characteristic and memorable phrases:

> They carried with them a portable canoe, very rightly advertised as collapsible, and a cast-iron stove, whimsically called by its maker 'The Inferno'. Each individual carried provisions enough to last him 48 hours if he ate without stopping. Each in addition was equipped with one mapping-pen, one umbrella, one instrument for removing tadpoles from the hosiery, one list of printed instructions for taking the bull by the horns, one Red Cross outfit in case he did, and one pneumatic compass.

As the expedition moved off,

> the remaining members were struggling to restrain the Siberian newt-hounds, which had pulled down and savaged a lower boy whose resemblance to a newt was indeed striking.

Whether Peter's mind was already dwelling on the possibility of travelling to distant places, it is impossible to say. But it is a curious fact that several of the features of the farcical Jordanian expedition (the small band of amateur explorers hacking its way up-river through high grass, laden

with expensive and useless equipment) were later reproduced in uncomfortably accurate detail when he himself went to Brazil. In another
Chronicle leader, too, he seems to have been fascinated by the idea of
travel and writing about it: though once again entirely un-serious, this
article also surely contained a hint of his real inclinations. 'All Yule is
divided into three parts, as Caesar very nearly said,' began his leader
'On the After Effects of Christmas'. Parts One and Two, he wrote, were
relatively tolerable, but the real snag was Part Three, the problem being
how to get rid of all the presents:

> the boomerang so kindly sent by Uncle Lemuel ... and that book of
> travel, *Up the Dnieper in a Biltong*? And that other book of travel,
> *Down the Pemmican by Sampan*? All these things lie about one's room,
> mutely reproachful, like corpses after a battle.

Throughout his life Peter retained a strangely prophetic capability—a
knack of writing (usually in jest) about events which at the time were
fictional but which later actually happened. Although he could never
explain this gift, he enjoyed possessing it; and here, in his flippant but
persistent references to exploration, there sounded odd pre-echoes of
his own career.

His success as the Editor of the *Chronicle* further enhanced his reputation in the school. Even so, he was by no means universally popular. To
his friends he was a wonderful source of fun—irrepressibly facetious, a
non-stop fountain of jokes; but to those further from him he could seem
altogether too much of a good thing—too good-looking, too smooth,
too successful, too arrogant.

In supposing that he was arrogant his enemies were entirely mistaken;
what they took for pomposity was in fact nothing but the façade of
nonchalance which he carefully maintained in order to conceal his own
acute shyness. His determination to turn everything into a joke sprang
from the same cause: rather than display his real emotions, he took
cover always in frivolity. His speech and even his voice reflected the
same tendency. He used stock, clipped, Bulldog-Drummond-type phrases
and talked in a languorous drawl which was so amusing (or so irritating,
depending on the hearer's affinities) that scarcely anyone realized that
its purpose was to obviate the need for emotional commitment. Imperturbability was his aim, and imperturbable he made himself appear to be:
by the time he left Eton he was already a master of the peculiarly English
art of understatement.

During his last two halves—Easter and Summer of 1926—he was
immensely busy. Apart from his other commitments, he was by then a

Cadet Officer in the School Corps, and he took his duties as Captain of the Oppidans seriously—a shade officiously, some people thought—making a real effort to invest the office with some point. 'The whole system of administration by boys at Eton is so vague, intangible and loosely woven,' he wrote afterwards, 'that the Captain of the Oppidans, if he works on the right lines, can take and use a very great deal of power.'

Peter was never interested in power as such, but he did have a strong and almost puritanical sense of duty, and was far more strict about discipline than his normally facetious attitude might have led one to expect. On one occasion, when four boys were detected receiving 'somewhat immoral papers from Paris', he sent for them and beat them 'very hard but very privately' in Pop Room. 'They got what they deserved,' he commented later, 'and no scandal was caused.'

One thing over which he took particular trouble was the cinema. Films were then a considerable novelty: the boys were not allowed to go to the cinema in Windsor or Slough, and the only shows they could see were those organized once or twice a half by the Captain of the Oppidans. When Peter took office the whole practice had fallen into disrepute, for his predecessor had allowed meetings to degenerate into riots, and he had some trouble in persuading the Head Master, C. A. Alington, that further shows were desirable. But this he eventually managed 'by a nicely calculated policy of apologetically irritating persistence', and the new arrangements that he made proved extremely efficient. He organized strict crowd-control and issued different coloured tickets for each of the three entrances. 'The doors were opened punctually, and within *five minutes* an audience of roughly nine hundred were in their seats,' he reported. 'The result was that everyone had a chair to sit on; the atmosphere was less reminiscent of the Zoological Gardens; and there was no danger in case of fire.'

The start of his final half was interrupted by the General Strike of May 1926. In an old, buff-coloured car procured from the ancestral stables at Joyce Grove he set out every morning soon after first light for Reading Gaol. There he collected copies of the Government newspaper the *British Gazette* which he ferried to Swindon, armed with a riding crop and accompanied by a pallid student called Blather.

Back at school, he applied himself energetically to the organization of the biggest event with which he had so far dealt—the Fourth of June. For this festival he professed, on several occasions, an almost pathological loathing. He hated pomp and formality in any case, but his particular dislike of the Fourth of June was probably provoked partly by the fact that he, as a member of Sixth Form, had to take part in the archaic ritual of Speeches, and partly by fear of the sartorial outrage which his mother was almost certain to perpetrate. On ordinary days there was a sporting chance of keeping her more or less away from the public gaze; but on the Fourth there was none.

The traditional pattern of celebrations left little room for original manœuvre, but Peter did make one or two innovations. Because no band would stay late enough to play the National Anthem at the conclusion of the firework display, he omitted the conventional portrait of the King from the set-pieces and had it replaced by another—'The Cats on the Tiles'. He also had flares set up on College Field to illuminate the approaches to Fellows' Eyot, the island from which the audience watched the fireworks. This, he wrote later, 'considerably diminished the number of dowagers who annually precipitate themselves into the abyss which separates the Eyot from the mainland.'

His tense feelings about the whole occasion found expression in a splendidly satirical leader, in which a Cynic describes the events of the day as he sits on Pop Wall in the morning:

In a few hours the buildings and grounds of this noble college will be flooded by a downpour of rain unequalled in relentless fury since Negretti met Zambra. Instead of going to bed at once, large numbers of so-called students will put on new and uncomfortable clothes and shoes of a shininess passing belief, and will hurry out into the rain, wearing in their buttonholes great gouts of vegetable matter, which, although unfit for human consumption, are sold by Yiddish horticulturists at half-a-crown each. On the arrival of the fashionably-dressed crowd of friends and relations, of whom the majority travel by car, a few by train, and hardly any on bicycles, the student perhaps shepherds his party into Upper School, where they hear a series of uncouth and incomprehensible sounds emitted by young gentlemen dressed like undertakers with a secret penchant for the Russian ballet. The remainder of the day is spent in fighting with other and equally determined sections of the fashionably-dressed crowd for places where food and shelter may be obtained. Later, under cover of darkness, a number of students, propelling their frail craft in a somewhat inaccurate manner over the inky surface of the Thames, assume a position as nearly vertical as their ludicrous costume and immoderate supper will permit: while on the one side myrmidons in the pay of the Captain of the Oppidans instigate a number of deafening explosions and allow an intermittent hail of charred

rocket-sticks to patter on the irascible heads of a crowd too numbed
by cold to raise any effective protest.

As the end of the half approached he felt acutely sad at the idea of
leaving the place in which he had done so well and enjoyed himself so
much. Half way through a frivolous letter to Sybil, in which he was
suggesting theatre-going plans for the holidays, he suddenly hit a
serious note: 'I've been writing out invitations to my leaving breakfast:
it's all very depressing, not to say expensive. I shall hate leaving this
place.' A few weeks later another letter repeated the sentiment almost
exactly: 'It was perfectly awful leaving Eton: I hated it.' Hardly ever
did he permit himself so open an expression of his feelings.

That summer he wrote to Sybil repeatedly, addressing her as 'Dearest
Sybil' or 'Dear Old Sybil', and in September he lured her to North Uist,
where he went with his family and her half-brother Bill to shoot snipe.

'She is awfully nice and intelligent,' he wrote from there to Rupert,
'and we so to speak split a cradle (in childhood, of course). Bill is
extremely witty. The amount of rot—utter rot—talked in this house is
simply amazing.'

No wonder he kept her close to him; for by then he was extremely
fond of her, and in any case she formed a living bridge between the
comfortable certainties of the past and the uncharted reefs of Oxford
that lay ahead.

3
Oxford

When Peter went up to Christ Church in the autumn of 1926 he soon began to repeat almost exactly the pattern of his Eton career: once again he excelled scholastically and socially, but it was by his writing and acting that he attracted the most attention.

At nineteen he was slim but wiry, and about five feet nine inches tall. Very dark, with straight black hair and an almost simian breadth of mouth and upper lip, he struck girls as devastatingly handsome; and his physical attractions were enhanced by the fact that he was supposed to be enormously rich. Although this idea was false—for he had no capital of his own, and depended on the allowance his mother gave him—he was certainly well off and had, or could get, almost anything he wanted.

The odd thing was that he seemed to want so little. He did not, like many of the richer undergraduates, have a car of his own, but shared with Ian a Morris two-seater known as William. He wore, for preference, a decrepit tweed shooting-jacket that Sybil had patched for him; having no sense of taste, he cared nothing for food, and sought out two things only—sausages and marmalade. He would drink as much as anyone if the occasion demanded it, but never did anyone see him incapable: even though his companions might finish an evening under the table, he himself always seemed exactly the same as when they had started. Although he was no prig, it simply never occurred to him to tell a dirty story; and when he swore he never used obscenities, preferring instead some deliberately archaic expletive—'Hell fire!', 'Curses!' or 'God's boots!' Altogether he seemed a great deal more mature than most of his contemporaries.

His rooms in Christ Church were on the first floor of Peckwater Quad, where he installed a portable gramophone and a large green lizard called Perkin Warbeck. Immediately above him was an old friend from Eton—Peter Cazalet, already celebrated as one of the best ball-game players of his generation—and his closest friend of all, Rupert Hart-Davis had simultaneously gone up to Balliol.

During their first term Peter and Rupert together took up a habit that both kept for life—smoking pipes. Having bought pipes and tobacco from Messrs Fribourg and Treyer in the High Street, they retired to Rupert's rooms to experiment. Rupert was violently sick, but Peter managed to maintain his normal sang-froid, and thereafter he smoked pipes continually, clenching his teeth so fiercely on the stems that usually he bit clean through them. For years he would smoke nothing but an American brand of tobacco called Edgeworth, which produced (according to Rupert) 'an odour reminiscent of motor-tyres burning in syrup'. From that first term at Oxford his pipes were part of his life.

As at Eton, he must have worked hard and unobtrusively, for now, reading English, he mastered the infinitely tedious Anglo-Saxon (which had to be *learnt*, and on which there was no chance of bluffing) while at the same time shooting on a great many winter afternoons, going for immense walks on Sundays, and taking an ever-increasing part in the activities of the Oxford University Dramatic Society.

In spite of his crowded curriculum he did not much enjoy his first year. The trouble lay not in any deficiency of Oxford's, but in his own emotional difficulties; for by then he was in love with Sybil, and she with him, and his mother did not hesitate to show her disapproval. Sybil, an orphaned (or rather cast-off) French girl, was by no means the sort of person she expected her eldest son to marry; ruthlessly ambitious on his behalf, she wanted a duke's daughter for him, at least (Peter once remarked in a bitter moment that only if he had been able to carry off Princess Elizabeth—the future queen—would Eve have been fully satisfied). That Peter and Sybil were in love meant nothing to her. Nor was Sybil the only one to feel the iron frost of her dislike: the Harley sisters, too, were soon withered by it. As long as they were young enough to constitute no sort of a threat, she was wonderfully kind to them; but the moment they became attractive young women—and therefore, as she supposed, presented a challenge to herself as well as a potential threat to Peter—she drove them off mercilessly.

Peter, however, was not so easily prized away from Sybil. In determination he was already a match for his mother, and for the time being he held out against her opposition. But the strain of doing so clearly did not help him settle down at Oxford, and during his first year he thought seriously about going down.

In January 1927 he was temporarily diverted by a ridiculous theatrical experiment—two performances of *Bulldog Drummond* given at the Electric Theatre, Newport Pagnell, in aid of the orthopaedic clinic there. Enthusiasm for the production was raised by the Harley girls, who were great hands at amateur theatricals and often put on plays in which Peter joined. In *Bulldog Drummond* Dido played the long-suffering Phyllis, and Primrose Irma Peterson, wife of the villain. The rest of the parts were taken by friends, among them Peter as Drummond, Ronnie Shaw-Kennedy as Carl Peterson and Frank Pakenham as James Handley.

The performances were much enjoyed—at any rate by the actors. 'I am still feeling more or less shattered,' Peter wrote to Rupert a week later. 'I more or less neglected the text—with which in any case my acquaintance was only superficial—and gagged with marked success. The fight was a terrific effort, and went down awfully well. The best feature of the whole thing was Frank Pakenham's rendering of a sort of Third Murderer part—his stealthy movements being reminiscent of an immature pachyderm which had fallen unexpectedly into a morass.'

Some of the cast saw a certain irony in the fact that Drummond, who was supposed to be as powerful as an ox, scarcely had the strength to bundle Carl Peterson into a bath, which in one scene the text required him to do. Peter was visibly annoyed by the fact that he was not any stronger; but apart from this he obviously enjoyed every minute of an episode quite bizarre enough to have taken his fancy.

His unhappiness returned as soon as he was back in Oxford, for Rupert left Balliol prematurely, stricken by the death of his mother after a long illness. In letters that now strike a slightly pathetic note Peter tried to comfort him by means of facetious jokes; but, knowing how hard he had been hit, could barely bring himself to be flippant. 'Oxford without you is trying to a degree,' he wrote, 'even more so than with you. Frankly, I shouldn't be too precipitate, as the University is being thinned out by frostbite, and it is now necessary to have the British Ski Association badge (3rd Class) in order to visit the bathrooms ... Sybil came down yesterday, thus helping matters considerably.'

Occasionally he cheered up enough to let off a real firework of wit. 'Went out to lunch with Harbottle,' he wrote one day to Rupert (Harbottle, or George Harwood, being a mutual friend of theirs) 'and a man called Jennings said "What do you think of Nietzsche?" I said that, speaking offhand, I thought there were more consonants to the square vowel in Knightsbridge, which is quite true.'

But his dissatisfaction persisted through the spring and early summer, and in May he wrote: 'Oxford is at its bloodiest ... I'm sorry this isn't a better letter. I'm not in the mood. Blast everything. Only two more years here.'

By then, however, he was deeply involved in the affairs of the O.U.D.S., and his passion for the theatre gradually assumed such proportions as to make him happy enough to stay on.

In those days the Society made a practice of inviting leading professional producers to direct its plays, and in February 1927 it brought in the celebrated Theodore Komisarjevsky to produce *King Lear*, which he proceeded to do on a steeply-raked set reminiscent of the Mappin Terraces at Regent's Park Zoo. Peter was originally given the part of the Duke of Cornwall's servant, but after an upheaval in the cast caused by the expulsion of the poet John Betjeman (who, until he lampooned the O.U.D.S. in the University newspaper *Cherwell*, had been going to play the Fool) Peter was elevated to be the Duke himself.

He does not seem to have been much of a hit. He looked, according to one contemporary report, 'like a hurriedly constructed Fifth-of-November Guy Fawkes. And instead of being the cold, brutal, domineering Duke, he was a fussy, shrill blusterer.' Even so, he won a measure of notoriety by getting himself cut quite badly one night in the fight with his servant (Osbert Lancaster)—an accident which, as Osbert wrote later, 'lent dramatic emphasis to his exit-line "I bleed apace!"'

The O.U.D.S.'s summer play that year was *The Tempest*, which was to be performed by the lake in the gardens of Worcester College. Peter tried for the part of Prospero, and his irritation at seeing it go to Julian Hall (his predecessor as Captain of the Oppidans at Eton, and someone for whom he had no great respect) burst out in a spirited letter to Rupert:

I have as bloody a part as you could wish to find—Alonzo, King of Naples, who wears a beard and indulges in conversation as limited as it is irrelevant. I missed getting Prospero by the breadth only of the most attenuated capillary attachment: all the other fairly amusing parts I might easily have got had by that time been filled with histrionic riff-raff, so I find myself confronted with the depressing prospect of saying 'Peace, prithee,' or, alternately, 'Prithee, peace,' at intervals of 100 beautiful lines. Occasionally, stirred to the very depths of his soul by some gaucherie in blank verse, Alonzo, throwing off his cloak of taciturnity, bursts into impassioned rhetoric, delivering sometimes as many as five or six words consecutively— e.g. 'No more, I do beseech you.' But for the most part he remains silent, and on one occasion falls into a profound stupor or coma. I hope to convey the effect by assuming a horizontal as opposed to a vertical position: otherwise, who would know?

Once again there were reshuffles of the cast, and Peter found himself eventually as Antonio, the villain of the piece, 'who, though fairly tongue-tied and ineffectual, is better than Alonzo.' He also understudied Julian Hall as Prospero, and at the very last moment he almost had to take over, for Hall was put out of action by a car crash. In the end, however, the part was read by Harman Grisewood (President of the O.U.D.S.) from the Temple text. Peter's O.U.D.S. début was thus a modest one, but the experience served merely to whet his appetite for further theatricals.

Far more depressing than indifferent reviews of the play was a plan which his mother had hatched for the summer vacation. Its ostensible purpose was to enable him to learn German, but its real objective— scarcely veiled—was to keep him away from Sybil. First Peter was to go to the Tennerhof in Kitzbühel—the experimental school run by Ernan Forbes Dennis and his wife, the novelist Phyllis Bottome, to which Ian had been sent the year before. Thence he was to proceed straight to Ireland, where Eve had taken a place called Ards House, in County Donegal, for the autumn shooting and fishing. In its elaboration—and obvious futility—the scheme was entirely typical of Eve's machinations.

Peter went to Austria on June 6th. To the Forbes Dennises, of course, he betrayed no hint of the struggle that was raging inside him. Having wrestled—in the end successfully—with the intransigent Ian the summer before, they found Peter a wonderfully quick and easy pupil who learned at lightning speed and never made a fuss. Little did they realize how he hated Kitzbühel and his incarceration there. 'I simply loathe this place,' he wrote to Rupert at the beginning of July. 'This really *is* a bloody place.' And then again on July 15th:

God, I do hate this place. It rains most of the time, and in the intervals one gloomily climbs a mountain. I do about three or four hours' German a day and read masses of the Bard and write to Sybil and long for bedtime. Mama has given orders that I'm to be kept here till the 31st ... the idea being, of course, that, dead or alive, I must reach Ireland without seeing Sybil. To that end she has also written to Mabel [Mabel Barry, Sybil's foster-mother] asking her to issue no invitations to me and not to allow Sybil to go up to London to see me, as the less we see of each other the better ... Of course I shall see Sybil, somehow, even if it means tying a sporran on the Morris and throwing a Lochinvar: but it's all pretty hellish really.

You can't imagine how depressing this place is: Mr Forbes Dennis is very nice, and the other inmates—such, at any rate, as are not completely imbecile—are kind and fairly honest. I simply loathe it. Still sixteen days to go, too.

At the end of the month he escaped and travelled straight to Ireland, as instructed. There, in spite of the presence of a contingent of friends, including the Harley girls, Rupert and his sister Deirdre, he still felt wretched. 'The atmosphere of the Fleming house is becoming daily icier and more strained,' he wrote in a letter on August 20th, and a week later he fired off an ironic broadside at Rupert, who by then was back in London:

Yesterday we walked for eight hours and saw fifteen grouse, of which only one survives ... I wanted to go and stay with Sybil in Scotland when we leave here, but was of course refused permission. I shall try again. There is still no indication of whether I am to be sent to Bessarabia to learn shorthand, or to Prague to study economic defenestration.

Try again he did, and somehow he managed to change his mother's mind, for on September 11th he wrote:

I leave here on the 24th with the car for a week at Black Mount, and then—marvellous prospect—go on to stay with Sybil for the rest of the time. I'm only allowed to on condition that we don't 'make love'.

As at last he set out in her direction, his spirits rose steeply back towards their normal plateau of exuberance, and from on board the Burns-Laird line ferry he wrote:

It is now 8 pm; the saloon is deserted, save for three bounders and a bearded woman—all devouring, with every appearance of relish, some so far unclassified species of fish.

At the beginning of October he reached Ardmore, in Ross-shire, where Sybil and her family were staying, and his joy was unbounded. 'I'm so happy I can hardly put pen to paper,' he wrote on the fifth. 'It's unspeakably marvellous being with Sybil again.' For the moment, at any rate, his mother had been routed.

When he returned to Oxford in October, 1927, he took with him the text of a one-act play called *King's Evidence*. This was something with which he had struggled intermittently for more than a year: he had begun it at Eton and fiddled with it at Joyce Grove, before eventually finishing and copying it out in Ireland. Doubtless, the fact that he had written a play enhanced his standing at the O.U.D.S., and for the spring production— Romain Roland's *The Fourteenth of July*, which Komisarjevsky was again hired to produce—he secured the solid part of Hulin. 'Mr R. P. Fleming was admirable as the Swiss Hulin,' the *Oxford Magazine* reported. 'Thanks partly to his ability, partly to his pipe, he succeeded in being far more natural and easy than most of the other men, and he kept his voice well under control.'

Peter must have devoted a high proportion of the spring term to theatrical activity, for no sooner was *The Fourteenth of July* off the boards than he set about rehearsing three one-act plays for performance in the Playhouse on April 2nd in honour of the Fourth Universities' Congress. Besides writing one of them—*King's Evidence*—and producing all three, he acted in two of them (the others were *Vigil* by Emlyn Williams and *Five Years* by John Fernald and R. P. Brown). According to *The Times*, *King's Evidence* was the best of the bunch, and Peter 'acted in it with success'. The *Morning Post* reported that two crowded houses applauded the proceedings 'without restraint'.

Such were Peter's enthusiasm and industry that during the summer term of 1928 he was elected President of the O.U.D.S. Nor did his obsession with the theatre end when the academic year came to a close: during the long vacation he arranged two performances each of O'Neill's *Where the Cross is Made* and Galsworthy's *Escape*. He himself played the leading role in *Escape*—Matt Denant, the convict on the run—and many of his friends considered this his best theatrical performance. According to one contemporary newspaper report, he 'showed himself a very finished actor, fully equal to the handling of every situation'.

His life was made even more hectic by the fact that since the beginning of 1928 he had been writing regularly for *The Isis*, the more respectable and magazine-like of the University's two journals (the other, *Cherwell*, being more of a knockabout tabloid newspaper). *The Isis* of that day was a dreadfully frivolous and inbred organ, and the level of seriousness can be judged from one issue's Social Notes:

Major 'Harry' Puce, the polo-player, has left London, thank God.

Unctua, Lady Vastly, has gone to Berlin for the Bezique season.

Mr Alaric Fitchew, the poet, has gone to Llandudno for the Celtic twilight.

Mr Peter Fleming has gone to Ashby-de-la-Zouche for the fun of it ...

The performance by the house-party at Feeblepoke Towers, of Lady Feeblepoke's romantic drama *Through Roundhead Ranks*, has luckily been prevented by an outbreak of foot-and-mouth among the cast.

Peter contributed vacuities of this kind readily enough; but he was capable also of far more serious writing. In February he produced a powerful short story called *Wild Justice*, set in Argyllshire, in which he used elements of his own background to good advantage: a Highlander sets an ambush in a shepherd's cottage and shoots the man dead as he comes home, but then panics and in the morning shoots himself. If the action itself is melodramatic, the atmosphere of the hills bound in the grip of winter is finely realized; both the setting and the language carry strong echoes of Buchan and Conan Doyle.

In May Peter wrote an outspoken attack—indeed, by the standards of *The Isis*, a violent one—on Buchmanism, the religious cult which had just established itself in Oxford. Here there was not a trace of his normal flippancy, but instead, deeply felt anger and disapproval:

The theory of Buchmanism we do not presume to judge; but the effects of its practice we deplore. They are extremely unpleasant ... Quite obviously this theory, even if put into practice (as it never is) calmly and conscientiously, must undermine individuality and destroy free will.

This is exactly what it is doing, particularly in the women's colleges ... The authorities appear to be alarmed, but remain apathetic. It is time something was done about it.

The tone and content of the article were exceptional enough to be noticed by the *Daily Telegraph*, which next day reprinted long extracts, and a week later *The Isis* returned to the attack, giving the Buchmanites (as Peter inevitably put it) a second barrel.

He did not often strike such a high moral tone; but he had begun to display a certain intellectual arrogance, and he had no time or mercy for anyone who he considered was making a fool of himself. When Julian Hall published a book called *Alma Mater, or The Future of Oxford and Cambridge*, he sought to demolish it with a sharply barbed attack:

Mr Hall's authoritatively classical style and his rarely obtrusive self-confidence combine to conceal the fact that Mr Hall has very little to say worth hearing and takes some time saying it.

Another target was Alec Waugh:

In spite of the publishers' assurances to the contrary, Mr Alec Waugh is a third-rate writer. *The Last Chukka* contains fourteen short stories and 276 pages, and is not worth reading ... The publishers inform the reader that, both in England and in America, 'Mr Alec Waugh is now one of the most sought after of modern short-story writers.' I hope they catch him.

In February 1928 precedent was confounded when Peter was elected to the Bullingdon, a club limited mainly to Old Etonians and dedicated to drinking, hunting and steeplechasing. 'I consider it a goodish joke,' he wrote to Rupert—but it was more than that: it was a unique phenomenon.

High society at Oxford was then divided into sharply opposed camps, aptly summed up by Osbert Lancaster in his autobiographical *With an Eye to the Future*:

On the one hand were the hearties, grey flannel-trousered or elaborately plus-foured, draped in extravagantly long striped scarves indicative of athletic prowess; on the other the aesthetes, in high-necked pullovers or shantung ties in pastel shades from Messrs Halls in the High, whose hair in those days passed for long and some of whom cultivated sideburns. Apart and consciously aloof were the Bullingdons and their hangers-on, always in well-cut tweeds and old-Etonian ties, or jodhpurs, yellow polo-sweaters and hacking jackets slit to the shoulderblades.

For a high-ranking member of the O.U.D.S. to be a member also of the Bullingdon was unheard of—yet Peter managed it. For a hearty (which to some extent he was because of his constant shooting and frequent appearance in tweeds and plus fours) to be also an intellectual was equally impossible—yet Peter achieved this too. By sheer force of character—by doing what he wanted and by being himself—he broke through all the traditional social boundaries. Part hearty, he was also an intellectual, and thus was part aesthete; and yet he was more of an anti-aesthete—not because he was too oafish to entertain aesthetic feelings, but because he chose deliberately to show no feelings at all and cultivated the ultimate non-aesthetic response.

As at Eton, very few of his acquaintances realized that this urbane and witty young man was still tortured by shyness. Yet to a few close friends he admitted that he longed to be able to wield in conversation the fluency that he commanded in his writing. 'I can write what I want, but I can't say it,' he once confided to Peter Cazelet. He found it particularly difficult to talk to women (and most of them found it *impossible* to talk to him), and sometimes at dinner-parties, if the conversation took an awkward turn, he would break out into a cold sweat of embarrassment.

Fewer people still appreciated with what rigid control he kept his emotions in check. Except to Sybil, and occasionally to Rupert, he would never reveal what he was feeling, and friends found that he kept his inner self unapproachably withdrawn. Even with Bill Barry, whom he knew extremely well after innumerable shooting forays, he maintained an elaborately artificial façade. He and Bill never discussed life or ambition or indeed anything serious at all; almost all their conversation was frivolous, and to an outsider would surely have seemed quite imbecile, consisting as it did largely of clichés from Victorian books of travel and field sports. A woodcock was never referred to as a woodcock, but always as 'Master Longbill'. A pair of duck was never a pair of duck, but 'the mallard and his dusky mate'. Water was invariably 'the precious fluid'. Once, when an excitable gun discharged into the undergrowth, Peter's voice was heard from the depths of the covert saying in its most cutting tones, 'I shouldn't do *that* again', and thereafter the phrase was used as a joke on every conceivable occasion.

With other friends, such as Peter Cazelet, Peter spoke perfect Bulldog Drummondese. 'Pipes drawing well, a move was made to the gunroom,' was a stock way of saying that it was time they got up from breakfast. 'Bedfordshire' meant it was time to go to bed, and the words 'useful' and 'effective' became formal terms of approval by means of which the speaker could admit that he was in favour of something (or someone) without opening himself up emotionally to the extent of saying that he *liked* it: thus not only could a person be described as 'effective'; the word could be applied equally to a tie, a picture or a view. In the same vein Peter developed a whole series of one-word answers which put paid to conversations which he saw no need to prolong: '*Exactly*,' he would say; '*Absolutely*,' '*Pity*,' '*Never mind*'—all with an emphasis that forestalled retort. To those who indulged in it all this artificiality was tremendously amusing and many people sought to imitate Peter in the perfection of his unshakeable urbanity.

His friends also eagerly repeated his aphorisms—among them that most debutantes seemed to consist of 'two hot hands and a heavy silence', and that the inside of the British Broadcasting Corporation resembled nothing so much as 'a cross between a transatlantic liner and a lunatic asylum.'

There can be no doubt that his mother's behaviour greatly increased his natural reticence, for she tended to stifle any admission or show of sensibility. Just as she—a talented violinist—did her best to stop her daughter Amaryllis playing the cello (at which, none the less, she became expert), so Eve mounted a roundabout campaign designed to stop Peter acting. This she did by persuading one of the dons at Christ Church, whom she knew, to tell Peter that his father would have strongly disapproved of his participation in the affairs of the O.U.D.S. Peter naturally ignored this clumsy manoeuvre, yet it further reinforced his determination never to tell his mother what he really felt, and—whatever the causes—he grew up with a strangely limited range of aesthetic response. Although his verbal appreciation was acute, he had very little feeling for poetry, practically none for pictures, and none whatever for music (the fact that he was tone-deaf was well known in the family, and once during a concert in Henley his Uncle, Lord Wyfold, leant across to him and groaned in a stage-whisper: 'Peter, singing is an *awful* thing.').

In May 1928, to celebrate his coming of age, his grandmother gave what he described as a 'lugubrious ball'. Much more to his liking was his mother's present—a pair of 12-bore Purdey shotguns (the most expensive obtainable) which he used and cherished for the rest of his life.

In the autumn he made his usual trip to Scotland, and again stayed with the Barrys at Ardmore. Already he was a formidable long-distance driver: in his little Morris he did 440 miles on the first day, and 160 by lunch-time on the second. 'I was shot in the back yesterday by a particularly bloody man,' he wrote to Rupert on August 11th, 'but the wound was "but a scratch".' At the end of the month he went down to Black Mount, but later returned to Ardmore, whence on September 24th he wrote to Rupert again in 'a stupor of contentment for which Sybil is largely responsible.' By then they had decided to get married and were unofficially engaged, but Peter's mother was still fighting a dogged rearguard action and making vague but menacing pronouncements about there being no question of his marrying until he was twenty-five—in three and a half years' time.

Back at Oxford for his final year, he tackled an extraordinarily full programme with his customary apparent lack of effort but in fact with immense concentration. Not only did he have to start working in earnest for his Schools the next summer: he was also President of the O.U.D.S. and Editor of *The Isis*.

Once again he returned to Christ Church with a one-act play that he had written during the vacation. *Iconoclasm* was performed during the Michaelmas term, and like *King's Evidence* won a good reception: set in a newspaper office, it portrayed an Editor whose habit was to receive twenty of his readers every week and talk to them 'straight from the shoulder'. At the end of one such gathering the editor's villainy was suddenly exposed when one of his guests, revealing himself as the man whom he had done down years ago, pulled a gun and shot him. In its mixture of satire and melodrama, the play can be fairly described as a typical piece of Oxford Fleming.

The main event of the O.U.D.S. year was the spring production of *Othello*, which was given in February 1929, and produced by the American, Brewster Morgan. Othello was played by Valentine Dyall, and Peter took the part of Iago. At that time the O.U.D.S. annual play was treated with immense respect and seriousness by the national press, and *Othello* was widely reviewed, attracting a whole column in *The Times*. Most of the critics were favourably impressed, and the production was certainly a considerable financial success. Peter himself won mixed notices. The *Daily Telegraph* was cool, and described his Iago as 'brisk and chatty, and with an odd staccato utterance'; the *Daily Mail* thought him 'too off-hand and conversational. He looked tremendously handsome, but never gave one the idea of guile or cruelty.' The *Oxford Magazine* considered his Iago 'a solid and conscientious piece of work … Mr Fleming gave us the calculating rascal, but not the monster. But his performance was a studied and skilful one, and in some scenes he was excellent.' The *Sunday Times* praised him for avoiding 'the primrose path of hissing villainy', and the *Observer* was even more enthusiastic: 'Mr Fleming's study of Iago, direct, unhesitating, strong even when his evil world fell in pieces, was the finest piece of acting in the performance.'

These careful and on the whole eulogistic assessments diverge strikingly from the memories of Peter's contemporaries. To them *Othello* was a disaster, a shambles pulled through only by Martita Hunt's highly professional Emilia. Nor is it easy, now, to see how Peter's acting can have won such acclaim, for his friends remember him as being quite embarrassingly bad. Tom Boase, who was then a junior don at Hertford and Auditor of the O.U.D.S., recalled with agony the difficulties they had over Peter's voice: he could not get the rhythm of the blank verse, and never managed to throw off his habitual drawl. To Osbert Lancaster Peter's renderings of Bulldog Drummond and Iago were indistinguishable: in both parts he was still Peter Fleming, unchanged. Many of his friends thought it almost pathetic that someone could be so passionately keen on acting and yet so frightfully bad at it.

After leaving Oxford Peter scarcely acted again, except in one or two family films. Yet his experience with the O.U.D.S., reinforced by his reading of English, left him with a deep knowledge of dramatic literature and an interest in the theatre that lasted all his life.

While Peter grappled with Shakespeare in Oxford, Rupert Hart-Davis was working out a similar enthusiasm for the theatre in London. After leaving Balliol in 1927 he had joined the Old Vic as a student, and a year later went as an actor to the Lyric Theatre, Hammersmith. It was through him that Peter first met a young actress who had just made her début as Sarah in Shaw's *Major Barbara* at the Theatre Royal in Huddersfield and was clearly bound for stardom: Celia Johnson.

Rupert himself first met Celia at the end of January 1929, and quickly became very fond of her. On April 1st he and Celia, together with Peter and Sybil went to the matinée performance of C. B. Cochran's review *Wake Up and Dream*. At the end of April they all met again. But these early encounters between Peter and Celia do not seem to have made any particular impression on either, and for the moment the main beam of Peter's attention was focused on Sybil.

He sailed through his finals with his usual imperturbability, and when he went down from Oxford in June 1929 he was regarded as one of the ablest men of his year. A popular triple bet of the day prophesied that he would be the next editor of *The Times* but one, Elizabeth Pakenham the next socialist Prime Minister but two, and David Mathew the next Pope but three. Though none eventually came off, all seemed sporting bets at the time, and the first was the safest of the three.

Golden prospects were all very well, but Peter was in a double difficulty; first, he did not know what he should do; and second, his family did. His mother and grandfather had joined forces in a plan to put him into the family business of merchant banking, and it was decided that in September he was to go to New York to serve an apprenticeship in a firm of stockbrokers. The prospect appalled him, partly because it would mean being separated from Sybil for several months, but mainly because the intricacies of business and finance were to him impenetrably arcane and of positively stupefying boredom.

Before having to face reality, he took off with Rupert for a motor tour through France and Spain. This he conducted with the combination of restlessness, originality and high good humour that was to characterize all his later travels. They set off in William, Peter's two-seater Morris, on

July 17th and took a cargo-boat from Dover to Calais; and somehow, although they fully intended to camp out, and were well equipped to do so, they ended the first day at the Trianon Palace Hotel at Versailles, one of the most expensive and comfortable in France. Opening his suitcase there, Peter found it full of what he pronounced to be 'fine loam'. This proved, on closer inspection, to be coffee, which his mother had pressed upon them in case they could find none drinkable, and which had burst from its bag during the journey.

From there they went to Poitiers, Angoulême, Bayonne, Biarritz, St Jean de Luz, and so into Spain, Peter driving all the way. Sometimes they camped, and sometimes they stayed in hotels; whenever Peter was forced to fill up a hotel register, he entered his profession as 'Sanitary Inspector'. The whole trip was coloured by the constant breakdown of the car's steerage, by endless hunts for Edgeworth tobacco, and by the difficulties of communication with the natives. Considering that he had read modern languages at school, and carried off so many prizes, Peter's grip on French seemed remarkably weak. 'La direction est un peu disloquée,' he would inform the mechanics in the latest garage; and once he paid the penalty when, more out of ignorance than out of bravado, he defied a warning sign that proclaimed GOUDRON FRAIS and took a corner at full speed, only to find the road awash with red-hot liquid tar, with which he, Rupert and the car were instantly plastered.

In Spain, Peter's Spanish proved still more rudimentary than his French, and in his diary for July 20th, in Bilbao, Rupert noted that 'last night's dinner was none too easily ordered.' Back in France, on July 23rd they reached Pau, where they bought a copy of *The Times* and discovered that Peter had got a First in English. Next day in Tarascon Peter warned Rupert against *vol-au-vent* as 'a mound of dough filled with pieces of bird not usually connected with the table.' Surviving this, and many worse gastronomic experiences, they drove through Nîmes, Avignon, Aix-en-Provence and Cannes to Nice, where they met Peter's mother and Ian, and whence all four took ship to Corsica.

There they stayed in the Castle Inn at Algajola. Ian, characteristically, discovered two *louche* English homosexuals living in a cottage near by and went off to play bridge with them. Peter, soon restless after a day or two's inactivity, set off on an abortive boar-hunt. Nor could he be persuaded to stay long: on August 4th, scarcely a week after arriving, he left for home, determined at all costs to reach Black Mount for the start of the grouse season on the 12th.

This he accomplished easily enough, doing nine hundred miles and the two crossings in three days exactly. In Scotland, however, he was disappointed to find his usual long stalking and shooting holiday severely curtailed. Early in September he despatched the faithful William to London 'lashed to the cow-catcher of the Midnight Express', and himself followed on the 11th. Three days later he sailed out of Southampton for New York.

No doubt the decision to send him to America was inspired by his mother's determination to separate him from Sybil (he could just as well, or better, have learnt finance in London); and now at last her plan succeeded, for his departure finally brought to an end their long romance. Clearly the parting caused both Peter and Sybil great unhappiness; but Eve's intransigence—whatever its motive—did eventually prove beneficial to him. Had he married and settled down at twenty-two or twenty-three, as he wanted to do, he might never have travelled; and had he never travelled, he could not have written the books that made him famous.

4

Casting About

'Long Island represents the Americans' idea of what God would have done with Nature if he'd had the money,' Peter wrote to Rupert on September 29th, 1929 from the Piping Rock Club in Locust Valley, where he spent the first weekend of his stay in America.

Go to Bilbao, go to Crackenthorpe, frequent Carcassonne, take up your residence at Blackpool, but never, NEVER have anything to do with New York ... New York is ugly, noisy, dangerous, hostile and expensive. I start work tomorrow—four months from nine to five daily (nine to one on Saturdays): I have to go downtown in the Subway, which is forty million times more horrible than the tube and so crowded that only the most powerful and unscrupulous (it is said) ever reach their destination in time.

The great American depression seemed to Peter as nothing compared with his own: Wall Street collapsed a few days after his arrival, but his own spirits sank even lower as he struggled to understand railway finance, at which, he knew only too well, his grandfather had been a genius. In a room with 'Research' marked on the door he made surreptitious efforts to write plays, and found solace in firing off spirited letters to Rupert. News from London that arrived at the end of October made him want to

talk absolute nonsense for half an hour. Gosh, one does miss one's nonsense in this life ... For four weeks now I have grappled with railway statistics from nine to five in steam heat and electric light: my fellow-workers have all the intelligence of a tapir but lack that creature's delicate sense of humour. I had no idea that work could be one tenth as boring. Anglo Saxon was a feast of fun for young and old in comparison ... I simply wouldn't think twice about chucking the whole business if it weren't for the endless complications of family responsibilities and expectations and so on ...

This is an incredible life ... one gets very little sleep and about as much fresh air as a mole with no sense of direction: in addition to which I play squash every evening and drink too much ... I get no time to read, except *Anna Karenina* in the Subway. I shall probably go on being an unpaid wage slave till the spring: by which time I shall know the number of lavatory attendants per cubic passenger on all the railroads in America.

By the middle of December his morale was even worse:

This is the most God-awful existence. I don't get nearly enough to do, and my national sport is perforce introspection. My aversion to Business and all that it stands for grows almost hourly, and I know beyond any shadow of doubt that I shall never be any good at it or happy doing it ...

Comic things occur periodically, though not between the hours of nine and five. I've now worked, or gone through the motions of working, five and a half days a week for three months and disliked it all the time ... My nerves are very bad, my trousers very shiny, and I have given vent to a fitful moustache ... I read nothing, write nothing, and live entirely on oysters ... The only people here with a sense of proportion are the bootleggers, and the only people with a sense of humour are dead.

It is a marvellous place for names. John [Fox-Strangways] and I are hot on the tail of a debutante called Ruth Quackenbusch. Almost everyone in society is called Biddle. I am being pursued by a young German countess, but outwit her at every turn.

The buildings in the financial district are of a truly immense height: it is wonderful to stand among them and to reflect that they are packed from top to bottom with hundreds and thousands of Crashing Bores. Not only that, but if one of these Bores decides to commit suicide by jumping out of the window (which they quite often do) it is almost morally certain that, on reaching the ground, he will injure or destroy two or three creatures as crass and beef-witted as himself.

It is monstrous the way people here talk: they go on roaring and quacking out facts as if they were doing it for some considerable wager. But I must say that a lot of them are nice.

'I know beyond any shadow of doubt that I shall never be any good at it or happy doing it.' Peter's decision, after that first bitter taste, to abandon business struck different people in different ways. Some saw it as the first great failure of his life—a failure to come to terms with reality and settle down to an adult existence; a failure, moreover, that caused much chagrin in his family. Others, however, took exactly the opposite view: that the decision was a triumph over his family, and a victory over the forces of convention that were trying to coerce him into a normal mould. But to those who knew him best, the decision was simply inevitable: it was inconceivable that someone so original and individualistic as Peter would ever be comfortable within the confines of a routine office existence, and his revolt was only a matter of time.

This is not to say that he had no qualms about defying his family's wishes. His loyalty to the clan, and particularly to his mother, was deep and devoted. But his conscience was eased by the knowledge that Uncle Phil had taken over the running of Robert Fleming & Co., and by the fact that his own brother Michael was already showing a flair for finance. Nor is there any doubt that Peter made a real effort to understand the mysterious processes of Wall Street: the trouble was, he just could not take himself seriously as a financier. Towards the end of 1929, at Phil's request, he sent home a brief, scribbled report on a company called Drug Incorporated in which the London firm was interested. After some rather uneasy use of financial terms, in which he virtually recommended takeover, Peter ended his note with the characteristic paragraph:

PS. I've shown this to an extraordinarily sound man here; he says it is not misleading, and that he was all for Drug when it was over 100. He knows what he is talking about, which is more than I do.

By Christmas his mind was made up, and although no letter survives he evidently wrote home telling the family of his decision to quit. But there was no urgent reason for him to return to Europe, and immediately after Christmas he went south to Alabama for a week's quail-shooting. This he thoroughly enjoyed. With his American host he rode from nine in the morning till dusk on horses 'of unobtrusive sagacity and great comfort', while pointers worked in pairs. 'The country', he wrote in his game-book:

was pleasantly broken and varied—swamps and cotton fields and little hills with pine and sage. You carried your gun in a sort of scabbard under the saddle-flap. Galloping home in the dusk was great fun ... I shot only moderately, but was considered phenomenally good.

Back in New York on January 5th, 1930, he described to Rupert in greater detail his 'hygienic and welcome' week's exercise, which yielded 123 quail:

> This entailed sitting from 9 a.m. to 6 p.m. on a horse so accommodating that you could almost strike matches on it, and from time to time discharging a nonchalant broadside into a cloud of these Semitic delicatessen. The weather was ideal, and the country populated entirely by charming negroes. Two of these rode with us to manage the dogs: they were called Hog and Oscar, but to me they will always be Swan and Edgar. On New Year's Eve I went out 'possum hunting with a negro called (and how rightly) Fluke ...
>
> My host in Alabama and his friend were, I believe, the best type of businessmen, but you might as well share a house with a yoke of oxen for all the amusement or companionship they afforded. You have summed up their social value and their human appeal when you have said they are house-trained.

For his next excursion—a trip to Guatemala—Peter took advantage of a slender business excuse. Uncle Phil wanted a report on a company called International Railroads of Central America, which ran a Guatemalan railway carrying bananas, and Peter volunteered to investigate its operations. His mother, characteristically, opposed the venture on the grounds that it would be dangerous and demanded that someone should go with him; but he silenced her with a breezy cable—MENTALLY STAGNANT MORALLY STALWART PHYSICALLY NIMBLE DEFINITELY WANT GO GUATEMALA COMPANION UNESSENTIAL —and set off.

Once again he laced the report he wrote with disclaimers—'Remember that all the above is based on ignorance and superficial observation'— but he clearly enjoyed the trip, whose highlight was a shooting foray on the 11,500-foot volcano of Atitlan. 'This was a very odd venture,' he reported in his game-book:

> The expedition consisted of myself with a ·350 rifle—an unknown quantity [and suitable for big game]; four charming Indians from San Lucas with muzzle-loading shotguns; and three small dogs, of whom one went home and one was lost. The first day we had a hard climb and tried a deer-drive on the shoulder of the volcano;

one *venayo* appeared (I do not know the correct name for these deer) but no one got a shot at it. We then went after *lardias*: the word meant nothing to me, and I hoped they might be 'possums or racoons. I shot one a long way off with the ·350 and the remains proved to be those of a rather decorative squirrel. They were collected, cooked and eaten. Two of the Indians got four miserable little doves, the size of thrushes. We ate those, too. It was very cold that night. A mountain lion came quite close to the fire. We heard it and found its tracks. Dawn was incredibly beautiful. I almost burst over the last thousand feet, never having been so high.

In many ways—in its improbability, its wild natural setting and its violent physical demands—this was exactly the sort of shooting that appealed to Peter most. He never greatly cared for elaborate and highly organized shoots: he was always happiest on his own, or with one or two companions, and if he got one old grouse on a stravaig at Black Mount, or a single, wily cock-pheasant at Nettlebed—or merely one squirrel with a big-game rifle on a Guatemalan volcano—he was far more pleased than if he had stood in a line of guns and killed a hundred birds driven over him.

In March 1930 he returned briefly to New York, taking passage for the first time in an aeroplane on a flight from Guatemala City to Mexico City. 'A very large number of people assembled to bid us godspeed,' he wrote later. 'In this valedictory throng the Latin Americans crossed themselves repeatedly as we prepared to take off; many were in tears.' In the air he 'wrote blasé letters home', among them a card to Rupert:

March 16. Am in aeroplane. Below me country alleged to be Mexico … Have just eaten small bit of Guatemalan cheese: propose shortly to die of thirst. But may be frustrated in this by pilot, who appears fatigued and listless.

Returning to England in the spring, he worked for two months in the City before finally deciding that he could not face that kind of life. The family were dismayed, and could not help him find another job, for he wanted nothing in any of the areas of which they had experience. The result was that he spent most of that summer in a desultory and depressing search for employment.

In July he signed on for an expedition to the Eastern Caribbean islands; its aim was to resuscitate the once-flourishing salt industry, 'with the idea', in the words of the organizer, 'of supplying Newfoundland and Nova Scotia with Empire salt, instead of the Spanish article which takes first place at present.' This promised to be just the kind of faintly ridiculous expedition that Peter would enjoy, but unfortunately it came to nothing.

In September he applied for a job with the British Broadcasting Corporation, supporting his application with the backing of two enthusiastic referees. 'He is regarded by us as far and away one of the most promising of our younger writers ... He will, I think, go far,' wrote Nancy Pearn of Curtis Brown, the literary agents; and Lord Clarendon (with whose son, Lord Hyde, Peter had been at Eton and Oxford) described him as 'an exceptionally intelligent young fellow, well worth trying to get hold of.' He was given an interview and made a good impression, but as no job was immediately available the best the B.B.C. could offer him was the hope of some post in the future.

Between these various disappointments he joined the Grenadier Guards and became a second lieutenant in the supplementary reserve of officers. He also wrote short stories, but again in a desultory manner, without managing to get any accepted for publication. He lived in London, at Turner's House, and spent many of his weekends at Joyce Grove, whence, one Saturday and Sunday, he walked the whole way to Sutton Veny, in Wiltshire, where Rupert was staying; he did twenty-five miles the first day and fifty the second, and although he himself arrived in fine fettle, his dog had to be revived with brandy.

Late in September he went north to Black Mount, and some of his restlessness came out in a letter to Primrose Harley:

> I do hope you're having a very good summer. The shadow of unemployment has hung rather heavily over mine ... How is Art? Literature, I find, obstinately refuses to be a commercial proposition, or anything like one.

A few weeks later, when Primrose had gone to America, he wrote to her again:

> I thought it was a very good thing to do—to go out there entirely on your own. It must have felt quite like an adventure; and the sensation is worth seeking out, in these deplorable days.

Adventure was what Peter craved; and when he did eventually find a job in the Economic Advisory Council, he must have realized that it was only a stop-gap. At the time, however, it seemed a considerable relief to have got something, and he described the job to Primrose as 'sort of in the Cabinet Secretariat. It looks like being rather amusing backstage stuff: and a lot of work.' All that survive from his time there are two immense reports—one on the trawler industry and one on the tsetse fly—from which almost every trace of his style and wit has been ironed out by heavy bureaucratic hands. But at least the writing of them kept him occupied through the winter and stopped him brooding too much about his future.

Then, in the spring of 1931, thanks to Rupert, he at last hit on something far more congenial. Rupert had by then left the stage and become an office boy at Heinemann's, the publishers: one day he was approached by Barbara Back, wife of Ivor Back, the surgeon, who asked him if he wanted a job as assistant Literary Editor on the *Spectator*. He said no, but he knew who did: Peter Fleming—and so began an association that lasted, on and off, for the rest of Peter's life.

In 1931 the *Spectator* was both owned and edited by Evelyn Wrench, whose name might have come out of Waugh and whose manner out of Wodehouse. Peter later described him as 'an idealist with a high-pitched voice and a rather fluttery manner'; in common with other young members of the paper's staff, Derek Verschoyle among them, he found it hard to take Wrench seriously. 'I do not think he was a very good editor,' he wrote afterwards. 'An amateurish atmosphere pervaded the sage-green interior of 99 Gower Street, and the paper lacked bite.' Nor did Peter think anything of Wilson Harris, who, though officially the paper's political editor, was effectively in charge for much of the time, since Wrench was often away.

On the staid and vapid journal that these two produced Peter's arrival made a sharp impact. Under his own name and the pseudonyms Moth, Scadavay and Apemantus he began producing articles of such incisive wit and cynicism that the older hands on the paper became seriously alarmed. Wilson Harris, he used to say, carried his articles about as gingerly as if they had been sackfuls of ferrets. One of Scadavay's first pieces was a furious attack on hotels, and, as a result of it, all hotel advertising in the paper ceased instantly. So flippant was Peter on religious subjects that dozens of clergymen wrote enraged letters cancelling their subscriptions, and the paper's religious adviser, Mrs Evelyn Underhill, implored Wrench to suppress him. He nearly *was* suppressed altogether by Harris after writing:

It is the proud boast of the editorial staff that no two issues of the *Spectator* have ever been proved identical. Sometimes it is the phraseology that is different, sometimes the order or titles of the articles are changed. If the same thing is said, it is said in a different way. If the same words are used, they are used of something else.

That has always been the tradition. If not variety, then at least divergence. *Semper idem, sed nunquam verbatim.*

Variety was certainly Peter's own strength. Besides the Moth column, 'A Penny of Observation', he reviewed books, plays and films. Much of his film criticism now strikes a tiresomely intellectual and pedantic note; but whenever he discussed a subject that genuinely interested him— such as a production of *Othello* at the Old Vic, or a new edition of Colonel Peter Hawker's *Shooting Diaries*—he dropped all pretension and wrote from the heart in a far more engaging manner. So delighted was Eric Parker, editor of the Hawker diaries, with Peter's notice that he wrote to thank him:

> You won't mind an old journalist telling a new recruit to the paper on whose staff I used to be that yours is much the best-written review of all that I have had of the Hawker book—and indeed of all the reviews I have had for a long time past.

In Gower Street, then, Peter found a vantage-point from which he could begin enjoyably to flex his literary muscles. But still he was restless. Mary Pakenham, a close friend of his, found him boiling with energy yet extraordinarily tense and neurotic. In June and July he spent four weeks with the Grenadiers at Pirbright, training there in the morning, driving to London at lunch-time and working at the *Spectator* in the afternoon. He would then take Mary to the theatre, go on to supper (often at Rules), drive her home, and finally motor back to Pirbright.

Such full days, however, by no means satisfied him. To Mary it seemed that he was still worried by the disappointment of his family, who had not yet come to terms with his peremptory abandonment of the career they had ordained for him. But the real trouble was that wanderlust was upon him: his taste of North and Central America had sharpened his appetite for far places, and in the summer of 1931 he planned his first expedition to the East.

It is no longer clear how, so soon after joining the staff, he managed to secure four months' leave of absence from the *Spectator* without losing his job; but somehow he arranged it, and in September he set off as one of two honorary secretaries delegated by Chatham House to attend a conference being held in China by a body called the Institute of Pacific Relations. This was his ostensible reason for the journey, but he planned also to stay with John and Tony Keswick—two brothers who working in the family firm of Jardine Matheson in Shanghai—

and the trip as a whole was designed to be what he later called a 'swan'—a general look round.

'Off at crack of d. tomorrow,' he wrote to Rupert from Turner's House on September 19th:

> Wish you were coming. Will write really facetious letter from poop of vessel ... Have examined plan and can find no trace of masts—surely indispens. adjunct? Otherwise, what origin of well-known phrase 'going to sea Before the Mast'??? Cannot accept Bumtrap's emendation 'going to Sea before the Mast is Fitted'. Am at loss.

All this was nonsense, for the only ship on which he sailed was the cross-Channel steamer, and his main means of transport was the train—first the express to Berlin and Moscow, and then the Trans-Siberian. Although he kept a diary, he wrote scarcely a word about the trip for publication, evidently considering it insufficiently memorable.

Crossing the frontier into Russia for the first time, he was immediately enveloped in the suffocating blanket of Soviet Communist bureaucracy. Round the walls of the customs-house at Niegoreloge, he noted, ran the deathless exhortation 'Workers of the World, Unite', in gold letters and four languages; but the second half of the slogan—'You Have Nothing to Lose But Your Chains'—had been omitted. It would represent, he wrote in his diary, 'a highly conservative estimate of one's potential losses in that place.'

Moscow's drabness depressed him, as did the 'startling and universal ugliness of the women'. But he observed the city and its inhabitants—'oddly colourless and oddly likeable'—with amused detachment, and reflected on the Muscovites' chronic inability to do anything in style:

> The Kremlin, castellated and cupolaed with dentifricial abandon, has the splendid, compelling assurance of a strong place that is also a beautiful one. From the river bank opposite one admires its crouching outlines unreservedly. But why, oh why, does the clock which crowns a central tower announce the time as 12.15 when it is really half-past five? Why do they *never* carry things off?

In those gloomy surroundings—where 'the bath in his [the visitor's] hotel is out of commission, the lavatory is under repair. The lift does not work. The service is awful. The telephone exchange is impossible. Only one match in three strikes'—he conceived a kind of masochistic affection for the Russians which he retained ever afterwards.

The Trans-Siberian Railway appealed to him in a similar way, in spite of its shortcomings; and later, in his book *One's Company*, he wrote an evocative description of his mode of travel on it—a passage that combined elements of his first journey, in 1931, with some from a second trip two years later:

You wake up in the morning. Your watch says it is eight o'clock; but you are travelling east, and you know that it is really nine, though you might be hard put to it to explain why this is so. Your berth is comfortable. There is no need to get up, and no incentive either. You have nothing to look forward to, nothing to avoid. No assets, no liabilities ...

You lie in your berth, justifiably inert. Past the window plains crawl and forests flicker. The sun shines weakly on an empty land ... There is always a magpie in sight.

You have nothing to look at, but no reason to stop looking. You are living in a vacuum, and at last you have to invent some absurdly artificial necessity for getting up: 'fifteen magpies from now', or 'next time the engine whistles'. For you are inwardly afraid that without some self-discipline to give it a pattern this long period of suspended animation will permanently affect your character for the worse.

So in the end you get up, washing perfunctorily in the little dark confessional which you share with the next compartment, and in the basin for which the experienced traveller brings his own plug ... Then, grasping your private pot of marmalade, you lurch along to the dining-car. It is now eleven o'clock, and the dining-car is empty. You order tea and bread, and make without appetite a breakfast which is more than sufficient for your needs ... After that you wander back to your compartment. The *provodnik* has transformed your bed into a seat, and perhaps you hold with him some foolish conversation in which the rudiments of three languages are prostituted in an endeavour to compliment each other on their simultaneous mastery. Then you sit down and read. You read and read and read. There are no distractions, no interruptions, no temptations to get up and do something else; there is nothing else to do. You read as you have never read before.

And so the day passes. If you are wise you shun the regulation meal at three o'clock, which consists of five courses not easily to be identified, and during which the car is crowded and the windows blurred with steam. I had brought with me from London biscuits and potted meat and cheese; and he is a fool who does not take at least some victuals of his own. But as a matter of fact, what with the air-

76

less atmosphere and lack of exercise, you don't feel hungry on the Trans-Siberian Railway. A pleasant lassitude, a sense almost of disembodiment, descends on you ...

At the most westerly stations—there are perhaps three stops of twenty minutes every day—you pace the platforms vigorously in a conscientious British way. But gradually this practice is abandoned. As you are drawn further into Asia, old fetishes lose their power. It becomes harder and harder to persuade yourself that you feel a craving for exercise, and indeed you almost forget that you ought to feel this craving. At first you are alarmed, for this is the East, the notorious East, where white men go to pieces; you fear that you are losing your grip, that you are going native. But you do nothing about it, and soon your conscience ceases to prick and it seems quite natural to stand limply in the sunlight, owlish, frowsty, and immobile, like everybody else.

At last evening comes. The sun is setting somewhere far back along the road you have travelled. A slanting light always lends intimacy to a landscape, and this Siberia, flecked darkly by the tapering shadows of trees, seems a place at once more friendly and more mysterious than the naked, non-committal flats of noon. Your eyes are tired, and you put down your book. Against the grey and creeping distances outside memory and imagination stage in turn their struggles of the past and future. For the first time loneliness descends, and you sit examining its implications until you find Siberia vanished and the grimy window offering nothing save your own face, foolish, indistinct, and as likely as not unshaved. You adjourn to the dining-car, for eggs.

Just as the darkening window of the train reflected the outlines of Peter's face, so this last paragraph reflects a little of his character: a romantic, who would scarcely ever admit that he entertained romantic ideas; a person with so little emotional confidence that if ever he allowed a trace of sentimentality to creep into his writing, he must instantly puncture it with self-mockery.

As his remarks about trying to talk to the *provodnik* make clear, his Russian was monosyllabic (once on the Trans-Siberian his request in sign-language for a boiled egg was 'fulfilled, three-quarters of an hour after it had been expressed, by the appearance of a whole roast fowl'). His Chinese was just as basic; but the moment he entered China for the first time he felt himself unexpectedly but pleasantly at home. The reason was simply that in his nature (although until then he had never

77

had cause to notice it) he possessed many Chinese characteristics: in his patience, in his even temper, in the impassivity of his features, and above all in his skill at calculating, preserving or yielding degrees of 'face', he met the natives on their own ground.

A discovery that pleased him less was that his arrival in Manchuria had coincided with a full-scale invasion by the Japanese, who were in the process of overrunning the entire country. Shenyang had been occupied on September 18th, 1931, less than a fortnight before he arrived, and he got there to find everything in turmoil.

> I've just had my first bath since I last saw you, and am in conse-
> quence pardonably elated, [he wrote to Rupert from Mukden on
> September 30th.]
> There is the best part of a war going on here, though not the best
> from my point of view since it achieves the inconvenient but falls
> short of the spectacular ... The railway journey from here to
> Peking, though it recommends itself to me very strongly, is really
> not worth attempting unless one is what they call Alone in the
> World. Yesterday all the passengers were robbed and two killed,
> and the day before the Japanese shot it up with an aeroplane ...
>
> I'm longing to crack a joke, I don't mind telling you. But at the
> moment the ecstasy of having a bath and a bed to oneself are
> sufficiently overpowering. I must say, everything has been very good
> value so far, and I wouldn't have missed it for anything.

He duly went to the conference in Shanghai, but then proceeded to enjoy himself, both in Peking, which he thought 'incredibly lovely', and in Shanghai, where he stayed with the Keswicks and shot snipe and duck. In November he travelled farther south to Swatow; there he spent ten days living on a boat with the representative of a tobacco company, and on November 10th he wrote to Primrose:

> We visit remote and smelly villages and eat shark's fins to repletion
> with the native dealers ... Most of the time we shoot, sleeping on
> the floorboards at night with our guns theatrically but apparently
> wisely loaded, on account of the bandits.

Writing to Rupert four days later he added:

> I am having fun here shooting. You live in a motor boat, caked in
> mud, very much under the stars, which are curiously plentiful.
> There are millions of intractable ducks and also geese, but these last
> live where the bandits are, in paradoxical safety.

His aim throughout had been to be back in England by Christmas, and in the second half of November he set off by sea for Singapore. Thence he drove up through Malaya with Archie Rose, a banker going the rounds of his branches, and from on board the S.S. *Talamba*, which he had just joined at Penang, Peter wrote Uncle Phil a long letter of down-to-earth information and advice about rubber. The slump, he reported, had driven the producers to their wits' end—'no very great distance, I imagine'—but after a few such cracks he got down to offering a serious report which he obviously hoped would be of some commercial value in London.

He reached Rangoon on December 1st, and thence, via Delhi, Baghdad and Istanbul, he returned overland to London. By the time he reached the Bosphorus his passport was filled from end to end with endorsements and visas. His permit to leave Istanbul occupied the final page, and the inside of the back cover had to be pressed into service for the remaining stamps. In three and a half months he had travelled some fifteen thousand miles and had acquired for China an affection that never deserted him.

After a swan of such proportions, London and the *Spectator* must have seemed very tame, but for a few months he settled back into the office with the effective, if not the official, position of Literary Editor. It was he, at any rate, who had to arrange the book reviews, and he was not always successful in attempts to secure particular critics. 'Dear Mr Shaw,' he wrote to T. E. Shaw (formerly Lawrence) on January 15th, 1932:

> Will you review for us *Arabia Felix*, Mr Bertram Thomas's book, when it comes out? I do not suppose you will want to. Please don't bother to answer this if you don't.
>
> Yours sincerely,
>
> PETER FLEMING
> Literary Sub-Editor

He supposed right—but at least he got an answer, scribbled on the bottom of his own sheet of paper:

> This would be entirely improper. I've been feeble enough to write the introductory note for Thomas! And shall regret it, continually.
>
> T. E. SHAW

This letter was one of the few pieces of paper that Peter treasured, and some thirty years later he wrote about it: 'It is typical of the amateur standards of those days that I didn't know what a sub-editor was.'

Amateur he may have been, but his writing showed more and more sparkle. Reviewing C. B. Cochran's *Helen!* at the Adelphi in February, he started off:

Helen! Not *Oh, Helen!* or *Say, Helen!* or anything crude like that. Just *Helen!* A short title.

It might have been shorter. ! would have been enough. At first the exclamation mark may strike you as rather *arriviste*, rather too much in the Walk Up! tradition. But really it is the clue to the whole production. It compels your gasps as would a drawn sword.

A title less explosive would have been hypocritical.

In March he reviewed P. G. Wodehouse's *Louder and Funnier* enthusiastically and was rewarded by a letter from the author at home in the Alpes Maritimes:

Dear R. P. F.,

Thanks awfully for your kind review of *Louder and Funnier*. The local peasants as I pass whisper to one another '*Il me semble que Monsieur Vodehouse est satisfait de lui aujourdhui!*' I am half-way through a full-length Jeeves novel. What will the harvest be?

The young men at 99 Gower Street gave the older inhabitants little chance to relax. Wilson Harris, never at ease when Peter was about, fortunately did not realize that he had invented and given spurious renown to a contributor called W. B. Tizzard. The name was one that Peter made up to sign a review of some miscellaneous books by L. A. G. Strong, but in due course the *Authors' and Writers' Who's Who* sent Tizzard a form to fill in, and for many years his entry appeared in their pages, with his recreations given as baseball, demonology and tricycling.

It was not long, however, before relative peace returned to the *Spectator*, for in April 1932 Peter saw and answered an advertisement in the Agony Column of *The Times* that was to take him abroad for months and determine the course of his entire life.

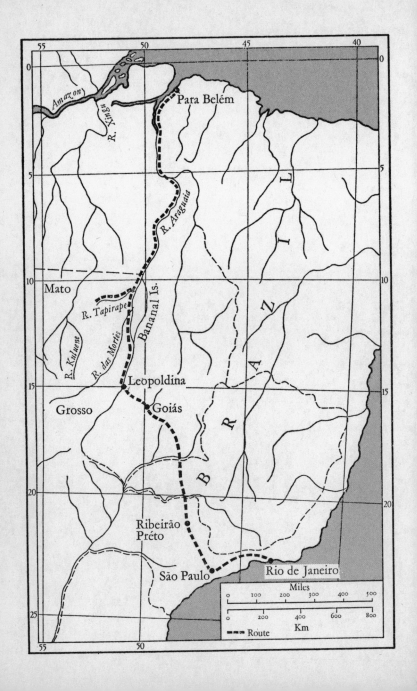

5

Brazil

In 1932 *The Times* carried nothing so mundane as news on its front page; the paper's face was given entirely to advertisements, and of these by far the most celebrated was the collection of personal wants, offers and *cris de coeur* known as the Agony Column. As Peter often remarked, he made a practice of reading the Agony Column first, greatly preferring its stimulating eccentricities to the stodgier fare of the editorial pages; and one morning in April his eye was taken by an announcement just far-fetched enough to appeal to him:

> Exploring and sporting expedition, under experienced guidance, leaving England June to explore rivers Central Brazil, if possible ascertain fate Colonel Fawcett; abundance game, big and small; exceptional fishing; ROOM TWO MORE GUNS; highest references expected and given—Write Box X, *The Times*, E.C.4.

Though strongly tempted, for ten days Peter did nothing except think about Brazil and gaze 'with all possible detachment' at maps of South America. But then on April 26th *The Times* carried an article about this very expedition, giving an outline of its plans and speculating about the fate of Colonel P. H. Fawcett, the explorer who had disappeared in Matto Grosso, searching for a lost city, seven years before.

This was too much. 'I was still careful to pretend to myself that it would be out of the question for me to go to Brazil,' Peter wrote later:

> It would cost too much and take too long; and it would be the act of a madman to throw up the literary editorship of the most august of weekly journals in favour of a wild-goose chase. All the same, I

argued, it will do no harm to find out a little more about it ... So I wrote to Box X asking for particulars, and presently got an answer from which it appeared that neither the time nor the money involved were as far beyond my means as I had expected.

Within a few days he had signed on, and he at once began searching for a friend to fill the second vacant place—mostly by the simple expedient of going up to people in the street, or wherever he chanced to see them, and saying: 'Come to Brazil.' It was thus that he enrolled Roger Pettiward, a tall, gangling, red-haired artist, with a drawl nearly as pronounced as his own. On May 20th it so happened that Pettiward was walking down Gower Street on his way to the Slade School and passed the offices of the *Spectator* just as Peter came out—a meeting inimitably recorded in *Brazilian Adventure*:

> At Eton and Oxford I had known him only by sight. In the last three years I had met him three times. But here was a fine large chap with an eye for comedy: so I called across the street: 'Roger, come to Brazil.'
>
> 'What?' said Roger: playing, I dare say, for time.
>
> 'You'd better come to Brazil,' I said, getting into a car.
>
> 'Why?' said Roger cautiously (or perhaps incautiously), also getting into the car. We set off down Gower Street: past the Royal Academy of Dramatic Art: past the School of Tropical Hygiene. I talked rapidly. At the end of Gower Street Roger got out.
>
> 'I'll let you know for certain on Monday,' he said. But his fate was sealed.

In a few days Pettiward too had signed on, as a surveyor—a capacity in which he had already done some work. The organizer was Robert Churchward, who had (according to Peter) 'the most tremendous difficulty in distinguishing between the real and the ideal'. The other members were Noel Skeffington-Smyth (another surveyor and also an Old Etonian), Arthur Humphreys (a mechanic), and two who could lay claim to no title save the general one of 'explorer'-Blunt Mackenzie and Neville Priestley. Neville was the only other one whom Peter already knew-a fourth Old Etonian, big, blond and ebullient, who had in fact done more exploring than the rest of them put together; on this occasion he already had plans for collecting animals for zoos from South America, and he travelled out to Brazil on his own. Each member of the expedition except Churchward (whose financial contribution was said to be already 'considerable') paid £400 into a central fund; and although Churchward was the official leader, he would, he said, be assisted in Brazil by one Captain J. G. Holman, a British resident of São Paulo with allegedly unsurpassed experience of the interior.

From the start there was a fundamental misunderstanding about the expedition's objectives. Already (in 1931) Churchward had travelled with Holman in Brazil, and his aim in mounting the new expedition was to further Holman's scheme for setting up a safari agency, which would arrange shooting tours in the interior. To Churchward, therefore, the purpose of the trip was mainly sporting, and in his advertisement he had included the sentence about looking for Fawcett only as an extra attraction. Because the time available was limited, he knew that any search they might manage to carry out could be only a bare reconnaissance.

To Peter, however, Fawcett was by far the most fascinating element in the whole venture, and the hunt for the lost explorer seemed to him the main point of the journey. Had a precise statement of the party's aim been formulated in England, much acrimony might have been avoided; as it was, the expedition set forth with a wide (and perhaps not fully realized) divergence of expectations.

The Times also found the idea of looking for Fawcett an attractive one, and a member of the editorial staff approached Churchward to ask if one of his team would write about the journey. As a result Peter was appointed the paper's Special Correspondent (unpaid) covering the British Matto Grosso Expedition – the first of many occasions on which he travelled as a special representative of Printing House Square.

Journalistic interest in the Fawcett story was strong, for in March a Swiss traveller called Stephen Rattin had emerged from Matto Grosso with an extraordinary tale of how he had discovered an elderly white man, who described himself as a colonel, apparently being held prisoner by Indians. Having told his story in São Paulo, Rattin almost immediately disappeared again into the interior to rescue the man—by then believed by many people (and certainly by popular newspapers in England) to be Fawcett.

Here were the makings of a fine journalistic race: the British Matto Grosso Expedition might, by a miracle, find Fawcett first, and if they did, Peter would have a considerable scoop. In an attempt to make more certain of it he suggested to *The Times* that the plans of the expedition should be adapted so that he could follow Rattin down the Rio Arinos in a canoe with a crate of carrier-pigeons; then, even if the Swiss did find Fawcett first, the British would have a swifter means of exporting the news to the outside world.

This suggestion was declined, but only with what Peter described as 'a wistful, a hankering look' in the paper's 'august official eye'. Another idea of his which did find acceptance was that he should use a code, based on the violent scene in Act IV of *Othello* in which Iago persuades the Moor to strangle Desdemona, for sending back any information which might have to travel secretly. *Othello* was to stand for Fawcett, *Iago* for Rattin. *Goats* would mean that the British had found Fawcett alive; *monkeys* that Rattin had done so. *No goats* would show that the British had found Fawcett dead; *no monkeys* that Rattin had done so. *Ape* would mean that Rattin had turned back, *two apes* that he had been killed. *Buck* would announce that the British had found definite traces of Fawcett, *heat* that they had overtaken Rattin, *arrow* that they had been attacked by Indians. The addition of the word *thanks* to a message would indicate that they were pressing on, and *yes* that they had been forced to turn back.

All this sounded splendidly precise; but when it came to telling *The Times* how and when he proposed to file dispatches, the best Peter could propose was a highly speculative scheme:

Aug. (first week, with luck) We reach a mission station at the mouth of the Tapirapé. From here I shall try and send a long local colour dispatch down to Belem by canoe. Allowing the canoe six weeks, you should get this by the end of September.

The plan, such as it was, ran as follows: from Rio they would go up-country by road and rail, via São Paulo, to a small town called Leopoldina. There they would embark on the Araguaia, an immense river that flows almost due north for fifteen hundred miles until it debouches into the delta of the Amazon. Having descended the Araguaia for some three hundred miles, they would turn left (south-west) up one of its tributaries, the Rio das Mortes, establish a base-camp on its headwaters, and from there make an overland trek into the area where Fawcett was thought to have disappeared.

Several such areas suggested themselves, for many different accounts of Fawcett's demise had been put forward; but the one they chose was the area pin-pointed by a former officer of the Royal Navy, George Dyott, who had led a well-equipped American search for Fawcett in 1928 and had, he thought, come within a few days' march of the spot on which the colonel, his son Jack and their other young companion had been massacred by Indians. Peter, it need hardly be said, had scarcely

heard of Fawcett before he took an interest in the expedition; but once
he applied himself to the subject he learnt it as fast as he had learnt
Anglo-Saxon, and by the time he left England his knowledge of the
saga was probably unrivalled.

At the *Spectator*, meanwhile, he had made such arrangements as he
could to secure his position when he returned. Derek Verschoyle was
to assume the post of Literary Editor in his absence; but Wrench by
then was planning to get rid of Wilson Harris, and held out hopes to
Peter that he might eventually become Editor; Peter therefore brought
in an ally in the form of Frank Pakenham, whom he left working under
Verschoyle while he was away.

In the middle of settling these journalistic details he signed a contract
for a book with Jonathan Cape, of whose firm Rupert Hart-Davis,
ascending rapidly from the position of office-boy at Heinemann's, had
recently become a director. Cape himself, with characteristic caution,
offered Peter no advance until such time as the manuscript should be
complete; then he would get £150, with a further £150 to follow when
the book was published. Yet it could also be said that it was a considerable act of faith for Cape to commission the book at all, for he had no
evidence of Peter's ability to produce anything except elegant and
amusing articles.

In commercial matters the budding author's naivety was remarkable.
'Thank you very much for helping me like this,' he wrote to Cape when
he returned the signed contract. 'It is awfully kind of you.' Nor did he
take advantage of a counter-offer from a rival publisher, Hamish Hamilton, who wrote:

> Unless you have definitely committed yourself to Cape, for whom,
> needless to say, I have enormous admiration as a publisher, I hope
> that you will allow me to bid against him. I am prepared to guarantee
> to spend a large sum on advertising the book, and probably a good
> deal more than he will promise.

Instead of using this letter as a lever for forcing up the terms he had
already been offered—as many a less scrupulous author might have done
—Peter sent it to Cape with the comment: 'I thought that perhaps you
ought to have it: if you don't I shall certainly lose it.'

All Peter's preparations were invested with still greater urgency by
the fact that he was once again in love. During the past year he had seen
more and more of Celia Johnson, and although he had not discussed
marriage with her, he had certainly thought hard about it. Now that he
was about to disappear for months into the Brazilian jungle, he feared—

though he could not bring himself to tell Celia so—that their association was finished; and this apprehension naturally made his departure that much more traumatic.

Not that everything about it was grim: even at this stage farce intervened, in the form of a letter from a member of the New Victorian Club in London asking Peter to keep a sharp lookout for her nephew, whom she had last heard of six years before in Buenos Aires.

'I must apologize for writing to you so fully on matters anent a perfect stranger,' she fluted:

> My nephew and I have the 'Scotch' second sight, and each time he has been in great trouble I have 'seen' him calling me. The last time there was this telepathic communication was on this Jan. 1, early in the morning. Since then nothing. I argue that he has either left the earth or lost his memory ...
>
> Strongly made, broad shoulders, in appearance he resembles the Duke of York (though his relation is through the Duchess) ... charming, persuasive manners and address, beautifully shaped hands and feet. He has the Bowes-Lyon nose ...
>
> Should you hear ANY particulars. I should beg you to tell them to me. Nothing you could tell me would horrify or repel me or cause me the sentimental sorrow which many women would feel. I am a steady reviewer of fiction (2 books per day) and this does not encourage illusions, nor blind one's eyes to life in the raw.

Peter wrote back promising to keep the sharpest possible lookout—and with that his preparations were complete. They were, as he himself said, 'grotesquely unprofessional, to put it mildly', as were those of the rest of the party. All the same, an article by him setting out the expedition's objectives, which *The Times* published on June 17th, gave the whole project a spurious importance, and it was with the highest hopes that he went to Tilbury on June 18th 1932 and embarked on the S.S. *Andalusia Star*: the start of a venture for which, as he himself later put it, 'Rider Haggard might have written the plot and Conrad designed the scenery.'

The voyage to Rio was due to last fourteen days; but on only the second day out he was smitten by remorse about the way he had abandoned Celia, and he poured out his agitation in a letter to Rupert:

> It is bloody awful having given her such a smack in the eye and not being able to do anything about it. She has been so lovely to me ...
> I feel very bad to have ripped through an emergency exit into the

fantastic, leaving her at the mercy of stale and familiar surroundings. I miss her terribly ...

The British Matto Grosso Expedition, like non-stop variety, offers easy escape. They are all very likeable, as well as splendidly improbable, and Pettiward is really good value.

The voyage bored him; but as they drew closer to South America he wrote again in much better fettle:

> This voyage is said by some to be nearing its end. As for me, I have lost all count of time. So has the Royal Geographical Society's patent, air-tight, unbreakable, snake-proof Chronometer, on which the whole of our surveying depends. Guaranteed never to swerve in its loyalty to Greenwich by so much as a second-hand's breadth, it has suddenly fallen back one hour and fifty minutes into the past ... Pettiward and I have tried boiling it, dashing it against the binnacle, kicking it along the deck, holding it up so that it can see the flying fish, putting it in Coventry, singing obscene songs to it, dipping it in gin, not dipping it in gin, lending it to a Brazilian political exile, shouting at it, jumping on it from behind bulkheads, and praying for it. But it is no good. None of the orthodox remedies seem to work.

They reached Rio at sunset on the evening of July 3rd, to be met by a rush of photographers and by their local leader, Captain Holman, whom Peter described as 'a tall, thin man of about forty, with a ragged moustache and phenomenally small ears,' with 'something of the camel in his gait' and 'short, mouse-coloured hair'. His appearance, he said, was 'in no sense attractive. But you would, I think, have been intrigued rather than repelled by that scarecrow figure.'

Next day the newspaper *El Globo* carried a photograph of the party and a fulsome note about its members, who were described as including the 'jornalista B. Fleming, do "Times," de Londres,' and 'Lord Blhunt Mackenzie,' to whom no profession could be ascribed save that of 'millionario'. Their aim was to leave at once for São Paulo, but in this they were frustrated by the customs officers, who argued about the expedition's baggage for six days—a dispute caused largely by the prodigious number of weapons, from sawn-off shotguns to revolvers, that had been considered necessary for survival. (Fortunately their large consignment of tear-gas bombs had been thrown overboard shortly before they reached Rio; otherwise the delay would certainly have been even greater.)

The wait naturally irked Peter, but it also gave him a chance to observe Captain Holman at close quarters, and he was not much taken with what he saw; for Holman, although good at dealing with the Brazilian bureaucrats, proved disconcertingly evasive when it came to discussing details of what the expedition was going to do. Within a few hours of their arrival he had begun hinting that he had vitally important new information about Fawcett, but he would not divulge what it was: his maps and papers, he said, were in his office in São Paulo, and he could not discuss plans until he reached his base there. So apprehensive did Peter become that he and Pettiward considered resigning from the expedition there and then; at last, however, he persuaded Holman to share his precious secret, and this proved so interesting that it instantly gave him and Roger an excuse 'for continuing on an enterprise which otherwise, under the gathering shadows of anti-climax and fiasco, our consciences and our common sense would have obliged us to abandon'.

Holman's new evidence was a typewritten statement that purported to come from Murika, the chief of a Kalapalos Indian village on the Rio Kuluene; it described how Fawcett and his two companions had arrived in the area in 1925; how Fawcett had insisted on pressing ahead into the unknown country east of the river, even though the two young men were in bad shape; how the Indians had seen the smoke of their fires for eleven days but on the twelfth day, seeing no smoke, had followed up and eventually come on 'traces of a massacre' at Fawcett's final camp.

The point of all this was that it independently confirmed, and in some places amplified, the account of Fawcett's end which had so far seemed most plausible—that of the American expedition led by Dyott. The discovery pleased and excited Peter greatly, for it meant that two separate pointers now directed the expedition towards the same place—the country east of the Kuluene—and the chances of discovering something about Fawcett seemed to have increased dramatically. Yet at the same time the document made Peter even more apprehensive about their leader, for he quickly realized that Holman's knowledge of the Fawcett saga was very slender indeed, that he was not familiar with the details of Dyott's theories, and that consequently he did not fully appreciate the importance of the new evidence which he himself had produced. Nor, Peter soon felt certain, had Holman the literary powers to have composed the statement from Murika, as he claimed to have done; still less could he have prepared the neatly marked map which he produced— another document of which he claimed to be the author.

In spite of these disquieting lapses Holman seemed to know a good deal about the country for which they were heading, and he made sensible proposals for changing their plans in the light of the new evidence. It would be far better, he said, not to ascend the Rio das Mortes, as they had originally intended, but instead to go up the next tributary of the Araguaia, the Tapirapé, from whose head-waters they could march across 150 miles of unexplored country towards the area in which it seemed that Fawcett had met his end. The idea struck Peter as a good one, and he outlined the new proposals in a cable to *The Times*; this—as previously agreed—he submitted to Holman for his approval, which was readily forthcoming.

It was thus in an atmosphere charged equally with hope and suspicion that the expedition eventually started up-country. At the first stop, in São Paulo, they were joined by Neville Priestley; and he, Peter and Roger Pettiward formed a natural trio who clung together ever tighter as the enterprise gradually accelerated towards fiasco and disintegration.

In São Paulo Holman announced that the difficulty of the country for which they were bound was such as to render useful survey work impossible, so that they had much better leave behind their bulky theodolite. This they did—and later they were glad to have done so; but the decision did, in Peter's words, strip the expedition 'of its never very convincing façade of scientific purpose; it would no longer be possible to offset a failure in the Fawcett hunt by brandishing a nice, new, accurate map.'

In São Paulo, also, they were overtaken by a revolution. Peter was not a little piqued by the fact that it occurred without his noticing it: as he later remarked, to be in the middle of a revolution and not to know anything about it until eighteen hours after it had started 'seemed to argue a certain want of perspicacity'. From the practical point of view it was a thorough nuisance, since it threw the railways into chaos and halted the expedition for another five days. At last, however, they set out on the night train to Ribeirão Préto, and thence they travelled by road, in a series of convulsive spurts and stops, via Uberaba and Goiás to Leopoldina, the point at which they were to embark on the Araguaia. Their progress was much hampered by revolutionary activities and suspicions: at least once they were assumed, because of the weight of their armament, to be the spearhead of some political force, and at Goiás they were becalmed for five further days by the fact that their baggage had been impounded a hundred miles behind them.

Through all these difficulties Holman kept his composure admirably, and he unravelled the knots of bureaucracy with skill and patience. But during the wait at Goiás Peter's doubts about him were suddenly intensified, and he became almost certain that Holman had no serious intention of looking for Fawcett at all. What gave Holman away was the fact that Peter understood more Portuguese than Holman realized, and overheard him conversing with some local Brazilians. His remarks gave the impression that the expedition was no more than a shooting party, and he humorously disclaimed any plans for searching out traces of lost colonels.

In an attempt to draw him into the open, Peter composed, ostensibly for *The Times*, a fake dispatch that he never meant to send, and in which he repeatedly ascribed to Holman the plan for making a trek of 150 miles across virgin country: at this, he felt confident, their evasive leader would surely baulk. But he did not. Far from it: he reaffirmed that the project was a reasonable one to undertake and passed the article for print.

Although he felt he had marginally increased their chances of achieving something worthwhile, Peter was still uneasy; and the strain of so much uncertainty was greatly increased by a fierce emotional struggle which was going on inside him. He could not, apparently, unburden himself even to Roger Pettiward, to whom he was then very close and his only outlet was a letter to Rupert which he wrote from the Grande Hotel Portugal in Goiás on July 25th:

This I regard as a pretty important letter ... The point is about Celia. I must try and take my mind off this bloody comic circus (which is hard) and think sensibly about serious things.

I love Celia as much as I see myself loving anyone: which is not enough to marry her. I know now, even better than I knew in England, that this would not work ... I miss her frightfully, and there will not seem to be much point in coming back to England and not to her. I really love her as dearly as I may. But one must (as they say) face the facts, and in a practical way. The facts are that on the latest evidence available I am bumming up her life. The means are pleasant, and more, but the end is bad. I can hardly bear to think of not seeing her again ... but this I think is what ought to happen. And so would you too, if you were me.

The thing is how to hurt her least. There has not been (or at least I don't suppose there has been) any breach in the continuity of things for her, to make it easier. On paper, to say goodbye when I come back would seem bound to make things more unbearable. But to do it from out here, by letter, not knowing her state of mind, might well be crueller. (It is bloody, this being out of touch). I can only hope for a change in her heart or some other fluke; or failing these a wise

decision on my part when I get your letters ... I have had a hell of a
time lately (though damned funny) and am really in no state to
write.

PS. Probably you won't say anything to Celia about this letter.
But whether you do or not, tell her that I shall always love her.

In its indecision and the nakedness of its emotional expression, this
letter was thoroughly uncharacteristic; it shows what pressure Peter had
been under—first that he could write such a note, and then that he could
post it. Probably by the time Rupert got it, and certainly by the time
Peter returned to England, he had completely changed his mind.

At last, after apparently interminable delays, the expedition got
moving again. Two decrepit cars and a lorry were procured, and the
party covered the last 130 miles to Leopoldina in a single day of ferocious
discomfort. They reached the place as the sun was setting, and as they
drove round the final corner came suddenly on the great river—a
moment which Peter never forgot:

> The Araguaia was there, in front of us, and beyond it was a redden-
> ning sky. The trampled open ground on which the twenty houses of
> the village stood ended abruptly at the lip of a perpendicular bluff.
> Beyond that, and forty feet below it, was the river: a river half a
> mile wide and more: a river so big, so long expected, and so pheno-
> menal in every way that it seemed hardly possible to have come on
> it so suddenly ... a river fired and bloody in the sunset: a river that
> we loved instantly, and learnt at last to hate. We gaped at this river.
> There was exaltation in the air.
>
> It ran slowly but strongly, making no sound at all. The trees on
> the farther bank stood up, a dark plumed horde. Our own bank—
> as your own bank always does—seemed terribly commonplace by
> contrast. We beheld for the first time, and in the most appropriate
> of circumstances, the frontiers of Matto Grosso.

Next morning they ferried all their stores and equipment by canoe
across to a *praia*, or sandbank, in the middle of the river, where they
slept that night on hammocks. At noon next day, July 30th, accompanied
by a motley crew seven strong, part Indian and part Brazilian, they set
off downstream in a convoy of four boats—two *batalõas* (capacious
clinker-built craft some thirty feet long), one smaller clinker-built
vessel, and a dug-out canoe.

For three weeks they glided down the Araguaia, establishing a daily
routine that became as familiar as if they had known it all their lives.

They slept on the sand of the *praias*, woke before dawn, had a cup of coffee, went off into the jungle to shoot for the pot any bird or small deer that might present itself, and returned at the call of a tin trumpet to a breakfast of rice and black beans sprinkled with *farinha*—coarse flour made from the mandioca root, which Peter described as tasting 'like a disheartened potato'.

After breakfast they packed and pushed off. The crews kept the boats close to the banks, and a good deal of shooting was to be had during every voyage, particularly for the men in the leading boat. Their choice of targets was regrettably catholic: almost every creature that moved— be it fish, reptile, mammal or bird—drew fire. Many of the birds, it is true, were edible—and eaten—among them several types of duck and the *jacu*, a kind of dowdy pheasant. But the explorers also shot (out of curiosity) the *jaburas*—white storks with black heads, beaks and legs, and dull scarlet throats, which, according to Peter, paced the *praias* gravely 'with long, meditative strides: their heads are bowed, their shoulders hunched, their mien preoccupied. Theirs is the gait of the quadrangle or the terrace.' No other bird, he said, so successfully created something of the Lost World atmosphere for which they were all secretly longing.

The most satisfactory targets, however—objects, at first, of vindictive hatred—were the alligators. To start with, the explorers pursued them at night and shot considerable numbers by torchlight. Gradually they realized that the creatures were far less of a menace than they had expected, and they persecuted them less vengefully: even so, they still shot any they came across, and alligators (as Peter recorded in his book) were a feature of all their river journeys:

> Every hour or so [going up the Tapirapé] there would be a burst of fire and a jubilant shout of '*Matou!*' from one or other of the canoes. Then the whole convoy would utter a wailing and ironic cry of '*Viva o Brasil!*' in tones of burlesque enthusiasm. This was one of the expeditionary jokes and never failed to please the men.

At about noon they would stop for a meal of *farinha* and water mixed with *rapadura*, a toffee-like product of the sugar-cane which was manu- factured and sold in rectangular blocks. After this sickly snack they went on again, paddling with the current through the afternoon until at about four they began looking for a suitable *praia* on which to spend the night. One found, they landed and pitched camp—no very arduous undertaking, since all they had to do was to scoop shallow holes in the sand in which to sleep. Then, while the Indians cooked supper, Peter and Roger would take to the jungle in search of game and exercise.

Later, after a heavy meal, they had nothing to do but sit and talk and listen to the 'maddeningly familiar repertoire' of their portable gramophone:

> It was the chief disadvantage of that life, that night came too early, outstripping—after a comparatively inactive day and half a pint of black coffee—the desire to sleep. We had no light to read or write by, and in the darkness the boundaries of our little world contracted, the uncertainties which were its only permanent furniture domineered over idle imaginations, and the gramophone, which on the voyage from England had provided an accompaniment for doubts and misgivings, was, after all these weeks, providing it still ...
>
> Eventually you lay down in the sand to await sleep. Everything was lovely, clear and dramatic in the brilliant moonlight. The great river slid silently past. The frogs made a steady mechanical *tok-tok-tok*, very like the hammering of a Lewis gun. Birds called, sadly or in fear. In the jungle behind you a wolf barked. Between your head and the teeming stars night-jars cut the air with a whickering of wings. The world seemed very empty. You went to sleep.

During this stage of the journey Peter and Roger perfected a system of communication that was at the same time both practical and absurd. To other members of the expedition it seemed tremendously novel, but anyone who knew Peter well would have realized that it was merely an extension of the jargon which he used anyway with his close friends, and that it served a similar purpose. Just as in ordinary life he used stock expressions to avoid emotional involvement, here in the jungle he resorted to parody in order to preserve some kind of detachment and sense of proportion. 'Much of what we saw and did was clearly too good to be true,' he wrote afterwards:

> In self-defence—in instinctive pursuance of that policy of *nil admirari* which is the joint product of repression, sophistication and all the hot air one hears—we turned to Parody. If Indians approached us, we referred to them as the Oncoming Savages. We never said 'Was that a shot?' but always 'Was that the well-known bark of a Mauser?' All insects of harmless nature and ridiculous appearance we pointed out to each other as creatures 'whose slightest glance spelt Death'. Any bird larger than a thush we credited with the ability to 'break a man's arm with a single blow of its powerful wings'. We spoke of water always as the 'Precious Fluid'. We referred to ourselves not as eating meals, but as doing 'Ample

Justice to a Frugal Repast'. To anyone who did not think it as funny
as we did it must have been an intolerably tiresome kind of joke.
But it made us laugh, and thus served its purpose. It became an
important feature in that private code of nonsense which was our
chief defence against hostile circumstance.

Laugh as they might, they became increasingly worried about what was
going to happen when they reached the Tapirapé. Captain Holman—
'bland, irrelevant and enigmatic', as Peter described him—sidestepped
all their questions and refused to discuss what he proposed to do.

They found out soon enough. When they reached the Island of
Bananal, at the point where the Araguaia is joined by the Tapirapé,
Holman came into the open and announced that he had no intention of
proceeding up the smaller river.

At once the expedition was divided. Peter, fired by his natural sense
of duty and by his obligations to *The Times*, emerged as the leader of the
faction in favour of pushing on, which consisted (predictably enough)
of himself, Roger and Neville Priestley. The rest were content to follow
whatever lead Holman gave them. Tense, sarcastic arguments broke
out, in the course of which Peter reminded Holman that it was to make
a serious search for Fawcett that they had come all the way from England
(and paid nearly £500 apiece), and that the first clause of the contract
they had all signed in Rio read: 'The object of the expedition is to
ascertain the fate of Colonel Fawcett as far as is humanly possible.'
Under this pressure Holman agreed to make a quick journey up the
Tapirapé, but not to undertake an overland trek. At this—an improvement, but not a good enough one—Peter and Roger offered to resign
from the expedition and to go and look for Fawcett on their own.

This shook Holman badly. He became very angry; and when, next
morning, the expedition did start up the Tapirapé, the atmosphere was
highly charged. The *bataloãs* were sent down the Araguaia to the mission
station on Bananal, to await the expedition's return, and the seven
explorers, accompanied by six Indians, set out upstream in the smaller
clinker-built boat and three dug-out canoes. As Peter showed afterwards
in his book, he was under no illusions about their chances of success:

Few ventures of a similar kind can have been so firmly rooted in the
ludicrous. From the mouth of the river to its head-waters, where
we should meet the Indians, was said to be a six days' journey. It
would be a difficult, and perhaps even—on account of the lowness of
the river—an impossible journey; and it was freely admitted by all
to be a useless one, unless we did a great deal more than simply

paddle up to the Indian port and paddle back again. Our leader did not want to make the journey at all, and at intervals said so to those members of the expedition with whom he was still on speaking terms. Furthermore, it turned out that our supplies had somehow or other been limited to food for sixteen days. I was filled with a kind of forlorn glee when I reflected that all this would one day have to be translated into that impressive, non-committal prose, with its slightly technical flavour, in which the activities of explorers are recorded in *The Times*.

Besides supplies for sixteen days, we had with us a largely irrelevant assortment of medicines and a box of presents for the Indians — tobacco, cutlery, necklaces and some rather silly toys. In addition everyone had the irreducible minimum of personal equipment: a blanket, a mosquito net, a revolver, and in some cases a change of clothes.

For various reasons they made little progress the first day, and, finding no suitable *praia* at nightfall, were forced to camp in a clearing in the jungle. Next morning, to Peter's unbounded elation, Holman suddenly announced that he himself was turning back: the rest, he said, could go on if they wanted, and he would await their return at Bananal. He disappeared downstream with one of the Indians in the smallest canoe. 'We', wrote Peter, 'went the other way, suppressing with difficulty a tendency to break into ribald song. From the ashes of our first camp on the Tapirapé a thin plume of smoke rose towards the laced branches, like the most delicate of exclamation marks.'

Shorn of its vacillating figure-head, the expedition made (by its own standards) startling progress, reaching São Domingo, the port of the Tapirapé Indians, in five days, instead of the six which it had expected to take. For the first time the going became really strenuous for the Europeans as well as for the Indians. All day they paddled up the twisting river, which became ever shallower and was frequently blocked by overhanging branches, through which they had to cut their way. Mosquitoes and alligators were far more numerous than on the Araguaia, and a new natural hazard appeared in the form of *arrayas*, or fresh-water sting-rays. Yet for Peter the river was a lovely place, a fairyland in which the humans were trespassers.

São Domingo proved to be no more than a series of empty clearings in the jungle on the river bank: Indians, it was clear, had been there recently, but the place was deserted. This the explorers had expected. Their plan was to split into two parties: one would continue up the river, mapping it as far as they could go; the other, consisting of Peter, Roger, Neville and two Indians, would march across country to a village where they knew they could contact the Tapirapés, and there hire guides for the trek towards the Fawcett country away to the south-west.

The river party left as planned, but the land party had scarcely set out when they met four naked brown figures coming the opposite way— the advance guard of the entire Tapirapé tribe, which was on its way down to the river. Back at São Domingo, the white men shared the one and only building—a missionaries' hut—with dozens of the natives who slung their hammocks under the roof. Next morning Peter distributed the presents—necklaces, mirrors, knives, forks, toys, tobacco, empty tins, brass cartridge-cases and lengths of black-and-red typewriter-ribbon —and after considerable problems of communication secured the services of the tribe's two 'captains' as guides for a journey lasting an unspecified number of days to the south-west.

Although he was greatly taken with the Tapirapés as a people, much appreciating their sense of humour, Peter had no great hopes of the two chiefs, who appeared shifty, irresolute, and (worst of all) entirely ignorant about the country for which they would be heading. Nevertheless, he decided to start next day at dawn. That evening, August 25th, he sat down in a hammock and wrote three letters, scribbling in pencils on sheets torn from an exercise-book. In one, to Holman, he, Roger and Neville formally resigned from the expedition, and asked that money for their passage from Belém back to Europe should be left at the mission station at Bananal. The second letter was to Bob Churchward, who had gone on up the Tapirapé; it informed him of the resignations, and laid plans for a reunion later. The third was to Barrington-Ward of *The Times*—a long, clear and dispassionate explanation of why the expedition had broken up. 'This letter will accompany the swan-song of the British Matto Grosso Expedition,' it began, 'a dispatch which I hope to have sent off from Belem by airmail via New York.' Having rehearsed the steps which led to their present position, Peter went on:

> Our own journey is not likely to be a long one. I doubt if we shall get beyond the limits of the Tapirapé country. But we may possibly get in with other Indians and go further towards the Xingu: in which case we shall be away and out of touch for some time. It is just possible that I shall find out something about Fawcett. Although we may be out of touch for some time, there is no need for any anxiety, for we are fairly well equipped and exceptionally well

accompanied. As soon as we smell an impossibility, we shall turn back.

What worried Peter far more than the physical hazards of this situation was the possibility that Holman would beat him back to civilization and publish a distorted account of what had happened, and much of his letter to Barrington-Ward was given to urging that nothing should appear in the paper until he himself reached England. 'I am sorry to be so long-winded,' he concluded, 'but there is a good deal to explain; and I should be very sorry indeed if this attempt to dodge the label "bogus" [that is, his projected cross-country journey] was frustrated by anyone's indiscretions in London.'

All he could do with this letter (and with the brief, non-committal despatch that accompanied it) was to send it downstream to Bananal and rely on Holman to forward it. But Holman, characteristically, did no such thing; fearing (with reason) that it might be derogatory to himself, he suppressed it, and handed it back to Peter weeks later when its contents had been rendered obsolete by the passage of time.

In describing the situation to Barrington-Ward, Peter minimized the difficulties in his usual way. The facts were that the party was neither 'fairly well equipped' nor 'exceptionally well accompanied': indeed, these statements were gross exaggerations. He and his two fellow Old Etonians were alone in the middle of one of the biggest countries in the world, and six weeks at least by water from Belém, the nearest point at which they could hope to get help; their capital amounted to £2; they had very little food and practically no equipment; they could scarcely communicate with the natives, and the Indians for whose territory they were aiming were reputed to be hostile.

Yet in all this Peter found cause for elation. The days that followed were days of fierce physical strain, of considerable privation and risk, of real exploration—the best days, Peter said later, that he had ever known. Off they went—three white men and three Indians—all heavily laden, marching on compass-bearings across the *campo*, or grassy, tree-studded, open country away from the river. The first day they covered some fifteen miles, but by the evening it was clear that the Indians were lost, and the day ended in a frantic search for water, which they found just before darkness caught them. Peter was not surprised when the two Tapirapé chiefs announced that they would go no farther; but the real blow fell next morning when Neville, trying to pull on his boots, found that his feet were so sore (from some kind of blood-poisoning) that he too decided he must give up and return to São Domingo.

This setback pared the British Matto Grosso Expedition down to three men: Peter, Roger and Queiroz, an excellent one-eyed Brazilian with a face 'like a malicious hedgehog' who had accompanied them all the way down the Araguaia. Their armament was also sadly depleted, and now consisted of a battered ·22 rook rifle held together by sticking-plaster and string, a ·45 service revolver with which none of them could hit anything, and an ancient ·44 rifle whose barrel had been ruined by neglect. The ·22 had proved invaluable for killing small game for the pot, but for purposes of defence it was all but useless since (Peter later remarked) 'the wounds it was capable of inflicting were calculated to enrage rather than to incapacitate the Oncoming Savages.' The other weapons were all but useless for any purpose. Their food was practically exhausted.

Yet still Peter refused to give up. For four more days he led his little party on towards the south-west. First they hacked their way through the jungle along the banks of a river which they took to be an uncharted tributary of the Tapirapé; then for two days they waded naked up the river itself. On the last day they took once more to the open *campo*, occasionally firing patches of scrub so as to leave smoke-columns on which they could take back-bearings. By then they were constantly finding traces of other Indians—Vestiges, as they called them—and often their fires were answered by columns of smoke in the distance ahead. In the day they were baked by the sun, and at night tormented by mosquitoes. Several times they were drenched and battered by elemental thunderstorms—the forerunners, Peter feared, of the rains, which, when they broke, would certainly put an end to their enterprise.

Eventually, on the fifth morning after Neville had left them, they agreed that there was no point in going on. Their only hope of achieving further useful progress lay in making contact with the next tribe of Indians; but the Indians, though not far off, were clearly avoiding them, and must be presumed to be at least passively, if not actively, hostile. Without their assistance they could not go much farther, for they had food for only three more days—just about enough to see them back to São Domingo.

'Were we justified in chancing our luck and using that food for a further advance of two or three days, relying on our digestions and the ·22 to get us home on a purely meat diet?' Peter asked in his book:

> We decided that we were not ... But it went against the grain to turn back on that clear and lovely morning. We were certainly

within a hundred miles of the place where Fawcett met his death,
and the distance may have been considerably less if he made good
progress on those days when the Kalapalos were watching his fires.
Provided the rains held off, we could very easily have kept going for
two or three days until we ran completely out of food. But we should
have had a very bad time of it on the way back, and I hardly think we
should have done much good. If one of us had gone lame, or if
anything had happened to the ·22, it is improbable that we should
have got out at all.

But I felt very sorry to be giving up this ridiculous scramble;
it had been great fun. As we strapped on our still sodden loads an
enormous alligator, the biggest I have ever seen, came quietly gliding
up the narrow channel opposite our camp ... Here was a chance to
work off some of our resentment against unkind circumstances;
and as it drew level I took careful shot with the ·22 and got it in the
eye.

That was probably the most phenomenal result ever produced
with a rook rifle. The peaceful river boiled. The alligator thrashed
its head from side to side in agony. Then, as the tiny bullet touched
(I suppose) its brain, it reared itself out upon the further bank and
lay there, killed with a crumb of lead.

There was no time to strip off my load and wade across to measure
it: though I should have liked to do this, for it really was a very
big one. We left it sprawling there, to mark the futile end, reached
with much difficulty, of a hopeless quest. If those secret Indians
came to our camp after we had gone (as I expect they did) I hope
they were suitably impressed by a monster so mysteriously dead.

The quest was dead as well; but the journey was far from over. Having
returned safely to São Domingo, they discovered that through a misunderstanding all their vital stores—food, blankets, mosquito-nets—
which they had left in a cache had been taken on down-river. Even
Peter, who consistently played down any discomforts they suffered,
afterwards admitted that by then they were in a bad state:

By day we went naked, for it was very hot and we were always
having to jump overboard and drag the boat. But at night we put
on all our clothes against the cold and bandaged the rents in them
against the mosquitoes. Neither of these precautions was very
efficacious; we would have given anything in the world for a couple
of blankets and a few feet of gauze ... We had very little food,
and we felt terribly the need for something with fat in it; the rice,

of which we had a certain amount, left us bloated but unsatisfied. However, we were lucky with the game, necessity lending a phenomenal accuracy to our aim. We got duck, and pigeons, a plaintive but delicious water-hen, and once a huge clutch of turtle's eggs.

I do not remember that we were conscious of any strain, but I think that perhaps we were more tired than we knew. I cannot otherwise explain the policy of *laissez-faire* and non-aggression which we adopted on discovering that there was a *sucury*—an anaconda—in a hollow tree on the *praia* where we had camped. We could not see it, but a sound between a moan and a hiss issued rhythmically from the trunk, and we knew that it was there. There were any number of things we could have done; if it had proved impossible to cut open the tree we could have lit a fire underneath it and killed the snake when it came out. But a curious kind of indifference had come upon us, probably the result of weakness and lack of sleep: and we contented ourselves with emptying a revolver lackadaisically into the tree, which quickened the tempo of the moaning hiss but produced no other result.

Back at the mission station on Bananal, there occurred the long-awaited confrontation with Captain Holman. Having been stuck for three weeks in that dreary place, he was exceedingly angry, and abusive exchanges took place. Holman then began by handing the three members who had resigned a letter couched in terms as hostile as they were ill-expressed:

Please note as each of you signed an agreement in which you agreed to abide by my decision as your leader, I have nothing further to say to you at present other than I consider you three to be dishonourable and not worthy of further consideration.

Presumably before you decided on this mad scheme of yours you realized what you were liable for, financially and otherwise, also it proves you did not consider me or even worry as to the effect or loss of prestige that may follow; so I tell you frankly I reserve my action until after consulting my solicitor and the British Consul in Belem.

Paragraph referring to your passage money. You can take your three passages out of the 200£s (two hundred pounds) owing to me by your friend Priestley which will be more readily recovered as you have more facilities for receiving on your side than I on this side of the Globe ...

Your baggage if not found at Belem will be due to revolutionary activities and at first opportunity will be forwarded to England...

You will also realize any publication other than has been approved by me will be duly contested, to ensure *The Times* will be aware of this I shall cable from Concession on Radio.

Yours Truly,

CAPTAIN J. G. HOLMAN

'Captain Holman's behaviour at this juncture was so extraordinary that I think it must be attributable to ill health,' wrote Peter in a letter he drafted, but never sent, to the British Consul at Belém:

He said that we could have a *batalõa* in which to make the 1,000-odd mile journey to Belem, but that he would return us no money (he knew we had none of our own with us). He was eventually persuaded to leave us 550 milreis [the equivalent of £10], and departed down-stream with all the expedition's funds, almost all the expeditionary property, and two large envelopes containing private correspon-dence belonging to Mr Pettiward and myself ...

You will of course regard it [this letter] as strictly confidential, but we all thought it as well that some person in a responsible posi-tion should know the truth about this remarkable expedition; for Captain Holman's recent behaviour has been so unaccountable that it is difficult to know what his attitude, in private or in public, might be. We hope that you will do what you can to correct the grosser misapprehensions with regard to our conduct which—though admittedly in moments of great excitement—he has threatened to circulate.

Thus, with a few last highly charged exchanges, the expedition finally disintegrated. It was the seizure of his letters that really annoyed Peter, and as Holman drew away in his *batalõa*, taking with him the only two members of the party who remained loyal, Peter waded out to the boat and demanded the return of the correspondence for the last time. Holman refused again, and, as Peter wrote later, 'there was very nearly an ugly scene. Very nearly, but not quite. That far-seeing man, we discovered, had borrowed our revolvers. The flagship of the expedition dropped downstream, the target of invective only.'

There followed a tremendous race: a marathon over more than a thousand miles of the Araguaia to Belem, on the Atlantic coast. This Peter and his truant colleagues eventually won—after a voyage which in itself was another epic of privation and endurance—by no more than a few hours. All the way they were haunted by the fear that Holman would reach civilization first and broadcast to the world a false account of what had happened; so, at the first opportunity—on September

13th—Peter sent off to *The Times* a cable which carried only one sad trace of the Shakespearian code in which their hot news was to have been couched:

EXPEDITION UNSUCCESSFUL SEARCH OTHELLO POLITICAL
CLIMATIC CAUSES HOPE REACH LONDON VIA BELEM
MIDDLE OCTOBER GOOD MATERIAL PHOTOGRAPHS PUBLISH
NOTHING TILL I COME DISPATCHES HELD UP ALL MEM-
BERS WELL INFORM PARENTS WHERE POSSIBLE

They reached Belém on October 5th, and were overjoyed to find first that they had beaten Holman to the post and second that the liner on which they had hoped to sail for home, but which they feared had left that very day, had been delayed twenty-four hours by repercussions attending the end of the revolution. On the morning of the sixth, before they embarked, they brought Holman to bay in the presence of the British Consul and all signed an agreement settling their financial dispute. In his elation Peter sent off a cable to Rupert:

BACK TWENTYSEVENTH ... FIERCE FUN ABOUNDING HEALTH
STARK MELODRAMA NO MAIL MONEY LUGGAGE OR REGRETS

And then, having heard no word from home since leaving England fourteen weeks, he boarded the ship for Europe.

In London little had changed. Rupert, fortunately, had had the sense to say nothing to Celia about Peter's letter from the jungle, and he returned to her joyfully. At the *Spectator* Wilson Harris was still firmly in control; Frank Pakenham had proved so incompetent that he had been sacked, but so, in effect, had Peter, for Derek Verschoyle had settled in as Literary Editor, and Harris told Peter bluntly that he valued him more for his writing than for his administrative ability.

For once Peter was visibly taken aback; but the deprivation did not worry him for long, since he already had a full-time job on his hands—the writing of his book. He discharged his obligations to *The Times* by means of two long articles which appeared on November 29th and 30th, the first accompanied by a whole page of his photographs; but this was a perfunctory account of what had taken place—non-committal and almost humourless—and gave no hint of the fireworks that he was about to produce. Luckily, however, interest in the Fawcett story was still strong: scarcely had Peter returned to England than the *Empire News* published an interview with Mrs Fawcett in which she said that she was expecting her husband to emerge from the interior of Brazil at any moment, having been rescued by Rattin; and a few days later a popular weekly carried a piece suggesting that Fawcett's son Jack had been made into some kind of Buddha. All this lent Peter's articles, bald as they were, a welcome topicality and prevented his feeling that he had given *The Times* short change.

Not that his turnovers pleased everyone: on December 8th a lady of definite views opened fire on him from Highgate:

Dear Mr Fleming,

I have read your articles in *The Times* & I think they are a waste of time. The reason for my thinking it is that I have once met a very nice woman who met a man who actually found Colonel Fawcett & he told him to mind his own business as he didn't want to be found at all.

I think it is a shame to pester people like that and my advice to you is to leave the poor man alone—after all he wouldn't say things like that for nothing—or would he?

Yours truly,

ISADORA PERRILLI.

It escaped this correspondent's attention that the British Mato Grosso expedition *had* left Fawcett entirely alone, and had accomplished precisely nothing in the way of establishing new details about the explorer's fate. Even so, in December Peter was elected a Fellow of the Royal Geographical Society, and he pressed ahead with his account of the fiasco. When Jonathan Cape wrote in the middle of the month inquiring about progress, he replied in typically self-deprecating terms: 'The book is getting on terribly slowly. I am afraid it is going to turn out to be very palsied stuff; but perhaps it isn't as bad as I think.' In fact he must have been working at enormous speed, for he finished a typescript of some 120,000 words in little more than two months. When he went north to Black Mount on December 23rd to shoot hinds and blackgame over Christmas, the work was almost complete, and he put the finishing touches to it in Scotland.

In writing it he had one great difficulty: that of adequately portraying the foolishness and (as he saw it) downright dishonesty of Captain Holman. Had he made a direct attack, Holman would surely have sued him for libel or defamation; and yet, if Peter failed to show the man up for the ass that he had proved, he would be unable to explain why the expedition had broken up in the way it did.

He solved the problem by a brilliant stroke: he saw Holman, in any case, as a split personality, and instead of portraying him as one person, he showed him as two. The sensible, efficient long-term resident of São Paulo, the organizer whose skill and persistence got the expedition up-country through the chaos of the revolution—he described as Captain J. G. Holman; but the boastful, evasive and cowardly poseur, whose presence ultimately proved disastrous to the expedition's chances of achieving any real success—this man he described as Major George Lewy Pingle, 'an American citizen holding—or claiming to hold—a commission in the Peruvian army'.

Only once, right at the beginning, when he first introduced Major Pingle, did Peter hint at the device which he had adopted. 'That is not his name,' he wrote. 'You can regard him as an imaginary character, if you like. He is no longer quite real to me.' Thereafter he treated him as a real person, merely substituting 'Major Pingle' for 'Holman' whenever the man's behaviour became unwarrantably idiotic. So cunningly did he fashion the story that ninety-nine people out of a hundred would read it without realizing what he had done; but somebody exceptionally observant might notice that Holman—supposedly in charge of the whole enterprise—gradually fades from the picture as the expedition approaches the Araguaia, and, once it has embarked on the rivers, never appears again. The device served its purpose admirably, for it scarcely detracted from the immediacy of the narrative, and it enabled Cape's solicitors to pass the text for publication.

The first title Peter chose was *Brazil Through the Agony Column*; after he had finished the text he called it *Trespassers in Hell*, but then he evidently felt that this was too melodramatic, and changed again to the more laconic *Brazilian Adventure*. The dedication of the book, 'To C', concealed from most people, (and certainly from his mother, whom he had learnt from bitter experience to exclude as far as possible from his romantic affairs) the identity of Celia Johnson.

Brazilian Adventure was published in August 1933 and was greeted by rapturous reviews. 'This is the adventure book which one always dreams of reading and no one ever writes,' announced James Agate in the *Daily Express*. 'It must enthral everybody.'

'This is an extraordinarily good book,' wrote Sir John Squire in the *Sunday Times*. In the *New Statesman* David Garnett was equally enthusiastic: 'Mr Fleming has the most delightful sense of humour and he writes brilliantly.' To Sir William Beach Thomas Peter appeared as 'an incurable parodist. The careless grace and humour are inimitable ... the best book of travel published for years.'

J. B. Priestley felt the same: '*Brazilian Adventure* is the best travel book

I have read for a long time. It is crammed with sound observation, good writing, humour and a unique blend of disillusion, foolhardiness and high spirits.' Even the more intellectual Harold Nicolson, reviewing for the *Daily Telegraph*, found the book irresistibly engaging. 'Obviously Mr Fleming and his two companions did a most foolhardy and provocative thing,' he wrote, describing their final breakaway. But then he praised 'the slim neatness' of the author's style and expressed his certainty that the book would appeal to every type of reader.

One of the main reasons for the book's success was Peter's splendidly original attitude. Until he came on the scene, travel and travel books had been treated with excessive reverence and solemnity; but then, with a single, sustained burst of self-mockery, *Brazilian Adventure* blew the whole genre sky-high. Readers—and reviewers—could scarcely believe that a travel book could be so funny.

And yet, among the chorus of praise and excitement, there sounded one warning note, oddly enough in the *Spectator*. This came in a favourable but sharply perceptive review by another up-and-coming author, Evelyn Waugh. '*Brazilian Adventure* is an arresting and absorbing book,' he began. 'It is the narrative of a highly exciting expedition written by a man with unusual literary gifts, an austere respect for accuracy, a clear mind in collating evidence and assessing probabilities, a sense of the dramatic, the beautiful and the comic ... I am putting it in the highest class.' He went on to praise Peter's account of the return journey to Belém—'a chase as exciting as Jules Verne's *Around the World in Eighty Days*'—and his skill in describing relations with Major Pingle. So fascinated was Waugh by Major Pingle, in fact, that he called for information about how accounts with him had been settled and demanded that he should be forced to read the book. (It was perhaps no coincidence that the end of Waugh's own novel *A Handful of Dust*, which he finished in 1933, was set in the heart of Brazil, where, in circumstances extraordinarily similar to some of those described by Peter, the hero Tony Last is detained in the jungle by a crazed white settler who forces him to read Dickens aloud.)

Amid his commendations, however, Waugh raised several points 'for comment and regret', principally that the book was so intensely self-conscious. Having mentioned the parody language which Peter and Roger invented, he went on:

I can imagine how enlivening that kind of joke was in Matto Grosso, but it expresses an attitude of mind that seriously cramps a work of literature. For the truth is that Mr Fleming has a really

exciting story to tell, but he almost spoils it by going to the extreme
limits of depreciation in his anxiety to avoid the pretentious ...

Mr Fleming's shyness continually intrudes on the reader ... he is
afraid to let himself go: there is a tentative, luminous phrase followed
by immediate recession. He is afraid of purple patches. That is all
very well when one has little to describe; but Mr Fleming has an
eyeful, if he would only give it us.

Here Waugh singled out prophetically what was to prove the one serious
weakness in Peter's literary armament—his fundamental and inhibiting
dislike of self-advertisement. But at the time, in the general enthusiasm,
Waugh's remarks passed unnoticed, and the book at once became a
phenomenal success. In the last few months of 1933 it raced through
eight impressions; in 1934 it went through another four, in 1935 another
three. By 1946 it had been reprinted in various hardcover editions no
fewer than twenty-five times. In 1966 it was chosen as a set book for
schools, and in 1973, forty years after its original publication, it was
still in print, having sold altogether some 123,000 hardback copies.

On its first appearance in England it became a Book Society Choice,
and in America a few months later it made an almost equal impact,
being selected by the Book of the Month Club as its choice for January
1934. Foreign rights were sold all over the world. All this acclaim brought
money pouring in: in its first two years the book earned Peter more than
£5,000 (the equivalent of some £25,000 in 1974), and for the first time
in his life he was rich.

One of the last people to hear of his success was the author himself;
for he, characteristically, had not waited for publication day, but in
June 1933 had gone off again on a second visit to the Far East. Thus it
was only from out-of-date newspapers and the occasional letters of
friends that he discovered he had become famous overnight.

Forty years later *Brazilian Adventure* still seems sharply fresh and
amusing. It can be criticized on several counts; the narrative line is less
clear than it might be, and there are too many irrelevant asides; but the
main impression given by the book is one of buoyant originality—in
the author's observation, in his frame of mind, and in his language.

Peter's humorous writing made use of two different techniques. One
was to describe some relatively commonplace object in deliberately
ridiculous fashion—witness his account of one of the statues in Rio:

Victory has got a half-Nelson on Liberty from behind. Liberty is
giving away about half a ton, and also carrying weight in the shape
of a dying President and a brace of cherubs. (One of the cherubs is

doing a cartwheel on the dying President's head, while the other, scarcely less considerate, attempts to pull his trousers off.) Meanwhile an unclothed male figure, probably symbolical, unquestionably winged, and carrying in one hand a model railway, is in the very act of delivering a running kick at the two struggling ladies, from whose drapery on the opposite side an eagle is escaping, apparently unnoticed. Around the feet of these gigantic principals all is bustle and confusion. Cavalry are charging, aboriginals are being emancipated, and liners launched. Farmers, liberators, nuns, firemen, and a poet pick their way with benign insouciance over a subsoil thickly carpeted with corpses, cannon-balls and scrolls.

The other technique which he used to great effect was almost exactly the opposite—that of describing bizarre and outlandish things and creatures in the most ordinary way possible. Thus the one and only armadillo he saw he described as cantering along 'with a *dégagé* air'. He claimed never to have seen a snake in the whole of the trip, and the alligators, he said, were a fraud. Of the occasion when a toad was detected climbing into his trouser pocket as he lay asleep he wrote: 'If I knew my job I should say it was a man-eating toad; but I cannot slander so trustful a creature.' The *piranhas*—allegedly vicious man-eating fish among which he waded for days up the Tapirapé—excited his particular admiration:

We could not but admire the rigid self-control with which they ruled their blood-lust. We noted the ascetic, indeed the almost apprehensive glances which they cast at our tempting calves. Sometimes, if we stood still, a small shoal, a kind of deputation, would approach and hang diffidently suspended in the translucent water, staring at our legs with a wistful, perhaps a slightly covetous awe: as shopgirls stare at the sentries outside Buckingham Palace.

The expedition as a whole left him outwardly unchanged, but it taught him a good deal about himself—that his powers of leadership, for instance, were considerable, and easily asserted themselves in a crisis; that his physical endurance was equal to anybody's, and his tolerance of discomfort astonishing: the myriad thorns and insect-bites had worried him less than anyone else, and he consistently went bare-headed without ever getting sun-stroke. But the most important thing which the trip taught him was that he had a great need to excite himself with adventure: in going to a wild place, in exposing himself to its dangers, and then in writing about the experience, he found enormous satisfaction and set the pattern of his life for the next few years.

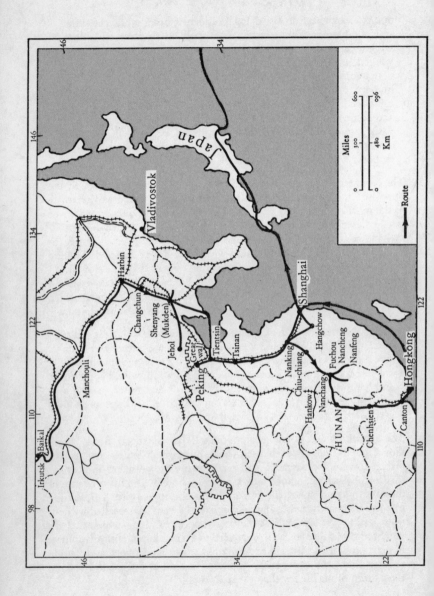

6

Bestseller

As soon as Peter returned from Scotland with his book complete he plunged into other literary and journalistic projects. On January 9th, 1933, he wrote to Jonathan Cape proposing that the firm should publish a selection of pieces from the *Spectator* edited by himself and Derek Verschoyle; Cape liked the idea, and in due course *Spectator's Gallery* appeared—to the surprise of Wilson Harris, who first knew about the project when he saw the book in a shop. The volume contained several of Peter's own essays—the first book in which any of his work appeared.

In February he took the top flat at 20 Danvers Street in Chelsea, directly above the distinguished bacteriologist Alexander Fleming, who was already well known for his discovery, six years before, of penicillin. The two Flemings were not related, but their accidental proximity caused postmen fearful confusion.

It was from Danvers Street that Peter sent Cape another idea for a book: a collection of three specially-commissioned biographical sketches, possibly called *The Abhorred Shears*. The studies, Peter proposed, should be 'of young men in whom the expression of genius was cut short by an untimely death, and they will be written by men equally young, and, I hope, equally accomplished.' Eric Linklater, he suggested, should write on Marlowe, Graham Greene on Chatterton, and John Sparrow on Shelley. No record survives of Cape's reaction to this proposal, but the idea came to nothing.

While writing for the *Spectator*, Peter began also to inquire about the chances of a full-time job in the B.B.C. Though he knew from his own brief experience in front of the microphone that his voice was against him as a broadcaster, he applied for the job of drama critic in February 1933. Getting no definite answer, he wrote again at the end of March, asking his contact in the B.B.C. whether there had been 'any developments in the matter of my deplorable voice'; and although this particular job eluded him, he eventually signed on as an assistant in the Talks Department—an appointment he would take up in the autumn.

While he waited for the B.B.C. to make up its mind, he began seriously to cultivate his contacts at *The Times*, where he soon formed an easy relationship with the Editor, Geoffrey Dawson. In those days *The Times* still wielded great power and influence: Westminster awaited every pronouncement of its leading articles, and the Editor was the confidant of the highest statesmen, Prime Ministers included.

Dawson had been Editor, in two spells, for more than fifteen years, and to the younger members of the staff he seemed an Olympian figure, to be approached (if at all) with reverence and formality. Yet Peter somehow cut straight through the normal barriers and dealt with him on a man-to-man basis, to the amazement and good-natured envy of his junior colleagues. He and Dawson had a good deal in common, not least their background as Old Etonians and their love of shooting. Before long Peter was on Christian-name terms with his Editor, and he often went north in the autumn to shoot grouse at Langcliffe, Dawson's home in Yorkshire. For Peter this was the first of several rewarding relationships which he formed with men old enough to have been his father: later friends included General Sir Adrian Carton de Wiart and Field Marshal Sir Archibald Wavell, both of whom saw in this dashing young man a reflection of their own early selves.

Peter was not yet attached to the staff of *The Times*, but he began to try his hand at writing Fourth Leaders—the light and elegantly-turned humorous essays which at that time were one of the paper's features. Although he later became a master of this form of *belles lettres*, he was not immediately successful, as is shown by a letter from the Editor written on April 2nd, 1933:

My Dear Fleming,

   I am afraid this will not do. You must study our leader style rather more closely. Seven paragraphs is too many for a short article of this kind, and the editorial 'we' (which you employ more than once) is always a nightmare to me. Have another shot.

Yours sincerely,

GEOFFREY DAWSON

Greater luck attended his plans for another visit to the Far East. Making the most of the fact that he had been in Manchuria during the Japanese invasion the year before, he painted a graphic picture of the fascination and importance which the Chinese political scene would hold that summer: in the north the Japanese army of occupation was containing with difficulty a huge population of bandits, and in the south the Communists, inspired by their young idealist Mao Tse-tung, had entrenched themselves in 'Red Areas' so securely that the Nationalist forces appeared to have little hope of dislodging them. All this, said Peter in Printing House Square, should surely be reported by *The Times*.

His interest in politics—then as later—was minimal. What he wanted was to travel again, and if possible to see some fighting; yet he played his cards so skilfully that *The Times* accepted his proposal that he should go to China with a roving commission as its Special Correspondent. The paper would pay well for any articles he wrote; he also managed to extort an advance of £50 from the *Spectator*, besides £100 from Jonathan Cape against his royalties from *Brazilian Adventure*. With Cape also he signed a contract for another book about the journey ahead.

Once again he found it hard to leave Celia; but the wrench of parting was softened by her staunchness. Already she knew him well enough to see that, no matter how much he loved her, his nature would force him to go off on long, solitary journeys, and on this occasion she faced his departure with a steadfastness that touched him deeply. He charged Rupert with the task of looking after her while he was away, referring to her in his letters as 'the Crackwit'.

He left England on June 2nd, armed with a ticket to Manchouli, on the border between Russia and Manchuria, and a copy of a signed letter from Stalin which his brother Ian had acquired a year before in Moscow while covering for Reuter's the show trial of the Metro-Vickers engineers. This document Peter tried on several occasions—though never with any marked success—to use as a kind of super-visa with which to bluff his way out of awkward situations.

After a brief halt in Berlin he went on to Moscow, where he spent four days talking to diplomats and journalists. *The Times*, at that date, had no correspondent in Moscow: because it refused to submit to the Soviet censorship whereby all resident foreign correspondents were controlled, the paper was obliged to report its Russian news from Riga, the capital of the independent state of Latvia. A short stay in Moscow was enough to convince Peter of the folly of this arrangement, and a few days later, when he reached Harbin, he wrote to Dawson about it:

The Russians are very keen that you should have a man there [in Moscow] ... because they think (this is the official view) that your Russian news from Riga is carrying less and less weight—that more and more people are beginning to doubt the possibility of covering the biggest country in the world from a town outside its frontiers ... My own personal opinion (which I would not quote but for the fact that it represents that of all my contemporaries) is that it is a sad pity, both from its own point of view and from the point of view of the public, that *The Times* has no correspondent in Russia ... I think you ought to get hold of a first-class man and send him out.

How many men of twenty-six, setting out on their first full-scale assignment for *The Times*, would have had the nerve to write the Editor a sentence like that last one? And how many would not merely have got away with it but have been warmly thanked for their outspoken advice? (*The Times* eventually stationed a man in Moscow in 1941.)

In Moscow Peter boarded the Trans-Siberian for the second time and at once slipped gratefully back into the routine which he had found so agreeable two years before. Later, in his book *One's Company*, he wrote:

Everyone is a romantic ... and for a romantic it is, after all, something to stand in the sunlight beside the Trans-Siberian Express with the casually proprietorial air of a passenger, and to reflect that that long, raking chain of steel and wood and glass is to go swinging and clattering out of the West into the East, carrying you with it. The metal curves glinting into the distance, a slender bridge between different worlds. In eight days you will be in Manchuria ...

As I settled down in my compartment, and the train pulled out through the shoddy suburbs into a country clothed in birch and fir, the unreal rhythm of train life was resumed as though it had never been broken. The nondescript smell of the upholstery, the unrelenting rattle of our progress, the tall glass of weak tea in its metal holder, the unshaven jowls and fatuous but friendly smile of the little attendant who brought it—all these memorable components of a former routine, suddenly resurrected, blotted out the interim between this journey and the last.

This time the trip was enlivened by the appearance of a young Russian intellectual called Assorgim who had been dispatched by the Soviet Commissariat of Culture to found a national theatre in Outer Mongolia; day after day he earnestly questioned Peter about the theatre in general and Shakespeare in particular, dwelling for hours on the play he knew as

Gamlet. Then, as he was about to leave the train, he implored Peter to teach him a modern English song with which he could add verisimilitude to one of his forthcoming productions. He wanted the kind of ditty that 'two Englishes ... two clubmen' might sing together when 'after long absence, much sorrow, great jobs of work, don't you know, they meet again.' After some hesitation, and with considerable technical difficulty (for he was tone-deaf, and could scarcely sing at all), Peter taught him the Eton Boating Song—with which Assorgim was delighted:

> We parted with many expressions of mutual esteem, and I gave him all the biscuits I could spare. I often think of him, a distant, gesticulating figure, teaching the Eton Boating Song to the inhabitants of Outer Mongolia.

At six o'clock on the last morning of the journey Peter was wrenched violently from the depths of a nightmarish dream:

> There was a frightful jarring, followed by a crash ... I sat up in my berth. From the rack above me my heaviest suitcase, metal-bound, was cannonaded down, catching me with frightful force on either knee-cap. I was somehow not particularly surprised. This is the end of the world, I thought, and in addition they have broken both my legs. I had a vague sense of injustice.

What had happened was that the train's brakes had failed on a long downward slope; a pointsman had seen that it was out of control and had switched it into a siding, where it had run off the rails and sprawled down an embankment. It was, as Peter remarked, the best sort of railway accident: the weather was ideal and no one had been badly hurt. In only four hours another engine was produced, and one of the coaches salvaged; in this the most important passengers proceeded on their way. By the time they did so Peter had covertly taken a number of photographs of the wreck; in this, however, it seemed that he had not altogether escaped notice, for when the truncated train reached the frontier post at Manchouli a posse of five customs men descended on his compartment and ransacked his luggage for threequarters of an hour. By a variety of stratagems he managed to keep the films of the train from them, and later some of the photographs were published in *The Times.*

After that nerve-racking incident he changed trains and proceeded through Manchukuo (the new name bestowed on Manchuria by the Japanese invaders) aboard the Chinese Eastern Railway to Harbin, which he found still terrorized by bandits, though less effectively than during the previous autumn. Having sent off his first dispatch to *The Times* (described by himself, needless to say, as 'a bad article'), he went on to Hsingking (Changchun), the newly-designated capital of Manchukuo, and there began a series of political interviews.

The ostensible purpose of these was to glean information for further articles, but his ulterior purpose was to obtain permission to accompany the Japanese army on a punitive anti-bandit drive. Back in April, when he had planned the trip, a full-scale battle had been in progress in the passes of Jehol, where the Japanese had been attacking the Great Wall; but by the time he reached the scene the fighting had died down, and a purge of the bandits seemed to offer the best chance of seeing some action.

He began, accordingly, to intrigue for the necessary permission, and when in due course he reached Mukden (Shenyang) his persistence was rewarded. Lietuenant General Koiso, the military governor of Manchukuo, told him that a small flying column would be leaving secretly in a week's time for the mountainous district to the east, and that Peter might accompany if it he liked.

This was exactly what he wanted. He filled the days of waiting with various diversions—among them a wild *geisha* party and a trip by air to Jehol to see that city's celebrated temples—and on July 5th he wrote to Rupert from the Yamato Hotel in Mukden.

> I shan't be able to write any letters for anything from one to three weeks, and you must see to it that Celia doesn't worry. I have written to her and said that I am going out on some sort of manoeuvres with the troops, but actually it is a sort of campaign against the bandits and I am afraid I may have talked about the prospects of it in my previous letters. So pretend that you have heard from me and that I said it was exactly like Pirbright [the Brigade of Guards' training camp] or something like that … Actually of course there is very little danger and I don't suppose anyone will smell any powder. There is, however, a million-to-one (literally) chance that I may not reappear, owing to being choked by the Japanese rations or eaten by my pony while asleep: in which case tell her that I loved her frightfully. But the occasion for these melodramatics will not arise, and I shall be back in a few days, I expect. It's going to be damn funny.

Together with an English peer, who was also courting adventure in the Far East in much the same way as himself, though on even more slender journalistic pretexts, Peter set off by train from Mukden attached to a column of mixed Japanese and Manchukuo troops some six hundred strong. He had been told to travel light, and did so,

> putting into a rucksack a shirt, shorts, two pairs of socks, a bottle of whisky, Boswell's *Life of Johnson*, and half a pound of cheese, the sole indomitable survivor of my Trans-Siberian victuals. This, with blanket, camera, films, field-glasses, and water-bottle, made a load which in case of necessity could be carried on foot.

They stayed the first night in an inn at Fushun, which Peter described as the Sheffield of Manchuria. Before dawn the next morning a car whisked them out to the barracks, and there they joined the Manchukuo column—'a soft-footed river of little slouching men in grey.' Given, at first, a large and aged Siberian charger, Peter soon swapped it for a little white pony ridden by a Russian, and this 'pretty, wise and completely tireless animal' served him impeccably during the march that followed.

The expedition, as it turned out, accomplished almost nothing: for ten days the column advanced as stealthily as possible, but the bandits, though constantly reported to be just ahead, kept disappearing like water into sand. No enemy force was defeated or even engaged, and only a couple of prisoners were captured. Even so, for Peter the excursion was thoroughly rewarding; afterwards he recalled with the keenest pleasure

> those silent early hours as we filed along the bottom of a valley, and the breeze which met us when we climbed a pass under the fierce eye of noon, and the muffled sound of men marching in dust, broken by the discreet clink of accoutrements, and my white pony standing in the moonlight, and many other things as well.

In spite of the lack of action, one or two macabre incidents did occur. Once, when the column had stopped for its midday halt in a filthy village, Peter noticed, hanging from a rafter in the house where they were resting, a little hammock covered with a cloth 'on which the flies crawled two-deep'.

> Presently something stirred beneath it; the flies rose with a buzz, then settled again. But now there was a child's hand sticking out, a small, hot, wretched hand, of which the wrist was pitted deeply. Everyone was asleep, or nearly asleep, except the Adjutant. I called his attention to the hand, and we pulled back the cloth. In the hammock a child lay dying of the small-pox. Five minutes later we were on the march again.

A few days later in another town they found, trussed and tied to posts, two bandits who were going to be shot that evening. Peter photographed them both 'without compunction but not without a vague feeling of embarrassment':

> The conventional part of me found something queer and awkward in the thought that those two trussed bodies would be food for worms long before some chemist in a dark room brought to light the figures they had cut on the threshold of death and dissolution. It was a situation which would have put Donne's muse on her mettle.

By the end of the march Peter—who had gone hatless, as usual—had been burnt to such a rich chestnut brown by the sun that his appearance caused bystanders no little astonishment. His colour put him in a different ethnological category from the normally pale-faced missionaries: 'The more educated onlookers inclined to the belief that I was an Indian,' he reported, 'but most put me down as a devil.' The rigours of the expedition had been almost too much for his companion who had succumbed to dysentery, and even Peter had been plagued intermittently by fever.

After two days' recuperation in Mukden he set out southwards for Shanghai, pausing for ten days in Peking to stay with Nancy and Harold Caccia, who had been posted to the embassy there. In Shanghai he again stayed with the Keswick brothers, and caught up with his mail. Potentially the most important piece of news which it brought was that his grandfather had died. 'I'm rather sad about my grandfather, who was a sweet old man,' he wrote to Rupert on August 12th, 'but I haven't worked out at all what difference his dying will make for me. In fact I'm being quite irresponsible and not bothering about anything.'

This indifference was not feigned: throughout his life Peter remained astonishingly uninterested in money, and he made no immediate attempt to discover whether he had been left all, some or none of his grandfather's considerable fortune. In fact he had been left none; for Robert, wrongly believing in his dotage that his grandsons all had capital of their own, left his entire estate to his own surviving children—Phil, Dorothy Wyfold and Kathleen Hannay—with a life-interest for his widow Kate.

At Tony Keswick's suggestion Peter equipped himself with some visiting cards; but, not being able to read Chinese, he did not for some time realize why the officials to whom he handed them were sometimes shaken by ill-concealed mirth. Then at last he got someone to translate the characters which Tony had had printed, and discovered that they meant 'Silly Young Fool'. His proper cards, when he got them, proclaimed that he was Fu Lei-ming, or Learned Engraver on Stone, and that he was the Special Correspondent Officer of the Newspaper for the Enlightened Apprehension of Scholars.

Just before Peter reached Shanghai—at the beginning of August—*Brazilian Adventure* had been published in London, but for the moment he knew nothing of its success. The only book that caught up with him was a proof copy of *Variety*, a collection of his articles from the *Spectator* hurriedly put together by Cape and illustrated with drawings by Roger Pettiward.

'This Moth book I think definitely fails to come off and is lousy,' he wrote to Rupert. He added four paragraphs of comments designed to improve it, but concluded fatalistically: 'I don't think it greatly matters what you do to this book.' Time proved him right, for *Variety*, even though it followed in the wake of *Brazilian Adventure*, proved a comparative failure: stripped of their original slight topicality, the featherweight essays appeared more facetious than urbane and did nothing to enhance Peter's reputation.

In his same letter from Shanghai he drew Rupert's attention to a possible new author for Cape:

> Oh, look here, before I forget, there is a man out here called Gerald Yorke, who was Captain of the Oppidans just before we went to Eton ... Gerald is out here with no money at all, and is now living in a temple with a bandit who is his servant ... By all accounts he is a pretty good chap and has certainly written a damned good account of the Jehol campaign, which I am sending you. It looks to me as if he would write a good book, especially if he can be kept on the move and not allowed to meditate and read Chinese poetry, which is what he runs to. He is impervious to discomfort and lives closer to the Chinese than any other literate person I have heard of.

In due course Cape did indeed publish Yorke's book *China Changes*; but Peter's immediate gain was that he had hit on someone who might make an excellent companion for his journey to the Communist-held areas in the south. The excursion was—journalistically speaking—the most important part of his entire trip, for the Chinese Communists were the most interesting figures on the political scene and offered Peter the best chance of being able to send *The Times* one or two substantial features.

By the summer of 1933 the strength of the Red armies was thought to be some 70,000 men, and they had taken over a large part of the Kiangsi province. From this mountainous and apparently impregnable enclave they launched occasional raids to win booty and food; the Nationalist forces had more or less given up hope of dislodging them, pursuing instead a policy of attrition and containment. Peter's object was to travel as close as he could to the front and see, if possible, 'what the Chinese Soviet Republic looked like to its immediate neighbours'.

He left Shanghai by car and drove via Hangchow to Nanking, the capital of China and the seat of the Nationalist Government. There he obtained a series of official interviews and a promise that a message would be sent to Marshal Chiang Kai-shek, the commander-in-chief of the Nationalist forces, asking him to make any arrangements he could that would expedite the passage of *The Times*'s Special Correspondent to the front. Chiang, at the time, was living in the mountain town of Kuling, so this became Peter's next objective.

Before he left Nanking he was joined by Gerald—'a large young man of saturnine appearance, equipped with a knob-kerry and a Chinese servant called Li'—and the three of them set out together on a river-steamer up the Yangtse. During the journey that followed Li proved invaluable, for he not only served as an interpreter but also guarded their interests with fanatical loyalty, bargaining endlessly to ensure that they were not cheated and manoeuvring in a thousand subtle ways to avoid any demeaning loss of face.

Disembarking after two days at a place called Kiukiang, they hired an ancient Ford and drove it in the direction of Kuling until the road ended. Then they took to their feet up the steep paths, paved with flagstones, which had been carved out of the hillside. After the sticky heat of the plains Peter found the keen, cool air and exercise extremely welcome.

In Kuling they were rewarded by an extraordinary slice of luck. Presenting themselves at the gate of Chiang's modest house, they found that none of their messages had reached him and that their arrival was entirely unexpected; but while they were parleying at the gate Madame Chiang appeared, saw them, and sent an aide to discover who they were. A few minutes later Chiang himself left the conference which was in progress to grant them a short but fascinating interview—one of the first he had ever given to a foreign journalist.

He came into the room quickly and stood quite still, looking at us. He wore a dark blue gown and carried in one hand a scroll, evidently part of the agenda of his conference ... His eyes were the most remarkable thing about him. They were large, handsome and very keen. His glances had a thrusting and compelling quality which is very rare in China ... As a rule contact with the great brings out the worst in me ... But before Chiang Kai-shek I retired abashed.

Although the Marshal's replies were rather perfunctory, and his attitude to the Communist threat so optimistic as to be almost patronizing, he proved invaluable to Peter, for he said he would wire the Governor of Kiangsi immediately and instruct him to grant the two Englishmen every facility for visiting the front. It was thus in a mood of some elation that they set off downhill from Kuling—to be greeted almost immediately by a scene that to Peter was quintessentially Chinese:

Half-way down we met a young man who was driving a pig up to Kuling. The unhappy creature was no mountaineer, and at last its forelegs had failed in their office, though the hind ones still had some strength left in them. The pig lay prone in the gutter, squealing, while the young man thrashed it incessantly with a switch, uttering loud and angry cries.

As usual it was a question of face, that dominant factor in Chinese life which I can never hope to define, but only to illustrate. The young man was a cut above the coolie class, and therefore could not demean himself by adopting the obvious and only practical course of carrying the pig up the mountain slung from a pole across his shoulder. Nor could he allow himself to be defeated without a struggle by the pig's collapse.

So he made a loud noise (which always helps to give you face, as the Chinese artilleryman well knows) and flogged the pig mercilessly, though he was aware that no amount of corporal punishment would get it any farther up the hill, as yet only half scaled. His face expressed a fiendish rage, but only for the sake of appearances. He was waiting for The Mediator—for some passer-by who would intervene in the strained relations between him and the pig, and effect a compromise. The whole incident was cut to a traditional pattern.

Chiang's word had evidently gone before them, as he promised it would, for when they returned to Nanchang they were received by the Governor of Kiangsi and by other senior officials charged with the task of suppressing the Communists. Next morning they left for Nanfeng, the most advanced post held by Government troops, which had recently been besieged by the Communist forces. So far, their travels had been uncomfortable rather than dangerous. The main enemy was the heat,

which even Peter found trying; most of the inns in which they stayed
were filthy, and every now and then they were smitten by food-poisoning.
For Peter, however, there was another wearing factor—Gerald's
loquacity. Although in many respects an ideal travelling companion,
Gerald did talk a great deal; Peter was naturally far too polite to remon-
strate, but soon he was sending off cables to his friends which began
with—or sometimes consisted solely of—the words CORK YORKE. Later,
when he called his book about the trip *One's Company*, the title was—in
part at least—a mild joke at Gerald's expense.

The farther south they went, the greater were the signs of fighting:
they passed numerous burnt-out villages and an overturned train, and
columns of troops straggled along the road. In Nancheng, the last town
before Nanfeng, they were almost halted by general irresolution and the
refusal of the Chinese to take responsibility for them.

> Maps were produced—maps on which the southward road ran
> between two perilously converging seas of red, and around which
> was built up a very pessimistic estimate of our chances of reaching
> Nanfeng alive. The Japanese-trained officer ... coined for the occa-
> sion rumours of an impending Red attack on Nanfeng. Even if we
> got there, he now said, we should never get out again. Someone
> else weighed in with the all too plausible theory that we might get
> in and we might get out, but we should never get back; spies would
> report our arrival, and our car would be ambushed in the hills on
> our return journey.

The potential hazards, it is clear, were by no means invented, and not
all that much exaggerated; but Peter was determined to reach the front,
and after a whole day of prevarication and intrigue he managed to out-
manoeuvre their craven and perfidious interpreter, Mr Chen, and to
obtain a military pass to visit Nanfeng directly from the military governor.
As they drove down a road flanked by slit-trenches, through fields in
which all cultivation had been abandoned and into country which grew
steadily wilder, Peter could not restrain himself from pointing out to Mr
Chen how admirably adapted to an ambush was almost every one of the
road's sharp and numerous corners. 'Mr Chen's large face', he wrote
afterwards, 'was disconsolate, and pale green in colour.'

'But nothing', he added in a phrase later widely quoted by reviewers,
'ever seems to happen to me,' and they reached Nanfeng safely. Scarcely
had they done so when a telephone message reported that firing had
broken out half way along the road they had just travelled; but Peter,
judging this to be merely a rumour designed to expedite their return,

proceeded to inspect Nanfeng's defences, and to look out on the high and densely wooded mountains in which the Communists were so securely established. That evening they drove back along the same road without so much as a false alarm.

Dissatisfied with this lack of action, Peter at once planned another foray into the Communist territory, this time by driving down the second of the two roads that penetrated the Red areas. This expedition proved, in the end, even less fruitful than the first, but it brought them nearer to death than any of their experiences so far, for the man who drove them was drunk and proceeded at a terrifying pace. For Peter the journey was a nightmare, for something he had eaten the night before had 'got under the guard of a normally ostrich-like digestion', and he would happily have welcomed death:

> The driver gave me every chance of doing so. The Chinese peasant has about half as much traffic sense as a Buff Orpington, and peasants were for some reason plentiful that morning. Some of them had brought their water-buffalo with them, some a flock of geese. This substantial proportion of the agrarian population the driver dismissed as figments of his imagination. There can be little doubt that, in some form or other, they *appeared* to him, for he acknowledged their existence by a savage increase of speed, whenever an increase of any kind was possible. He pressed his foot on the accelerator almost subconsciously, as he might have passed his hand across his brow, to banish what he took to be an hallucination ... We reached Hsinkan, by a miracle, with no blood on our hands, and still in possession of our lives.

By then, although again disappointed in his search for fighting, Peter had collected plenty of material to discharge his commitments to *The Times*, and the rest of his journey consisted of a leisurely return to Shanghai, via Canton and Hong Kong. Once more he came close to extinction when, as he and Gerald were walking over the hills towards the Pei river, he stopped to take a photograph in a cutting and got left behind the rest of the party. An explosion from high above him drew his attention to the fact that blasting was in progress, and, looking up, he saw an immense boulder bounding down the hill straight towards him. Above it was 'a wildly gesticulating fresco of manikins', who had no doubt that the rock was going to land on him:

> The prospect of a game, however short, of catch-as-catch-can between me and a large segment of South China clearly appealed to

the spectators but left me cold. I decided that, if one had to be squashed, it was better to make, figuratively speaking, no bones about it. I descended, with all possible dignity, into a cranny between two boulders and shut my eyes.

With a sound to which the Fall of the House of Usher was as the dropping of a pin, the mass of rock landed among the boulders ten feet away and lay, miraculously, dead. It hardly splintered at all, and none of the splinters came my way. We continued our journey.

That walk was further distinguished by an extraordinary coincidence. Peter had been telling Gerald about his quest for Fawcett the year before, and they were discussing the apparently deathless fascination which the explorer's fate exerted on the mind of the public. Suddenly Gerald stooped down and picked up a scrap of newspaper, printed in English, on which the only complete paragraph 'announced the return, empty-handed, of yet another American expedition from the jungles of Matto Grosso ... Gerald and I pointed out to each other what a small place the world was. It is always better to observe the rites.'

In Canton, Hong Kong and Shanghai they found themselves hailed as the greatest living authorities on Communism—a role which, in spite of his natural diffidence, Peter felt reasonably well qualified to play, since he honestly believed that his information was the best obtainable by foreigners. In Shanghai, where he shot snipe with the Keswicks and stayed on their luxurious houseboat, he had the delicious experience of discovering that he was a best-selling author. Lying on a bunk, he read two months' accumulation of mail with characteristically self-critical reactions:

A sheaf of reviews [of *Brazilian Adventure*] produced in me a feeling, not at all of elation, but rather of embarrassment. Nicolson, Lynd, Squire, Priestley—the giants of contemporary criticism, men whom I had hitherto held in considerable respect—praised this book to the skies. A cable summoned me to New York, where it had been chosen Book of the Month. 'Which month?' I wondered. But more I wondered 'Why?'

Still, here was a copy of the book itself. Clamped between tasteful covers and approached with a fresh mind, perhaps it would justify the giants and reveal unsuspected virtues. I read it. It revealed nothing of the sort. But I have a theory that a young man should put himself as frequently as possible in situations where a maximum number of comic things are liable to happen to him, and it was apparent from the rest of my mail that the position of a successful author, however little he deserves his success, has its compensations.

A bout of fever in Shanghai curtailed what would have been a more leisurely visit to Japan, and, passing through Tokyo and Yokohama in only two days, Peter took ship for the west coast of America. In Seattle, he contrived an agreeable evening with Brewster Morgan, his former colleague and producer in the O.U.D.S.; so strongly did the conversation flow that he missed the North Coast Limited express, on which he had booked a seat to New York. Undaunted, he chased the train in a taxi, caught it at a level crossing, and proceeded across the United States, deprived by the sudden dash of all reading material save for a copy of Sir Thomas Browne's *Religio Medici*. In Manhattan he was fêted by his publishers, Scribner's, and made a quick visit, part derisory and part nostalgic, to Wall Street. Then, at the end of October, he sailed for home once more.

Again the trip furnished him with the material for a bestseller. *One's Company* was published in August 1934, almost exactly a year after *Brazilian Adventure*, and although it did not make quite so sensational an impact, it confirmed Peter's reputation as one of the most promising writers of his generation. Again the reviews were numerous, long and enthusiastic.

'Mr Peter Fleming, as the reading world now knows, is an adventurous young man with an acid and scornful mind, a fresh and vivid style, and a conviction that he bears a charmed life,' began Vita Sackville-West in the *Spectator*. '"Nothing," he complains, "ever seems to happen to me."' If *One's Company* was a shade less fascinating than *Brazilian Adventure*, she went on, 'that is not to say that Mr Fleming has not again written a travel book in a thousand.' In the *Daily Mail* Compton Mackenzie praised Peter's 'power of observation, his command of the vivid simile, and his individual point of view.' In the *Evening Standard* Howard Spring pronounced that the book came off 'as brilliantly as before'; and in the *News Chronicle* Robert Lynd declared: 'The good-humoured contumely with which he writes of his fellow-creatures is a continual delight.'

Once more, however, a warning note was sounded—substantially the same note as had been struck by Evelyn Waugh a year before. Writing in the *Daily Telegraph* under the portentous headline A WORD OF WARNING TO MR PETER FLEMING, Harold Nicolson pointed out, at some length, the essentially negative and destructive character of his writing:

Mr Fleming stands at the end of that long line of iconoclasts who have rendered English literature so intelligent and so uncreative. I had imagined that the literature of negation could go no further than Aldous Huxley. Mr Fleming carries it further. I have a feeling, however, that he has carried it towards its last lap. Mr Fleming will have to encounter a 'new birth' if he is to find some affirmative. It is sad to reflect that so young and gifted a writer may merely be dropping the last clods upon the coffin of a movement which is gloriously dead ...

It would be a pity if Mr Fleming were unable to devote to less negative purposes the remarkable literary gifts which he possesses ... Mr Fleming, I feel convinced, possesses every gift, literary and intellectual, yet he is muscle-bound in the region of the head.

So high-pitched an intellectual tirade (of which these paragraphs are only a small part) was perhaps rather hard on an author of only twenty-seven who had already produced two best-sellers and shown himself capable, in his chapters about the Communists, of mature political judgments. Yet Nicolson's remarks did contain many grains of prophetic truth.

Even so, they were lightly regarded at the time. Far more instantly memorable was a phrase created by Nicolson's wife Vita Sackville-West. One read Fleming, she wrote, 'for literary delight and for the pleasure of meeting an Elizabethan spirit allied to a modern mind'; for her review a sub-editor at the *Spectator* conceived the headline 'A Modern Elizabethan', and it was as this that Peter was intermittently known throughout the rest of the 1930s.

Undoubtedly the critics were right in pronouncing *One's Company* less fascinating than *Brazilian Adventure*. Its main flaw was that the story broke into three uneven parts—the journey out, the anti-bandit campaign, and the chase after Communists—and thus lacked the straightforward narrative thread that had made the first book so exciting as well as so funny. Yet it contained many ridiculous incidents, and many fine descriptions of the Chinese landscape, some of which (in spite of Peter's deliberate rejection of aesthetic passages) painted pictures as delicate and memorable as Chinese water-colours.

Above all, the book enshrined the author's affection for China and its inhabitants. Something about its landscape struck a deep chord in him, as did something in its people's elemental struggle with the earth; and a little of his feeling came out in a passage at the end of the book in which he described the view from the Keswicks' boat:

A pale sunlight lay on the paddy fields. In some of them the rice had been cut and lay in swathes on the thin layer of water which covered the mud; in others men and women were working with scythes. The country was dead flat. As far as you could see there was nothing but dykes and fields, fields and dykes, with here and there a clump of dark trees round a tomb, or the ribbed sails of a junk moving stiffly down some unseen waterway, or a magpie flying slowly. A single tall pagoda stood up in the distance.

On this huge, green, unlovable chessboard the workers were small blue automata. The mud hid their legs to the knee, and when they stooped they had the blind, shapeless look of parasites. You felt that if the world were suddenly overturned—if the landscape before you were suddenly tilted sideways—they would still be clinging to it: still working inch by inch in their appointed squares: still working while the pagoda fell, and the magpie flew off into space, and our houseboat with its Union Jack was swept away: still working until the earth, their sole, most grudging ally, flawed and disintegrated beneath them.

There would not be an end of China until the last of them was dislodged.

Launched by the still-strong momentum of *Brazilian Adventure*, *One's Company* started off even faster than its predecessor, and by the time it went out of print in 1946 the book had sold nearly 90,000 copies.

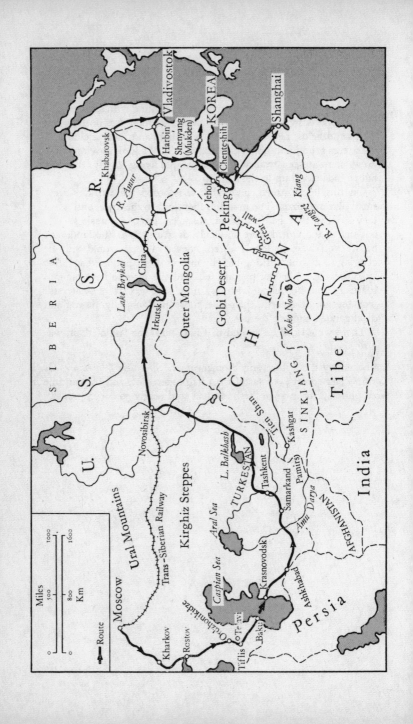

7

Back to the East

Returning to England in October, 1933, Peter discovered that he was a literary lion. *Brazilian Adventure* was going like a rocket and fan-letters arrived in shoals. *The Times*, of course, was delighted: having taken a gamble on sending a novice to China, the paper now found that its Special Correspondent was a best-selling author with a name already famous, and in November and December it gave considerable prominence to three series of his articles—one on Communism in China, one on China's foreign relations, and one on his own journey.

All this he found pleasant and flattering, and it must have been a severe frustration to have to buckle down to an office job with regular hours. But his sense of duty would not allow him to back out of an agreement to which he was already committed, and on October 23rd he joined the staff of the B.B.C. for a probationary period of three months as an assistant in the Talks Department at a salary of £450 a year. He did well in the job from the start; yet he had no intention of staying longer than his contract obliged him to, and in December he wrote to the Director of Talks to say that he had decided, with the greatest reluctance, to resign as soon as his probationary period was over:

> I like working here enormously, and I don't want in the least to sever my connection with the B.B.C. But I find myself—by a fluke which could not be foreseen when I applied for the job—in a position to earn, by writing, at least four times what the B.B.C. pays me. Economics apart, I should be a fool not to make the most of the artificial value temporarily attached to my pen. In short, I must have time to write, and a full-time job here is therefore impossible.

He duly resigned from the full-time staff on January 23rd, 1934, but he remained employed by the B.B.C., part-time and on half pay, until the end of March. During those three extra months he acted as producer for two series of talks, one of them called 'The Far East'. His increased freedom enabled him, at the end of January, to accept one of the many offers being thrust at him—that of a part-time 'editorial executive' on the *Evening Standard*. This appointment proved nebulous and undemanding, although Peter did, in the course of the next few months, contribute several feature articles to the paper and also worked for some time on the Londoner's Diary column. His main preoccupation during the winter was the completion of *One's Company*.

Among the new friends he made about this time was George Buchanan, a playwright and novelist of the same age as himself who was working as a sub-editor on *The Times*. Having met him in Printing House Square, and admired his book *Passage through the Present* (a portrait of the state of England done in diary form), Peter suggested that they should write a play together. The setting was to be a large liner at sea, and Peter's plan was that he should contribute the ideas and the action, while Buchanan wrote the dialogue. Not surprisingly—for Buchanan's style and mode of expression were far more aesthetic and intellectual than Peter's—the project never came to fruition, although both authors devoted several sessions to it. In spite of the failure Buchanan remained fascinated by Peter—the romantic hero, the man of action.

Meanwhile the success of *Brazilian Adventure* had delighted Peter's family. Philistine though many of them were, they keenly appreciated the advantages of literary fame, not least Grannie Katie, who boasted about the book and gave away copies with the same benign abandon which had characterized her descriptions of the boys' achievements at school.

After Robert's death she continued to live at Joyce Grove, and there at weekends the boys congregated with their friends. It was not unusual for the huge house to contain four or five disparate and largely incompatible groups. Peter's mother, together with his half-sister Amaryllis, then aged eleven, would generally occupy the nursery wing; Eve would play her violin, indoctrinate her daughter with anti-Grannie propaganda, and make occasional sallies to visit her smart friends in the surrounding country. Peter would be entertaining literary or shooting friends; Ian's set was predominantly one of golfers and bridge-players; and Richard and Michael, both of whom were working in the City, would have their own friends along. Each group amused itself, paying little or no attention to what the others were doing.

Peter's mother was still scheming to find him a suitable bride; but unfortunately for her he had by then become adept at handling her machinations. Of the many introductions which she engineered for him only one prospered at all—that with Lady Caroline Paget, daughter of the Marquess of Anglesey. Peter very much liked Caroline; he was fond also of her sister Rose, and he often stayed at Plas Newydd, their home in Anglesey, where he acted enthusiastically in several of the family's amateur films. But he never had the slightest intention of marrying either of the girls. For one thing he did not see the advantages—so obvious to his mother—of becoming a Marquess's son-in-law; for another, he was firmly attached to Celia.

It now seems strange that Eve did not realize the strength and depth of this alliance; had she done so, she would certainly have fought against it, for Celia, although undeniably beautiful and talented, came from a respectable middle-class family with none of the advantages such as titles, money and land that Eve considered indispensable. As it was, Peter concealed his fondness for Celia so effectively that his mother never realized how serious it had become until it was too late for her to intervene. It may have been that Peter's habit of repeatedly disappearing on long journeys encouraged her to believe that he could not be seriously attached to anybody; yet if she thought this, she completely underestimated the tenacity both of her own son and of the girl with whom he was in love.

Celia, by this time, had established herself as one of the brightest young stars of the London stage. 'What charm and oddly attractive looks that young actress has, and how well she acts,' wrote one critic of her performance in *The Vinegar Tree* in July 1932; and in 1934 another declared that 'Celia Johnson, with her tall and slender elegance, her lovely spaniel eyes, her quick sympathy, her lively intelligence, her humour and her wistfulness, is the Modern Girl at her most gracious.' The play that finally confirmed her reputation was Merton Hodge's comedy *The Wind and the Rain*, which opened on October 18th, 1933, and in which she gave more than nine hundred performances as the heroine. Thus, in the spring of 1934, when Peter was finishing *One's Company* and beginning to think about another journey, she was in the middle of an immense run, and she stayed in the play until Peter eventually returned to England in November, 1935, after fourteen months' continuous travel.

Although at times he was sorely tried by his mother's eccentricities, Peter remained staunchly loyal to her, never breathing a word of criticism or betraying his embarrassment more than he could possibly help. To most of his friends his devotion seemed completely blind; yet he felt instinctively that Eve—maddening though she might be—really was doing her muddled best on his and his brothers' behalf. If any of them doubted her love, she set it out for them to see in a letter which she addressed to Peter, for all four of them, in the winter of 1933:

My Darlings,

I am writing this because I find it easier than talking. I am afraid of breaking down and making an idiot of myself and embarrassing you.

I think the time has come when I should tell you that my task as far as you all are concerned is practically finished. I can do little more for you. You know what is right and what is wrong, and I have tried to instil into you the great truth (which is not preaching but simply common sense) that to do right is the only happy way of life and therefore the only sensible one, and as soon as the wish to learn and the power to appreciate and understand leave us, life is over ...

I have tried to bring you all up with the best possible education, and without ostentation, or more money for your use than was good for you—always with an eye to a possible future with very little.

When Michael is 21 I might marry. I vowed about a year after Mokie was killed, when marriage was discussed, that I would not marry till he was of age. They all said (including Grandpapa and Grannie) that I should never be able to bring you up without a man to help me, but when I came to think over it I found that the will made it impossible for me to do so conscientiously. It is a bad will ... and it left me an enormous trust. I have done my best to carry it out, and if I have sometimes failed it was because it was too difficult for me not to make mistakes in this gigantic task. The aim and object were always high and the strivings were always *meant* for your good ...

As you know, Mokie and I married for love and we only grew more in love as the years went on, and he wrote to me every single day of the war. I have never recovered from the shock of his death, and I don't suppose I ever shall.

As I said before, I can do little more for you. You are grown men, and for all the faults in your upbringing or in me I would ask your forgiveness and ask you to remember that the task was a great one for a woman alone, and without any real help and a good many hindrances.

'The heights hold peace.' That is what I put on Mokie's cross, and I would have you keep that before you all your lives. May they be happy, and may you make them as great as is within your power by aiming always at the highest and by not being satisfied with less than that.

I am immensely proud of you all, and that I love you all deeply goes without saying. I am very ambitious for you because you are Mokie's sons, and that you should ever allow yourselves to slide into mediocrity would distress me terribly. I would like you so to act and to be that men will have confidence in you, and I do hope and pray that you may make such places for yourselves in the world that humanity may be the better for your company. God bless you all ...

Your loving and devoted MOTHER

Although this letter was obviously written at a moment of personal crisis, when its author was seriously contemplating marriage, Peter was touched deeply by it, and throughout his life he followed its main precepts, maintaining the highest possible standards in all he did.

As far as his own future was concerned, the way ahead seemed clear: his love for Celia notwithstanding, he must travel more and write more —both articles and books—and sometime during the spring of 1934 he conceived a plan for the most ambitious journey of his life. He would go to China again, for a start, once more as a Special Correspondent of *The Times*. But this would be only the beginning. His ultimate ambition —which he confided to no one in England—was to walk or ride back the whole way from China to India: an immense trek of some 3,500 miles through the heart of Central Asia.

Various impulses inspired him to this aim: one was the romance implicit in the idea of crossing Tartary; another was the fact that relatively few foreigners had accomplished the feat before. The last traveller to have reached India from China had been the American Owen Lattimore in 1926-7, and since then the Chinese province of Sinkiang, which lay astride the most direct route, had been ravaged by a succession of civil wars, so that political uncertainty reinforced the already formidable physical barriers and thus (in Peter's eyes) rendered the project even more inviting.

Of his real intentions, however, he breathed not a word in London, and in Printing House Square he gave out merely that he wanted another free-ranging assignment in China. The great difference between this and previous expeditions was that his renown now enabled him to call the tune far more precisely than before, and on June 13th, he wrote to Dawson with a number of explicit requests:

My suggestion is roughly this: *The Times* should give me a roving commission in the Far East on the following basis:

1. All expenses paid (in this connection it is worth noting that last year a five months' journey through Russia, Manchuria, China, Japan and America cost me only £330 altogether).

2. My itinerary to be subject to your approval and vetted by your Staff Correspondent on the spot.

3. The arrangement to be terminable by you, with my fare home guaranteed.

4. The American copyright of my articles to be at my disposal. The circumstances you ought to bear in mind when considering this suggestion are:

i. I have no money except what I earn.

ii. I am at present earning—apart from my books—more than £1,500 a year by journalism.

iii. I could—you must take my word for this—get a similar assignment from Beaverbrook and make a profit on it.

You see, what I want is an opportunity to travel, in a good cause, without having to think all the time, 'Well, I'm not paying my way. I must go back and earn some more money.'

Points in favour of my suggestion are:

1. I have, though I do not deserve, a 'name' among the reading public. By August—what with this Book of the Month nonsense and all—I shall be a still better name. [*One's Company* was to be the Book Society's Choice for August.]

2. The potential imminence of a Russo-Japanese war.

3. The fact that, if all goes well, I shall spend most of my time in the interior, where travel is cheap.

4. My alleged (by me) ability to make an article worth reading on its 'local colour' value alone, apart from its topicality or importance.

5. The fact that, on and after my return, *The Times* would have the benefit of my experience for what (if anything) it was worth.

I hope the idea appeals to you. I am pretty sure it wouldn't run you into a heavy expenditure, but if you think it would perhaps we could work out some other arrangement, though something like the basis indicated above would suit me best.

Perhaps I ought to add that this journey or journeys would not have as even their secondary object the writing of a book. I want to get out of that rut and/or racket, and—though I may do another travel book if the material inspires me—I shall not start with a publisher's contract in my pocket.

No doubt the disclaimer in this last paragraph was designed to allay suspicion that he might be using the paper merely as a convenient means of financing the research for his books. He himself was very sensitive about this point: he often worried that his articles for *The Times* were too thin and that he was not giving value for money. On this occasion he must have felt fairly certain that another book would emerge from the trip, whatever form it might take—and indeed the journey did eventually inspire two books (*News from Tartary* and *A Forgotten Journey*). For the moment, however, it seemed wise to push further literary projects firmly into the background.

His policy certainly had its desired effect on the paper, for on July 17th, the Manager of *The Times* sent him precisely the sort of *carte blanche* he had been seeking:

Dear Mr Fleming,
    Our agreement with regard to your projected journey cannot, in the nature of things, be stated in precise terms.
    You are to proceed to Mongolia and to contribute to *The Times* such articles as the circumstances permit, and if events develop in or around the area you will be at the disposal of the Editor to deal with them. As we see it at present, the journey would occupy not more than nine months and we are prepared to pay you a sum not exceeding £650. Before your departure we would place this amount at your disposal in any way you choose.

By the time these details were settled Peter had already met (at a night-club in London) the girl who was to share his most arduous journey. Ella Maillart, known always as Kini, had already made a name for herself as a solitary traveller endowed with endurance and enterprise every bit as formidable as Peter's. A French-speaking Swiss, she had distinguished herself in an extraordinary variety of fields: captain of the Swiss women's hockey team, she was also an international skier; she had acted in plays and a film, taught French in Wales and Germany, made herself an expert sailor, walked through the Caucasus and ridden a camel through the Kizil Kum desert in the depths of winter. She had done a good deal of journalism and had written two travel books, of which the second had been a considerable hit in Paris. Her position, when she met Peter, was oddly similar to his: she had established enough of a reputation as a writer to be able to finance further travels by means of journalism, and when she came across Peter in the summer of 1934 she was planning extensive journeys in the Far East, just as he was.

Tall and angular, she struck people as far more feminine than her achievements might have led them to expect. Peter felt little for her physically, but he did immensely admire her guts and enterprise, and when he said casually 'See you in China' he doubtless genuinely felt that it would be by no means a disaster if he did in fact come across this resourceful fellow-journalist in the East. Unfortunately (as it turned out) he took it into his head to tease Celia at the time by pretending he had been greatly taken with Kini—a joke that was to cause him much embarrassment later.

After a few fruitless approaches ('Come to Mongolia,' he said to George Buchanan one day) he hit on two congenial companions for the first stage of the journey. With George and Mogs [short for Imogen] Gage, whom he already knew quite well, he planned a shooting expedition to the Caucasus. Viscount Gage was then a Lord in Waiting to King George V, and a more English figure could hardly be imagined; Peter used afterwards to describe with relish a fracas that had broken out on some continental railway station where, threatened with detainment because of some irregularity in their documents, Gage had walked up and down the platform announcing at the top of his voice in a brutally Anglo-Saxon French accent: '*Ils peuvent m'arrêter, mais je ferai un bruit incroyable.*' With Mogs Peter got on exceptionally well: they talked incessantly and laughed wildly at each other's jokes.

One's Company was published on August 3rd, to general acclaim, and Peter, who hated parties at which he was the centre of attraction, was glad to escape from the hot-house of literary London three weeks later. Together with the Gages he left England on August 24th, armed, as usual, with only the flimsiest of plans: he hoped to get some shooting in the Caucasus and to proceed from there to Manchuria via the Turksib Railway through Russian Central Asia. He also vaguely hoped to get permission to visit Outer Mongolia. But he began the journey without the visas necessary for either enterprise, and it weighed on his conscience that, unless one or the other came off, he would have a hard job in producing enough for *The Times* to justify the paper's investment in him.

The Gages were surprised by the amount and weight of his equipment: they had expected him to travel ultra-light, with the economy born of long practice. Instead, they found that besides clothes and books he had brought a typewriter and a gramophone, to say nothing of his usual supply of potted grouse and Stilton from Fortnum & Mason. He typed the entries in his diary on the sheets of a loose-leaf notebook which Celia had given him, inscribing inside the front cover: 'To One Who's My Idea of Company.'

'Holland no less flat,' he wrote on the first page. The party stopped first in Berlin, where they stayed in the Adlon (of which, Peter wrote, 'I know of no more depressing hotel'); among the people they met were the Military Attaché, Brigadier Sir Andrew Thorne (an old friend of the family), and Douglas Reed, *The Times*'s resident correspondent. In Moscow they stayed in the National Hotel and combined some intensive sightseeing with attempts to procure the necessary travel documents from the State travel bureau Intourist—already an organization, though still in its youth, of legendary incompetence. They toured the Kremlin, went to the Museum of Western Art, watched a marriage being performed in the State registry office and did their best to mock the Anti-God Museum, which struck Peter, however, as 'not as funny as it ought to be', because many of the exhibits were ambiguous. The sight of some huge Siberian tigers in the zoo excited him a good deal, and he began trying to arrange, through Intourist, an expedition to shoot one when he reached Vladivostok. The sight of Lenin, lying embalmed in his tomb beneath the walls of the Kremlin, moved him to record that he 'seems to have shrunk since 1931'. On September 1st—a date, in his estimation, 'arbitrarily fixed to coincide with the opening of the partridge season'—he saw Stalin take the salute at a march-past in Red Square marking the twentieth anniversary of the International Youth Movement.

Between these diversions he kept up a running battle for visas with both Intourist and the Mongols. His hopes of visiting Outer Mongolia—never high—gradually faded away, mainly because the Mongolian legation was continually deserted and there was nobody with whom he could do business; but suddenly he got permission from the Russians to travel on the Turksib Railway. This lucky break delighted him: it was, he said, 'a great and unexpected thing'. Another event which brought much pleasure was the arrival of a letter from Maurice Baring, who was then aged seventy and had included in his long journalistic and literary career a spell as a war correspondent in Manchuria. 'I have just finished *One's Company* and feel impelled to write and thank you for the pleasure and entertainment it gave me,' the old man scrawled in writing so shaky (from Parkinson's disease) as to be barely legible. He too, he said, had travelled the Trans-Siberian, so that he could sympathize with Peter and see how accurate his account had been. He went on to urge Peter not to shrink from describing things, even though those things had been described by others before—he urged him, in effect, to let himself go a little more in his writing. 'But who am I,' he concluded, 'who should give advice? A very ignorant and idle man who wasted unique opportunities of seeing places all his life.'

Having talked at length with the resident journalists and dined at the British Embassy, Peter boarded the train for Kharkov, together with the Gages and an interpreter called Boris. As he recorded in his diary, the start of the journey was not auspicious:

> I shared a compartment with an enormous Ukrainian lady, of whom at the outset I gave to Mogs a very uncomplimentary description in English. Throughout the journey she maintained a gloomy silence and a *fatale* air. At the close of it she said, 'Excuse me, please,' in perfect English. It was a bad break.

In Kharkov, while George had some official interview, Mogs and Peter 'went miles away and bathed with some difficulty in a stormy river which did us a lot of good and strengthened the impression of eccentricity which I hope to create.' Thereafter, stopping frequently to inspect factories, collective farms and palaces of culture, they made their way south into the Caucasus via Rostov and Ordzhonikidze.

The farther they went, the wilder the country became and the more unpredictable their progress. They left the train at a place called Breslan and proceeded in a variety of ancient cars, on horseback and on foot into the alleged hunting areas. The shooting itself proved something of a farce, for the arrangements made on the visitors' behalf were constantly being changed, and the local experts were almost always so severely incapacitated by the previous night's drinking that they kept failing to make the early starts essential to success. Even so, Peter enjoyed everything immensely, for he conceived a great liking for the Georgians, with their wild, spontaneous hospitality, and the hunting forays took place in country so spectacular that they provided some of the most ferocious exercise he had ever had.

The entries in his diary, growing progressively more staccato, reflect the increasing strangeness and excitement of the surroundings:

September 12

Up at six. Roared up the Georgian Military Highway towards the clouds ... Splendid bit of (Tsarist) engineering, which wound up gorges with a steep drop on the off side. Driver reckless but very

good. Damn cold. Terrific scenery. Stopped and drank brandy at
Kasbek ... Dropped tortuously down to Passanour, a little village
where we had some food and picked up two guides and some
three-legged horses ... We set off, mostly on foot, up a valley
towards the Hevsur territory. After a long wait while another horse
was scrounged out of some eyrie in the crags, we went on. It began
to rain like stink. At 5.30, soaked through, we reached some sort of
village and quartered ourselves in a two-storey building ... Here
we ate our cold food and boiled some Oxo, the water for which I
procured by the simple expedient of holding the saucepan under the
gout of rainwater from the eaves. My thick sweater had been lost,
but one of the men rode back and found it. It was very cold, but my
Baghdad sheepskin coat was a godsend and much admired by the
natives. I slept in it, and my clothes dried on me ... There was a
mysterious deposit of bantams' eggs in our room, and a fair showing
of rats.

At noon next day, as they started off after a midday rest, Peter discovered
that his haversack, which, among other essentials, contained his passport,
had fallen off a led horse sometime during the morning. Leaving the
others to go on, he rode back in search of it and was rewarded only by
a rumour that a man had been seen departing into the mountains with
some object found on the trail. By the time he caught up with the rest
of the party again he had ridden or walked more than thirty miles,
dragging his horse a good many of them, and his return felt 'awfully
like coming back from stalking'. That evening they drove down to
Tiflis, and there invaded a hotel 'in a curious procession—me in my
savage furs, Mogs looking like an eccentric step-dancer in George's
trousers, and George in his stockinged feet carrying his shoes'.

The shooting proper began on September 16th, when they reached a
place called Telav in the early morning, ordered breakfast in one restaurant and ate it in another—sour milk, cocoa, mutton and wine.

'General impression strongly in favour of the Georgians,' Peter
wrote in his diary:

Nobody knew where our house was, so we waited about on a
balcony in the sun. Then suddenly people appeared, fairly heavily
armed, who said they could not imagine why we had been sent to
Telav. It was all a mistake. We must go and live in a palace at
Tsinondali, where the shooting and the accommodation were much
better. We piled once more into the car ... the palace had belonged
to the Chavchavadzes and was a squat, creeper-covered building

with deep tropical verandas, standing in a sort of garden-park with many different kinds of trees. We were installed in the so-called Museum apartments. In George and Mogs's room there were five beds, twenty-one Empire chairs in olive-green silk, five tables, three sofas and a large number of curious spittoons fitted with a pedal. Mine is less magnificent, being a passage room between one occupied by a Russian writer and his wife, and the bathroom, which they tell me smells. There are three beds, and although I go to bed alone there is always some absolutely unexplained man sleeping in one of the other beds when I wake up.

When we had settled into these fantastic quarters we went out shooting. A painful drive in the car, which in addition to us contained seven armed men and a dog called Rosa. Then a long, aimless walk, never in line, through a wilderness of weeds, maize-fields and scrub. Total bag: two quail and two very small doves. I was shooting with an old English 16-bore, of which the second barrel seldom fired. We should have had two or three pheasants. The best moment was when Constantin, our bodyguard, fired at a hen pheasant with his Mauser [a pistol]. The range was about three hundred yards and the bird was flying strongly.

Next morning they were up at five, but Boris and the men, having had a blind the night before, could not be rallied until much later, and by the time they eventually set off, accompanied by nine men and a pack of dogs, most of the pheasants had retired to the safety of impenetrable undergrowth:

> After wandering along and putting up one or two pheasants in dense cover, the expedition got completely lost in a thicket. The dogs disappeared, allegedly in pursuit of a wolf, and morale was low.

In spite of the disorganization, Peter again thoroughly enjoyed himself, particularly when one of the men, Santino, attempted to recall his dog by blowing his gun-barrels like a horn—a process which (Peter wrote years later), though it had no effect whatever on the dog, 'emptied many a Caucasian corrie of less insouciant quadrupeds'.

> We sagged on, in no sort of formation and on no sort of plan, seeing little and getting nothing, until we came to the river (Alazan) where droshkies were waiting for us. Here we ate mutton and eggs and chicken and cheese and drank a good deal of wine. After lunch fairly heavy firing broke out. Mogs, though claiming to be blind,

broke a bottle at the first attempt. I put a bottle on a tree and tried out the Mauser ... People were standing about and shooting quite vaguely in every direction. In the end Mogs shot two pheasants rather unexpectedly, and I got a quail and a hare, whose throat Santino cut. The expedition got lost several times and was also frequently attacked by savage sheepdogs. Santino had two shots at fish in the river, one with a gun and one with a rifle ... Among the rank-and-file of the expedition some rather wanton small-bird shooting broke out. A puppy turned up from somewhere. A snake was caught and put in a bottle.

That day ended with prodigious eating and drinking. Most of the next was spent planning a bear-hunt which never came off, but on September 20th the party finally took to the steep, wooded hills in search of deer and boar:

The men wore old military overcoats ... and shambled steaming through the mist like bears. All were heavily armed. The two drives came to nothing at all ... We had a sharp slide down, and an una-accountably bad dinner. The usual burst of target practice in the middle of the shoot.

On the 21st, later than ever, we marched out along the foothills in blazing sunshine, had one promising but blank drive where deer were seen, and camped idyllically quite low down in the woods. It really was lovely. We tore up chunks of meat and swigged wine in front of an enormous fire. The men got rather drunk on some kind of vodka and did wild Georgian dances to their knives, singing like fiends and clapping their hands ... They are all good on the hill, though foolish.

On the 22nd they set off for the high tops in pursuit of *tours* (mountain sheep like *moufflons*), and for the next three nights camped in magnificent surroundings:

At last we came out of the trees on to a high, bare spur, palely dotted in the moonlight with autumn crocuses. Big peaks all round, and the world a long way below ... We went on and on, to camp at last on a sheep-trodden ledge where stood a semi-circle of ruinous huts used by the shepherds in the summer. The dirty, cream-coloured horses looked as romantic as anything. We ate some soft-boiled eggs and drank some fine water and some brandy and lay down to sleep round a fire, George and Mogs in their little tent. Owls cried, and the men made me come and drink with them ... I was up at five.

The moon was still on the mountains ... There was a little cloud in the valley. The men lay like headless black furry monsters in their *burkas*. Presently the dawn came and a wren sang somewhere nearby.

In going which was so precipitous that everyone wore climbing-irons, the party slithered and scrambled about the mountains with more hope than success, although one or two small deer were bagged and Peter did in the end dispatch an enormous boar, part of which was promptly turned into *shashlik*. Every day was violently strenuous, and on the toughest they went hard for fourteen hours with scarcely a break. By the end Peter was burnt black in the face, thin, and 'in cracking good condition'.

He was extremely sorry when the whole wild expedition came to an end: seldom had he faced such an intense physical challenge; never had he shot in such outlandish country with so improbable but agreeable a gang of companions. 'Life has been fantastic,' he wrote to Rupert on September 30th from Tiflis:

> One day sleeping in a disused palace, the next lying four-deep round a fire with a lot of Third Murderers on a mountain top; one day eating five-course meals, the next subsisting on brown bread and gherkins. It is very important that you should ring up Beachcomber for me and say that he was in many respects right about the Caucasus ... tell him also that, coarsened as we were by camp life, his name was not forgotten; my huge Kurdish fur coat, in which I constantly slept, was called Hamilton after the ape which stood in one of his bye-elections.

As if to round off the whole episode, the police by some miracle found and returned Peter's lost haversack, minus only his razor-blades. 'An astonishing and undreamed-of slice of luck,' he recorded in his diary:

> The Gages go to Armenia probably tonight, I go to Baku tomorrow. I shall miss them sadly They are damn good value and we have got on wonderfully ... Wrote this up and saw the Gages off. Very sad.

As he remarked in his letter to Rupert, Peter felt that *The Times* 'might reasonably think the Caucasus rather irrelevant', and he now set off on what he hoped would prove journalistically a more valuable stage of the journey, crossing the Caspian on the ferry from Baku to Krasnovodsk, and there catching the Trans-Caspian Railway to Samarkand. Food on the train being scarce, he depended partly on Fortnum & Mason but mainly on the milk, chickens, melons, grapes, bread, tomatoes and mutton which were on sale in the stations through which they passed.

Reaching Samarkand after dark one evening, he took a *droshki* to the largest and newest hotel, where there ensued a fine farcical episode of which he later gave a splendid description in a radio talk. The hotel was so new that its restaurant was not yet functioning, and just as the blowzy blonde at the reception desk was assuring him that no food was to be had, a wizened charlady appeared and took him off to a night-club where a band was playing western jazz, vilely, and where she badgered the management into providing a large meal of sausages and vodka. As Peter was finishing this unexpected but welcome repast, a young officer in the Red Air Force called Nikolai appeared and greeted him warmly, mistaking him (it afterwards transpired) for a Russian pilot who had recently carried out a daring rescue in the Arctic. Undeterred by his error, Nikolai called for more sausages and more vodka and became exceedingly convivial; but it was not until they lurched out into the street that Peter realized quite how drunk he was:

'England,' he cried, 'is a very cultured country. I salute her!' and drawing an automatic pistol from his holster he fired three rounds rapidly in the general direction of the stars. Two men who were coming down the street towards us turned and ran off as fast as their legs could carry them ...

'Come along now,' said the old charlady, whose philosophical outlook had in no way been affected by this *feu de joie*; and she took him by the arm. I took his other arm and we proceeded towards the hotel in an atmosphere heavily charged with international goodwill. Nikolai kept on saying what splendid people the English were, and I, with typical Imperialist duplicity, kept on trying to get hold of his pistol.

When we reached the hotel Nikolai made a bee-line for the blonde behind the reception desk, with whom he began an ardent though one-sided conversation. I got my key, and the old charlady helped me carry my luggage up to the bedroom. As I came down for the last of my suitcases a beggar appeared in the hotel entrance and stood peering not very hopefully into the lighted lounge. Nikolai, who was making little headway with the blonde, saw this apparition and for one reason or another took a pot-shot at it. He missed, the beggar vanished with a howl of dismay, the blonde screamed, Nikolai slapped her face and in the resulting confusion I managed to grab the pistol and withdraw to my room.

The hotel was now in a state of some tumult. Doors were opening, bells were ringing, feet were pounding along the corridor. All this gradually died down as I undressed, and peace would have reigned once more over Samarkand if I hadn't started to worry about the safety-catch on Nikolai's automatic. Was it cocked, or wasn't it? It was a Russian pistol and I had no means of telling. In the matter of firearms my upbringing was a strict one, and I decided that, rather than risk leaving a cocked pistol lying about my bedroom, I had better find out whether it was on safe or not. So I opened the window, pointed the pistol at the sky and pulled the trigger.

There was a deafening explosion. Once more doors opened, bells rang, feet pounded down the corridors. And I, as I got into bed and fell into a dreamless sleep, reflected that life in Samarkand seemed from my brief experience of it to have a rather unusual flavour.

Next day he visited the city's sights, among them the tomb of Tamburlane, and when Nikolai appeared, not much more than half conscious, went with him to the bazaar where he bought a Red Army cavalry overcoat which he thought very fine and which made him look like 'a cross between Rupert of Hentzau and Lot's Wife.'

'Autumn has suddenly come, if not winter,' he noted in his diary on October 9th. 'It is bright and cold and the leaves are beginning to fall. Samarkand is a good place.'

As always, however, he would not linger, and two days later he took the train to Tashkent, where he boarded the Turksib Railway for Novosibirsk, sharing a four-berth compartment with Boris and an ever-changing assortment of strangers. At Novosibirsk (the junction with the Trans-Siberian) Boris left him and returned to Moscow, while he went on alone to the east, enjoying the comparative luxury of the long-distance express. As usual on his journeys he indulged in a little mild espionage, and when the train reached the shores of Lake Baykal he managed, through the help of a young journalist, to get a ride on the engine so that he could better observe the lie of the permanent way: some of it was in tunnels and some on extensions built out over the water of the lake, and he wanted to assess its vulnerability to air attack in the event of a second Russo-Japanese war.

A week later he reached Vladivostok, to be met '*en prince* by the entire staff of Intourist ... Got my first mail for two months and my first bath for three weeks.'

Elated by his return to creature comforts, he wrote to Rupert from the Commissar's Arms Hotel on October 23rd:

I have just arrived here via the celebrated Amur Railway ('It may be Amur, but it isn't *propre*,' as the poor dear Tsarina used to say) and it is grand to be out of a train. I am down to my last two ozs of Edgeworth, and God knows how I have got that much left. Rear bumf I remember as a kind of myth or legend, and the sound of a Good Old English Voice runs it pretty close ...

I could perfectly well write a funny book about the journey up to date, a bit thinner than the last but more facetious. But I should never get into Russia again if I did, and I think we've had enough thin stuff from Fleming. Not that we shall have anything else, alas. Oh, and look here ... I will try and remember to enclose a cheque for £25, with which I would like you to buy the Crackwit another watch and give it to her on her birthday ... don't tell her in advance, on pain of death.

> Your scrofulous pal,
>
> PETER

Intourist had made prodigious efforts to arrange the hunt for a Siberian tiger which Peter had inquired about in Moscow, but the inefficiency of the organization now proved so disastrous that he was brought nearer to complete frustration than ever before. He was kept sane—'though only just', he noted in his diary—by meeting a sea captain from Orkney with whom he had some pleasurable conversations.

His agitation was not produced solely by his failure to get a tiger: he was by no means desperate to shoot one, but rather was using his genuine passion for shooting as 'a useful ticket on which to try to travel in areas to which foreigners were normally denied access.' His rage sprang from the intolerable mess which Intourist made of the arrangements: he spent more than a week rattling futilely back and forth in local trains, and never even looked like seeing any action. He was profoundly grateful to cross the border into China on November 1st.

In Manchukuo the situation was much the same as when he had been there last: the Japanese were still trying to consolidate and invest with an air of respectability their illegal conquest. Once again Peter travelled about collecting information of military and political interest.

At home, meanwhile, his mother had been intriguing on his behalf with J. L. Garvin, Editor of the *Observer*, and on November 9th she sent him a cable via the British Consulate in Mukden:

GARVIN OFFERS YOU THE EDITORSHIP OBSERVER WORK-
ING UNDER HIM FIRST PRIVATE MIE

Peter's reaction was typical. 'You have probably heard (if it is true) that Garvin wants me to edit the *Observer*, the poor mutt,' he wrote to Rupert the day he got the telegram. 'I am waiting for details.' A week later he added in another letter: 'Garvin's offer I have hardly thought about, but I must say it sounds flattering, though ill-advised.' He seems never to have taken the proposition seriously—nor, indeed, to have sent Garvin any firm answer. Garvin, however, did not easily give up his idea, and on December 7th he wrote Eve Fleming one of his characteristically elliptical notes from Gregories, his home at Beaconsfield:

My preference unswervingly fixed, so we shall wait until summer at need for Peter. How familiar his pangs. Every writer with imaginative force and acute literary sense thinks what he has done or is doing the worst thing he ever did. When the giving-out tortures cease, he is radio-active no more. Trial? Let him come if he will for three months or six. But that's not it. If he *likes* it and doesn't feel clipped-winged by it, he'll be able to swing it in a couple of years. There's a mighty lot more to be learned inside, but it's powerful lore.

A more important piece of news, as far as Peter was concerned, was that his mother had bought a small estate in Oxfordshire—Greys, a lovely house, mainly seventeenth-century but with parts much older, which was faced, across a sweep of drive and lawn, by the romantically ruined towers and walls of thirteenth-century fortifications. The place was only about three miles from Joyce Grove, and its ground marched on one side with the land which the Fleming family already owned. 'I hear we have bought a house in the country,' Peter wrote to Rupert. 'Ring my mother and tell her I told you I thought it was a grand idea, because that will reassure her if she needs it.'

He himself was having a fine time where he was. 'Harbin is a fantastic place,' he told Rupert—

stiff with intrigue and decay ... It is brilliant bitter weather, very highly strung, and wakes one up early ... I now cut a pretty considerable dash in my Russian cavalry overcoat, which brings tears to the eyes of White Russian women—always easily moved—and inflates the notebooks of Bolsheviks and Japanese detectives. Nobody can make me out, and I don't blame them.

He next spent a few days in Mukden, working furiously to finish a series of articles on Russia for *The Times*, and on November 13th he sent them off at the same time as a letter to the Editor:

I am sending you under separate cover five inferior articles on the more irrelevant parts of Russia. Part of the first and part of the last are all right, but the others are worth very little; Russia today is no place in which to prosecute a quest for certainties, and the dusty answer which is its only reward consists merely of statistics which, even if I understood them, are 100 per cent unreliable. Still, you may be able to do something with the stuff.

The letter went on to offer serious background advice about the possibilities for the immediate future in Manchuria, and ended on a faintly nostalgic note:

Give my love to everyone. I envy you nothing in England except the pheasants which you are doubtless shooting in large numbers. Tell your daughters that I will try and bring them back a bandit as a pet.

The Times did indeed manage to 'do something' with the articles, and ran the series prominently for four days from January 2nd, 1935, preceded by no fewer than three little trailer-articles. Once again, in spite of his own disparagement, Peter had made the most of his slender material.

He, meanwhile, had been greatly stimulated by the sudden appearance in Harbin of Kini Maillart. She, too, was travelling as the Special Correspondent of a newspaper (*Le Petit Parisien*) and her plans were flexible enough for her to fall in with Peter's idea for a series of relatively short journeys in northern China, one of them to the Mongols of Manchuria. Kini's presence—apart from giving him someone to talk to —was a great linguistic advantage, for besides French, German and English she spoke good Russian, and this powerfully reinforced Peter's own faltering Russian and Chinese. At his behest she had visiting cards printed with her surname translated into Chinese characters: Fu Lei-ming, the Learned Engraver on Stone, was thus improbably reinforced by Ma Na-ya, the Horse of International Goodwill.

For the rest of the year they travelled intermittently together, sleeping on the k'angs—or heated communal platforms—of Chinese inns, or in the smoky felt yurts of the nomads—a time of which Peter later wrote an evocative description:

Winter—cloudless and windless—gripped the yellow land, laced here and there with silver by a frozen river. Smoke rose with great deliberation in the sparkling air. At night footsteps fell with a curious and sullen emphasis upon the frosty ground.

They witnessed some bizarre sights—not least the Mongols killing sheep by slitting open their bellies and plucking out their still-beating hearts. When Kini got a bad sore throat, they made a medicinal visit to an opium den. In the course of those few weeks Peter discovered what a formidable traveller Kini was: as impervious to discomfort as himself, endlessly inquisitive in the right way, fearless, indefatigable. Another discovery, still more important, was that she too was secretly hoping to walk the whole way back to India; and although they discussed their plans freely, it was some time before either would admit that he or she was beginning to entertain the possibility that they might make the great trek together.

At the end of December Peter flew south to Shanghai and spent Christmas on the Keswicks' houseboat, shooting snipe and duck and much enjoying the brothers' hospitality. 'A lot of good jokes and a grand Christmas,' he recorded in his diary. 'Those two couldn't be nicer.'

The turn of the year found him once more in Peking, staying with the Caccias. Behind him were four months of strenuous travel and many thousand miles—to most people an adventure in itself. For him, however, all this was no more than preliminary manœuvring; and as 1935 came in he stood poised to set out on the long walk which had come to mean so much to him.

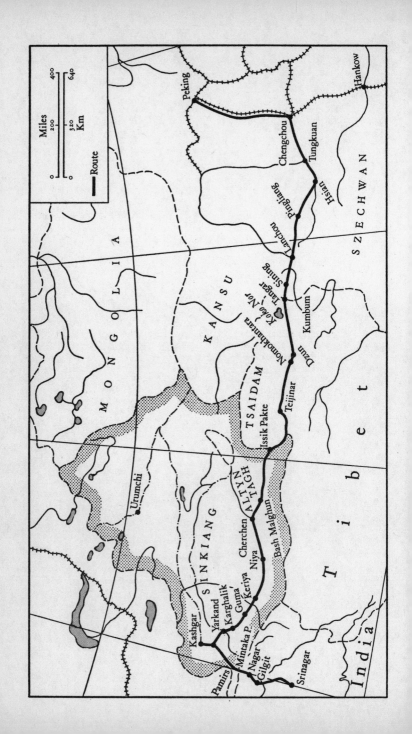

8
Tartary

'I have now been travelling for some four and a half months,' he wrote to Dawson from Peking on January 2nd, 1935. 'I do not feel, and I certainly do not look, any the wiser for having done so. I have however been wise (you must take my word for it) in sending you back nothing save the pitiable articles on Russia.'

The situation in China, he went on, was so complicated that it would be folly for him to pronounce about it prematurely: before he could write serious political articles he must go to Japan 'to ask a few awkward questions' in Tokyo, and then complete his study of Japanese–Mongolian relations with a short expedition to Dolon Nor. 'Thereafter,' he added, 'I aim for Sinkiang. The situation there sounds interesting ... The chances of getting into the province are extremely poor, so I would be glad if you would treat my plans as confidential, since I disapprove of talking destinations until they have been reached. If I can I shall return across country; but I almost certainly can't.'

Thus casually, almost surreptitiously, Peter mentioned for the first time to the paper his ultimate ambition of walking to India. For once he was not being unnecessarily deprecating about his chances of success, for the province of Sinkiang, or Chinese Turkestan, had been closed to foreigners by a series of civil wars, and there was no chance whatever of obtaining official permission to travel through it. With the normal caravan routes closed by the fighting, all that reached Peking were rumours that the administration of the entire province had been taken over by Soviet Russia; and at the beginning of 1935, as Peter wrote later, 'Sinkiang, if you substitute political for physical difficulties, shared with the peak of Everest the blue riband of inaccessibility.'

This alone made him determined to discover for himself what was happening there, and although he devoted much of January to securing the rest of the information which he needed for his articles on Japan, Manchuria and Mongolia, his mind was playing constantly on the great journey ahead. He duly went to Japan and then to Inner Mongolia, but all the time he was sifting the possibilities of routes through the far west and collecting such scraps of information as he could pick up.

Kini Maillart, meanwhile, was doing the same. It is no longer clear exactly where or when they decided to travel together: although, as Peter remarked, they had been happy enough to potter about Manchuria together, neither was keen 'to commit himself or herself to the other's society on a journey which was not only very long and allegedly dangerous but which had for each of us (I think) a curious kind of personal importance.' For a while they postponed a decision, pretending (and believing) that they would go by different routes. Peter favoured the Old Silk Road, to the north, through Mongolia and Urumchi, the capital of Sinkiang, while Kini wanted most to go through Szechwan, in south-western China, and then through the east of Tibet. Soon, however, it became clear that neither of these routes would be possible, and that the only hope of getting through would lie in slipping into Sinkiang on the flank, as Peter put it, along some trail not officially recognized as a route at all.

The catalysts who finally transformed their plans into action were a White Russian couple called Smigunov, and it was Kini who found them. In Peking she met a young Swede called Erik Norin who had been working as a geologist in the southern oases of Sinkiang when the Tungans, or Moslem fanatics, rose in rebellion. Forced to flee abroad, Norin had escaped with the Smigunovs, who had been running a small but profitable trading business in the immense plateau of the Tsaidam. Now, Norin told Kini, the Smigunovs were languishing in Tientsin and longing to return to their haunts in the Tsaidam, and they would be only too glad to act as guides over what, in terms of distance alone, would be at least half the journey.

Summoned to Peking, the Smigunovs accepted with alacrity the proposals which Peter and Kini put to them: they would guide them at least as far as the western boundaries of the Tsaidam, and then as far on towards India as political conditions would allow. Stepan Ivanovitch—described by Peter as 'a tall, burly man with a florid face, a black moustache and a fierce expression'—spoke Mongol, Turki and a little Chinese, and since he knew the Tsaidam well, his arrival seemed suddenly to render the whole expedition a great deal more realistic.

It was the signing-on of the Smigunovs that finally drove Peter and Kini together. She, having discovered them, had first call on their services, and he realized that they represented too good a chance to miss. Besides, he enormously respected Kini's courage and integrity. She for her part (as she recorded in her book *Forbidden Journey*), appreciated his

> brilliant intelligence, his faculty of being able to eat anything and sleep anywhere, and also his sure grasp of the kernel of any situation, of the essential point in any argument. I appreciated still more his horror of any distortion of facts and the native objectivity with which he recounted them.

Each, inevitably, saw disadvantages in the other. In Kini Peter had detected a regrettable tendency to chatter and (worse) to sing. Kini did not care for Peter's drawl, for his eternally-smoked pipe, for his obsession with shooting or for his opinions on dramatic art. But by far the biggest and potentially most serious difference between them lay in their attitude to travel, and in particular to the journey which they were about to undertake: Peter's aim always was to press on, to waste no time, to get through. Kini, by contrast, wanted always to loiter, to study the people along the route and to absorb the atmosphere of the places through which she was passing.

Both were well aware of this difficulty, and so were their friends among whom they made their preparations in Peking: not unkindly, it was pointed out that Peter's last book had been called *One's Company*, and Kini's *Turkestan Solo*. Both saw, however, that the difficulties ahead were likely to be so formidable that they would need each other's help; and thus was formed the unlikely partnership between (as the Chinese knew them) Fu Lei-ming and Ma Na-ya.

When Peter went to Brazil he himself described the preparations he made as 'grotesquely unprofessional', and the same phrase might well be applied to the equipment which he assembled for his 3,500-mile trek across Tartary. He was, admittedly, pushed for time as he struggled to collect the material for, and then to write, two series of articles for *The Times*; even so, the arrangements he made struck friends in Peking as grossly improvident.

His amateurish attitude extended even to his weapons, over which he might have been expected to take the most trouble. Having left the search too late, he scoured Peking in vain for a sporting rifle until, at

the last moment, Sir Eric Teichman, the Counsellor at the British
Legation, offered him the loan of a little old Winchester ·44 together
with three hundred rounds of ammunition which Peter described as
'past its prime a decade ago'. Trying out this ancient weapon on the
Legation range, he found that it was reasonably accurate up to fifty
yards but useless at targets beyond that distance. He decided to take it
with him largely for reasons of face.

What he really wanted was a successor to the ·22 which had proved so
admirable for filling the pot in Brazil; and, finding that 'the rook rifle
market in Peking was sluggish to the point of stagnation,' he sent a
last-minute telegram to the Keswicks in Shanghai. They, by a miraculous
fluke, managed to 'undermine the coastal defences of the Chinese
Republic by buying the indispensable weapon from a lighthouse keeper,'
and put it on a train for Peking. The train, however, left the rails
at Tsinan, and what was to prove the expedition's most important
single item of equipment reached Peter only a few hours before he set
out.

Guns apart, Peter deliberately travelled as light as possible, arguing
that a mass of baggage would excite not merely the cupidity but also
the suspicion of officials through whose hands the expedition passed.
Apart from his Leica camera, portable gramophone, typewriter, compass,
clothes and a few books, he took only the following supplies:

> 2lbs of marmalade, 4 tins of cocoa, 6 bottles of brandy, 1 bottle of
> Worcester sauce, 1lb of coffee, 3 small packets of chocolate, some
> soap and a good deal of tobacco, besides a small store of knives,
> beads, toys etc. by way of presents, and a rather scratch assortment
> of medicines.

His most useful garments were the Russian cavalry overcoat, bought in
Samarkand, which proved ideal for riding and sleeping in cold weather,
and a pair of knee-high soft-leather boots with a formidable system of
laces. These, Peter wrote afterwards, were 'splendid boots, boots beyond
compare'. He had bought them cheaply in a store on Broadway when
he had the sudden chance of escaping from Wall Street to shoot quail in
Alabama over Christmas in 1929. Since then they had carried him to the
top of the Guatemalan volcano of Atitlan, through the jungles of
Mato Grosso, through bramble-infested shooting days at Nettlebed,
through Manchuria in search of bandits and through the paddy fields of
South China in search of snipe. Now they were to carry him through
Tartary.

Rather than take a mass of Mexican dollars with him, he obtained from the Chinese Post Office a cheque which he would be able to cash in Sining, the last town before the uninhabited wastes beyond. Kini, thinking already of the Himalayas, put ten English pounds in her pocket so that she would not arrive in India penniless.

In Peking Peter took care not to disclose his intentions or his ultimate destination: knowing that there was no chance of obtaining visas for Sinkiang, he gave out only that the party was going on a relatively short trip to the area of the huge lake called Koko Nor, and obtained papers which would take him as far as the Province of Kansu. Thereafter, he had no idea what might happen.

Thus, in the middle of February, he found himself setting out from Peking as the leader of an expedition whose whole nature and constitution were so typical of his character that its essential points are perhaps worth brief elaboration:

1. He had no detailed plan, and had told scarcely anyone what he was trying to do.
2. He had virtually no hope of achieving his objective.
3. He was deliberately heading for a country which he knew was closed and hostile to foreigners, and which he had no passport to enter.
4. He was under-armed and absurdly under-equipped.
5. Apart from a few words of Chinese, he spoke none of the languages which he would meet along the route.

All this makes him sound recklessly irresponsible—and indeed in a way he was. Yet, as those who knew him well realized, such meagre physical precautions as he bothered to take were reinforced to an extraordinary degree by the power of his personality. Somehow, by refusing to admit that obstacles were insuperable, he reduced them all to a manageable level; by playing down difficulties that would have brought other people to a standstill, he removed them entirely from his path. Moreover, the sheer force of his character communicated itself to the people—no matter how primitive they might be—through whose territory he passed: Chinese, Mongols, Turkis, Tungans—all seem to have sensed the exceptional nature of this young travelling stranger, and, rather than attempt to detain or rob him, one after another they let him go.

Peter's last few days in Peking were filled with feverish activity. Early in February he sent Dawson a series of five articles on the general political situation in the Far East and, on February 13th, two heavyweight political turnovers on Mongolia, accompanied by a characteristic note:

> Herewith two absorbing and incomprehensible articles on Mongolia. These must be temporarily regarded as my swan-song, although I may fire off an article on the somewhat melodramatic subject of Sinkiang in the course of the next three weeks, when I hope to find myself in the neighbourhood of its borders. I leave in two days for the Koko Nor, on the other side of which I may possibly emerge into India via either Sinkiang or Tibet proper; but the chances are over-whelmingly in favour of my having to turn back ...
>
> I must say, you made the best of a bad show with those articles on Russia. I think these and the Manchurian ones are a bit better, though the former, being written under the influence of three anti-typhus injections, each comprising the essence of thirty lice, lack that light touch for which I am unjustly renowned.
>
> Give my respects to your family and to Printing House Square.

The party left Peking by train at midnight on February 15th. The winter wind, Kini remembered afterwards, whistled about the horned roofs of the station, and the scene was rendered more fantastic by the fact that the friends who saw them off had come straight from a fancy-dress ball, so that the platform was full of masks and feathers which loomed in and out of the clouds of magnesium-smoke released by a French photographer taking flashlight pictures.

Their first train—the express to Chengchou—was comfortable enough, but it arrived a few minutes late and missed, by a whisker, the connection with another express on the Lunghai railway. Dumped thus at midnight on the platform at Chengchou, Peter was determined not to wait twenty-four hours for another express, and decided to take the slow train to Hsian due in an hour and a half. When it arrived it was packed to the open doorways, but a friendly policeman kicked a space clear and Peter's team forced its way aboard, thereby raising the number of people in that carriage to seventy-two. For nearly twenty-four hours they rattled slowly along in acute discomfort before disembarking at a place called Tungkuan, where they spent the night. Next day Peter got up early and caught the slow train to Hsian, leaving the others to follow later.

For the next stage of the journey, the four hundred miles from Hsian to Lanchou, the only practical means of transport were lorries, and Peter booked his party on to one, obtaining a worthless guarantee that the trip would not take more than six days. The trucks were old and decrepit and already, when he found them, groaning under mountains of freight.

'They did not look as if they would leave next day,' he wrote. 'They did not look as if they would ever move again.'

But move and leave they eventually did; and—to cut short a long and agonizing story—the expedition reached Lanchou alive and reasonably well only eight days later. Of the hideous discomfort of that drive Peter later gave a vivid account in *News from Tartary*. Kini, for the first three days, managed to secure a seat beside the driver, but Peter spent all eight clinging to the top of the pile of baggage, covered in dust, frozen and smitten at intervals by cramp but unable—because of the press of humanity and the continuous danger of being flung off—to move or change position.

Occasionally there was a pleasing incident, as when they slithered down a muddy valley in Kansu:

> The lorries plunged and lurched wildly, and one of the less likeable of our companions, losing his grip on the bucking freight, shot like a cannon-ball into the morass.

For the most part, however, the journey was misery, exacerbated by punctures, breakdowns and numerous other unexplained delays. By the penultimate day the number of passengers on Peter's lorry had risen to twenty-eight, and the man next to him was sick from time to time. As Peter recorded in a jewel of understatement, 'We had a somewhat wearing drive.'

> The sun still shone, but dust rose in clouds, and the clouds, thanks to a light following wind, were not easily left behind. Everyone clung or squatted or sprawled in the closest possible proximity; the slightest change of position affected half a dozen neighbours. Nothing more vividly brought home to me the degree of over-crowding to which we were subject than the sight of a large louse, some four inches from my nose, crawling majestically up the back of a minor official. The minor official was far too tightly wedged to reach it; my only disengaged arm was fully employed in keeping me from falling off the lorry; and an outsider, a man from another pudding of humanity altogether, had to be called in to arrest the louse's progress and destroy it ...
>
> A woman was sick with extraordinary persistency all day; and my neighbour ... was not always able to contain himself. We looked forward with longing to the infrequent halts; but when they were over a brisk hand-to-hand engagement had to be fought before everyone was once more settled in their places.

Throughout the ordeal by lorry Peter had many hours for introspection, and his conscience evidently began to plague him, for when he reached Lanchou he wrote a long letter of explanation to Rupert:

I am a fortnight gone on my way home; it has been a pretty tough passage so far ... If you look at your map, you will see there is a place called Koko Nor ... Well, the idea is to go through that and at the end of it bear either (a) left into Tibet proper, which is impossible, or (b) straight on through the Ladakh into India, which is impossible, or (c) right-handed into Sinkiang, which is also impossible. Any of the three would be well worth doing, and a really major thing if brought off; especially the last ... In the south, which might concern me, Lawrence is confidently supposed, though not by me, to be active among the Moslem rebels ...

As far as personnel goes, the expedition is an unlikely one. It consists of a White Russian ex-officer and his wife ... a nice but childish couple. The fourth member is a dashing Swiss girl, who (this is important) may take some explaining to the Crackwit if she hears about her. Her name is Maillart ... I met her in London in the summer, said 'See you in China,' and forgot about her. But at the time I ragged the Crackwit about her, pretending to have been greatly struck, and that is why I have said nothing to her (the Crackwit) about this woman ...

Maillart is tough, thirty-one, and slightly wolf-like in appearance. She is a very good traveller, and we get on fairly well, but I would not have had her on this trip if she hadn't got a prior lien on the services of the White Russian, who is the only chap who knows the way. Also, she speaks Russian reasonably well and is thus fairly essential.

She is an international skier, captain of the Swiss women's hockey team ... We remain on speaking terms without difficulty, but as far as the Affections go she will never mean more to me than a yak. All the same I feel guilty towards the Crackwit and worry a lot about not having told her about the Other Woman, though I'm sure it was better not to. So if, Peking being what it is, the news comes through and the Crackwit asks with a forced laugh 'What about Peter's Swiss?', will you explain? It's a silly situation and would never have arisen if I hadn't cracked jokes about the girl last summer.

On re-reading this, I seem to have been unduly derogatory about the Swiss. She is very enterprising and what you might call a good trouper. It's just that she isn't my cup of tea.

Do impress on her (Celia) that this circus, if successful or even moderately so, is very well worth while from my point of view. Being what I am, it would be silly not to have a crack at it, though I'm afraid it won't be more than a crack ... So the great thing to do is to see that nobody worries, and also *not to talk* about what I hope to do, partly because it is so unlikely to come off, and partly because the alarmists might start putting the wind up interested parties. You can imagine the fuss there would be if the Greek Ambassador told my mother that piles were rife in Northern Tibet. Actually, it is a very safe and salubrious country, and as usual I'm going to be no fool. But June looks at the moment like being a fairly optimistic date, so don't arouse anyone's hopes. Except to those like Celia and my mother who are supposed to be in the know, say that I am doing a journey in NW. China and hope to be back in the summer.

Soon Peter had more to worry about than the possibility that Celia might be upset, for in Lanchou the expedition all but foundered. Soldiers took away their passports and searched their luggage, suspicious that they might be Bolshevik agents, and for six days the travellers sat becalmed while increasingly sinister rumours multiplied. All travel to the west, it was said, had now become impossible because of the twin threat of the Chinese Red armies on the rampage to the south and the ever-spreading tentacles of Russian influence reaching down from the north: the last foreigners in the area had been bundled out ignominiously. In vain Peter tried every ruse he could think of, leaving his card with various officials and writing an elaborate letter on *The Times*'s paper to the Governor, who never answered. Had Peter been able to produce a copy of one of those days' issues of the paper, he might have gained some face, for *The Times* was at that moment prominently running his articles on Manchuria.

The blow, when it fell, was not unexpected: Fu and Ma, it was announced, might go on, but the Smigunovs, being Russian, must return under open arrest to Tientsin. With one stroke the expedition had been cut in half—and it was the expert half that had been turned back. Only the amateurs might proceed.

For Peter the news was more than a serious blow to his hopes: having brought the Smigunovs all this way and raised their hopes so high, he now felt responsible and terribly sorry for them. Their naive enthusiasm for the Tsaidam, and their joy at the prospect of returning, had touched him deeply. Taking Stepan with him he went to the Chief of Police and made a stormy scene, managing in the end to rattle the man but obtaining no satisfaction. There was nothing he could do but leave the Smigunovs behind.

And yet, crippled though the expedition was, there seemed to him no question of turning back; so he and Kini hired three mules and at ten o'clock in the morning of March 6th, together with a man named Wang, set out westwards along a track that followed the crumbling bank of a river in the direction of Sining.

The fact that they were moving again, and in the right direction, brought them both a wild elation, and they celebrated their unaccustomed good fortune by announcing to Wang that they would reach Sining in five stages instead of the six which he had proposed. This they achieved —by starting in the icy cold before dawn and keeping on for marches of ten, twelve or even fourteen hours, staying in filthy inns and living almost exclusively off *kua mien*, described by Peter as 'a kind of spaghetti violently flavoured with red pepper.' Although Kini rode for much of the time, he himself walked almost all the way in an effort to get fit.

'Life', he wrote afterwards, 'had become a very simple, soothing affair: so soothing that we forgot our complicated ambitions and the difficulties that lay in store for us. It was enough to be crawling westwards in the bright, clean mountain air; food and sleep were the only things that seemed important.'

They sighted the walls of Sining at the far end of a shallow, open valley in the middle of the afternoon, but it was not until dusk that they reached the gates:

> On the bastions above them little sentries armed with stocky automatic rifles were silhouetted against the fiery west. Bugles brayed thinly. We passed like dusty ghosts through streets where rich food-smells hung on the frosty air and paper lanterns were golden in the darkness ... We were dog-tired but happy. Happy because we had done another stage—the last stage, almost, before roads and houses finished and the wilds began; happy because we had done it in five days instead of six; happy because we were not defeated yet.

Again their euphoria was quickly punctured. Again the trouble was over their passports and their lack of visas. Lanchou, they found, had taken no decision, but had merely passed the responsibility down the line to Sining, and there for ten irritating days they dangled on a slender thread of hope. Each morning they spent hours sitting on the k'ang in their inn. While Kini sewed or read, Peter played endless games of patience; if a set came out (which was almost impossible), it meant that they would reach India. Ten cards left over meant gaol in Turkestan, twenty—with black predominating—an ignominious return to Peking. Later in the morning they would repair to the back room of a burly, bear-like photographer who had befriended them and there pick up the latest gossip. From time to time Peter paid a call on some official who might possibly help them. It was a dreary and demoralizing time. Kini pined for the spring skiing that would then be at its height in Switzerland, and Peter thought wistfully and with a touch of guilt about the offer from Garvin at the *Observer*, of which, for the sake of attempting this apparently futile journey, he had airily postponed acceptance.

Perhaps it was mainly in an attempt to cheer himself up that he wrote Geoffrey Dawson a note on March 17th:

> I find myself within biscuit-toss (but without a biscuit) of the top right-hand corner of Tibet. I will let you know within ten days my chances of getting further west. They are slender, but existent. Things, which have gone very badly so far, might still be worse. But I am afraid that India is out of the question.

Peter could not afterwards remember exactly when or how it was that they heard they were to be granted visas for their alleged hunting trip to the Koko Nor. He recalled only their 'incredulous and fearful joy'. It seemed that they had played the role of innocent tourists so successfully that the central government in Nanking had finally delegated the task of issuing visas to the local officials in Sining. Peter prepared for the wilds by converting a large slice of their capital into a single piece of gold, the size of a bar of chocolate, and most of the rest into silver dollars.

Still there was a snag: their permits, it was said, would be ready 'in a few days'. What did that mean? But the delay, as it turned out, was providential, for Peter and Kini used it to make a one-day trip to the south-west and visit the great Tibetan lamasery of Kumbum (which means 'a hundred thousand images'). It was during this detour that they met the man who finally set them on the desert road.

At Kumbum, where they stayed in the lamasery, Peter felt for the first time 'something of that dark and powerful glamour with which Western superstition endows the sacred places of the East'. Sceptical and irreligious though he was, he experienced 'that tight, chill, tingling feeling which I suppose is something between spiritual awe and physical fear.' In Kumbum, too, they encountered for the first time a substance with which they were to become all too familiar in the weeks ahead:

The tea was brought in and with it, flanked by slabs of butter, a pyramid of some drab-coloured powdery substance. In the dim light we could only guess what this was. First we thought it was sugar, then we thought it was salt, finally we decided it was very fine grey ash, of the kind you see in portable braziers in Japanese inns. Then we tasted it and agreed that it was sawdust, possibly sawdust from the holy tree. It was only gradually that it dawned on us that this was *tsamba*, or parched barley meal; *tsamba*, which was to be our staple food for three months ... We were very green.

A day later they walked a mile across to the Chinese trading post of Lusar, where they introduced themselves to Ma Shin-teh, a rich and powerful Moslem merchant whom Smigunov had known and highly recommended. He now proved wonderfully helpful. In a room that harboured eight 'far from unanimous' clocks and was graced by half a dozen of Ma's sons, a long conversation (which sorely tried Peter's staccato Chinese) brought an eminently satisfying outcome: one of Ma's agents, called Li, would be leaving for the Tsaidam with a Mongol caravan in eight or nine days' time, and Peter and Kini could go with it. Li would cook for them and look after their animals. Li was promptly summoned—'an awkward, likeable young man, with a weatherbeaten face and very slit eyes'—and a rendezvous was arranged in Tangar for March 27th.

Glowing with gratitude and triumph, Peter and Kini returned to Sining, only to find that their visas were still not ready. Undeterred, they set about assembling their stores:

Flour and rice, and bricks of tea and coloured cloth to barter with, and a cooking pot and a utensil approximating rather remotely to a frying-pan, and a long piece of wire to use as a cleaning rod for the rook-rifle, and sugar and *mien* and many other things.

At five o'clock that evening Peter paid the last of his many visits to the governor's *yamen* (or headquarters) and was handed 'a big flimsy sheet of paper on which a rectangular scarlet seal ratified the dancing characters.' It was not, as he later discovered, the right sort of passport, for it was written only in Chinese and should have been in Tibetan also; but at least—and at last—it was a passport. At dawn next morning they loaded everything into two Peking carts provided by the authorities and set off on the day's journey to Tangar.

By then, Peter reckoned, they were due for a slice of luck. Always rather fatalistic in his outlook, he was a great believer in luck and argued that, so far on this trip, they had had discouragingly little. Everything, in fact, had run slightly against them, from the missing of the first train connection.

In Tangar his theory was justified, and the very best of luck appeared in the form of a Protestant missionary couple called Urech—he Swiss, she Scots—who not only insisted that the travellers should stay in their comfortable house for as long as they wanted, but also gave them invaluable assistance with their final preparations.

These were extensive, and comfortably filled several days while they waited for news of the Mongol caravan promised by Ma Shin-teh. They bought two Tibetan ponies: 'an ungainly, gentle-mannered bay' for Kini, which she named Slalom, and 'a rufous, raw-boned animal' for Peter. With his came a battered foreign saddle, but Kini bought a wooden Chinese saddle covered with red and blue padding.

> There were many other things to buy; hobbles, spare horseshoes, copper kettles to fetch water in, soft sheepskin boots to wear in camp, a little chest for our medicines, a round iron fire-place—in short, a lot of important odds and ends.

Eventually, worried by the absence of news about the caravan, Peter rode down to Lusar again, accompanied by a convert of the Urechs. He would have been amused to know that in London *The Times* had chosen that very day to publish the first of his articles about Sino-Japanese relations, under the title 'An Eye-Witness in Mongolia' and accompanied by a whole page of his photographs, the most striking being a splendid panorama of Mongolian cavalry charging across a plain in front of a background of crumpled hills. Totally ignorant of the author's whereabouts, the paper confidently proclaimed him to be in Peking.

In Lusar Peter found that the caravan, which belonged to the Prince of Dzun, was indeed assembling, and that Li, their agent, was planning to leave for Tangar the following day. That evening he chartered four camels for a journey of sixteen or eighteen days 'for about as much as it would cost you to charter four taxis from Hyde Park Corner to Hampstead and back again.' He spent that night in the house of Li's family—an experience he much enjoyed—and next day rode back to Tangar—a gruelling, seven-hour trip through bitter cold, during which he was fortified by the prospect of being able to break to Kini the excellent news that at last they really did seem to be on their way.

That night they sat up long after the missionaries had gone to bed, writing the last letters that they would have a chance to post for several weeks. One of Peter's was to Dawson:

> I said I would let you know my chances of getting further west ... At the moment they are bright. I am leaving tomorrow with the caravan of a Mongol prince for the Tsaidam, a region which most maps cover with those little explosive symbols which are usually supposed to connote a marsh or bog; actually I believe it is a desert. It will take me about a month to get to the middle of it (my destination is called Teijinar, but I doubt if it is hallowed by a reference in *The Times* Atlas), and from there it may be possible to get across the frontier into southern Sinkiang ... It sounds a fairly difficult road, and I think you can bet on me having to turn back. In any case you won't hear of me for a bit, as (a) there will be no postal facilities and (b) there will be no news ...
>
> I hope I shall be back in time for the grouse; it may be much sooner. This is rather a good part of the world.

Writing to Rupert, he hit a jauntier note:

> I have just written three other letters, and cannot bring myself to explain for the fourth time where this preposterous place is ... Each camel costs as much as a taxi to Golders Green and back, and carries a load equal to the weight of the whole Royal Family; so I think they are pretty cheap. I have got a passport of sorts, though I fear not the right one; but for it, as for all paper, a use will eventually be found. I have two ancient rifles with which to intimidate the fauna ...
>
> I have hopes, though not high ones, of getting through to India. But whether I go on or turn back, you may depend upon it that I shall be *ventre à terre*; I hope to meet you in the Royal Enclosure at Lord's, Forsyte. If on the other hand my camels get spavined, or the Swiss gets the vapours, thus causing delay, neither worry yourself nor allow anyone else to do so; there is no danger of any sort except the danger of delay ... The Swiss is bearing up well, and we remain on speaking though not always in my case on listening terms; she is an honest soul and quite useful. I do hope Celia is all right. Everything here is so uncertain and remote that I have almost succeeded in giving up worrying, though not quite.

Next day—March 28th—they were up at dawn, but hung about for hours until at last their camels appeared, 'shaggy, and supercilious', and

Mongols conjured up by Li adjusted their loads. Then, reluctantly refusing the Urechs' invitation to stay to tea, they set off:

> We followed the camels through the narrow streets and out of the South Gate. We watered our horses in the last sea-bound river we were destined to see for the next four and a half months. At the bridge we said goodbye to the missionaries, wishing with all our hearts that we could express one tenth of our gratitude; they had been wonderfully kind to us.
>
> Then, with joy and incredulity, we remounted, turned our horses' heads in the general direction of India, and cantered after the camels.

Now at last they were beyond the clutches of officials, travelling through Central Asia at the pace of Central Asia, unchanged for thousands of years. At first it seemed to Peter infuriatingly slow: the camels advanced at about two and a half miles an hour, and in the first short day they covered only six miles. When they woke next morning it was snowing, and again the day was a short one. On the third, after vigorous haggling, Peter bartered his red horse and twenty-four dollars for a smaller Tangut pony which he christened Greys, 'after the house in Oxfordshire towards which he had to carry me'. The animal proved something of a demon, for although it kept going gamely enough it seemed to be markedly xenophobic: it was perfectly quiet with Mongols or Tibetans, but whenever Peter tried to mount, it made foolish and dangerous attempts to bolt, and once, careering off when he had one foot in a stirrup, almost broke his leg with a random kick.

On the afternoon of the fourth day they came up with a party of Mongols bound, like them, for the Prince of Dzun's caravan. They camped that night with them, Peter and Kini pitching for the first time the tent which she had designed and had made in Sining. Nine feet long by five wide and four high, it looked so small and flimsy as to resemble (in Peter's phrase) 'some abstruse kind of practical joke'. But in fact it served its purpose admirably, affording them what they needed most at night—shelter from the unceasing and bitter wind.

At noon the next day they rode over a ridge and saw below them a cluster of drab cones—the tents of the main caravan:

> The country for miles around seemed to be dotted with camels and horses grazing … a crowd, the wildest you could wish to see, formed quickly round us—Mongols garbed unwieldily in their great sheepskins, one shoulder bare, one hand on the hilt of a Tibetan broadsword: Chinese Moslems, more trimly dressed but still

barbaric, with hard, cunning, cruel faces, the cruellest faces in the world.

Soon they were bidden to an audience with the Prince, who received them in his modest tent—a cryptic young man whose movements reminded Peter of a cat. During the exchange of formalities he showed no emotion; nor did he soften perceptibly when Peter presented him ceremonially with a small, second-hand telescope which he had brought specially as a gift. But at least the Prince accepted the strangers into his company, and they travelled with him for the best part of three weeks.

They set out on April 1st. 'Tents were struck and loads lashed on in the chill half-light, and presently a mile-long column of two hundred and fifty camels, in strings of anything from four to ten, went winding westward through the silent wintry desolation.' In the middle of the morning they sighted the immense frozen waste of the Koko Nor—a huge lake lying more than ten thousand feet above sea level. For days Peter and Kini had argued as to whether its water was salt or fresh, and Kini was delighted when a trial proved conclusively that it was salt, for she thereby won a bet of a hundred Mexican dollars.

For another three days they crawled along the southern shore of this inland sea. Starting always in the searching cold of the dawn, they marched through the long morning and pitched camp in the early afternoon, whereupon Peter would set off alone on foot with the ·22 into the surrounding wastes in search of duck, geese and hares. As in Brazil, his skill at stalking with the little rifle consistently filled the cooking-pot, and he brought off several prodigious flukes, twice knocking down antelopes at about four hundred paces. While he hunted, Kini read, wrote, darned or slept in camp, attempting to doctor, in the intervals, the Chinese who brought her an endless variety of complaints, many of them indescribable or imaginary, or both. Her own and Peter's health remained astonishingly good. At one stage one of Peter's eyes became badly inflamed, and later Kini was tortured by a recurrence of old-established rheumatism; but those—apart from sundry kicks and bites—were the only real maladies they suffered.

Living as they were in a state of almost permanent hunger, they looked forward ravenously to the evening meal, which Kini cooked over a fire of dung. When it was ready,

we put the great black pot just inside the tent and Li brought his bowl and we got our enamel plates and dinner was served: rice or *mien* or a kind of noodles which we called by its Russian name of *lapsha*, and whatever meat we had in hand. How we ate! We did not speak. We shovelled the food down until the pot was empty and we were distended. It was my misfortune that I had only a teaspoon to shovel with ... but it is wonderful what you can do with a teaspoon when you are in the mood.

As soon as they had eaten, somnolence would overtake them. If they washed at all, they washed in the frying-pan—the only suitable receptacle they had. Then they would take off their boots, wriggle into sleeping-bags, cover themselves with greatcoats and drift off to sleep. Peter, thinking perhaps of Matthew Arnold's *Sohrab and Rustum* and the 'hushed Chorasmian waste', memorably painted the scene:

The wind dropped at night. Outside the iron land froze in silence under the moon. The silver tents were quiet. The watchman moved among them squatly, like a goblin (thinking what thoughts, suppressing what fears?). A wolf barked. A star fell down the tremendous sky. The camp slept.

For seventeen days they made steady progress with the Prince's entourage, but then, at a dreary settlement called Dzun, where a few mud huts surrounded an ancient lamasery, the caravan halted and they were left to their own devices. By then they were in the vast basin of the Tsaidam, so warmly spoken of by the poor Smigunovs, which turned out, as the maps had promised, to be a salt marsh, pitted with bog holes and dotted with tamarisk scrub. In Dzun (which Peter soon christened 'the end of the world') they were stuck for three days until they could procure new camels and new travelling companions. Then, three days farther west, at Nomokhantara, which lay on the border between the Mongols of Dzun and the Mongols of Teijinar, they had to change animals once more, and were again delayed by the surliness of the inhabitants, who refused to hire them camels until Peter made such a nuisance of himself that they gave in.

Nomokhantara consisted of a few yurts scattered about an enormous grove of tamarisk, or some such shrub, which grew to a height of about twelve feet. Several of the Mongols were living away from their tents in 'curious open bowers' scooped from the lee side of these bushes, and the whole place was strangely deceptive:

The little trees (if you could call them trees) did not grow thickly; there were ten to twenty yards between each, and at every step fresh devious glades presented themselves, tempting you to explore further. This it was very unwise to do. There were no landmarks, no tracks, and every tree looked exactly like the next ...

The first day we were there a boy ... went off into the tamarisk and never came back. Search parties ranged by day, huge bonfires blazed by night, and the lamas put in some fairly intensive clairvoyance, chanting and throwing dice to establish his geographical position. I interrupted, by special request, a game of patience and put the problem to the cards, one suit standing for each quarter of the compass. But the boy was never found; he must have died of hunger and thirst, perhaps only a little way away.

They spent six days trapped in that tamarisk prison. Peter whiled away many hours stalking hares with the ·22, always getting as many as he could carry, and one evening he heard, with startled incredulity, a sound that took him straight back to the woods and hedges of Oxfordshire: a cock pheasant crowing. He followed the bird and shot it, and later got two more.

At last their new camels came and they started westwards again, reaching a place called Gorumu in six stages. From there another six days would bring them to Teijinar, beyond which lay the borders of Sinkiang, the forbidden state. What they would do when they reached Teijinar, they had little idea; but the good spirit of Smigunov was still with them, and they had one last card of his to play: in Teijinar, he had told them, there was living a White Russian exile, a Cossack called Borodishin, and he would be able to advise them on the best way of infiltrating the closed frontier ahead.

By this time Peter was deriving huge satisfaction from the journey. No longer annoyed by the leisurely pace of progress, he found positive satisfaction in going so slowly. 'We had left the twentieth century behind with the lorries at Lanchow,' he wrote afterwards—

and now we were up against the immemorial obstacles, the things that had bothered Alexander and worried the men who rode with Chinghiz Khan—a lack of beasts, lack of water, lack of grazing. We were doing the same stages every day that Marco Polo would have done if he had branched south from the Silk Road into the mountains ... Those scientific expeditions which scour the desert in caterpillar tractors, with film cameras whirring by day and broadcast music in the tents at night, bring back a mass of valuable data; but I doubt if they know what the desert feels like. In all else ignorant, we at least knew this.

His relationship with Kini had settled into an effective working partnership, and perhaps he now privately regretted some of those sharp remarks he had made in the letters to Rupert, for he found her an astonishingly good travelling companion. Already they had lived together for three months in the closest proximity and considerable discomfort, and they went on doing so for another four months, yet they got on extraordinarily well together—for reasons which Peter generously summed up in his book:

By all the conventions of desert island fiction we should have fallen madly in love with each other; by all the laws of human nature we should have driven each other crazy with irritation. As it was we missed these almost equally embarrassing alternatives by a wide margin ... While we were outwardly very different, we had certain fundamental things in common. The most important of these was a liking for the kind of life we were leading. We neither of us particularly minded discomfort and uncertainty and doing without most of the things which civilized people consider, or imagine they consider, essential to the conduct of a rational life; and we both liked fresh air and exercise, of which we got plenty. We were both adaptable and fairly phlegmatic; and we were both fatalists, as all travellers, and especially travellers in Asia, ought to be.

Perhaps one of the main reasons for our getting on so well was that Kini always had a certain friendly contempt for me, and I always had a sneaking respect for her; both sentiments arose from the fact that she was a professional and I was eternally the amateur. The contrast showed all the time. Kini believed that the best way to get a thing done was to do it yourself; I believed that the best way to get a thing done was to induce somebody else to do it.

It was I who shot the hares; but it was Kini who, noticing that if Li or a Mongol skinned them, the liver and kidneys were always thrown away, taught herself to do the job. If anything wanted mending or making fast, if a box needed repacking, if one of the saddles was coming to bits, it was always I who said 'Oh, that'll be all right,' always Kini who expertly ensured that it would ...

I suppose I was the leader, because I made decisions more quickly, guessed more quickly, knew more quickly what I wanted than Kini did. But she did all the work that required skill or application and almost all the work that was distasteful or annoying rather than merely arduous, the work that gets left undone if there are only second-rate people to do it; we both knew that she was, so to speak, the better man, and this knowledge evened things out between us, robbed my automatically dominating position of its power to strain our relations. We had complete confidence in each other.

Kini was often irritated by me; and sometimes when I called her a bloody fool I thought I meant it. But we were both essentially what the Fox-Hunting Man [Siegfried Sassoon] calls 'solitary-minded', and the detachment in our natures prevented us from interfering with each other's lives; we had come to take each other as much for granted as we took our horses. It was only at times that one would remember, fleetingly, how valuable the other's presence was, how trying the journey would have been alone. Perhaps we were less independent of each other than we felt.

Kini, for her part, found Peter more irritating than he realized. Early in the journey she began to wish that she had come alone, and as the weeks went by she became increasingly irked by the basic divergence in their approach to what they were doing. 'United in our craving to succeed in our enterprise, we had come to a perfect understanding,' she wrote in *Forbidden Journey*:

> Yet we did not see things from the same angle. Every night Peter would repeat his refrain: 'Sixty *lis* [about twenty-five miles] nearer to London.' He did it to annoy me, and I would tell him to shut up, for I wanted to forget that we had, inevitably, to return home. I even lost the desire to return home. I should have liked the journey to continue for the rest of my life.

Kini could not understand Peter's passion for pressing on: he was, it seemed to her, less afraid of 'finishing up in the depths of an Urumchi prison than of getting home too late to shoot grouse in Scotland'. What she did not appreciate was that the need to forge ahead formed a fundamental trait of Peter's character—a compulsion which not even he could begin to explain.

When they reached the great salt marsh of the Tsaidam, Kini longed to break away from the homeward route and explore the mountains whose peaks stood glittering in the south, and she planned to put one of the enforced delays to good use by making an excursion in that direction:

> Ever since we reached the flat solitude of the Tsaidam those mountains had been beckoning me, but there was no persuading Peter to sacrifice a week to exploring, and I had given up hope of getting to know them. Now, with my rucksack on my back I could spend three days in going at any rate some little distance up the valley. It was a

way of becoming my own master again, of ceasing to be a mere fragment of a caravan. Of course Peter was chivalrous and pretended that I was very useful, but he could not realize how much I longed to shake off the inertia that had taken hold of me since I had been travelling with him. I no longer took the lead, no longer shouldered any responsibility. I was one of a group, and my capacity for decision was blunted.

But it was no use. Peter returned from his hunting, happy at having had a good day while I minded the house ... Peter said he wanted to get on.

One fact of life which did unite them was hunger, and an increasing obsession with food. Lovingly they would discuss the meals that had delighted them in childhood: Peter the mountainous teas, with sausages and mashed potato, which he had gorged in his room at Eton, and Kini the *Roschtis* with eggs and bacon which she had devoured in Swiss inns after skiing. Instead of these delights, they had to subsist largely on *tsamba*, which they moistened with water or butter and kneaded into sticky lumps, and on their evening meal of meat and noodles. Even Peter—one of the least greedy people imaginable—had started to take the closest interest in all kinds of food. 'With the exception perhaps of an hour after the evening meal,' he recorded,

> there was no single moment in the day when we would not have eaten, and eaten with the greatest relish, anything that appeared remotely edible. Dog biscuits would have been welcome. A plate of cold tapioca pudding would have vanished in a flash. Your dustbins, had we come across them, would not have been inviolate.

Hungry as they were, they had by far the toughest part of the journey still ahead of them. At Teijinar the invaluable Li finally left them to return home, but their luck held and they found another priceless ally in the form of the Cossack Borodishin, a lonely and disconsolate figure who was living in a pair of yurts some two hours west of the settlement of Teijinar, still dimly hoping that one day he would see again his wife and children, whom he had last heard of in Siberia seven years before.

Borodishin's knowledge of events to the west was disappointing: he had not heard what was happening in Sinkiang—whether the Moslem rebellion was still in progress, or whether peace had been restored. But he did, as they had hoped, have ideas about how they should proceed: there was one obvious route into Sinkiang, he said, but this would almost certainly be guarded by the Tungan rebels; the best plan, therefore, was to avoid this road, and go by another route, to the south, which was far more difficult but unlikely to be watched, since it was reckoned to be impassably short of grazing for animals in winter. To follow it they would have to strike south-west into the mountains and then head west up the gorges of the river Boron Kol. Twelve marches would bring them to Issik Pakte, where there was a Turki encampment. Borodishin himself would lead them as far as Issik Pakte, although he could go no farther than that, having no papers.

So they bought four camels, at an average price of four pounds apiece, refurbished their supplies, and set out in the smallest party with which they had travelled so far—three humans, four camels and the two horses. Leaving in hot sunshine, they were soon enveloped in blinding storms, first of sand and then of snow. The snow made it far too cold to ride, and they 'tramped with numb feet and stiff faces, silent automata plastered in front with white'. When the snow suddenly stopped they found themselves crossing 'a bleak tableland towards a sudden jagged cluster of little peaks which the Mongols called—aptly enough, we thought—the Black Cold Mountains'.

For day after day they picked their way through this trackless upland wilderness, at altitudes which ranged from nine thousand to fifteen thousand feet; they camped uncomfortably in rocky hollows, and in the icy dawns Peter himself had to catch and load the camels, there being no servant to help him. Yet that harsh country, tough as it was on the humans, was even crueller to the animals, for such water as could be found was of poor quality, and there was practically no vegetation. After going well for weeks, Peter's pony Greys, which he had grown very fond of, suddenly collapsed and had to be dragged along behind one of the camels.

On May 23rd, as Peter casually put it, 'a bad time was had by all.' They marched all day across a grey desert at about fifteen thousand feet above sea level, and in the afternoon they began looking for a valley in which Borodishin said there would be a spring. But when he reached the place, the spring was not there, and he admitted he was lost. Dusk caught them in a waterless gully, and after going hard for twelve hours they camped with no liquid to drink or cook with. Next morning, although they found the spring easily, Peter felt queer and was afraid that he had strained his heart. Two more marches brought them down to Issik Pakte: there they saw Turkis for the first time, and Borodishin, who had been to the place before, secured two guides to take them on to Bash Malghun. But Greys, it was clear, could go no farther, and Peter swapped him for an inferior little mare which he named Cynara—the title of a play in which Celia had appeared at the Playhouse Theatre, in London, in 1931, and which had done a lot to establish her as a West End actress. Insect life, Peter reported, was by then 'regrettably to the fore', and when Kini washed his shirt she found in it eight lice and a hundred and seventy-one nits, or eggs of lice.

By that stage they were well into Sinkiang, but still they could garner no news of the rebellion. All they could do was to hope for the best and keep going, with the oasis of Cherchen as their next major objective. After Borodishin's departure the language difficulty became acute; before he left he taught Peter some twenty basic words of Turki, and these had to suffice for dealing with their two new guides—one a pleasant, elderly man and the other a surly young fellow distinguished only by his shameless and disgusting greed.

Again their way lay across arid deserts in which water and grazing scarcely existed. On May 31st—Peter's twenty-eighth birthday—he celebrated by having a double ration of sugar in his morning tea and by walking all day, full of the odd elation by which he was periodically gripped. In the evening Kini cooked him a great feast of rice and curried antelope.

Apart from the anniversary, they had not got so much to celebrate, for the next day the harsh conditions began to knock out the animals. Soon after they had left their first watering place two of the camels started going slow, pulling back on their head-ropes, which were fastened, Mongol-fashion, to pegs driven through their noses. For half an hour the humans dragged and shoved the weaker of the two beasts along, but it was useless:

> With a last apologetic roar he knelt down and nothing we could do would make him rise. There was nothing for it but to leave him —to cast him on the gobi, as the Chinese say ... but it was horrible to leave him there, hunched, apathetic and somehow shrunken, with the snow plastering his inexpressive face ... Under a lowering sky we crawled on up towards the pass, uttering mechanically the abruptly ended yell with which the Mongols urge their beasts. The [second] sick camel moved with a faltering stride, roaring his grief.

That night the beast refused to eat, and in the morning he still knelt where he had gone down the evening before. Though they got him up and drove him forward for a few yards, the effort was in vain, for he knelt again with an air of finality, and he too had to be abandoned. The loads were redistributed on the remaining camels, and Peter lashed their suitcases on the little mare Cynara.

In twenty-four hours they had lost half their transport, and Kini's horse Slalom was also failing fast. For the rest of that day she and Peter dragged, shoved and coerced him forward, while the slovenly Turkis, leading the camels, drew farther and farther ahead. By the late afternoon the advance had become 'a miniature pageant of despair', Peter wrote:

> In front went Kini, bent almost double, dragging doggedly on the reins. Behind the tottering Slalom, I, also bowed, barged with one shoulder against his gaunt hindquarters; and behind me limped the little mare on whose burden of suitcases tattered hotel labels incongruously evoked palm trees and beaches, crowded streets and *confort anglais*.

They ended that day by dragging themselves and the pony over a pass and down into a long valley, and they pitched camp in freezing darkness.

> We had been marching for eleven hours, with no food since dawn; but we were not hungry. We drank some cocoa and as it warmed our bellies felt a faint reaction, a kind of drowsy triumph. So far it had been an easy journey; today, for the first time, we had faced crisis of a sort without assistance. And although it was no great achievement to have dragged a failing horse a few miles further than seemed at one time possible, we were pleased that we had done our best by Slalom and we hoped that we had saved his life.

Whether they had or not they never knew, for next day they were forced to abandon him on the bank of a river, where there was fresh water and a little grass. The parting moved Peter deeply:

> We called to the Turkis to halt and unsaddled him for the last time. He stood still as a stone, the ugly shadow of a horse, alone in the sunlight under the encircling hills; he had served us faithfully ever since Tangar. The camels moved off and I followed them. Kini stayed a little while with Slalom. I found that I was crying, for the first time for years.

The next day was the Fourth of June, and Peter, remembering the custom whereby far-flung old Etonians used to send the school cables of greeting couched in facetious Latin, 'wished snobbishly that I could send a wire from an address which could only be indicated in terms of longitude and latitude, and wondered how one could translate *tsamba* into Latin'. Kini, more practically, decided that the moment had come to sacrifice their one tin of crab, which had been presented to them by the Japanese Consul in Vladivostok.

On and on they went, in stages up to fourteen hours long. Even though he took it more or less for granted, Peter was astonished by Kini's endurance, and he himself began to wonder how much longer he could keep up walking more than twenty miles a day, for eventually the machine that worked his legs began to show signs of running down. But at last, on June 8th, after a dogged nine-hour stage across a glaring desert, they went through a belt of tamarisk and found themselves 'miraculously translated to another world. Real grass grew, in substantial quantities ... Flocks of sheep and goats pastured in sunlight which no longer irked our eyes by rebounding from the desert.' This was Bash Malghun.

Fresh bread and sour milk in a wooden bowl made the place seem like paradise, and its attractions were further enhanced when the inhabitants pronounced that the way through to Cherchen, six days ahead, was clear. For one brick of tea and five dollars they secured a charming guide, called Tuzun, and three donkeys to act as supplementary baggage-carriers.

Soon after they had set out again they met, coming the other way, a Moslem Chinese merchant bound for the Tsaidam, and through him they confirmed a rumour which they thought they had deciphered in Bash Malghun—that Cherchen was indeed in the hands of the Tungan rebels, that their leader Ma Chung-ying had gone to England, and that his place had been taken by his deputy, who had arrived at Khotan in an English aeroplane.

This scrap of unreliable gossip, Peter wrote, 'went to our heads, and we felt ourselves at the hub of events, with our fingers on the pulse of Central Asia'. After so many weeks out of all communication, he had acquired an 'unbridled lust' for news or anything that smelt like it, and it was in a state of pleasurably excited anticipation that they drew near Cherchen.

So ignorant were they of this place that they had no idea what to expect: it might, for all they knew be a collection of mud huts or a scattering of yurts. What they ound, in fact, was an oasis of almost inconceivable fertility:

Wonder and joy fell on us. I suppose that the earth offers no greater contrast—except that between land and sea—than the contrast between desert and oasis. We stepped clean out of one world into another. There was no phase of transition: we slipped into coolness and delight as smoothly and abruptly as a diver does. One moment we were stumbling in the open river-bed, plagued by glare and a grit-laden wind; the next we were marching down a narrow path under the murmurous protection of poplar and mulberry and ash.

Trees lined the path, which threaded a patchwork of neat little fields of hemp and rice and barley. Men of gentle appearance in white robes leant on their mattocks to watch us pass ... Everywhere water ran musically in the irrigation channels.

There was a brief flutter of worry over their passports, and they themselves were taken into a relaxed kind of open arrest as they entered the town. But, brought before the officer in charge of the garrison, Peter dissolved suspicions in his own inimitable manner:

Switching on my Chinese technique, such as it was, I answered in gay and deprecating terms. Oh no, we were not Russians. That was wholly incorrect. I was English, she was French. My humble name was Learned Engraver on Stone, hers was International Horse of Goodwill. My affair was the affair of Extra-Special-Correspondent-Officer to the Newspaper-for-the-Enlightened-Apprehension-of-Scholars. A great English newspaper. Had the Before-born heard of it? (The Thunderer's echoes rolled, alas, but faintly here: the Before-born's face looked blank and unimpressed.) We had come from Peking, a most strenuous journey. Now we were going to Kashgar, and after that to England. Our business? Oh, we were on a *yu li*, we were expeditionary persons.

Disarmed by this *tour de force*, the officer stamped their passports, even though there was on them no mention of validity for Sinkiang, and the travellers were free. That evening they were received and put up by the *aksakal*, or representative of the British Government—'a tall, venerable Afghan with a dignified carriage and a shrewd eye.' In his house, on 'a wilderness of carpets', and in the middle of a garden full of apricot trees and vines, they spent five luxurious days recovering from their ordeal and eating with bestial abandon.

After Cherchen the journey was never again fired by quite the same sense of urgency: although nearly three more months of travel lay ahead— much of it exceedingly strenuous—Peter and Kini were largely free from the anxiety that so far had been their constant companion. Now that they were well into Sinkiang, the chances of being turned back were minimal, and they knew, almost for sure, that they would get through.

Reaching India depended not so much on luck and diplomacy as on sheer endurance.

In Cherchen Peter's wildest journalistic hopes were more than fulfilled, for he was able to discover, in a series of interviews with local officials and commanders of the Tungan garrison, a great deal about the political situation which would make red-hot news for *The Times*. His inquiries confirmed many of the rumours which had been filtering through to him across the wastes of Tartary: the fighting had died down, but the Tungan rebels were in control of all the southern oases. More important still, they were being actively encouraged and abetted by the Soviet Government in Moscow, and Russian influence was in widespread evidence: Communist Russia, there could be no doubt, was making a determined effort to crush British interests in the province and to establish herself as the most benevolent foreign power in the area—the latest variant of her 'forward policy' in Central Asia which had worried British statesmen ever since the early nineteenth century.

On June 16th Peter wrote Dawson a cheerful though politically guarded situation-report, no doubt fearing that it might be read by the wrong eyes before it reached Printing House Square:

> This is just to let you know that all goes well, and that *The Times* is now represented in this much-discussed province for the first and I fear the last time for who can say how many years. Accompanied by a Swiss international skier (female), I got here through the mountains from the Tsaidam ... The expedition lost half its personnel in Kansu; and on the last stage we lost half our animals as well. But now prospects are fair; we should be in Kashgar in July, and over the passes into India in August. Conditions on the road are said to be very quiet, and the British popular; the local governor gave me four chickens last night. So it looks at the moment as if we shall get through; I never expected that we should.
>
> So far the journey has been uneventful, but it ought to make up into readable articles, simply on the rather bogus recommendations of its length, of the situation in Sinkiang, and of the fact that the regions traversed to reach Sinkiang are very little known. Nobody goes there, and hardly anybody lives there, and I must say I don't blame them ... Just eaten my first egg for three months. Hope the grouse are good. Perhaps I shall see you in September.

This letter, together with others which Peter wrote in Cherchen, did eventually reach England, but not until he himself had done so, and at home the long absence of news from him began—predictably enough—

to worry his mother. In the middle of June she started to pester *The Times*, and on the 22nd Ralph Deakin, the Imperial and Foreign News Editor, wrote to the Press Department of the Foreign Office asking if they could discover Peter's whereabouts:

> Peter Fleming, who went to the Far East as Special Correspondent of *The Times* last year, has not been heard of for some weeks, and we and his family are inclined to feel somewhat nervous at the absence of news ... Fleming is more than capable of looking after himself, but we thought it advisable to request that a telegram might be sent to the Consulate-General at Kashgar mentioning the absence of news.

Telegrams were sent, and received more or less heavily bowdlerized, but no news was forthcoming for several more weeks. In July Dawson sought the help of the Chinese Ambassador in London, Mr Quo Tai-chi, who readily agreed to put out feelers of his own. In a letter sent on July 19th to thank him for his help, Dawson wrote:

> It was exceedingly good of you to respond so promptly to the appeal of *The Times*. I only hope we may have good news before long, for he is a young man who can ill be spared.

By then there was serious concern about Peter's well-being, both at the India Office and in Printing House Square. On July 22nd, in an inter-office memorandum, a Mr Butler summed up the situation for the Editor:

> MacGregor, late of *The Times* and now of the India Office, called this morning to inquire about the movements and intentions of Peter Fleming. The I.O. is getting anxious about him, as the state of affairs in Sinkiang ... is disquieting. The province appears to be in the hands of the White Russians and is in a very disturbed condition ...
>
> Fleming stated [in a letter to Dawson] that he was starting on March 28 for the Tsaidam, a swampy region in N. Tibet. Since that time a letter has been received from him dated April 15 from Dzun Koko Nor, a lake in the eastern corner of N. Tibet, and no further news has reached England. You will see that in his letter to you Fleming mentions that he hopes to be back 'for the grouse'—i.e. in about three weeks' time, but that he would probably be back sooner.
>
> Fraser said the other day that he had warned Fleming against

178

attempting this route, as it is not a healthy one for strangers, and that he feared some mishap, as the farthest [he meant 'nearest'] telegraph from Koko Nor was much less than three months' journey. Fleming has with him Ella Maillart, a Swiss girl who knows the country a good deal better than he does and speaks some Tibetan.

The ignorance of events in Sinkiang displayed in this memorandum strikingly confirmed what a scoop Peter was carrying in his notebooks. Clearly, neither the India Office nor *The Times* had the faintest idea what was going on in the forbidden province: far from being very disturbed, it was almost entirely peaceful—and if it could be said to be in any Russians' hands, it was in the hands of Red Russians not White.

As all these agitated inquiries were being made, Peter and Kini were creeping steadily westwards, safe if not entirely sound. Soon after they had left Cherchen Kini was smitten by agonizing rheumatism, and it was only through her extraordinary courage that she kept up daily stages of ten or twelve hours. Although much of their way now lay through desert, the track was at least marked, and they spent most of the nights under roofs of some kind, rather than in the open. The main enemies were the ever-growing heat, the mosquitoes and the flies. For transport they acquired, at various times, a number of donkeys, but Peter soon tired of riding them. 'On a horse', he wrote,

> on a camel, even on a yak, your imagination soars without much difficulty; you are never for very long impervious to the romance of the road, such as it is. But the donkey ... is a sublunary mount for the adult. Its mean stature, its demure and patient aspect, above all the tripping rhythm of its gait—all these combine to take the gilt off the golden road. After a few days on a donkey you come to see life from the ignoble, the unstimulating point of view of a sack of potatoes.

On they went through the burning deserts from one oasis to the next— from Charklik to Keriya, from Keriya to Khotan. In every major centre of population they stayed with the *aksakal*, who invariably turned out to be an Afghan, and in the *aksakal*'s garden in Khotan a curious experience befell them:

> We ate our first cooked meal for five days and listened bemusedly to the squinting Afghan, who was telling us a long story. It was, to say the least of it, a sensational story, but at first we found it difficult to fit it into the political and geographical conditions obtaining in these parts. Comprehension dawned slowly: it was a synopsis of

M. Jules Verne's *Twenty Thousand Leagues Under the Sea*, which had
been translated into Afghan in Kabul.

By that stage of the journey Peter had developed to a high degree the
art of manipulating 'face' and using its subtle but very real pressures to
secure food, animals, free passage, or whatever the expedition needed
at the moment. As they entered Khotan, for instance, they needed
fodder for the animals. The mayor was out, and the

> shrewd old-fashioned Chinese in charge of his yamen was very
> properly alienated by my vagabond appearance—dirty shorts and
> Red Indian face and knees and arms. But I took his rebuffs coolly
> and, after referring to my friendship with several men of conse-
> quence in Khotan, I not too ostentatiously wrote down his name and
> rank; then I made as if to leave him, my demeanour expressing
> well-bred regret at such churlish treatment of a foreign traveller.
> This mild and oblique intimidation shook his nerve, and before long
> we got the fodder.

In the course of the four days they spent in Khotan, Peter brought off
another modest coup by interviewing Ma Ho-san, the twenty-two-year-
old commander-in-chief of the rebel armies. Then they took to the road
again. There was a nasty moment in Pialma when the commandant took
them for Russian spies, but Peter bluffed him 'by dint of making cheap
jokes with his staff, starting arguments on irrelevant subjects, and
generally playing the fool'. In Khargalik, the last major oasis held by
the Tungans, he scored another hit by outmanœuvring the recalcitrant
general whom he found watching a netball match and from whom he
wanted to hire animals.

> When the match was over the general waddled out on to the ground
> and with an air of condescension began to hit the ball into the net.
> When I went up to say goodbye he threw it at me playfully. It was a
> very light ball, and I sent it skywards with a prodigious punt; it
> fell like a bomb among the astonished crowd, who had never seen
> a ball kicked before. There was a roar of laughter and I made a
> creditable exit.

At Yarkand they found large parts of the town still in ruins as a result
of fighting during the civil war, and there they had one of the few real
rows of the trip: typically, Peter was determined to push on—to Kashgar,
site of the first British Consulate which they would reach—but Kini
wanted to loiter where they were. As usual, Peter won the argument,

and on they went, finding ever more frequent traces of British influence the farther west they travelled.

Nothing could spoil their arrival at Kashgar—not even the discovery that one of the donkey-boys had inadvertently allowed his animal to wallow in an irrigation ditch, so that their luggage was full of water, and that Peter's tropical suit, which he had husbanded carefully over the past three thousand miles for the express purpose of cutting a sartorial dash when they returned to civilization, was streaked from top to bottom with brilliant green dye.

'I had now to decide', he wrote afterwards, 'whether to enter Kashgar disguised as a lettuce, or looking like something that had escaped from Devil's Island. It seemed to me that if there is one thing worse than bright green clothes, it is wearing bright green clothes which are also soaking wet; I therefore sadly resumed the shorts and shirt of every day and prepared to let down the British Raj.'

Swallowing their disappointment, they rode into Kashgar on July 23rd, to be met by the Vice-Consul, Arthur Barlow, and to be luxuriously installed in the Consulate as guests of the Consul and his wife, Mr and Mrs Thomson-Glover. 'The raptures of arrival were unqualified,' wrote Peter:

> Discovery is a delightful process, but rediscovery is better; few people can ever have enjoyed a bath more than we did, who had not had one for five and a half months. Usually ... your return from a primitive to a civilized life is an affair of stages—a gradual process of transition, not a sudden step from one mode of existence to another ... But the end of the desert road was not like this for us. One night we slept on the floor, drank tea in mugs, ate doughy bread, argued with officials, were stared at, dreaded the next day's heat: twenty-four hours later we were sitting in comfortable arm-chairs with long drinks and illustrated papers and a gramophone playing, all cares and privations banished. It was a heavenly experience.

A radio message to London set fears there at rest, and back came a cable from Geoffrey Dawson: ALL IMMENSELY RELIEVED YOUR RE-APPEARANCE. Peter followed up this exchange with a letter to Dawson which summarized the journey so far, giving *The Times* enough to run, if it wanted, a trailer for the articles which Peter would write when he returned. 'The situation here is of the first interest and the first import-ance,' he concluded. 'I'll tell you about it when I see you.'

'The cub reporter has won through,' he wrote to Rupert.

In about a week we shall assault the Himalayas, once across which I shall board the largest aeroplane procurable and hurry home. The journey has been uneventful, and, believe it or not, swift. The Swiss has been A1; she is a good girl, but we shall part without the slightest difficulty ... I really am quite pleased about this journey.

After a fortnight of the Thomson-Glovers' hospitality, they felt 'fat and fresh and quite capable of taking the Himalayas in our stride'. This, in due course, they did, though not without many further delays and annoyances caused by unreliable animals and still more feckless Turki guides. By August 12th—the opening day of the grouse season—they were back in mountain country, and Peter suppressed his feelings of nostalgia, by observing that 'it seemed unreasonable and exorbitant to regret the Highlands when the peaks about you ran to 20,000 feet.' For him the 'high maze of empty sunlit valleys' through which they now passed was the most idyllic stage of the journey, and he was greatly stirred by the sight of the Himalayan giants blazing white against the blue sky, particularly the unconquered Rakaposhi and (later) Nanga Parbat.

On August 15th they had a great feast of macaroni and vodka to celebrate six months on the road—it was six months to the day since they had left that garish midnight party on the platform in Peking. Next day they tackled the pass of Chichiklik, 15,000 feet high and the biggest in the Pamirs. As they wound upwards among the boulders, 'the Turkis stabbed the wretched ponies midway between eye and nostril with long iron skewers which they carried for this purpose; this let a great deal of blood, and though it looked a cruel and barbarous practice it undoubtedly made the animals' breathing easier at high altitudes.'

A few days later an even stiffer climb took them up the Mintaka Pass, or the Pass of a Thousand Ibex, 15,600 feet above sea-level and marking the western extremity of China. Leaving the little caravan behind, Peter climbed on alone, leading his horse up the stony track, beside which the bones of less fortunate pack-animals lay whitening. At the top he found a stone shelter for mail-runners and sat down on its threshold to smoke a pipe, feeling sleepy and complacent. He and his stallion were on Indian soil.

The rest of the journey was enlivened by a series of parties. The travellers were received in Baltit by the Mir of Hunza, who entertained them with dancing and polo, and in Nagar by the Mir of Nagar with more dancing, more polo and a banquet. On September 1st they left Nagar and rode south in blazing sunshine, 'under the majestic, unbelievable Rakaposhi, towering inviolable, her peak for ever (it is said) protected by unclimbable walls of ice.'

Three days brought them to Gilgit, where they stayed with the Political Agent, and another eight to their final goal of Srinagar. On the last morning they jettisoned—'half in glee, half in regret'—the jam jar which had carried their butter for three thousand miles and the spare cocoa tin which had solved so many storage problems. Peter's faithful boots (which he had worn barefoot for the last thousand miles, his socks having fallen apart) were now themselves disintegrating, and he presented them to Wahab, the best of their guides. Then they set out for the last time in the 'crisp, gallant Himalayan air'.

> The track wound, almost too romantically, down a great valley between fir-trees. The pony caravans which we had passed frequently during the last few days were here more numerous than ever ... At noon we crossed the Pass of Tragbal, and turned in our saddles to look back at the great mountain system we had crossed, here shown as an undecipherable scribble of ridges in the narrow margin between the immediate horizon and the bottom of the sky.
>
> Then we rode a little further on and suddenly, amazingly, there were no more hills before us. Beyond the dark immediate spear-points of the nearest firs there lay—miles distant, thousands of feet below us—a flat vale, half hidden in a haze ... We plunged down the zig-zag track. Down and down, to and fro across a tiny section of the Himalayas' southern face ...
>
> The Vale of Kashmir absorbed us slowly. The track made its last zig-zag and flattened out. We rode out of the fir-trees into the edge of the plain. There were maize fields, and children driving humped zebu cattle, and tall thatched houses built with beams and little bricks. There was also a sticky heat. It was seven months all but three days since we had left Peking; we had covered about 3,500 miles, and the whole journey had cost us roughly £150 each.

Peter, by then, was rampant for home, and while Kini set off by Air France for the Lebanon and then Paris, he took the Imperial Airways flight to London, which in 1935 was a three-day journey. From Alexandria on September 20th he sent Rupert a telegram—DUE MONDAY TELL CHEYNE AND DEBAG SWISS CAT IF CELIAS COMING CROYDON—which, being interpreted, meant that he could tell Peter's mother of his movements and, if Celia was going to be at the airport, let out of the bag the news that her all-but-fiancé had spent the past seven months with another woman.

And so Peter came home from his greatest journey. 'Brown, older, tougher', George Buchanan noted in his diary on October 2nd. But otherwise the traveller was scarcely changed: still shy, still gauche at parties, still defending himself with a protective armour of non-reaction, still playing down himself and everything about him. And yet he could not altogether play down his passage to India, for no amount of understatement could disguise the fact that the feat he and Kini had accomplished was one of exceptional courage and endurance.

Of the leading *dramatis personae*, Borodishin was killed by bandits only two years later, but the Smigunovs made their devious way to Paraguay, whence Stepan wrote to Peter years later:

> When the Communists came we ran away on camels through Mongolia ... We had much to go through on this wonderful journey, but we were hard as steel, as they say, we did not break, nor let our courage go to pieces ... I am already sixty-two years old, and to be frank I am a little tired of wandering—although I would risk to travel to Tibet, see those stern cliffs, and die there.

Kini, never marrying, continued to travel widely. Sometimes when she came to London Peter would give her lunch or dinner, or try to help her create publicity for her latest book, and they maintained this irregular but pleasant form of contact for the rest of Peter's life.

9
Marriage

The things that had changed least of all during Peter's absence were his love for Celia and hers for him; and at last, having known each other for six years, they decided to get married. Well aware how strongly his mother would fight the idea if she got wind of it, Peter kept the whole business secret until the last possible moment, and Eve in the end paid dearly for her past attempts to arrange her son's affairs, for the news, when it broke, gave her an appalling shock.

For the moment, however, she knew nothing of it, and Peter got down to work. Fifteen months' travel had left his head and notebooks bursting with material, and as soon as he had touched down again in England he began to write. His diary of the Caucasian trip amounted almost to a book in itself, and he toyed with the idea of a facetious volume called *Sausages in Samarkand*; but this was put out of court by the superior importance and urgency of his impressions of Tartary, and he laid the Caucasian diary aside (it was eventually published, in almost its original form, as *A Forgotten Journey* in 1952). His most immediate commitment was articles for *The Times*, and in due course he produced no fewer than fourteen long turnovers. The first series—five pieces about the journey—was launched on November 18th, accompanied by a leader which described the author as 'this acute, observant and eminently calm explorer.' The second series—six pieces on 'Hidden Asia'—ran from December 5th to 10th, and the third—three articles under the heading 'Rivalries in Sinkiang'—from December 16th to 18th. Once more the paper must have felt well satisfied with its investment, for the articles, besides being highly literate and readable, represented a political and journalistic scoop.

After the first batch a spirited controversy broke out in the paper's correspondence columns about the weapons Peter had taken with him on his epic march, beginning on November 23rd, when Mr T. B. Money-Coutts attacked him for being so improvident as to arm himself with only the little ·22 and the defective ·44. Rather than allow its Special Correspondent to venture into the wilds with such inferior fire-power, he suggested, *The Times* should present him with a proper sporting rifle.

Next day Peter struck back sharply. 'Mr T. B. Money-Coutts's suggestion that *The Times* should present me with a ·256 Mannlicher is an admirable one,' he began. 'The rest of his letter is nonsense.' He went on to point out that in the circumstances in which he had started the journey the rifles had been the only ones he could get, and that in any case a ·22 was ideal for the kind of pot-shooting he had practised 'in country where the game has little reason to dread the rare human beings that it sees, and is more puzzled than alarmed by the discreet report of a ·22,' whereas one shot from a big rifle would have cleared the ground for miles ahead. No doubt Mr Money-Coutts had 'shot his way out of many a tight corner among the savage nomads of Hertfordshire,' he went on; but any attempt to have done such a thing in Tartary would have been suicidal.

Peter afterwards felt contrite at having mauled his critic so fiercely; but the argument was too tempting for readers of *The Times* to ignore. They opened up in scores from far and near, none more fruitily than Lieutenant-Colonel G. A. Anson, who wrote from the Naval and Military Club in Piccadilly:

> I wonder how those who look on a ·22 rifle as a childish toy would like to make a target of the plump part of their own back view at 100 yards—or even 150—for a good ·22 cartridge.

Criticism of a different kind came from the Communist *Daily Worker*, in which an ill-tempered series of articles by Richard Webb 'revealed' Peter's 'real motives' in making his journey through Sinkiang. 'The *Times*,' Webb trumpeted, 'gave to his otherwise worthless articles an extraordinary publicity such as has not been given to any other correspondent of theirs since the war.' The reason, he concluded, was simple: the British Government, 'alarmed at the moral influence and commercial supremacy of the Soviet Union in the border country of Sinkiang, is again adopting a "forward" policy in these regions, for which Mr Fleming's articles form the necessary barrage of propaganda.'

Ludicrous though this theory was, Peter was delighted that anybody should take him so seriously.

While the controversies raged, he was pressing ahead with the book to which, inevitably, the journey had inspired him. He may, at the outset, have really meant it when he told Dawson he did not intend to write another; but now he simply had to set down in order the myriad things, people and places that he had seen.

He was already well launched into the manuscript when, in the middle of November, he and Celia fixed December 10th as the date for their wedding. Now at last he told his mother—and a bad moment it was for her. She had already suffered one heavy blow the year before when her youngest son, Michael, had married Tish (short for Letitia) Borthwick, whose family lived just down the road from Joyce Grove in Oxfordshire and were, alas, though well off, untitled. Now her eldest son also proposed to marry a commoner. She simply could not countenance the fact, and when Peter took Celia to meet her, she ignored her, pretending she was not in the room. Even when they went to see Eve the night before the wedding, and Peter said: 'Now look here, Mama, about tomorrow,' she replied: 'What *about* tomorrow?' and began to talk about the curtains.

The couple never formally announced their engagement—a rare departure in those days—and successfully concealed their plans from the press. On December 2nd, after nine hundred performances, Celia slipped quietly away from the cast of *The Wind and the Rain*, giving out that her doctor had ordered her to take a rest, and on December 10th she and Peter were married at 9·45 in the morning in the Old Church, Chelsea. Only a few members of the two families and their friends were present, and the first the world knew of the wedding was a short news story published in *The Times* the following day under the heading 'Mr Peter Fleming Married—"The Wind and the Rain".' This revealed that the friendship was one of long standing, that the 'C' to whom Peter had dedicated *Brazilian Adventure* was none other than the girl he had now married, and that the Directors of *The Times* had given Peter a rifle ('make and calibre to be of his own selection') as a wedding present. (The weapon which Peter eventually chose was not a Mannlicher but a ·275 Rigby Mauser.) Before any other papers could descend on them the couple had escaped safely to Austria and were skiing in Zürs.

The only person definitely not happy was Eve. 'I am miserable about this wedding,' she wrote to Rupert on the day of the ceremony. 'Perhaps I take too jaundiced a view with fatigue and disappointment over this silly secrecy business, which has hurt me more than I can say.' Little realizing that it was precisely her own tactics which had led Peter to keep her in the dark, she went on to insinuate that it must have been Celia's influence which had made him so secretive. Then, with typical impulsiveness, she announced that she would sell Greys, where she had been planning to convert the Cromwellian Stables—a building separate from the house and encompassed in the old fortifications—into a flat and writing-room for Peter. She put the property on the market that very day, adding in her letter:

> I only bought it for Peter, really, and it's not going to be of any use to him now, so it is of no use to me. If only he had had his father here to advise him! I have done my best, but I seem to have failed at the critical moment.

Three days later she wrote again, struggling to be charitable:

> If Peter had done it in the right way and not with all this silly theatrical secrecy business I expect I should have felt better about it. It is so unlike him. I have wired him that I am sure he is right, and I do indeed hope he is. Anyway, he is very happy now, and long may it last.

Happy he certainly was: on December 21st he wrote to Rupert from Zürs:

> It is simply lovely here, and being married to the Crackwit is the best joke so far. I'm far happier than I imagined anyone was likely to be.

From Zürs also he sent another letter, equally ebullient, to Geoffrey Dawson:

> My Dear Geoffrey,
>
> Thank you very much for the charmingly avuncular and oracular manner in which *The Times* treated our wedding. Our press cuttings prove that the rest of the press failed to drop bricks for lack of straw. It all went with a swing, and we are both inordinately happy.
>
> Look here, have you got anything I could do for you in New York from February onwards for a maximum (I hope) of three months? They want Celia to go out in a fat part with a fatter salary ... I could, if there is anything like a vacancy, do a bit of work in your New York office, and put in a certain amount of travelling with New York as a base. It needs little percipience to see that what I really want is an excuse for going, and a bit of money ... but I might

write you something worth printing, and if I am ever going to
be any use to you it would be a valuable experience to have to
cope with an allegedly civilized people whose language (for once) I
know.

You might let me have an answer at once, and by telegraph if
you like the idea. The theatre people want a quick decision ...

Yours ever,

PETER

The familiar tone of the letter, and the phrase 'if I am ever going to be
any use to you', give a hint of how Peter's position at *The Times* had
developed since his return. He was now established as one of the most
brilliant young men on the paper, a special favourite of the Editor;
Dawson would presumably be succeeded in due course by his deputy,
Robin Barrington-Ward, but after him there was no established candidate
in the running, and soon the rumour of Peter's Oxford days began to
be strongly repeated—that he would one day edit the Thunderer
himself.

He joined the paper's staff, part-time, on March 1st, 1936, filling in
the routine questionnaire with a blunt pencil and putting under the
heading *Nature of past and present services to The Times*: 'Journeys to
China, Brazil etc. etc.' His job was that of leader-writer, and he moved
like a bright spark of life through the gloomy corridors of Printing
House Square. In those days an atmosphere heavy with tradition pervaded the old building: coal fires burned in the dark-panelled rooms, and
most of the staff were as old-fashioned as their surroundings, the senior
sub-editors insufferably serious, the assistant editors professorial. To
the young men trapped in the paper's web of tradition Peter represented
the embodiment of a dream: he was what they all wanted to be, and
gave them hope that *The Times* could be an adventurous and lively place
in which to work. He alone seemed to be able to defy the conventions
and get away with it. Iverach McDonald, who had joined the paper the
year before, was shocked out of his wits when Peter once, as he left the
Editor's office, murmured: 'OK, Geoffrey.' No other young man would
have dreamt of addressing Dawson so casually. Nor could anyone else
imagine quite how Peter managed to preserve his freedom so successfully: even when he joined the paper's full-time staff on October 1st,
he still came and went mysteriously, and people could never be sure
whether or not he would be in the office.

Even before he had formally joined the paper, his journalistic loyalties
had been rooted firmly in Printing House Square, but now he sought

actively to recruit other promising contributors. One of his most successful discoveries was Joyce Anstruther, whom he had met several years
before. It was he who suggested that she should write for *The Times*
articles about a typical British family—and this she proceeded to do
with enormous success under the name Jan Struther, creating, in Mrs
Miniver, a character so successful that she later devoted a whole book
to her exploits.

After their honeymoon Peter and Celia went to live in More's Garden,
a block of flats on the Chelsea Embankment only a little way along from
Turner's House, where their top-floor windows commanded a fine view
of the river. In 1936 Celia returned to the stage and made another great
hit in *Pride and Prejudice* at the St James's, and in the next few months
many of their friends remarked on how conspicuously happy they were
—a couple of dazzling good looks and talent, at the height of their
youthful success.

Their proposed trip to America never came off, and perhaps it
was just as well, for Peter went hard to work on his new book. For this
he negotiated a 20 per cent flat royalty, and he signed a contract with
Jonathan Cape at the end of March. At first he called the book *Two
Got Through*, but later he changed the title (very much as he had
changed the title of *Brazilian Adventure*) to the cooler *News from Tartary*,
and he dedicated the book to the memory of his father: 'To V.F.,
Killed in Action, May 20th, 1917.'

When *News from Tartary* was published in August, with the Chinese
characters for Fu Lei-ming emblazoned on the cover, it proved yet
another runaway bestseller: the fastest he had produced, it went through
seven impressions before the end of the year. The reviews were the best
he had ever had, and their general tenor can be summed up by passages
from a glowing notice written by Harold Nicolson in the *Daily Telegraph*:

> His latest book ... is to my mind the best that he has yet written ...
> Its political and informative value is considerable. Its entertainment
> value is immense. It will arouse great fury and cause much pleasure.
>
> These things are obvious and need not be stressed. No modern
> writer can equal Peter Fleming as a story-teller, as an astringent
> narrator of romantic and dangerous voyages through unknown
> lands. We all know that. Yet there is something more. I am not so
> much concerned with *News from Tartary* as a travel story; in that
> respect it will receive universal acclaim; I am concerned rather with
> this book from the aspect of literature and personality. Has Mr
> Fleming really discovered his own formula?

Obviously this book is written in a more sober and serious mood than *Brazilian Adventure* ... But does it represent a definite advance? I think it does.

I am now convinced that Mr Fleming, if he ever desires to do so, will produce something which is an important contribution to English literature. For the moment he is too shy and arrogant to do anything of the sort. His own stylistic capacity makes him blush. Yet he will before long rid himself of these schoolboy inhibitions and allow his love of writing to triumph over his dislike of showing off. There is nothing so damaging to literature as that appallingly second-rate bogey which is known as 'public school spirit'. Not that I deride that spirit: I admire it immensely: yet it should never be allowed to infect the style of gifted men ...

It is an amazing achievement of narration to be able to tell of the slow and unincidental caravanning of seven months, and to convey the sense both of monotonous continuity and of excited expectation ... It needs true literary power to turn a diary of diurnal endurance into an epic of adventure. Such is Mr Fleming's present achievement. And, to me at least, it places him and his book in a category apart.

No less striking a tribute came unsolicited in a letter from the author Eric Linklater:

This is simply fan-mail: I've just read *News from Tartary*—which is the best news I've read from anywhere for a long time. I'd like to be elderly and impertinent about it in this fashion: (a) from the writer's point of view it is a *tour de force* in that you maintain the reader's interest, without slackening, from start to finish ... Twice, while reading it, I looked on to the last chapter to make sure you'd got through safely. This is something I haven't done since I read *The White Company*, aet. 9.

(b) Your style has expanded: without *essentially* changing, it can do things like that lovely description of a night march or the excellent joke of the general in Kashgar who shouted 'YMCA!' And to describe the crack of your rook rifle as 'a diffident report' is an achievement that would have made Flaubert happy for a week ... It was a grand and miraculous journey, and the book's a perfect celebration of it.

And so it was; for Peter packed into his narrative an extraordinary wealth of human detail. As he himself repeatedly stressed, the expedition yielded absolutely no useful scientific or cultural data, and a disgruntled critic might justifiably have pointed out that the author showed no more than a perfunctory interest in the people and places through which he passed: his main interest—indeed, his only real one—was to get through. Nevertheless, *News from Tartary* is so rich in strange places and incidents, and so full of unforced humour, that it is still in print, still utterly absorbing, and in various hardback editions has sold 55,000 copies.

Its publication, piling on top of his other successes, made Peter one of the best-known young men in England, and he was soon aware of the advantages and disadvantages of having vast numbers of fans. Of the many letters he received, some brought only delight, as this one from Lady Diana Cooper, who was cruising in the Adriatic aboard the yacht *Nahlin* with King Edward VIII and Mrs Simpson:

> I've enjoyed reading it [*News from Tartary*] more than I can say. I read it aloud sometimes with Duff—I've laughed and gloated and cried over it too. I hated the journey to end, although it brought you back, and I hated the book to end. I loved Kini, and your writing about her is a masterpiece ... Yesterday was Montenegro, today Greece and an extra king to dinner.

Others were even more impressed. 'MAGNIFICENT HEARTFELT THANKS FOR GIVING WORLD SUCH A BOOK MAY I SAY MARCO POLO THE SECOND' cabled the ecstatic Walter Illingworth from Blackburn. 'Be an angel and autograph this beautiful thing for a crock who has been on her back ten years!' pleaded a lady living in the Royal Court Hotel, Sloane Square; and requests for autographs and photographs poured in from all over the world. Guilt was playing on one young lady's mind in Ebbw Vale:

> I borrowed a library copy of *One's Company*, and as the photograph of you above 'Siberia sometimes palls' was loose, I just took possession of it and framed it. Sometimes, as you look across at me grimly, I wish I had not stolen it ... If at any time you should feel like a holiday on a small farm in Wales, you would be welcome at my own and my parents' home.

No such inhibitions plagued Nancy Gardner of Glasgow, New Zealand:

> Heaven knows where you are at this hour, Peter Fleming, but may God be with you wherever you may be ... May you always be lookirg for a nice blonde round the next mountain. May you always be the kind of man who squeezes his toothpaste tube 'plumb in the

centre', and goes out bare-headed in the midday sun. Because that is how we like you, Peter Fleming, and that is how we would have you remain. Good luck, and thank you for past pleasures.

Not everyone, however, was quite so fulsome. 'Why the hell do you insist on calling the attention of your readers in nearly every chapter to your love of beer?' demanded an Irish missionary, irascibly and incomprehensibly (for Peter hated beer) from a station in Kathiawar. And a lady in New York found that *News from Tartary* left her in a state of some apprehension. 'It was awfully exciting and very interesting,' she admitted, 'but it seemed that after I had finished it all I got was a horrible dream about dead horses. If any of the books I am *going* to write ever make people dream of dead horses I will feel terribly dismayed.'

His most tiresome correspondent, undoubtedly, was a woman who wrote from Yorkshire to say that her husband no longer understood her, that divine providence had ordained that she and Peter were meant for each other, and that he must meet her in the bar of the Berkeley Hotel at 5.30 next Monday, when she would appear wearing a big spray of dark red roses and carrying a copy of *The Times*. 'I know you will not fail me,' she wrote. 'Our souls have been linked already—"You were a king in Babylon, and I was a Christian slave"—perhaps, who knows?' Peter did not keep the rendezvous, but he made the mistake of sending back a polite answer. Years later a handsome, middle-aged woman came up to him in the bar of a London theatre and declared herself as the author of the letter. 'I went to the Berkeley,' she said. 'We thought it was awfully wet of you not to turn up.'

'But who were "we"?' Peter asked. 'What was it all in aid of?'

'Get me a drink,' the woman answered, 'and I will tell you.'

The bar was crowded and the bell was ringing for the second time when Peter got back with the drinks. The woman had gone, and he never heard from her again.

As the social and political atmosphere of the late 1930s became increasingly uncertain, with the threat of war in Europe growing, and feelings of futility and disillusionment gaining an ever stronger hold in England, Peter stood out more and more as a figure of romance and escapism. To many people he seemed to have stepped straight from the pages of a Buchan novel. Handsome, rich (so people thought), aristocratic, he would slip quietly away like Sandy Arbuthnot to undisclosed destinations in Central Asia, reappearing months later in London strikingly sunburnt and weather-beaten but no whit less urbane, answering casual inquiries about where he had been with such cryptic and offhand replies that his missions seemed even more mysterious and exciting than they had been.

The author George Buchanan saw him as a kind of pointless hero, and in his novel *Entanglement* (published in 1938) he gave the minor figure Mark Shirwood many of the characteristics which he discerned in Peter. Mark, a rich, well-born young man whose easy passage from Oxford into business leaves him unsatisfied, takes to long-distance pioneering flights as a means of proving himself and putting some point into his life.

The author's description of Mark could have been transferred *in toto* to Peter: 'thin, fit-looking ... with a candid, self-deprecatory smile ... the dark, handsome Mark, who acted with traditional heroism in a changing world,' smoked a pipe, spoke with a drawl, and continued to sit casually at his desk when his boss came into the room, instead of leaping to his feet as other juniors did. But although 'he had mature readiness for outward action, when it came to inner emotional experience he was boyish'. One feature in which Mark differed greatly from Peter was his speech, which was gushing and ridiculous; in the novel his creator deliberately made him a rather dull person, and when his plane crashes and kills him it does not seem any great loss.

Peter himself never learnt to fly, but in 1936 he was involved by chance—and by his reputation—in the aftermath of an odd flying incident. A German aircraft with the number D-ANOY disappeared in Central Asia while pioneering a new commercial route across Chinese Turkestan. The German Embassy in London sought Peter's advice on the possibilities of mounting a rescue operation, and he at once wrote a long memorandum which, though on the surface splendidly esoteric, did in fact embody a great deal of practical advice:

If a search party goes in ... *on no account should it be large or well equipped*. Nor should it be composed of Germans, who will be suspect to Chinese officialdom on account of the German-Japanese pact.

The only Europeans that I know who might successfully undertake such a mission are the two brothers Söderböhm ... Serat, a Mongol who has travelled with Hedin and Teichman, might also be a useful man ... If anything were attempted through the Tsaidam, Lu Hwa-pu, a Russian-speaking Chinese photographer in Sining, might prove helpful. He is an honest and effective man. Gold, which can be bought in Lanchow, is the safest and most portable form in which large bribes can be carried ...

Everything should be done unobtrusively and casually. One good man with a good servant and preferably with an ostensibly commercial mission would stand a far better chance than a pukka relief expedition with tents and swastikas and expensive equipment.

I shall be very glad to do anything I can to help at any time.

It is no longer clear if Peter saw himself as that 'one good man', or whether he would have gone back into Sinkiang at the Germans' behest; perhaps he would have, even though he now had a wife and a steady job, for the assignment would have contained exactly the combination of improbability, risk and difficulty that most appealed to him. In the event, however, he never had to make a decision, for it transpired that D-ANOY and its crew were in good order: the aircraft had been forced down by engine trouble, but later managed to take off again and fly on to Urumchi. As a token of their gratitude for his prompt help the the Germans presented Peter with a small box made of some yellow quartz-like substance, and although in due course it got broken he kept a piece of the material, which lay about among the odd bits of junk in a drawer of his desk for the rest of his life.

In Printing House Square it was soon uncomfortably apparent that bizarre projects like the rescue of D-ANOY, or the maiden voyage of the *Queen Mary* to New York in the summer of 1936 (which he covered memorably for the paper), were what really took Peter's fancy, and that his interest in politics was practically non-existent. He could—and did, as in the case of his journey through Sinkiang—assume an interest out of journalistic necessity, but it never came naturally to him; and in the intensely political atmosphere of the late 1930s his attitude was all too often (in spite of his own attempts to take things seriously) one of incurable frivolity. Still worse, when the growth of the Nazi movement did begin to stir his natural instincts, they were directly opposed to the line that *The Times* was taking. As the threat of war grew, his instinct was to fight the thing that he disliked, and his powerful innate loyalty was converted for the first time into patriotism; but *The Times* was already pursuing the soft line which later became notorious, condoning the aggression of Hitler and Mussolini and endorsing almost daily the British Government's policy of appeasement. Peter found it increasingly hard to fall in with this anodyne attitude, and whenever he could he struck a blow against it—for instance with a leading article, whose title 'Three's Company' may have betrayed its authorship to some cognoscenti, in which he attacked the original Axis Pact between Germany and Italy.

It was Peter who persuaded Dawson that the paper should carry this unusually outspoken leader; and soon the two men were involved in an incident that touched on an even more controversial issue—the Abdication. It is tradition, rather than precise memory, that records the events of the night of December 7th, 1936; but that evening, at the height of the crisis, *The Times* published in its first edition an anonymous letter signed 'XYZ' which drew attention to some cruel lines in the fifth act of Racine's *Bérénice*. Under the heading, THE SLEIGHTS OF LOVE, two verses were printed in which Titus upbraids Bérénice (the translation being the anonymous author's own):

> Think not, dear heart, that, broken by my fears,
> At the long last my love will dry your tears
> In wedlock. No! However low I lie
> My glory tracks me down inexorably.
> It calls to my astonish'd soul: Beware!
> This marriage in thine Empire has no share!
> And after all the scandal and the strife
> Still less than ever can you be my wife.
>
> And think not, lady, in my bitter woe
> That for thy sake I'd let the Empire go,
> That glad in servitude with thee I'd stay
> And at the world's end sigh our lives away.
> Thyself wouldst blush to see so vile a thing
> Tied to thy train—a hopeless, throneless King,
> Loathsome to men below, to gods above,
> A sad example of the sleights of Love.

The poisoned arrow found its mark, for Mrs Simpson was by then in the South of France, and there she saw the paper's first edition, which caused her considerable distress. In London, however, the letter was withdrawn from subsequent editions, and very few people outside the office were aware of it.

Accounts now vary of how that malicious verse came to be printed and withdrawn. One version has it that Peter was in charge of the leader page that night, that he himself wrote the letter and slipped it in while Dawson was away at dinner, and that Dawson, returning, had it removed. But another version holds that it was Dawson himself who caused it to be printed, and Peter who removed it after he had gone. Of these alternatives the second seems the more probable, since Dawson did, it is known, sometimes indulge personal whims in early editions, and in any case the letter-column on the leader page was very much the Editor's preserve, especially at times of national crisis. Furthermore, Peter would certainly have had the nerve to remove a letter which he found offensive, even if he had no real authority to do so. Whether or not he did find it offensive is harder to establish: he had no very high opinion of the King, it is true, and being old-fashioned in his moral outlook did not approve of the way the monarch was sacrificing duty to love: yet at the same time his nature was essentially chivalrous and polite, and to authorize so wounding a personal assault would have been most uncharacteristic.

In any case, if he did have a difference of opinion with Dawson over the Abdication, it did not lessen the Editor's high regard for him, and at the end of 1936 the paper sent him off on a long tour of the European capitals. Taking Celia with him, he spent three months visiting Paris, Rome, Prague, Vienna, Berlin and Moscow—an experience which did nothing to increase his respect for the line which the paper had been adopting. The most notable incident of his tour was a row between himself and Douglas Reed, *The Times*'s resident correspondent in Vienna. Its immediate cause was a turnover article which Reed wrote about the situation in Czechoslovakia and which caused much ill feeling in Prague, where Peter happened to be at the time. Peter had been meaning to send Dawson a memorandum giving his own views on the Czech situation, but in order to save time he sent instead a copy of Reed's article annotated to show where he disagreed with the author. In no sense did he mean this to be a personal attack on Reed, but that, unfortunately was how Reed took it, and he wrote abusive letters both to Peter and to Printing House Square, claiming, among other things, that doubts had been cast on his impartiality.

This was precisely the sort of situation which Peter had done his best to avoid. He knew how irritating to old-established foreign correspondents the peregrinations of a young, amateur leader-writer were liable to be, and he had done everything he could to avoid giving offence. 'I am awfully sorry to have given you all this bother,' he wrote to Dawson from the Hotel Adlon in Berlin, at the end of a long letter of explanation. 'I will do my best to see that it doesn't happen again; but I must repeat that I have taken every possible precaution not to give myself airs or sail under false colours or make myself a nuisance. And everybody so far has been most charming and most helpful.' Dawson, not surprisingly, supported him, and wrote back in reply: 'The fuss about Prague really does seem to have been the most ridiculous affair.'

By then Peter's books were selling well in Germany, and during his time in the country the *Frankfürter Zeitung* ran extracts from *News from*

Tartary as a serial. He pressed home his advantage by means of a ten-day lecture tour ('my Rumblefest,' as he called it in a letter to Rupert), hopping from place to place by air.

At the beginning of March he and Celia went on to Moscow, and it was there that news reached him of the death of his grandmother. Though still extraordinarily energetic, even she had recently shown signs of fatigue, and her family had with difficulty persuaded her that a cruise to South Africa would do her good. As she was about to leave for Southampton she suddenly called for her beloved golf-clubs to be added to her mountain of luggage; in vain the family tried to persuade her that the amenities of the liner on which she was to sail did not include a golf-course, and in the end the clubs went with her. But that evening, before the ship sailed, she suffered a stroke and had to be driven straight back to London. Although she was still conscious when she reached Grosvenor Square, next morning she died peacefully, aged seventy-nine.

Blissfully unrealistic to the last, she had refused to countenance the fact that she might one day do such a tiresome and mundane thing as die, and she had never made a will. All Robert's estate thus passed automatically to Phil and his sisters, and Peter and his brothers were once again left without any share of the family capital. Of the four, Ian felt the deprivation most, and he was always complaining about being short of money. Peter minded least of any of them—partly because his books were earning handsome royalties, but mainly because he cared so little for money anyway. 'We are v. sad about my grandmother, who was nice and immemorial and a good joke,' he wrote to Rupert from Berlin on March 12th. 'I believe the usual brouhaha which crops up whenever I am disinherited is going on; but as far as I am concerned there are no complaints.' [He had not, strictly speaking, been disinherited; but the result of his grandmother's intestacy was certainly that the family money by-passed him and his brothers.]

Flippant though he might be, there was one piece of property in whose future he could not help being keenly interested: the Nettlebed estate. His Uncle Phil had never been able to devote much time to those 2,000 acres of beech-woods and flinty fields on the southern end of the Chilterns: a keen huntsman, he had always preferred more open country, living first at Grendon Underwood, near Aylesbury, and then moving to Barton Abbey, near Steeple Aston. There seemed no chance that he would come to Joyce Grove, and so it proved: recognizing that no future generation of Flemings would want (or indeed be able) to live in a pile of those dimensions, he gave the house to St Mary's Hospital,

Paddington, and it became first a training school for nurses and then a convalescent home. Before the transfer was completed the house ran for a while as a kind of free hotel, and members of the family continued to stay there at weekends, but the estate was left in the care of an agent, with only an absentee squire.

For the rest of 1937 Peter and Celia continued to live in More's Garden. She was busy acting, and he was reasonably well occupied with literary and journalistic projects in London. Apart from his work on *The Times*, which was now supposed to be full-time, he wrote reviews of plays and books for the *Spectator* and, in the autumn, helped launch a new glossy periodical called *Night and Day* to which he contributed a lively column signed 'Slingsbye'. (Intended as a London counterpart to the *New Yorker*, this glittered brightly for six months, but was then extinguished by two simultaneous libel actions.) Yet in Printing House Square he found life increasingly uncomfortable, for the paper was ploughing heavily along in the furrow of appeasement, and Peter could not find any enthusiasm for the way in which the paper shared and propagated the naivety of the country's rulers. Nor did he enjoy routine tasks such as sub-editing copy for the printer: mechanical jobs of this kind never appealed to him. No doubt he was secretly relieved when, in July 1937, Japan declared full-scale war on China and he saw developing in the Far East a situation which would engage his interest and his journalistic powers to the full. He seems to have had little trouble in persuading Dawson to send him out, and in February 1938 he set off by air, taking Celia with him and travelling for the first time as a fully accredited war correspondent of *The Times*.

The purpose of his fourth visit to China was twofold: the main one was to report on the war, which by then had reached immense proportions, the Japanese having captured large parts of Eastern China, including Peking and Nanking. But on his way to the war theatre he was to survey and report on the Burma Road, which the fighting had invested with an altogether new importance.

The result of the war in the East had been to sever China's principal supply-lines: with the Japanese in control of most of the ports—her normal outlets—she had to fall back on far more precarious lines of communication with the West, and of these the Burma Road was the only one over which the Western Powers could exercise any influence. The road ran from Yunnanfu, in western China, to Lashio, in Burma, through difficult mountain country, and when Peter arrived in March

1938 the Chinese were working feverishly to complete this vital link with the outside world.

Early in February Peter and Celia left London by Imperial Airways and flew in a series of short hops to Rangoon, arriving twice at Baghdad on the way because of unfavourable winds. 'We've both enjoyed this ridiculous trajectory a great deal,' he wrote to Dawson on the 9th while flying over Cawnpore. 'Seen from the air, the Lutyens edifices at New Delhi (on which we descended for breakfast this morning) look like a confectioner's nightmare; I do not think the colours are weathering as well as they might have.' Had he known he was going to spend three years working in one of them, he would doubtless have taken an even closer interest.

From Rangoon they took the train to Mandalay and Lashio, the end of the line, and thence went on by lorry along the new road to Bhamo—two hundred miles of a tortuous track which had recently been carved from the jungle and over which they averaged fifteen miles an hour for two excruciating days. Just beyond Bhamo the motorable road ended, so Peter hired four mules and two Szechwanese chair-coolies, who were to carry Celia when the sun got high in a *hua kan*, which he described as 'a simple but comfortable contrivance of bamboo and string', and he himself took gladly to his feet, delighted by the prospect of a long walk which, for once, really was necessary.

By the time he reached Yunnanfu on March 20th he was in sparkling form, as he showed in a letter to Rupert:

> We did the journey from Burma in spanking style, and after walking two hundred and eighty miles in seventeen days I am so muscular that it is freely said on the China coast that I can crack nuts between my buttocks. Tiny Johnson [Celia] turned out very tough and fierce and trudged most manfully; when not doing this she either rode on a porcine pony or was carried by two unhappy Szechwanese in a kind of gigantic lacrosse bat ... We topped things off with a four-hundred mile bus-ride, from which after three days we emerged gnarled and misshapen—but some of us were that already ...
>
> I have at last elicited some response from *The Times* who sent me a message yesterday saying WITHAM HANKOW SEEMS UNSUITED. Withal? Within? Women? Weather? And unsuited to what? I now think that it means that a person called Witham (why couldn't they put 'Witham Esq.' if he is a person?) is at Hankow and seems unsuited to *The Times*. I have wired them IS WITHAM A MAN OR A MISPRINT IF FORMER WOULD APPRECIATE PARTICULARS,

and there the matter is likely to rest until I get another message saying CHOLMONDELEY TASHKENT PRESUME CONTACTING. Well, well. What after all is a net but a number of holes tied together with string?

Last night we went to a Chinese dinner at six and a French dinner at nine, and I can feel the sharks' fins navigating unhappily in the Burgundy.

Three days later he wrote in a more sober vein to Dawson: news had reached Yunnanfu of Hitler's *Anschluss* with Austria, and Peter was stabbed by his conscience: he suddenly felt that if the situation in Europe was that serious, he should not be fiddling about in China:

It is fairly clear that the Far East is taking a back seat for the minute, especially as the military situation seems to have stagnated since I left London. Be that as it may, I am flying to Hankow the day after tomorrow and hope to keep China's abstruse and unpronounceable activities intermittently before the public.

For the next three months, while Celia stayed with various friends, he reported the war, first from Hankow, where the Chinese Government had established itself, then from Chungking, where the British and American Governments set up embassies, then from various parts of the 1,500-mile front, and finally from Canton, where the Japanese carried out a series of murderous bombing raids on the civilian population. Even his brief daily dispatches were full of characteristic phrases, and he sent home one memorable turnover article called 'Top Hats in Chungking' which described the official arrival of the new British Ambassador, Sir Archibald Clerk Kerr. Denis Allen, a junior member of the ambassadorial party, never forgot how

at the Consulate General in Hankow a swarthy and travel-stained young Englishman presented himself, with his wife, and, to the delight of those whose imagination had been stirred by *Brazilian Adventure* and the other travel books, announced that he was Peter Fleming, adding characteristically that he had 'just walked in from Burma' ... It was arranged that he and Celia should travel with us to Chungking ... I remember sitting one day with others on the veranda of a house on the south bank of the Yangtse opposite Chungking while Peter, undeterred by unhelpful suggestions from the rest of us, sat smoking his pipe on an upturned packing case and, with his portable typewriter balanced on another, tapped out that splendid account.

Two other observers on whom Peter made a vivid impression were W. H. Auden and Christopher Isherwood. Commissioned by the publishers Faber & Faber to write a travel book about the East, they too were wandering about trying to come to grips with the fighting, and Peter joined them for a short excursion to a sector of the front. To him the episode, though enjoyable, was worth no more than one short mention in a letter to Rupert: 'I did a brisk amusing trip with Auden and Isherwood (the Chinese always called him "Isherman", which made him sound Crimean and faded).' To the two intellectuals, however, the expedition demanded several pages of narrative in their book *Journey to a War*. Isherwood described their first encounter:

> A few minutes later [in Tunki] Peter Fleming himself walked into the room. 'Hullo you two,' he greeted us, with the amused, self-conscious smile of a guest who arrives at a party in fancy dress. Though indeed his dress was anything but fancy—for this occasion it was almost absurdly correct. In his khaki shirt, and shorts, complete with golf stockings, strong suède shoes, waterproof wrist watch and Leica camera, he might have stepped straight from a London tailor's window, advertising Gent's Tropical Exploration Kit.

When they wanted to interview a general, Peter arranged the meeting and 'handled the exchange of courtesies with consummate skill'. After supper he sat 'silently smoking and grinning', from time to time punctuating the conversation 'in truly Chinese fashion with a resounding belch'.

> Next morning the noise outside our doors made all further attempts at sleep impossible. The hotel servants were emptying buckets of refuse on to the heads of the washerwomen squatting along the river bank. Yells and curses mingled with the clatter of the servants' feet, which resembled the clumpings of a country dance. I went out on to the balcony to find, to my amazement, Fleming still fast asleep. His pillow was a hard satchel, in which he carried his writing materials.
>
> Fleming supervised our departure with his customary efficiency. One saw his life, at that moment, as a succession of such startings in the dawn. He stood pulling at his pipe, giving orders to the coolies, tying up loose ends, adjusting the weight of the bags, encouraging each member of the party with a joke or a word ...
>
> [As they ascended a pass] Fleming eyed the copses for signs of

game and delighted us by exclaiming: 'How I wish I had a rook rifle!' Our preliminary defensive attitude towards him—a blend of anti-Etonianism and professional jealousy—had now been altogether abandoned. He, on his side, confessed to a relief that we weren't hundred per cent ideologists. 'I'd expected you two to be much more passionate.' Laughing and perspiring we scrambled uphill; the Fleming legend accompanying us like a distorted shadow. Auden and I recited passages from an imaginary travel book called *With Fleming to the Front* ...

[After supper on a later evening] we drank cognac and began an argument on the meaning of the word Civilization. Had China anything to learn from the West? Peter thought not. 'The Chinese,' he kept repeating, 'have got everything taped.' 'Surely,' I protested, 'you can't pretend that the coolie is well off, in his present condition. Isn't he ever to hear Beethoven? Or see your wife act?' 'Oh,' said Peter airily, 'he's got them both pretty well taped.'

Peter, to our great regret, left Kin-hwa by train the same evening, for Nanchung. We had all three enjoyed our expedition together. As Auden said, summing it up: 'Well, we've been on a journey with Fleming in China, and now we're real travellers for ever and ever. We need never go farther than Brighton again.'

As usual Peter put himself as close to the fighting as he could, but as usual (to re-echo his own complaint) nothing seemed to happen to him, and he was never in any great danger except during the air raids, whose perils he shared with everybody else on the ground in Hankow and Canton. Even those he found it hard to take seriously, and at Easter he reported to *The Times* from Hankow:

The Chinese call bombs 'explosive eggs', and a seasonable variety has been delivered here over the weekend. The Hankow area has been visited eight times in the last 48 hours by Japanese bombers which operated in brilliant moonlight. The aim was poor, however, and ... so far the new tactics have been expensive and fruitless, but no more so than the old.

Twice in the course of his ten-week tour of duty he interviewed Chiang Kai-shek, the Chinese commander-in-chief, and by the time he went down to Canton at the end of May he had become a leading authority on the entire confused situation. After a quick visit to Hong Kong, he took Celia to Shanghai at the beginning of June, and with her sailed for Japan, where he was to interview members of the High

Command. On June 5th, aboard the 'not particularly good ship *Chile* (sans carne)' he wrote to Rupert:

> I am reunited with the Toast of Chungking and we are homeward bound ... The Toast claims that she is going to give birth (but to what? Naturalists the world over are agog).

On June 20th in Tokyo he secured an interview with the Japanese Foreign Minister, and that same day he sent *The Times* a long article summing up the state of the war. Although superficially a careful and impartial analysis, the piece was in fact strongly pro-China and reflected, in its urbane but sarcastic belittling of their achievements in twelve months' fighting, Peter's deep-seated contempt for the Japanese. He concluded his dispatch with a prophetically accurate paragraph about the future:

> At the front Japan will go on winning, and China losing, almost indefinitely. But it is still open to doubt whether Japan's digestive powers are equal to assimilating the fruits of victory without endangering the national well-being.

As he predicted, the war dragged on indeterminately for another seven years until, in August 1945, two atomic bombs ended Japanese aggression in China as surely as everywhere else.

At the beginning of July, with his agreed tour of duty successfully completed, Peter set off for home by air—but the journey was by no means the smooth, quick passage to which jet-age passengers are accustomed. A fragment of diary gives a sharp impression of the rigours of air travel in 1938:

> *July 17* Out very early [in Bangkok] to a dark river, from which we take off about 5.30 or 6 ... Land in a muddy creek from which the charms of Akayab cannot be guessed at and transfer to a hot lighter while they fill the tanks up. Then on to Rangoon ... another lighter ... come down at Calcutta some time after two and find it excessively hot. We traipse ashore out of the stifling boat, fill up a form or two, and traipse back again, sweating. On to Allalabad, which luckily proves cooler ... my stomach is bad these days and I do not eat much. Poor C is itching and unhappy.
>
> *July 18* Up at 3.15 which is early enough and drive out through heavy rain to the river, where we sit till past seven in an uncomfortable, unlit resthouse waiting for weather reports. Take off against a swollen stream and plug on against a headwind to Gwalior, where

we land on a nice, drab sacred lake ... then plug on again to another and more spectacular lake at Rajsamand. Finally reach Karachi about 6.30.

The autumn of 1938 was an exceedingly depressing time in which to arrive back in England. War in Europe seemed inevitable, yet Chamberlain, the Prime Minister, could not see what appeared so obvious to others, and in September he made himself notorious for ever by three times flying to Germany and signing his pact of non-aggression with Hitler. Worst of all, from Peter's point of view, *The Times* was still supporting the policy of appeasement with a devotion which strikes posterity as barely credible, and he found the atmosphere in Printing House Square most uncomfortable.

Fortunately he had pressing personal matters to distract him, for Uncle Phil, in an act of great generosity, had decided to give him the entire Nettlebed estate. Although the formal transfer did not take place for another eighteen months, Peter accepted the present joyfully. The decision to put down roots was in itself a major departure from his own precedents: hitherto almost the whole of his adult life had been nomadic. But now—prompted by the sudden hand-over of the estate, by the imminent arrival of Celia's first child, and perhaps also by the general feeling of insecurity—he chose to make a base of his own, and at once set about arranging somewhere more congenial to live than the impossible Joyce Grove. He could easily have enlarged and improved Bromsden Farm, a modest but pleasant house on the southern edge of the estate, which had fallen vacant at that moment. But he chose instead to let that to Rupert, and he commissioned Paul Phipps, the architect—and father of Joyce Grenfell—to design a new house for himself and his family.

The site, as he wrote years later, virtually selected itself, for there was one incomparable position almost in the centre of the land. At the head of a thirty-acre rectangular field which sloped gently towards the south, flanked on both sides by woods and offering a view, over innumerable tree-tops, of hazy ridges in the distance, there already stood an old wooden shelter known as Merrimoles Barn. Whether or not it had ever been accompanied by a dwelling, no one seemed to know; but the top corner of the field, just above the barn, was the obvious position for the new house, since it commanded a lovely, soft vista that would be rewarding at every season of the year.

Liking the odd name Merrimoles, Peter had some research done to try to discover its origin; but the only theory that emerged was the unconvincing one that the place had once been a smallholding belonging to a woman called Mary Mole, and so had been known as 'Mary Mole's'.

'I suppose', Peter wrote later, 'that the problems of siting a country house are analogous to those of siting a machine-gun;' and Mary Mole—legendary or real—had inhabited a perfect machine-gun site. 'To this agreeable spot', Peter wrote,

> we first conducted the architect on a very wet day. Rain fell implacably. Under his thundering umbrella the architect squelched meditatively to and fro upon the virgin turf.

All Phipps could think about, as he wandered beneath the deluge, was the bore of the only available water-main, which was too small, and the fact that if the new house caught fire the pressure would be insufficient to douse the blaze. All Peter could think about was that the building must have plenty of doors and french windows, so that dogs would be able to go in and out easily. As a friend of his remarked, he wanted the inside of the place to be as like outdoors as possible—a pleasant idea, but not one of any tremendous help to the architect.

The edifice that emerged was a neo-Georgian building of red brick, inoffensive if undistinguished. In comparison with Joyce Grove it was a mere cottage, and its rooms—though sizeable and of pleasant proportions—were so much smaller than Joyce Grove's that none of the old Flemings' furniture would fit into them; but by any other standards Merrimoles was a substantial house, with eight bedrooms and some twenty rooms in all. Work on it began towards the end of 1938 and continued slowly through most of 1939, the builders being much hampered by the appropriation of various supplies for rearmament projects. Yet, as Peter himself remarked, although on paper the time was not a propitious one for starting to build a home, it was in fact an excellent moment to have chosen, for he caught the tail-end of pre-war workmanship and prices. The total cost of the house was less than £10,000, most of which he had saved from royalties on his books; and the architectural feature which he was most proud of was the separate outside lavatory for the gardener.

In spite of the satisfaction of having a new house in the making, the turn of the year found Peter at a low ebb. At *The Times* he was underemployed; at home he could not get going either with a novel, for which he had an idea, or with the play he wanted to write, and in general he was oppressed by the air of irresolution and foreboding which invested the whole country. Probably it was the tension in the air that led him to start keeping records: on New Year's Day he began a diary, and later in the year he once more started to make entries in his game-book, which he had left blank since he began travelling in 1932. Remorse smote him as he considered the seven-year gap, and on the page opposite the last of the 1932 entries he wrote: 'I did a lot of shooting during these years, both at home and overseas, but was so foolish and casual as to keep no record of it. I regret this very much, and hope that if anyone reads these words they will serve as a warning against idleness.'

The first entry in his new diary reflected his general unease:

Jan 1 1939 Coming up this afternoon the Sunday paper bills were fairly unanimously preoccupied. 'Peace or War in 1939?' ... Yesterday shot pigeons (10) in Bix Larches [a wood on the Nettlebed estate]. The little birds make much of their presence in the silence, and a tree-creeper the size of your thumb is almost a riveter. (This sort of writing should always be referred to as the Questing Vole School, after Mr Boot in E. Waugh's *Scoop*). Spent about six hours, alone in the house, trying to make a start on a play, but one thing or another seems to have hamstrung my muse: I make no progress and feel disagreeably becalmed. *Must* get a play done in 1939 ... [Printing House Square] stagnant.

There was better news to report on January 3rd:

Last night at 7.30 [in the flat at More's Garden] Celia tentatively said maybe the baby was coming. We got hold of Sister Cooper [the midwife] at Salisbury after a delay on trunks and she just caught the last train, arriving at midnight, C having meanwhile reproached herself for making an unnecessary fuss. About two C started having pains and woke me with difficulty. Coop and I put up the bed in the sitting-room; then again at 5.30 C began to get the works, so she was transferred. The doctor was telephoned for about seven, and the baby born about nine.

Outside it was a fine rough winter dawn, with the seagulls dipping in the wind. I read *The Times* until the baby began to lament. Then soon I saw C, who had done it very neatly. She was awfully good in the pain while I was with her and insisted on smiling heroically: no mean feat. Women in real pain have much less self-pity than men. The baby had most of the sad attributes of a newly-hatched thrush. C was eating scrambled eggs less than half an hour after he was born.

In due course the boy was christened Nicholas Peter Val; for his first few years he was known as Nicholas or 'the Sausage', but when he was five or so the name became permanently abbreviated into Nichol.

Typically, Peter did not bother to tell anyone on *The Times* that the baby had been born. 'Peter and Celia Fleming have a son,' Barrington-Ward wrote in his diary for that same day, January 3rd. 'With customary nonchalance he left it to his colleagues to discover the news in the proofs … at night.'

At the end of January, with snow lying on the ground at Joyce Grove, Peter spent a day with his estate agent, Johnstone, going round about thirty tenants in the village trying to work out a reasonable maximum of refugee capacity. For him it was a novel experience to have close contact with English village people in his capacity as their landlord; he was touched by their readiness to help, and entered in his diary:

> One old couple (the man spruce and good-looking but cracking up) had one miserable damp spare room (out of four) and were pathetically contrite about not being able to help because they would have to get someone in to help if the old man got worse … The poor understand distress, the rich—familiar only with their own dissatisfaction—don't.

By then he had been in touch with M.I.2, one of the secret military intelligence departments at the War Office, and on January 31st he went to see Major-General F. G. Beaumont-Nesbitt, the Deputy Director of Military Intelligence, entering hopefully in his journal: 'M.I. are going to give chaps like me a preliminary canter soon.' Soon after this he did get a chance to do some lobbying for a more active Government policy —but in quite a different arena. David Bowes-Lyon, the brother-in-law of King George VI, asked him to form a small group which would approach the King 'in a ginger capacity', the main aim being to try to convince the Monarch that the country's defences were utterly inadequate, and that urgent steps must be taken to improve them. Peter agreed and brought in John Foster, a highly articulate lawyer, 'as a chap who can not only talk but can also get up a brief'. At the beginning of February their chance came, and they went to Buckingham Palace one evening for an audience with the King that (Peter's diary reported) proved more amusing than successful:

> We all had a whisky and soda and the only trouble was that John made him laugh too much with stories about the prevailing state of muddle. David and I had to keep on making prefectorial inter-

jections, stressing the seriousness of our purpose. The King himself only really got a word in edgeways once, and then he embarked on an anecdote about recruiting which nobody could even begin to follow. The little Princesses came in to say goodnight (we were there about an hour) towards the end. They wore girl guide uniform and both looked nice girls, especially Elizabeth, who has fine eyes and (I should say) a lot of character ... The King asked us to put some of our points on paper, and this John and I did next day.

Although the encounter produced no specific result, the ginger group stayed together through the spring and summer, reinforced by other friends, and did its best to wake the country up to the fact that war would surely come.

Peter's own life, meanwhile, was far too desultory for his liking. In February he made a quick trip to Oslo, where he lectured to the Anglo-Norse Society, and he continued to review plays for the *Spectator*; but his mood was accurately reflected by a short story called *A Tent in Tibet* which the *Times Literary Supplement* published in the summer. Although much of it was undisguisedly autobiographical, it probably told even more about the author than he intended.

An explorer called Richardson is dying of cold in his tent somewhere in High Asia. Eighteen months before, he had emerged from five years on the Changtung plateau to find that the newspapers, assuming him dead, had published obituary notices. 'He was in fact shy and clumsy, but he appeared only arrogant and dull ...' After each major journey he wrote a book. The first was a great hit, and he was lionized (although the book 'was as dull as ditchwater'). Thereafter the books did less and less well, and his audiences at the Royal Geographical Society steadily dwindled. Now, as he succumbs to the bitter winter, he faces death with equanimity and, for the sake of a few last minutes' warmth, burns his cherished diaries. 'Having met disaster, he found the encounter not unpleasant.'

Peter himself was nothing like as gloomy as his hero: his instinct for self-preservation was immensely strong, and he would never have tamely succumbed in the way Richardson did. Yet undoubtedly he saw himself as he described the man—appearing arrogant and dull, although really shy and clumsy, and he secretly dreaded just such a literary decline as he outlined. Also, he here produced another of his inexplicably accurate glances into the future: within a year he himself had been reported dead and read his own obituary notices in the press.

By the summer of 1939 his position on *The Times* had become thoroughly paradoxical. On the one hand Dawson told him directly that when he himself retired, which he was planning to do at the end of the year, he wanted him to take Barrington-Ward's-place as deputy editor; on the other, Peter was so bored and under-worked in Printing House Square that in May he and Rupert concocted a plot designed to precipitate some sort of a showdown. Together they drafted a letter which was ostensibly written by Rupert in his capacity as a director of Jonathan Cape, and addressed to Peter at More's Gardens:

Dear Peter,

Jonathan continues to show a keen interest in the project of a Buchanish novel by you, and the firm has been in conclave on the subject ... Jonathan ... after much talk, made the following suggestion in the form of a memorandum, which he wants me to pass on to you:

> PF *states that he gets very little to do at* The Times, *but this state of affairs is unavoidable as far as he can see; that his belief in himself as a writer and his earnings as such have been declining for some time; that he needs money; and that he has an idea for a book. Why does PF not take a few months off and write this book? We will give him £100 a month in respect of an advance on account of royalties, for a period not exceeding five months while he is writing it. This is, I imagine, more than he gets from* The Times, *and he could, presumably, go on writing his occasional Chinese editorials if* The Times *wants him to.*

I don't know what you will think of this. I personally would be very keen for you to do it, for obvious reasons. Leaving out the selfish ones, it seems to me that for a few months you would stop feeling that you were wasting most of your time and that you would make a bit of money and perhaps open up a fresh and profitable line of country ...

What do you think? I know you are not hopeful about the novel, but then you never are. Wouldn't it be worth sounding *The Times* to see whether they would let you break your contract (if you have one) and take leave of absence for four or five months? It would be a pity from every point of view if your literary output maintained indefinitely its level of the past three years.

With its carefully-planted disingenuities—'your contract (if you have one)'—this document should have had a useful block-breaking effect. But no record survives of its reception in Printing House Square, and it is uncertain whether Peter even showed the letter to Dawson. In any case, the political situation began to deteriorate so rapidly that there would have been no chance of Peter devoting four or five months to the novel even if the idea had been accepted by the paper. It is sad that he never got down to the task, for a letter to Jonathan Cape himself, in response to the firm's unparalleled gesture of paying most of the price of a new car, shows how finely months of frustration had whetted Peter's appetite for making jokes:

My Dear Jonathan,

This is just to express, as formally as a rough diamond can, the lively gratitude which Celia and I feel to you (and the boys) for giving us the best part of a good car. This quite uncalled-for act of generosity, besides being very deeply appreciated by the munificaries or munificats, has certainly saved from annihilation an indeterminate but substantial number of fellow-citizens; for it was not possible to stop our old car save by running into something. If the true facts were known, your progress down the road from London to Nettlebed, between cheering crowds marshalled by the insurance companies, would be a triumphant one; and it would be just too bad if you happened to meet Fleming at the wheel of his new juggernaut.

Seriously, we are extremely grateful to all of you. The car (on the prow of which the far-sighted manufacturers have inscribed the exhortation 'DODGE') will, until it falls to bits, be a pleasant reminder of how agreeably and profitably the Cape—Fleming Axis (small thanks to Fleming) has worked.

Yours ever,

PETER

Alas, the time for jokes and for literary endeavours was fast running out. In May he rejoined the Grenadier Guards' reserve of officers (from which he had resigned in 1936), and in June and July he did a month's training with the regiment. Immediately after that he worked for a month with M.I.2. Even the Oxfordshire landscape seemed to him to be oppressed by an air of foreboding. 'The usual 1939 afternoon, dank and blowzy,' he wrote in his game-book after shooting pigeons at Bromsden on July 29th. 'The corn is green, and few pigeons come to it.'

By the beginning of August, the question which faced him, as it did thousands of other young men, was not whether, so much as where and when, he would have to fight.

10

Into Action

When Chamberlain announced in his broadcast of September 3rd that the country was at war, his voice (Peter wrote in his diary) 'sounded like stale digestive biscuits'. But at least reality was being faced, and much as he might despise the Prime Minister, Peter positively welcomed the chance of going out to fight. For him the war started at a thoroughly convenient time: his civilian life was becalmed, and he had lost the inspiration which had made his early writing such a success; far from interrupting any work or plans in progress, hostilities opened just at the moment when he needed a new stimulus and fresh reasons for travel. He was admittedly at an awkward age: thirty-two was rather old for a front-line soldier—definitely too old for an infantry platoon commander—and he had had no experience which would qualify him quickly for promotion in an infantry battalion. Yet, as several of his fellow-officers were to discover, he harboured a burning desire to fight in the front line, to kill the enemy, and generally to emulate the unemphatic heroism for which his father was still remembered. Several of Peter's friends saw his ambition as a 'D.S.O. wish': yet in calling it this they misunderstood him, for his desire was not to win a medal so much as to serve his country finely.

The chance to fight, it turned out, was denied him—ironically enough by his own individuality. His brilliant intelligence, his record of long, solitary journeys and his knowledge of the East all marked him out as an ideal agent for intelligence work and special duties, and during the whole five years of the war he did no more than three weeks' home service with his regiment, the Grenadiers. For the rest of the time he was engaged in bizarre projects which took him to Norway, Africa, Egypt and Greece, and then repeatedly to India and China.

His help was sought by the War Office more than a month before the official declaration of hostilities. At breakfast time on August 1st he was rung up by a shadowy colonel who asked if he might come round. Half an hour later he came, and asked if Peter could leave for China in a fortnight's time. Peter said he would if it would serve any useful purpose, and within a few minutes had provisionally agreed to go out as the leader of a small party of officers whose mission would be to stir Chinese guerrillas into more effective action against the Japanese. Characteristically he did not disclose the plan to Celia, but a few days later he made some notes about it in his diary:

If I go in September for several months, there are the following disadvantages:

a. Geoffrey leaves *The Times* at the end of the year and I take B-W's place.

b. B-W goes to America in October for two months: so I am wanted badly before the change-over.

c. C starts rehearsing at the end of August: opens in the provinces at the beginning of October, and comes to London at the end of October.

d. Meanwhile Merrimoles begins to be finished in Oct–Nov and Joyce Grove to be evacuated about the same time.

e. Brown's [the gamekeeper's] teeming pheasants are left without butchers who will pay their way, and indeed without butchers of the right kind at all.

f. My novel becomes more still-born than ever.

At the request of M.I. (R)—a secret department which, under the guise of doing research (hence the 'R'), was in fact studying methods of guerrilla warfare—he wrote a paper entitled 'Notes on the Possibilities of British Military Action in China'. In this he proposed the infiltration of 'a small number of picked British officers into the Chinese forces, not merely as advisers at H.Q., but as fighting guerrilla leaders'. He also suggested—a tremendously Buchanish idea—that a force of British cavalry should be established in the Mongolian Corridor, the high grasslands to the north and west of the Peking–Kalgan–Paotow railway. In this sparsely inhabited country, 'which, since the days of Chinghiz Khan, has been the happy hunting-ground of irregular cavalry', the presence of a small British force would, he wrote, have a nuisance value out of all proportion to its size; moreover, the existence of such a unit would have an excellent effect on the morale of the Chinese rank and file, who would be pleasurably surprised to find foreign officers coming with them under fire; and it would be the surest way to overcome the obstacles of pride, jealousy and face which will be encountered in local commands. The average Chinese general will not take kindly to foreign direction or control, however tactfully imposed on him; but he will view with gratitude, respect and astonishment a foreign officer who undertakes in person, and with success, the distasteful task of fighting.

These notes, put together in haste, were received with enthusiasm and appeared (Peter noted later) 'to have been accepted out of hand as the British plan for intervention in China'. On August 8th two representatives of M.I. (R) came to More's Garden and discussed the project further, readily agreeing to his proposal that his departure should be deferred until the middle of November. Peter was delighted by the postponement—not least because it meant that he would be able to shoot some of his own pheasants—and he set about collecting recruits for a private army. Among them was Martin Lindsay, who had served ten years in the regular army and had made his name as an Arctic explorer; having once learnt Chinese in Shanghai, Lindsay set about refurbishing his knowledge of the language by hiring a Chinese to give him lessons.

For the next few weeks Peter lived a curiously indeterminate existence. 'I seem to be under but not of the War Office,' he noted; and on August 26th, after he had shot nine pigeons and a jay on the far side of the Nettlebed estate, he entered in his gamebook: 'Should have been shooting grouse with G. Dawson and Halifax, but the crisis is on us and one almost saves a cartridge for the German.'

Living in Chelsea and working long hours both at *The Times* and in Whitehall, he began to pine for action. 'The news so far this evening is bad,' he scribbled on a single sheet of paper at 8 p.m. on September 13th:

Anthony [Winn] and I went out to have a drink at 7.15. It was a lovely evening, cloudless and hot. Anthony said: 'What a lot of material for autobiographies is being provided.' We talked nonsense about what opportunities for shining the war might provide; and decided it was better to have two things to be frightened of simultaneously—then one didn't know which was frightening one more ... Telephoned to C to say that I might be later than midnight, but did it badly and alarmed her.

In the third week of September, after several weeks of detailed preparation, the plan for intervention in China suddenly fizzled out—apparently because the Foreign Office was anxious not to exacerbate the Japanese by taking even clandestine steps to help the Chinese against them. 'Should have left for China yesterday,' Peter wrote in his game-book after a modest partridge-shoot on the 23rd. 'Felt rather left in the air: so did most of the partridges.'

Soon after this he joined the staff of M.I. (R), instead of merely working for it, and it was not long before his fertile brain began to produce ideas for disconcerting the enemy. For months he had been pressing his conviction that Japan's ambitions in the Far East would ultimately be as dangerous to the Western world as Germany's ambitions in Europe, and he now produced a plan for drawing attention to Tokyo's real designs.

There should, he proposed in a memorandum marked MOST SECRET, be a second edition of the 'Tanaka Memorial'—a celebrated document which had appeared in 1926 purporting to emanate from the Japanese Prime Minister Baron Tanaka, and which had advocated to the Emperor the seizure of Manchuria and Mongolia as a prelude to the conquest of China, the defeat of the United States, and the creation of a Japanese world hegemony. 'It is suggested', wrote Peter, 'that the concoction and judicious release of an analogous document might produce valuable results on public and even official opinion in certain parts of the world.'

> For example, the revelation of Japan's dishonourable intentions towards American naval bases in the Pacific islands, the Philippines, the Aleutian Islands and the Panama Canal might well have an auspicious effect in the United States ...
>
> The document might purport to be a summary of the resolutions reached by a secret meeting of the KOKURYUKAI (Black Dragon) Society, attended by a number of influential naval and military leaders (probably unnamed) ...
>
> Publication might be effected by planting the document on an American foreign correspondent of repute. Rome (where there might be trouble with the censorship and therefore extra verisimilitude) might be a good place to do the planting.

The idea was never followed through; yet in putting up the scheme Peter showed extraordinary foresight. In effect, he predicted the Japanese attack on Pearl Harbor more than a year before it happened.

For the rest of 1939 he was stuck uncomfortably in London. At *The Times* Dawson decided not to retire after all, but extended his editorship indefinitely; the question of the succession was thus shelved for the time being, and Peter's presence in Printing House Square was no longer

1 Eve and her four boys in 1918: (left to right) Peter, Richard, Michael, Ian

2 'I have given vent to a fitful moustache' (1930)

3 Peter going up the Tapirapé in Brazil (1932)

4, 5, & 6 Tartary (1935): *left* Ella Maillart (Kini); *right* Peter playing patience;
below Peter riding Cloud, with Li on a yak

7 The shrine which Peter kept for Ian

8 Lucy and Kate Fleming with their father (1950)

9 The Squire (1965)

essential. By then, in any case, he was a full-time soldier, and could not have taken any significant part in the work of the office. He did however continue to write, and in the *Spectator* of November 3rd produced a viciously sarcastic attack on 'the thin yellow line of pacifism' which had recently manifested itself among the intellectuals of Bloomsbury. *Pax Bloomsburiana* was one of the most intemperate articles he ever wrote: clearly motivated by contempt, it abandoned altogether his normal urbanity and descended to largely indiscriminate abuse:

> Shrill, staccato, but in London so pervasive that it is on the whole (like cicadas) rather soothing, the chittering of the Stop-the-War Front makes itself heard ... Sir Oswald Mosley, on the right wing, cannot be said to be entrenched in depth. His shoddy claque is weak and too discredited to get or deserve a hearing ... The centre of the line appears to be held by politicians, either dim or formerly distinguished; by people who habitually court those politicians, by some rich women; by bores; and by a large number of people who, while not prepared to admit that anything that Mr Chamberlain has done or could ever do might be wrong, appear nevertheless anxious to put an end to the state of war which Mr Chamberlain declared to exist between Britain and Germany quite a long time ago. The centre of the thin yellow line contains no elements more engaging than these loyal but fumble-witted oafs, these governesses to a governess ... It appears to have been this action [the Russian Army occupying part of Poland] which swung Bloomsbury into the Stop-the-War Front like a great wave of used bathwater ... And Bloomsbury's motives? I don't know enough about Pond Life to attempt the undoubtedly complex task of defining them.

Predictably enough, the article brought a rush of pacifists to the barricades, among them Louis MacNeice. 'I have not yet decided what I think about this war,' he wrote in an answering letter in the *Spectator* the following week; 'but if there is one thing which might predispose me to joining Mr Fleming's "thin yellow line" it is the intolerant schoolboy smugness with which he attacks it.'

In spite of his aversion to pacifists of all kinds, at the beginning of December Peter accepted an invitation to shoot pheasants at Chevening, near Sevenoaks, the home of Lord Stanhope and a hothouse of appeasement. Perhaps the reason he went was so that he could observe at first hand the principal object of his contempt—for Chamberlain himself was another of the guests. No doubt Peter was perfectly polite to the Prime Minister: in such a situation he would not have dreamt of criticizing him or perpetrating the slightest incivility. But his good manners did not stop him making some disparaging notes on small sheets of the house's writing paper:

'Not forthcoming,' they say, and with reason. He has few graces and seems uninterested in us. He looks well and does not trouble, as he might, to invest himself with a faded air ... His humour is weak, evocative of drill halls and blue rosettes and laughter in brackets. At breakfast, unbending, he told us of the man who, his wife being ill, declared that he must take her to a genealogist. His brain is full of the raw material of the English tradition—facts about the Earl of Chatham's gout, anecdotes about the Delhi Durbar; but it is difficult to see in him the exponent of that tradition in these days. You have a feeling that he will never quite catch up with the contemporary racket, that he will remain to the end a missionary in the jungle, poking with his umbrella along what was once the right path, admonishing the carnivores in non-provocative terms.

He shot badly. He is slow and tends to let birds past him before he fires. He looks every inch the townsman in his rusty tweeds, handling his gun a trifle gawkishly. Is there something synthetic, a straining after the Baldwin touch, in our image of Chamberlain the nature-lover? He told us of a starling in St James's Park which, by whistling like a kestrel, scares the sparrows. I am inclined to disbelieve in this bird. Kestrels whistle rarely, except perhaps (I do not know about this) when the young first leave the nest. It seems unlikely that a starling would have the opportunity to learn, or a London sparrow have any reason to fear, so recondite a cry. This may all be nonsense; but the anecdote somehow struck me as phoney, the enthusiasm behind it as amateurish and far from the Fallodon tradition. [Lord Grey of Fallodon, who in 1914 had been Foreign Secretary, was a considerable ornithologist and in 1927 published *The Charm of Birds*.]

He asked me one or two questions about China of the kind that clubmen ask. And he told me that in the plane flying out to Munich he read a book on Dr Johnson and his circle.

Not for another four months did Peter get a chance to make an active contribution to the war. In the meantime he continued to write occasionally for the *Spectator*, and in March 1940 he contributed three signed columns to *Punch*. The middle one of these was a charming fantasy inspired by an entry which he had found in a library catalogue: 'Peter Fleming is best known for his crossing the Alps with his elephant.'

The beast's name in the stud book, he wrote, 'is Moral Rearmament II, but to me she was always Sophie ... I never found time to write a book about this journey, and the series of twenty-four articles describing it, which were to have appeared in *The Times* under the allusive title "Les Malheurs de Sophie", has been indefinitely suspended owing to the war.'

In the New Year Celia and the baby moved into Merrimoles—still not fully completed—and Peter was able to go down there for weekends. The transfer of the estate from Phil to himself became effective on January 1st, and in February he sent round a note to all the workmen and tenants, drawing their attention to the fact that he was now their landlord and employer, saying that he hoped to run the place on lines of which his grandfather, father and uncle would have approved, and seeking to dispel any illusions which there might be about finance. 'These are not easy times for any of us ...' he wrote. 'I should like to make certain things clear.'

It is many years now since the landlord has made any profit out of the Nettlebed estate ... I am not rich and, to be frank, I should be only too delighted if my property brought in a revenue which would supplement my earnings. But I regard it as more important and desirable that everyone connected with the estate of which I happen to be the owner should have a square deal ... and I shall do my best, both as landlord and employer, to ensure that this happens.

It is perhaps more likely to happen if it is generally realized that the estate no longer has behind it great financial resources and cannot therefore meet exceptional demands. In pointing this out, I do not seek to evade any of my responsibilities; I only ask for your co-operation in trying to create, in this corner of Oxfordshire, a non-artificial, unsubsidized example of what we would all like England to be. This will not be easy, and may prove an impossible task; but with luck and goodwill it may perhaps be accomplished, however slowly.

At the end of March he fell ill and had to spend a week in bed. This, to him, was an almost unique misfortune, for he always maintained the pretence that he never *did* fall ill: refusing to take the slightest precaution about his health, he ignored all the minor ailments to which other people are subject, and whenever he had a cold or influenza merely remarked that he had got swine fever again. Now, however, he had to take a week's sick leave—with, of all diseases, German measles.

Spurred on, no doubt, by the irony of the situation, he wrote a short satirical novel of some twenty thousand words which he called *The Flying Visit*. This describes how Hitler, goaded by his desire to gloat over the England which his *Luftwaffe* is pounding, has himself flown over London one night, only to be sabotaged by a time-bomb disguised as a Thermos-flask. Sole survivor of the shattered aircraft, the Führer parachutes down on to the Chilterns, finds himself in a beech-wood on an estate not a million miles from Nettlebed, gives himself up, is taken into custody by a blonde girl agent, and, by his sudden arrival, throws the British Cabinet into confusion.

His capture cannot be announced, the politicians argue, because the Nazis certainly have an identical replica ready in Germany to be marched on to the stage, and any claim that Hitler is a prisoner in England will be immediately derided as rubbish. Equally, there seems no point in keeping him ... Then an American newspaper correspondent breaks the story of his arrival, and the Cabinet decide there is only one course of action open to them: to send him back. So back he goes, this time in an R.A.F. bomber, to be parachuted into 'a wide, shallow bog in Eastern Germany.'

Peter had neither the time nor the inclination to work the story out in any great detail; but the idea behind it was highly original, as was his attitude towards the Führer. In the spring of 1940 the majority of people in England were greatly afraid of Hitler; but Peter, by contrast, lost no chance of belittling and deriding him. 'There he stood,' he wrote of the ceremonial which preceded his take-off for England:

> Drawn up to his full height of five feet seven inches, his right arm rigid, his cap tilted at an angle suggesting vanity without panache ... His eyes shone. His ectoplasmic face was vacant with exaltation. He looked as though he might burst.

Twenty-four hours after his parachute descent, 'this little Central European' has become 'a dim, swaddled figure, now capering soggily in an alien beech-wood under a dirty dawn.' Having tried to give himself up at the gamekeeper's cottage, but having been repulsed by the gamekeeper's short-sighted and crotchety wife, he withdraws into the woods again: 'Unhappy little bore! There he sat, with his eyes closed and his back against a beech-tree; pudgy, begrimed, pathetic; rather like a toad.' Several times he tries to shoot himself, only to discover that some well-wisher had loaded his revolver with dummy ammunition. When the blonde spy spirits him away to the large country house in which she lives, Hitler is locked into the downstairs lavatory.

To pick out these details is perhaps to make the book sound heavier than it was. It was, in fact, a soufflé, full of deft humour and containing some splendidly funny scenes, notably one in which Hitler wanders into a village hall where a fancy dress competition is in progress, takes to the stage, makes a speech, brings down the house and is instantly awarded first prize by the delighted revellers, who are convinced that he is an Englishman acting brilliantly. And yet, light as the novel was, it was toughened by the vein of contempt for its subject that ran through it from first page to last. It was published by Cape in July 1940 and dedicated to the infant Nicholas, 'in the hope that this book, when he comes to read it, will be no longer even remotely topical'.

By far the most remarkable feature of *The Flying Visit*, however, was its prophetic foreshadowing of the descent upon Scotland by parachute of the Deputy-Führer, Rudolf Hess, within a year of the book's appearance. Never was Peter's gift for anticipating the future more strikingly deployed, and when Hess arrived in May 1941 *The Times* printed a leader entitled 'The Flying Visit' which drew attention to the extraordinary parallel between fact and fiction, concluding that the case threw an interesting sidelight on Oscar Wilde's thesis that nature always tends to imitate art. Peter himself, though firmly disclaiming any gift of second sight, was always rather pleased with the trick that history played on him, and with what he called his 'involuntary excursion into prophecy'. In an introduction to a later edition of the book he wrote:

> The resemblance between the two episodes, one real and one imagined, is in fact superficial ... It is true that the Führer of Nazi Germany never landed in Britain by parachute; but at least the Deputy-Führer did. It is true that Hitler's aeroplane was not destroyed in 1940 by a time-bomb in a Thermos-flask; but at least an attempt was made to destroy it in 1943 by a time-bomb in a brandy bottle. And the conviction (which, though expressed by a dim, anonymous character, furnishes my story with its denouement) that Hitler was 'not going to do the Germans much good in the long run' proved, in the long run, correct.

Peter did not have to wait much longer, after finishing the book on April 1st, for an opportunity to take active steps against Hitler's armies — and the chance, when it came, was (to him) agreeably sudden. On April 9th, 1940, the Germans invaded Norway and within three days had captured all the major ports—thereby confounding one of Chamberlain's least fortunate utterances: that Hitler had 'missed the bus'. In London the Government hastily and recklessly decided to challenge the invaders on foreign soil, and, amid scenes of the utmost confusion, dispatched three separate expeditionary forces to Narvik, Namsos and Andalsnes. In Whitehall, as Peter later remarked, 'there was some uncertainty (that is to say, nobody had the slightest idea) whether Namsos was or was not in German hands, and it was prudently decided that a reconnaissance of this obscure little port ... should be carried out before an attempt was made to land there.' Happening to hear about the project, Peter volunteered to take part in it, and 'had practically no difficulty at all' in obtaining command of the reconnaissance party.

He got his orders on the evening of April 12th and was told to leave as soon as possible. Immediately he telephoned Martin Lindsay and said 'Come to Norway.' Lindsay agreed, and they prepared to set off by air next day. One of Peter's first actions was to ring up the Bank of England, where, as he put it in a later radio broadcast, 'someone very obligingly stayed up after hours packing a small fortune in Norwegian currency into a suitcase, rather as if they were cutting sandwiches for a picnic.'

Known as 'No. 10 Military Mission', the party consisted of Peter and Martin Lindsay, two young officers who spoke good Norwegian, and two signals-sergeants to work the radio set. Their orders were simply to discover whether or not the Germans had reached Namsos, and, if they had not, to signal the ships bringing the Allied expeditionary force to come in. A page of Peter's diary, pencilled in an army exercise-book, gives a good idea of the haste which attended the party's departure:

April 13 D.M.O.'s meeting at 9.30. Plan on but everything still pretty vague ... General flap throughout morning ... D.M.I. said goodbye and told me to keep a diary, which I am doing ... Got off reasonably punctually at twelve ... Left poor C seeming desolate but staunch and drove out to Hendon receiving the latest dope (which isn't much) from a pleasant Colonel Edwardes ... Martin bought food and beer at the canteen ... Took off at 1300 hrs [for Orkney] and had a lovely flight, mostly through an overcast kind of sunlight which gave the spring land a look of autumn.

Elated to be on the move again, Peter wrote to Rupert during the flight:

At last the well-known author, traveller and man about town is going to get some fresh air again. I must say I couldn't be more pleased. It is a wonderful job, promising good sport and virtually no danger at all. If the Crackwit hears anything to the contrary, you can point out that nobody, even in the War Office, knows exactly what the job is, and that what may sound alarming in general outline appears the opposite when the actual details are known ... Press home any chance of getting her to eat more.

They spent that night at Kirkwall, in Orkney, sleeping on stretchers because there were no more beds, and Peter noted with excitement the look of the men who had seen active service:

> The mess was composed of men who have been bombing Bergen in slow planes, leaving petrol and ammunition behind to make room for 500lb bombs. They have hard staring eyes and look fine. They are having another smack tomorrow, just before we leave. They saw off one cruiser for certain. I feel very good and the war seems suddenly quite different.

At 5.30 next morning they took off for Sullum Voe, the naval base in Shetland. Peter watched the wheel of the aircraft retract, spinning, into the wing among the empty bomb-racks beside him and wrote in his journal: 'Lost (so far) mackintosh, Trollope and ten copies of the code.' After a 'wonderful breakfast' on the depot ship of the R.A.F seaplane base, they took off for Norway in a Sunderland flying-boat and crossed the sea at low level. At 11 o'clock they came on a submarine which promptly dived, leaving them uncertain whether it was German or English, and an hour later they sighted a low-flying aircraft on their port beam which they took to be a Heinkel.

As they droned on across the sea, Peter became increasingly reluctant to relinquish control of 'the enormous and well-armed flying machine' which had been placed at his disposal: it seemed to him a great waste that the bombs which it was carrying should merely be taken all the way back to Shetland. And so, after consulting the pilot, he decided to ask for permission to fly down the road that ran south from Namsos to Trondheim, which was known to be in German hands, and to bomb any enemy columns which they found moving up it.

After an exchange of heliograph signals with the British warships lying off the coast, this permission was denied him, and a message from the cruiser H.M.S. *Glasgow* ordered him to proceed straight to Namsos and to arrange for four Norwegian pilots to come down to the mouth of the fjord that evening to guide the Navy in. The message ended with the words: ESSENTIAL OBSERVE COMPLETE SECRECY.

As Peter later remarked, a low-flying, four-engined seaplane is not the easiest thing to keep secret. But, having found the right fjord, they roared up it 'between the steep, white, jagged hills that ran down to the dark green water.'

Suddenly, swinging round a bend, we saw Namsos ahead of us: a little huddle of coloured wooden houses crouched between the mountains and the water. In a few seconds we were circling over it ... Smoke rose from its chimneys, trampled snow lay in its streets. A ginger cat walked meditatively down one of them. But apart from the cat there was no sign of life at all ... No. 10 Military Mission had been ordered ... to find out who was in occupation of Namsos. Here it was, hovering over the place like a kestrel over a rickyard, and for all it knew Namsos might have been occupied by the Tibetans.

After a few minutes they flew on over a ridge to another arm of the fjord, and there landed, 'wounding the still, dark surface of the water with that wonderful arrogant swish which a Sunderland makes'. As they taxied cautiously towards the landing-stage, with the crew standing to their machine-guns, a dinghy came out to meet them, 'sculled with such frenzy that it looked like an epileptic water-beetle.' In it was an agitated Norwegian who assured them that no Germans had yet arrived, so they sent an officer ashore who rang up Namsos and ordered the telephone exchange to stop all outgoing calls.

Then they took off again and flew back to the little wooden port. By the time they taxied in, an apprehensive crowd had assembled on the jetty, and Peter—the first British soldier to land in Norway—stepped ashore and made a short speech explaining the situation. By no means all his listeners were convinced by the story he told them: several believed he was a German in disguise, and their suspicions were not finally dispelled until, in the three hours of darkness that made up the whole of the dangerously short night, three destroyers slid in and disembarked the first wave of the Allied expeditionary force.

The force's commander was (as Peter described him) 'that legendary, admirable character', Adrian Carton de Wiart, who had 'only one eye, only one arm, and—rather more surprisingly—only one Victoria Cross.' With this indomitable warrior, a generation older than himself, Peter struck up a close and immediate *rapport* based on mutual respect. The general arrived with no staff officers at all, and Peter became not only his chief of staff but also his batman, driver and (on mercifully rare occasions) his cook. Together they lodged in a small wooden house perched high on the crags that dominate the port, looked after (until she had to withdraw to somewhere safer) by a beautiful Norwegian girl called Fanny. As General Carton de Wiart recorded in his autobiography *Happy Odyssey*, he was absolutely delighted to discover that Captains Fleming and

Lindsay had reached Namsos ahead of him. 'Whoever may have been responsible for sending them,' he wrote, 'I thank him now, for then and then I appropriated them, and a better pair never existed.' Peter, for his part, was equally pleased to have met the general, and wrote in his diary: 'He is a damn nice man.'

For six nights they contrived, with the skilled and enthusiastic help of the harbour-master Henrik Andersen, to keep the landings going without the Germans becoming aware of their presence. As soon as dusk gathered, ships came in and disgorged troops, who deployed southwards towards the advanced base at Steinkjaer (inevitably known as 'Stinker'), the aim being eventually to attack and recapture Trondheim, some 125 miles to the south, supported by a simultaneous attack from the other force which had been landed at Andalsnes. At the end of each disembarkation the shore party removed every trace of the night's work: every rope was re-coiled, every plank restored to its normal position. As a result, the German aircraft which carried out a thrice-daily reconnaissance saw nothing suspicious and left the place alone.

But then, on the night of April 19th, a brigade of Chasseurs Alpins were landed, and they, not appreciating that an elaborate game of hide-and-seek was in progress, foolishly engaged the first German aircraft of the morning with their machine-guns, thus precipitating the destruction of the town. More aircraft appeared in the middle of the morning, and by the evening two thirds of Namsos had been bombed and burnt into ashes. Peter's diary caught a vivid impression of the scene:

The first bombs fell at 10.15 on and round the station and railhead. '*Dispersons*,' cried the French, and took to the rocks like rabbits, annoying C de W who lounged about in his red hat and refused the disguise of a naval balaclava. No heroics but a genuine unconcern. The Germans were machine-gunning and killed one Frog. The station was going up in successive gouts of black, with timber flying above. The bombs floated down over our heads. Quite a few duds. They stuck to the station in a very gentlemanly way. We were above it and the blast was less bad than I expected ...

We went down to Steinkjaer about 12.30, after which they blew the town to hell with incendiaries. When we got back at seven-ish there was nothing but a loud fire. Church gutted, hours showing like a skeleton on the clock face ... No tears, no anger, no searching. Only a little petty looting.

Afterwards, describing that day to a friend, Peter enlarged on how angry Carton de Wiart had become at the behaviour of the French. Standing in the open, beneath a hailstorm of bombs, he had with great deliberation fished in his pocket for his cigarette-case, taken out a cigarette and lit it—no easy task, in any circumstances, with only one hand—muttering as he did so, 'Damned Frogs—they're all the same. One bang and they're off!' What Peter did not report, in his diary or anywhere else, was that he had behaved in exactly the same way as the general, strolling about in his Grenadier cap and battledress, without an overcoat, smoking his pipe. Whether he too did it out of 'genuine unconcern' or (as seems more likely) by means of iron self-control, the general loved him for it.

Even with Namsos gutted, the expeditionary force hung on for day after day in a situation whose futility became more and more apparent. Having no skis, the British troops could not go far from the roads, and even their specially issued clothes were as much of a hindrance as a help. If they wore their full quota of fur-coats, boots and extra socks, Carton de Wiart remarked, 'they were scarcely able to move at all, and looked like paralysed bears.' Some random notes which Peter scribbled under the heading 'General's Requirements' give an idea of the chaos prevailing: 'Need signals. No code. No ambulances. Little petrol. No artillery. No military police. Transport unorganized. No pipe. Fourteen days' food supplies? No casualties. N.C.O.s don't exist. No maps.'

The German air supremacy was such that the Allied plan for a pincer-attack on Trondheim—already vague—became utterly impossible. Every morning the Heinkels came over and pounded the remains of Namsos, pinning down the Allied troops, who sat, as Carton de Wiart put it, 'like rabbits in the snow'. Yet even in so desolate a situation his own standards never varied, as Peter showed in an article written for the *Spectator* thirty years later. One morning, while Peter shovelled snow into a saucepan to make tea, Carton de Wiart went down to see if he could scrounge some of the French rations for breakfast:

I watched him saunter down the steep hill towards the quay as the church-bells rang and the first air raid of the day was unleashed. A conspicuous figure in his red hat ... he maintained an even pace down the centre of the gutted street. Machine-guns chattered; smoke drifted from burning buildings; the Heinkels were flying so low that the bombs had no time to whistle before they burst. Carton de Wiart paid not the slightest attention. From safe bivouacs in the wooded heights around Namsos hundreds of men were watching him—French infantry, British base personnel, all in some degree shaken by their recent ordeals, all (at a guess) becoming a little more war-worthy as they followed his lackadaisical progress.

The *Luftwaffe* went home with empty bomb-racks. The General returned with some delicious sardines. His single eye surveyed my preparations for breakfast. Devastation was all around us. 'Better get rid of those eggshells somewhere,' he said. 'Don't want the place in a mess.'

Unshakeable though he was, even Carton de Wiart decided that no purpose was to be served by hanging on indefinitely in such a useless position, and on April 26th he sent Peter back to England with orders to proceed as fast as possible to the War Office and there discover the Government's real intentions for Norway. Thus, 'after much fiddling about on a bright morning', Peter flew to Invergordon, on the Cromarty Firth, but the Sunderland could not land there and took him far north to Sullum Voe, where he spent the night and completed his own report for the M.I. chiefs in London.

Meanwhile that same evening a Swedish radio station in Stockholm broadcast a report from the evening paper *Allehanda* that he had been killed in one of the air raids on Namsos. The source of the information was given as 'Swedes returning from the north'. At once the Stockholm correspondent of *The Times* flashed the news to London in a service message, adding carefully:

BRITISH LEGATION HERE SAYS LELAND STOWE CHICAGO CORRESPONDENT UP NORTH LEARNT FROM NORWEGIAN OFFICER FLEMING WAS KILLED WHEN BOMB HIT GRAND HOTEL NAMSOS SUNDAY. LEGATION SO FAR UNABLE GET NEWS CONFIRMED ALSO LIKE STOWE DOES NOT KNOW IF BOMB VICTIM WAS THE PETER FLEMING OR NAMESAKE.

In Printing House Square the report was handled with proper caution, especially as an official denial was issued by the War Office at 9.15 that night, and nothing appeared in the paper. But no such inhibitions cramped the style of the *Daily Sketch*, which knew a good story when it saw one and printed this one with maximum prominence. A banner headline on the front page neatly turned the rumour into almost solid fact: 'AUTHOR KILLED IN NORWAY' it proclaimed, and then, in smaller type, 'Radio Report'. Beneath, between photographs of Peter and Celia, the first paragraph of the story announced: 'Captain Peter Fleming, well-known author and explorer, has been killed in action north of Trondheim, according to the Scandinavian wireless.' There followed an obituary, short, trite and inaccurate.

The distress which the report caused Celia and other members of the family is easily imagined. But the first that Peter himself knew of the matter was when, arriving back in Scotland on April 27th, he found himself warmly congratulated on still being alive. For the moment he had no time to investigate the origin of the rumour, since his paramount need was to reach London as soon as possible. He flew from Shetland down to Invergordon where a bomber was standing by to hurry him south, but the weather was bad and after half an hour in the air the pilot turned back and landed him at Invergordon yet again.

By then he was in a state of some anxiety and impatience. The dispatches he was carrying should have reached the War Office twenty-four hours earlier, yet he was still five hundred miles from Whitehall, and the weather was growing even worse. He decided to catch the night train to London from Inverness, only to discover that he had already missed it. There was, he concluded, only one thing to do; and in the radio broadcast he made after the war he described how he did it:

> Hitler had missed the bus in Norway; I had missed the train at Inverness; but it didn't seem to have made much difference to Hitler, and I determined that it should make as little to me. I rang up the station-master and ordered a special train. I would sign for it, and I felt sure the War Office would be delighted to pay.
>
> The station master was a splendid man. Instead of asking a lot of silly questions, he asked the only one that mattered: What time did I want to start? I said I would like to get some dinner first, and he said: Very well, he would have the train ready outside the station restaurant at half-past nine. And there it was when the time came: an enormous railway engine, a sleeping-car, and one or perhaps two other coaches to keep it properly trimmed at high speeds. The sleeping-car was a special one, panelled with exotic timbers from different parts of the Empire; I think it had been in some kind of exhibition. It was a lovely train. And how pleasant to be able to say to various old friends that one met in the Station Hotel: 'You don't happen to want a lift to London tonight, do you?' And when the three or four who accepted were on board, with how casual, how proprietary, how smug an air one glanced at one's wrist watch and, leaning out of the window, said to a kindly railway official: 'I'm ready to start, if your people are.'

After this episode various authorities sought, with increasing irritation, to make him foot a heavy bill; but of course he never paid it, and eventually it disappeared harmlessly into the bowels of Whitehall.

In any case, early next morning he delivered his dispatches to the War

Office and had an interview with Winston Churchill, then First Lord of the Admiralty, whom he found in silk combinations smoking a cigar before breakfast. He was a little disconcerted when, about to light his pipe, he asked Churchill if he minded, and got the sharp retort: 'Yes I bloody well do!' But from this meeting he emerged with the feeling that 'there was at least one politician in London who knew how, and how not, to wage a war.' He managed to dash down to Merrimoles for the night, behaving, when he got there, as though he had just come from a normal week in the office.

His mother, however, was not fooled by his casual manner and realized that the situation to which he was bent on returning was one of considerable danger. In a characteristic attempt to preserve him she wrote to Geoffrey Dawson on April 30th:

> Dear Mr Dawson,
>
> We generally meet on the telephone when Peter is lost in some jungle! Now I venture to write and ask if you do not think that he is too precious to England to be sent to Norway where no doubt the Germans will get him if they can ...
>
> By the mercy of heaven I did not hear the report that he had been killed in action, but my second boy [Ian] had a ghastly time until he found it was not true ... It seems to me that we are doing the same thing that we did in the last war, and the bravest and best of our men will be killed. I know that he is of great use in the W.O. and if you feel, as I do, that he should be kept here, you may be able to do something. I can do nothing.
>
> In any case, I trust you not to let him know that I have written. He says, of course, that it is 'safe as houses, and *great fun*.'
>
> Yours sincerely,
>
> E. ST. C. FLEMING

Dawson was naturally powerless to intervene, but he sent Eve a soothing answer. 'Of course I entirely agree with you,' he wrote, 'though I know that nothing on earth would keep him out of Norway.' What he did arrange, however, was that Admiral Sir William Goodenough should write the paper a strong letter denouncing the *Daily Sketch's* irresponsibility in giving such prominence to the report that Peter had been killed, and this *The Times* printed on May 3rd.

Meanwhile, on April 29th, Peter had set out again for the snowy mountains of Namsos, bearing orders of a kind for Carton de Wiart and carrying a brown-paper parcel full (according to some people's memories) of explosive, but, according to others, of detonators. More explosive was certainly needed in Norway, not least to blow up a bridge which lay on the Germans' eventual line of advance; and Peter was certainly on the lookout for more, as a note in his diary records; but it seems unlikely that he would have been able to carry a useful quantity, even of the new plastic explosive which was just becoming available. In any case, whether he took explosive or detonators, he defied all the regulations with his usual sang-froid and kept the dangerous parcel with him throughout the journey.

'Ate to bursting point but had grave difficulty in getting a second helping of sausages, eyebrows being raised at so barbarian a request,' he wrote in his diary after he had taken the overnight train back to Inverness. Again he drove to Invergordon, whence he flew once more to Namsos.

There the same state of indecision prevailed, and not even Peter's messages from Whitehall brought much improvement. As Carton de Wiart wrote afterwards, Peter told him: 'You can really do what you like, for they don't know what they want done.' Soon contradictory radio-messages began to arrive from the War Office: first Carton de Wiart was told to evacuate his force, then to hold on, then to evacuate, then to retire towards Moesjen, a hundred miles to the north. Knowing that the road was deep in snow, he wired Whitehall to say that no such move was possible, but at the same time sent Peter and Martin Lindsay to reconnoitre the route, and they took twelve hours to cover forty miles.

In that hopeless situation, when there seemed no chance of inflicting any physical damage on the enemy, Peter's mind turned to deception as a means of at least disconcerting the opposition. 'We must do *something* to annoy the Germans,' he said to Johnny Bevan, an intelligence officer with whom he was to do much business later in the war; and with Bevan's help he concocted some typewritten messages which he put among other documents and then carefully half-burnt. The remains suggested that the Namsen bridge, which the Germans would be using, had been wired up with an explosive device set on a time-fuse, and that a machine-gun had been dug in on top of a mountain, trained to fire along the road. Whether or not this bluff had any effect they never knew; but it showed Peter's natural enthusiasm for deception at which he later became an expert.

At last, on May 1st, there came a definite order to evacuate, and during 'that last, endless day,' as Carton de Wiart called it, he got a message from the Navy to say that they would take off the whole of the force that night. He judged the task to be impossible, but the ships, creeping in through a dense sea-mist, accomplished it, the only casualties being one French destroyer and the Tribal class destroyer *Afridi* which were spotted and bombed by German aircraft as they left the fjord in the early morning. Peter came off with Carton de Wiart in the *York*—but not before he had left a lasting impression on Vice-Admiral J. G. F. Vivian, who was in charge of the evacuation. As he stood anxiously on the pier, which itself was burning, in a setting eerily illuminated by the blaze from a huge and inextinguishable heap of coal, the Admiral found himself next to Peter and asked him if he had any information about a unit for which they were waiting. Peter had none, but was as usual imperturbable and said to Vivian: 'You were once Naval Attaché in Japan. Come and tell me about it.' And so they stood there, chatting about Japan and China—a diversion for which the Admiral was for ever grateful. As the ships drew away, the bridge—for whose destruction Peter had nursed his brown-paper parcel—exploded satisfactorily, to loud cheers.

Norway was a fiasco. As Peter remarked afterwards, the campaign *felt* hopeless from the start. 'The errors were so gross, the muddles so pervasive and the whole affair over so quickly that there wasn't really a great deal to be learnt from it.' He himself emerged unscathed, with his reputation, if anything, enhanced, and with a mention in dispatches. Yet although at a personal level he enjoyed the episode (as he had told his mother) he felt the sting of defeat bitterly. He was sickened by the inefficiency with which the campaign had been mounted, and by the fact that the Allies had been forced to retreat so tamely. It was believed by many of his fellow-officers that the report which he deposited in the War Office contributed in no small way to the downfall of Chamberlain, who resigned on May 10th and was replaced as Prime Minister by Churchill.

Back in London, Peter found that on May 4th Sydney Carroll, the Editor of the *Daily Sketch*, had replied in the letter-page of *The Times* to the attack on him by Sir William Goodenough. The retort struck him as contemptible, and on the leaf of a notebook he began to draft a scathing reply, which for some reason he never finished:

Mr Sydney Carroll defends himself, with manly unction, against Admiral Sir William Goodenough's charge of causing unnecessary grief to a number of people by publishing in the *Daily Sketch* a third-hand news agency report of my death in Norway which had been officially denied by the War Office at 9.15 p.m. on the night in question. It is as difficult to answer Mr Carroll's letter—delightful document though it is—as it would be to play squash-rackets with a poached egg.

One of his supporting arguments is that the headline 'Captain Fleming Reported Killed in Norway' 'would not cause even the most sensitive of Captain Fleming's relations more than a momentary apprehension.' We Flemings are a hard-boiled lot; but even so …

For a while he returned to the stagnant waters of the War Office, but his existence was soon enlivened by a curious incident at Whitsun. It was, as he later wrote in the *Spectator*, a time of great general alarm. 'The evacuation of Dunkirk had begun … aliens were being rounded up, signposts taken down, milestones uprooted, street-names obliterated.' Whitehall was being deluged with sinister communications, and among them came a letter, purporting to have been written by a German agent, which gave, in considerable detail, the plans for an attack on the east-coast resort of Southend by a battalion of parachute troops, to be delivered at 0100 hours on Whit Sunday.

Everything about this letter seemed genuine, from its odd spelling and grammar to its naive psychological attitude, and the authorities took its message seriously, arranging what they could in the way of a makeshift defence for Southend. But Peter and Ian (who by then was Personal Assistant to Admiral John Godfrey, the Director of Naval Intelligence) discerned one serious omission in the official plan: unless some reliable eye-witnesses were present, they claimed, the Battle of Southend would result in a propaganda victory for Dr Goebbels, no matter what the actual result of the fighting. Since the German radio would be sure to announce the paratroop attack immediately, it was essential that a reliable British report should be produced with equal celerity. The point was taken, and Peter and Ian found themselves bowling down to Southend on the afternoon of Whit Saturday in a small camouflaged staff-car. Expecting to find, as Peter later wrote, 'deserted streets; loopholes in the front parlour of "Seaview"; tanks unobtrusively leaguered behind bathing machines,' they came instead upon a seaside resort in full Bank Holiday swing, packed with evacuees and weekenders. 'Bands played in Palm Court lounges, courting couples strolled along the front, queues stood outside cinemas. Phlegm, we felt, was being carried a bit too far.'

After dark the perfunctory defences were strengthened when a company of the Pioneer Corps dug itself in on the beach, and Peter and Ian withdrew to the roof of a large hotel, where a naval observation post had been established.

Here, soothed by the muted strains of 'South of the Border' and 'The Lambeth Walk' from the blacked-out ballroom below us, we waited for history to be made. But somehow, as the night wore on, we found it increasingly difficult to take the whole business seriously. In London it had been easy to visualize an airborne attack on Southend in the middle of the night; in Southend, in the middle of the night, it became impossible to do so, and when, soon after one o'clock, a report came in that there was no unusual air activity anywhere, the Official Eye-Witnesses sought out their car, put the elderly driver, who was dead drunk, in the back seat and made for London.

Afterwards we used often to speculate about the identity, and the motives, of the man whose anonymous letter sounded the tocsin in Whitehall and took us, for the first and last time in our lives, to Southend. He was, in his own rather specialized field, something of an artist.

Immediately after this abortive excursion Peter was assigned another unorthodox task, even stranger than the one he had undertaken in Norway. The commander of XII Corps, General Andrew ('Bulgy') Thorne, a fellow Grenadier whom Peter had met in Berlin in 1934, had been charged with the task of defending the south-east of England against the German invasion which seemed imminent during the summer of 1940; and he asked General Ismay at the War Office for an officer who would raise and train a body of troops to stay behind, literally underground, in the wake of the German advance and harass the invaders from the rear. Ismay's choice was Peter, who thus found himself in charge of an operation to which his own long training as a small-game hunter in the woods round Nettlebed fitted him particularly well.

Furnished with a detachment of Lovat Scouts, two leading aircraftmen with portable wireless sets, and a sapper subaltern in the person of the formidable Mike Calvert, he created an organization known as the 'XII Corps Observation Unit'—the prototype of the numerous 'Auxiliary Units' which soon came into being, and the first active cell of the entire British resistance movement. In conditions of the utmost secrecy he began to raise and train a clandestine army.

During and after the war many legends grew up about the part Peter himself played in the preparations for the last-ditch defence of southeast England: he strode about, it was said, in polished riding-boots and achieved such proficiency with a bow and arrow that he could kill deer at a hundred paces. Moreover, some of his underground hideouts were fashioned with diabolical—not to say Heath Robinsonian—cunning: in order to obtain entry to one of them, the story went, a visitor had first to find a marble hidden in some leaves near the entrance and then to insert it in what appeared to be a mousehole. The marble would roll down a long pipe and drop into a tin-can, thereby signalling the resident troglodytes to open the trap-door, which itself was concealed in the roots of an ancient tree.

All this, as Peter ruefully reported afterwards, was nonsense: he never wore polished riding-boots, and he was a hopelessly bad shot with a bow and arrow. Only once did he manage to hit a deer, and he never got it: having wounded it far back (at a great deal less than a hundred paces) he followed it up for hours but eventually lost it. Nor were any of his hideout entrances triggered by a marble.

Even so, he did attack the problem of going to ground with immense enthusiasm and ingenuity. Armed with a suitably potent and mysterious letter of authority signed by the general in charge of the Tunbridge Wells area of the Local Defence Volunteers (forerunners of the Home Guard), he recruited whatever men he liked. The document authorized him to approach certain selected L.D.V. units and to choose men for a special mission, 'which may necessitate their going with Captain Fleming or his subordinates in the event of an emergency'. He quickly built up a network of rural contacts, and his notebooks were filled with the names of gamekeepers and foresters, until he knew exactly who was in charge of, or likely to be at large in, every stretch of country in his area.

His strategy was based on the assumption that the Germans, having landed, would overrun the conventional defences in the south-east. The ports, it was hoped, would hold out, but the other defenders would fall back to the stop-line, on the southern outskirts of London, where they would prepare a counter-attack. Kent would thus be left temporarily in enemy hands, and it was in this situation that Peter hoped to operate, lying low by day and emerging to make quick sabotage attacks at night.

At Calvert's suggestion Peter's units mined a whole belt of bridges so that they might retard, however briefly, the German advance. They also constructed a large number of booby traps, filling milk-churns and sewage-pipes with explosive, into which fuses could be inserted at the last moment, and they mined a number of country houses which they thought the Germans might use as headquarters. Their main task, however, was the construction of underground lairs.

One at least of these was fashioned from an old badger sett, whose tunnels the men further excavated and enlarged until they had a tolerably comfortable home. At the time Peter never wrote a detailed description of these refuges, but in a novel called *The Sett* which he began but never finished soon after the war he left a vivid glimpse of some of the physical and psychological problems which they encountered in this strange return to the earth:

> Badgers must have used the place for hundreds of years. Their tunnels, the sides faintly scalloped by innumerable claw-marks, went deep into the chalk ... They [the men] took a pride in their place. They schemed endlessly and worked hard to improve it. Ventilation shafts, alarm signals, dustbins, lights, clothes pegs, bookshelves hollowed out of the chalk, washing-up arrangements— all these tactical problems they tackled with enthusiasm. It was not long, however, before claustrophobia and a general malaise set in, because they were civilized men who had suddenly executed a double somersault back into a cave existence.

Whatever the difficulties, the hideouts were most effectively concealed. In his book *A Very Quiet War* Ralph Arnold recorded how he went one evening with General Thorne (to whom he was A.D.C.) to inspect one of Peter's creations:

> He led us into the middle of a thick belt of woodland on the hillside above Charing. Stumbling along in the dark, we presently reached a clearing, and the Corps Commander was challenged to find the entrance to the Unit's hideout. We poked about unsuccessfully for a few minutes, and then our guide casually kicked a tree stump. It fell back on a hinge to reveal a hole with a rope ladder dangling into a cavern that had been enlarged from a badger's sett. In this cave, sitting on kegs of explosive and tins of emergency rations, were some Lovat Scouts and half a dozen hand-picked Home Guards ... It was pure *Boy's Own Paper* stuff, and the Corps Commander, whose brain child Auxiliary Units had been, simply loved it.

On another occasion, during an exercise, a neighbouring battalion deployed two whole companies against one of Peter's units to perfect their technique of mopping up odd parachutists. So confused were they by the wood—in which recent timber-extraction had created a pattern of rides entirely different from the one shown on the map—that the right-hand company finished up on the left, and vice-versa, and one section marched right over the heads of the men they were hunting, who sat tight in their burrow.

It was Peter's own idea to equip his men with bows and arrows. Should the invasion take place, and his friendly jungle become infested by enemy, he would need (he foresaw) some silent means of picking off any German who came in easy range. His men, as it turned out, never had a chance to engage a human target, but they did discover other uses for their bows and arrows—fitting the latter, for instance, with incendiary heads to set thatched roofs on fire, or strapping to them detonators and short lengths of safety fuse. A missile thus equipped and shot over the heads of the outposts would cause a 'brisk and unexplained explosion' and a certain amount of confusion within enemy lines.

Since the role of the Auxiliary Units would be almost entirely nocturnal, or at best crepuscular, they did a lot of training at night; and the notes Peter made in his diary give an idea of how thoroughly they learned the skills of moving under cover of darkness:

> Attack by night. Reverse many daylight principles. Avoid shrubbery, plantation etc. Often safer keep wrong side of hedge (but close to it) if the going is quieter than on the covered side ... Know all you can about the enemy's eating habits. Meal-times are a bottleneck, in all military establishments ... Nobody minds [going on] a fighting patrol as long as it patrols; but when it stops they hate it ... Take off piling swivels [part of the rifle]. Make a patrol march past and listen for avoidable creaks. Even at his stealthiest the British soldier emits a sound as of discreet munching.

From now on he adopted the military practice of writing all names in capital letters—'move to BILTING at 1030'—and in one of his pocket-books he listed some 'possible embellishments', many of which show how much he expected he would have to rely on small-scale tactical deception: 'German speakers, dogs, doctor, traps, bird calls, silencers, knives or sharp bayonets, fire extinguishers (no), pigeons, portable wireless, P.O. boxes, Very lights.'

He established a regional training centre in a farm called the Garth at Bilting, and his own headquarters was a hut in which the officers dined off boxes of gelignite, using other boxes of explosives as chairs. Peter's wide circle of contacts brought in many distinguished guests: there might be only bully beef to eat, but there might also be a Cabinet Minister to lunch, and once the unit entertained a brace of generals to dinner.

In the long hours of waiting Peter and Mike Calvert would endlessly discuss leadership. Peter, recognizing that he was a loner, doubted his own powers of command: he knew that he did not have the common touch, and envied the commander who could walk into a crowded NAAFI canteen and mix easily with his men. He was always trying to do this, but without much success. In many ways, however, he was first-class with the troops, for he took immense trouble always to talk to his men, to visit sentries at night, and so on: besides, his own fearlessness was an inspiring example to anyone who served with or under him.

It is impossible, now, to say how effective the Auxiliary Units would have been if the German invasion had come. Peter's own guess was that they would probably have justified their existence in the early stages, 'but that reprisals against the civilian population would have put us out of business before long. In any case, we would have been hunted down as soon as the leaf was off the trees ... I doubt if we should have been more than a minor and probably short-lived nuisance to the invaders.'

In spite of this rather pessimistic assessment, the form of subterranean base which he pioneered seemed, in the gloom of 1940, to offer a worthwhile extra weapon for use in the extremity of a German invasion, and the idea spread all over the country. Major Colin Gubbins, returning from Norway, where he had commanded the Independent Companies, to the task of creating a resistance movement in this country, found Peter's system already well developed in Kent, and adopted and applied it widely elsewhere. By October 1940 more than 3,000 men had been trained (albeit superficially) for this form of last-ditch warfare and were scattered at strategic points not merely throughout south-eastern England but on the east coast of Scotland as well. Even when the threat of invasion had receded, their hideouts were maintained, and the British resistance movement continued to prepare for the worst throughout the war—an organization so secret that its very existence was not officially admitted until ten years after the war had ended. It is sad that Peter never finished his novel *The Sett*, and so never left his own picture of the strange breed of troglodytic warriors which he founded.

For him by far the most melancholy event of the year was the death of his youngest brother Michael, who had gone to France as captain and adjutant of the fourth battalion of the Oxfordshire and Buckinghamshire Light Infantry. Three times his gallantry was mentioned in dispatches— on 20th, 22nd and 27th May—and, according to one of the citations, 'his complete disregard of danger and coolness under fire were a wonderful example to all at critical times.' Soon afterwards he was captured, and he died of his wounds while a prisoner on October 1st. His widow Tish moved with her three small boys and one girl to live at Merrimoles with

Celia, and for the rest of the war the next generation of Flemings sheltered under the same roof.

Peter was tremendously interested in, and fearful of, what might happen to the boys—both Nichol and his cousins—and by writing to them from abroad, and playing with them while he was on leave, he did everything he possibly could to protect them and promote their well-being.

II

Greece

At the beginning of 1941 Peter was ordered to raise yet another private army. The initiative, this time, came from Colonel George Pollock, head of Special Operations Executive in Cairo. Later in the war S.O.E. became a highly professional organization dedicated to fostering resistance to the Axis powers all over the world; but in early 1941 it was still seeking an individual role, and, while it felt its way, was taking on almost any task connected with sabotage or guerrilla warfare. Its head was that master of irregular operations, Colin Gubbins: fresh from pointing the British resistance movement in the right direction, he was struggling to work out the most useful career for his new charge—and having seen how efficiently Peter had established the first of the Auxiliary Units in Kent, he not surprisingly asked him to undertake the even more hazardous task which the Cairo office had suggested.

Pollock's idea was that among all the Italian prisoners captured by General Wavell in the Libyan desert there must surely be many anti-Fascists who could be trained to return home and foment revolution among their countrymen. A small party was therefore needed to go out and tour the prisoner-of-war camps in Egypt, select suitable men and train them for the earliest possible return to Italy.

Sent for by Hugh Dalton, the Minister of Economic Warfare (to whom S.O.E. was then responsible), Peter was told that he would be leading an absolutely vital mission to the Middle East. When he replied in deprecating terms, saying that he doubted if much could be accomplished, Dalton told him sharply that this would be a great opportunity. The plan, by then, had been drastically modified: Peter's task, besides recruiting potential Resistance fighters, had been extended to include the raising of an entire 'Garibaldi legion'—a force at least a thousand strong, whose members would accompany the Allies when they landed in Italy and would go ashore shouting 'Viva Garibaldi!' and other slogans— thereby, it was hoped, throwing the defenders into confusion.

Peter took all this as seriously as he could, and soon the normal Fleming recruiting tactics were brought into play. 'Come to Egypt,' he said to a dozen of his friends—and among those who accepted were a fellow-Grenadier called Norman Johnstone and Mark Norman, a second-lieutenant in the Hertfordshire Yeomanry. Another friend whom Peter asked was John Barstow, whose sister Nancy was married to Harold Caccia; John, however, was commanding a battery of the Honourable Artillery Company and could not get away, so his place was taken by his younger brother Oliver—also a gunner, but, being only a subaltern, with less responsibility. Soon six officers and six batmen were assembled, and it was typical of the disorganization prevailing at the time that only one of them had any command of the language in which, should they ever find any suitable Italians, negotiations would have to be conducted.

The little army—known as the Yak Mission—was dispatched post-haste to the Commando training school at Lochailort, in the Western Highlands, and there its members were given a crash-course in assassination and the use of explosives. For three days they were taught to kill with guns, knives and bare hands by instructors who had learnt their trade in the Shanghai riot police. Back in London, Norman Johnstone collected £40,000 in five-pound notes; with these he was to buy and bribe as necessary, but also to pay Peter's men, to whom it was held out as an extra inducement that they would not have to pay income tax while they were abroad. They, meanwhile, had assembled a formidable collection of explosives, booby-trap equipment and poison, to say nothing of two Tommy-guns, which were the first ones seen in the Middle East.

At that stage of the war, with the Germans in control of most of the Mediterranean, the normal way to reach Egypt was to take a ship to the West coast of Africa, and then fly north to Khartoum and Cairo. This Peter's force proceeded to do, sailing on a Commando troopship as far as Freetown, and there transferring to a Dutch freighter which took them to Takoradi, on the Gold Coast. In that decrepit and steaming port they had to wait for several days until aircraft became available: there was nothing to do but swim and play chess and pore over the Italian grammars provided by S.O.E. At chess their most formidable opponents were the Polish pilots who were flying the route to Khartoum and Cairo.

Eventually their chance came. Finding places in a number of single-engined aircraft, they set off for the north-east. All the way the pilots kept diving almost to ground level to point out the wrecks of aircraft whose engines had given out on earlier journeys.

No sooner had they arrived in Egypt than they realized that the Yak mission was going to be a dead loss. Although they visited several Italian prisoner-of-war camps outside Cairo, not a single man could be persuaded to volunteer for the job they wanted done, and the expedition withdrew in disillusionment to Mena House, by the pyramids at Gizeh.

Peter felt exceedingly frustrated. There he was, with a well-armed Commando force, but with nothing for it to do; so he marched himself in to Colonel Pollock and asked for a new assignment. A vague idea was propounded that he might go on to Yugoslavia (which was then still neutral) and there try to work up antagonism against the Germans, whose anti-Yugoslav pronouncements were becoming daily more menacing; but this plan came to nothing, and for several weeks he was stuck in Cairo, where the fecklessness and continued extravagance disgusted him.

On February 17, as he flew south to Wadi Halfa, he wrote a letter, all in capitals, to his five-year-old nephew Valentine, the oldest of Michael's children:

I EXPECT THIS IS THE FIRST LETTER YOU HAVE HAD THAT WAS WRITTEN IN AN AEROPLANE FLYING OVER THE DESERT. THAT IS WHAT I AM DOING NOW AND VERY DULL IT IS TOO—NOTHING BUT SUN AND SAND AND THE NOISE OF THE ENGINES ... WHEN I COME BACK WE WILL HAVE A HUGE FEAST. I HOPE YOU ARE GETTING ON WELL WITH YOUR LESSONS AND WORKING HARD. THE BETTER YOU ARE AT LESSONS, THE MORE CHANCE YOU WILL HAVE OF DOING THE THINGS YOU WANT WHEN YOU ARE OLDER.

A month later he hit a much more disgruntled note when writing to Rupert. Asking him in a tense, short letter to take £15 out of his account at Jonathan Cape and buy Celia a brooch in the form of a Grenadier badge, he added: 'I am rather bogged down here at present ... I am feeling too frustrated to write a good letter.'

The one useful contact which Peter made during this black period was with A Force, the team of strategic deception units which was already active in the Middle East, seeking to confuse the Axis powers by feeding them a mixture of true and false intelligence. From these clandestine weavers of intrigue he picked up many ideas which were to prove valuable to him a year later.

For most of the time, however, he was bored, and plagued by a guilty awareness of the fact that he was doing no good. It was not until he met Wavell, the Allied Commander-in-Chief in the Middle East, that he managed to get moving again. Wavell knew about him, had read his books, liked him at first meeting, and immediately granted his request that he should take his private army to Greece.

By then—the beginning of April—German preparations for the invasion of Greece were building to a climax: a *coup d'état* in Belgrade, whereby the anti-Nazi Serb party seized power, had made it certain that the Germans would invade Yugoslavia as soon as they were ready, and heavy concentrations of German armour and infantry were massing in Bulgaria. One of the main attacks, it was clear, would come due southwards through the Monastir Gap on the frontier between Greece and Yugoslavia, and Peter's idea was that he should proceed at once to the area and go to ground there, much as he had in Kent, in order to organize post-invasion resistance and harass the German lines of communication. The plan was both ambitious and exceedingly brave, for none of the party could speak much Greek, none knew the country, and no one in Cairo had the slightest idea of what conditions would be like in the far north of Greece.

Undeterred by the difficulties, Peter secured passages for his men and stores in a troopship which was taking a New Zealand brigade, including the Maori battalion, to Athens. There he met Harold Caccia, the First Secretary in the Embassy, and stayed a night in his flat. Also in Athens were Anthony Eden, the British Foreign Minister, and General Dill, Chief of the Imperial General Staff, still trying, at the end of the eleventh hour, to organize a Balkan bloc against the aggression of the Axis powers, and Peter had a talk with both of them.

Norman Johnstone, meanwhile, bought him an American car with some of his five-pound notes and procured two lorries into which they loaded all their stores, including a precious ton of plastic explosive which they had nursed all the way from England. Thus mobile, they set out northwards through brilliant spring weather in which spells of hot sunshine were punctuated by sharp snow-showers; and when they reached their objective they pitched camp on a site that commanded a magnificent view of the Yugoslav frontier only a mile away. Having sent S.O.E. a telegram which caused much delight at the headquarters in Baker Street—AM HOLDING MONASTIR GAP—Peter went off to tour the border itself.

The situation, he soon found, could hardly have been worse. A large force of German paratroops had just dropped on and captured Skopje, not much more than a hundred miles to the north, and a force many divisions strong was advancing straight towards the gap in front of him. It was clear that the ground on which they stood would be overrun in a matter of days, if not of hours, and that it was far too late to start training local resistance fighters. Once again his mission found itself faced by an impossible situation.

It was, Mark Norman remembered afterwards, a glorious day, and under the blazing sun, amid a profusion of wild flowers, the entire expedition sat down on top of a mountain and tried to decide what it should do. It was miles ahead of any other British unit, and not attached to any other part of the army: Peter, as usual, was completely on his own.

The only sensible course, he decided, was to turn back and offer his services to any commander who could make use of them—and this he did, involuntarily joining a retreat which quickly became a headlong rout as the Germans stormed southwards in a drive that pushed the Allied armies clean out of the country. The Yak mission still had its ton of plastic explosive, and this it put to good use, first by giving some of it to the Australian brigade who fought a bloody battle over the very ground on which the mission had camped, and then by helping some engineers to blow a major bridge. Soon afterwards they came on a cache of Greek dynamite, which they used to wreck a collection of some twenty locomotives in a small marshalling yard at a place called Amintion. Since the Germans were astride the railway line on both sides of the town, as much as possible of the rolling stock—which included two brand-new hospital trains—had to be destroyed, and Norman Johnstone and his colleagues enjoyed themselves immensely fitting charges to the driving-wheels and boilers of the engines. Towards the end, when their explosive ran short, they got up steam in four of the remaining engines, drove them out of town for quarter of a mile, and sent them full tilt back into the station, where, as Peter put it in a radio talk after the war, 'they caused further havoc of a spectacular and enjoyable kind.' He himself devised an elaborate booby trap in the improbable form of a double-decker London bus which he carefully positioned in the middle of a bridge over the Alcmaeon river and fitted up with a battery of flame-throwers, so that anyone who tried to move it would be incinerated.

Soon two other trains claimed the party's attention, this time in the town of Larissa, in the middle of the plain of Thessaly. Larissa had been, and still was being, repeatedly bombed by the Luftwaffe, for it had formed the Allies' main supply base in northern Greece, and, by the time Peter's party arrived, the station had been pounded into shreds. Even so, in a siding outside the town they discovered two intact ammunition trains, and Peter, knowing what a shortage of ammunition there was farther down the line, got permission from the brigadier in charge of the base to try and get one of the trains away.

All the engines except two had been put out of action by the bombing, and in the intervals between air raids Norman Johnstone, having scrounged some coal and water, got up steam in the larger of the survivors. 'All was going well', Peter reported afterwards, 'when one of the few really large bombs that came our way blew a hole in the track just outside the shed we were working in, thus, as it were, locking the stable door before we had been able to steal the horse.' Greatly disgusted, the party turned its attention to the other sound engine and eventually got it going. By the time they drove it out, along the only set of tracks still navigable, they had worked through—or rather in between—ten air raids.

In the siding they chose the bigger of the two ammunition trains, which consisted of twenty-six trucks containing 120 tons of ammunition and 150 tons of petrol—not, as Peter remarked, 'what you might call an ideally balanced cargo,' especially as no one seemed to want the petrol much. With Norman driving and Oliver Barstow stoking, they drove proudly through the town, picked up their kit at the station, embarked ten borrowed soldiers to act as brakemen, and, after repelling several parties of Greek stragglers who tried to hitch a lift, puffed their way out into the empty plain.

Alas—after only five miles or so on a slightly uphill gradient the needle on the pressure gauge began to fall, and nothing they could do would put it up again. The train groaned to a halt and ran back a few hundred yards before the brakes could be properly applied. Standing there in the middle of the plain, it made a tremendously conspicuous target, and it was only a few minutes before some passing aircraft spotted it.

Peter at once ordered the ten men in the guard's van to take cover a safe distance away, but he, Norman and Oliver stayed by the engine to make sure that the fire in its boiler did not go out. If they had their problems, he reported afterwards in his radio talk, so, luckily, did the enemy, who had clearly used up all their bombs.

They still, however, had their machine-guns, and three or four of the aircraft proceeded to attack us, coming in very low one after the other. But they all made the same mistake, which they might not

have made if we had taken evasive action and left the train. They all
attacked the engine, round which they could see signs of life, instead
of flying up and down the twenty-odd wagons full of petrol and
high explosive and spraying them with bullets, which could hardly
have failed to produce spectacular results. They concentrated on
putting the engine out of action; and the engine, as we ourselves
were just beginning to realize, was out of action already, all the water
in the boiler having somehow disappeared.

We used the engine in much the same way as one uses a grouse-
butt. Whichever side the attack was coming from, we got the other
side. The flying machine, making a terrible noise and blazing away
with its machine-guns, swept down on us, and as it roared overhead
—much bigger, much more malevolent, but not really very much
higher than the average grouse—we pooped off at it with our
Tommy-gun, to which the German rear gunner replied with a burst
that kicked up the dust a hundred yards away or more.

The only damage inflicted on either side was one bullet-hole shot in a
map in the cab of the engine. But the locomotive had expired of its own
accord, and when night fell the train was still stranded. Then, out of the
darkness, another train appeared, full of Australian gunners, and this
towed Peter's coaches to the next station, where a good engine driven by
a Greek picked them up and set off for the south.

Next day the weather was ideal for furtive movement—pouring rain
and low cloud—and no German aircraft appeared. Thus, only forty-
eight hours after Peter had volunteered for this unlikely project, the
ammunition reached its destination. 'It was a place called Amphikleion,'
he wrote afterwards:

'and here I formally handed over the train ... to the supply people.
Everyone was delighted with it. 'This really will make a difference,'
they said. We felt childishly pleased. The sun shone: it was a lovely
morning. And this marked improvement in the weather made it
comparatively easy for a small force of German dive-bombers, a few
hours later, to dispose of the train and all its contents with a terrible
finality.

No one had time to mourn the loss. Peter's little convoy—shorn of his
car, which had been stolen in Larissa by Greek deserters—pressed on
towards Athens along roads choked with other straggling remnants of
the Allied armies and littered with wrecks and the bodies of mules.
Every few miles a German air-attack sent everyone diving for cover, and

once, as Peter's men hurled themselves into a ditch, they found themselves next to an immensely stout general who turned out to be Jumbo Wilson, the allied commander-in-chief. Mark Norman afterwards remembered that hectic dash towards Athens as a time of immense excitement, every facet of it rendered the more memorable by the glorious weather and by the relish with which Peter seized every opportunity of scoring off the Germans.

Scarcely had Peter reached the capital when he was asked by General Wilson if his party could sever the coastal road between Missolonghi and Navpaktos, on the north shore of the Gulf of Corinth, so as to impede the German advance from the west. By then their own stock of explosive had all been used, and the only new source they could discover was a dump of 500lb bombs stacked on an airfield on the south side of the Corinth canal. The bombs were by no means ideal for the job, but they drove off and collected some, loaded them into a caique, crossed to the north shore of the gulf, and did their best to demolish both a bridge and a section of the road where it was cut out of the cliff above the sea. The attempt against the bridge was a failure, but they managed to blow off enough of the corniche road to create a difficult gap, and the German advance (they heard later) was held up for four days.

The journal which Peter had been keeping went, next day, to the bottom of the Aegean. But at this point he began another fragment of diary which somehow survived and in which he left a sharply focused snapshot of the chaos of the next forty-eight hours. Of his second retreat to Athens he wrote:

> Others [the rest of his party] delayed down Gulf of Corinth, first by a bomb on a lorry of 4th Hussars which they helped to clear up, second by a puncture in the van with attendant complications. I walk far and aimlessly along the road, creating much amazement, for a British soldier has never been seen to walk before. A hectic drive back along the Corinth–Athens road which has been bombed since this morning and almost cut in two places ... Hundreds of yards of transport unnecessarily immobilized by distant planes: nearly as bad as the Greeks ... Silly though human the way people run away from whatever they are doing under threat of bombing.

By the time they arrived back in Athens the Greek resistance was in the final stages of collapse. The King and his Government had withdrawn to Crete the day before, accompanied by the British Ambassador, and Harold Caccia had been left to close down the remains of the Embassy. Allied troops were being evacuated, and the harbour at the Piraeus had been wrecked, first by the explosion of an ammunition ship, and then by repeated air raids.

Peter reached the capital at about seven, called at the Caccias' flat, and then made his way to the Piraeus, where he found the expedition's kit being stowed on deck aboard the *Kalanthe*, a tubby little ship of some four hundred tons, camouflaged a muddy green, which had once been a private yacht but now had been requisitioned by the Royal Navy and assigned to the remains of the Embassy staff. She was commanded by Lieutenant-Commander Brass, the Assistant Naval Attaché, and Peter's unit had been asked to provide such armed protection as they could muster. The passengers included Nancy Caccia with her two small children, Doreen Blunt, the wife of the Military Attaché (who had gone ahead with the King) and her three children, and André Michelopoulos, a member of the Greek Government. Various other Greek officials and British Service personnel brought the total complement to about eighty.

The ship cast off at dusk. Just as it pulled away from the devastated quay a cat jumped ashore, and Peter remarked to Norman Johnstone that the animal must have had a premonition of disaster. As they sailed out of the harbour in a yellow after-glow, they could see the Germans dive-bombing Eleusis a few miles to the north-west.

Their destination was Crete; but by that stage of the campaign the *Luftwaffe* had absolute control of the sky: during the day German aircraft cruised ceaselessly on the lookout for targets, and for a small, slow boat to have moved during daylight would have been suicidal. The *Kalanthe* was too short-winded to reach Crete in a single night, so the crew aimed first for the island of Milos, in the Cyclades. This destination they reached safely in the first night, and they lay up discreetly for the day in a bay on Poliaigos, a tiny islet off the coast of Kimolos, which itself is a satellite of Milos.

Peter's unit provided crews, each of one officer and one other rank, for three of the ship's four Lewis guns, and all through that lovely, peaceful day they waited, hoping that nothing would happen. The ship rode easily about a hundred yards off the beach with the Greek crew below and the engines running in case she had to make a sudden move; the gun-crews remained on duty, but everyone not needed went ashore, including all the women and the five children, who made their base in a cave above a grove of olives. The others swam or hunted for gulls' nests.

At about eleven, after much far-off buzzing of engines, three aircraft appeared in the distance but went safely on. Peter sent a message to Mark Norman and Oliver Barstow telling them to stay where they were, and that he would signal if he wanted reliefs for the gun-crews. 'I have a hunch we shall get it this afternoon,' he wrote in his diary. 'Two p.m. is the time they generally recce Milos.'

Later we hear from some colourful guys in a boat, who sell us eight hundred eggs and a few nautically-minded sheep, that this morning's planes sank two small boats at Milos. Gin and lime on the bridge and a delicious omelette. Then the shore party turn up for lunch, not having got my message. I tell them both to go back after lunch and stand by with the motor boat. But Ol [Oliver] pretends to misunderstand and stays around, which I don't find out till later ...

Hot afternoon, bathing and reading, the blue water shining back on the underside of the gulls' wings. All quiet save for one or two distant drones (two planes fly straight over island about two o'clock) until Norman goes ashore about five ... We are just going to have a drink at six when trouble begins.

The *Kalanthe*'s four guns were mounted in pairs, two on the bridge and two in the stern. Mark Norman and Oliver manned the forward pair, each backed up by one soldier. Peter was in the stern, accompanied by Norman Johnstone's batman Isted (his own servant, Guardsman Loveday, having gone ashore in the latest exchange).

As they stood to, three bombers flew over high, but appeared to do nothing about them.

Then one comes along very low between the islands, half a mile away. We show up fine in the lateral evening sunlight, and soon we hear him coming back for us on the other side of the steep white island. Another comes over the bay from the south, and we know they are taking trouble and we are for it.

First attack comes over the hill from the east. He slants down straight for us, lets his bombs go far too soon, and they burst on the shore above and behind the women and children. He comes on machine-gunning hard, masthead high, and we engage him, eight men standing nakedly to the tall Lewis gun mountings. You really need a grouse butt of some kind for this sort of thing. He is shooting short, and when he has gone over his tail gunner sprays the water miles beyond us.

I think my gun has jammed, but it is only the cocking-handle forward. Nobody seems to have been hit. A Marine is coming aft to look at my gun. I send Clarke forward to take his place, then the second bugger comes into the attack, not giving us more than two minutes between doses. This time he has us. We see the white ribbons of smoke or rather I suppose vapour from his M.G. exhausts; they trail below him. He comes at the height of a driven partridge, and I daresay his bullets whistle round us but I don't remember noticing them.

Four bombs come out of him. Our fire has no effect. I *think* two bombs were short, one a near miss, and the fourth a direct hit just forward of amidships. For less than a split second I think we have got away with it, and looking round think I see large bits dropping off the plane and have a small spasm of exaltation and shout: 'Look at the bugger, he's hit!', or words to that effect. But the large bits must have been segments of the ship, which reacted violently to the near miss and blew up a second time (the boiler going) immediately afterwards at the direct hit.

The ship flies skywards in the middle. The air is black with smoke, steam, oil and coal. I find myself staggering, holding on to the tilted deck. I suppose my tin hat fell off, as a hunk of the ship fell on my head and made a cut which I noticed later because of the blood. Isted and the sergeant-major, two black men, are staggering in the murk. Wreckage goes on falling for a long time. We collect lifebelts and chuck the raft over ...

I have been shouting 'Anybody hurt?' 'Anybody left forward?' and now I hear somebody yelling. There is a biggish fire amidships, spreading. Then I locate Gilbert [Randall] swimming about (I imagine I locate Ol too) and Gilbert after shouting locates Mark somewhere forward and says he is not too good.

I call the sergeant-major who has climbed back on board and is cutting a boat loose and we go forward for Mark (there was an interlude before this when I picked up a Tommy-gun with the idea that I mustn't leave my arms behind. I also poked about for my battledress and leather jerkin, but without collecting either of them).

When we go for Mark I notice that blood has been pouring down my right leg, also from my head, blinding one eye. I think I am hit in the left shoulder, but nothing hurts and I have no idea how the wounds came.

The sergeant-major, who is splendid, comes along and we crawl past the fire, balancing awkwardly on torn, up-ended plates but getting there in the end. We find a black man with black hair, who is unrecognizable as Mark, huddled and bleeding from the head. He says he thinks he can move, and the sergeant-major gets busy on a cradle. I hail G who is now in a boat, then find myself liable to pass out, owing I suppose to loss of blood. Rather than leave two inert bodies to be got over the high bulwark, I tell the sergeant-major I will send a party up, scramble somehow overboard and slide down a rope.

I am very thirsty and have salvaged a water-bottle. Almost but not quite pass out on the floorboards, where I lie for a minute looking up at little soft white clouds, thinking of larches at Merrimoles and feeling in an unreal way that this is what it means to get into trouble at last. A Greek is in the boat shivering with shock. He maddens me and I send him aft. I also bawl out one of the dozy sailors who turns up smoking a cigarette ...

I tell G to take us ashore, which is a shorter distance than it was, the ship having drifted. I can get out and wade ashore on my own but feel weak and lie down beside a screaming, scalded Greek on a rock like a sea-urchin's back. Once more the sky and the little clouds and a dream-like feeling.

Nance [Caccia] looks fierce in a bust-bodice with blood on her cheek. I tell her about Ol [her brother] but I think she knows already. There are about eight of us stretched on the white rock with the boat burning seventy yards away and the S.A.A. [small arms ammunition] going off continuously like a Chinese feast ... Huge faces loom from all angles offering whisky, which I refuse, and water, of which I drink a good deal.

Then someone says the ship is going to blow up, which I say is nonsense, but sure enough it does while we are all being lugged over the tufts of prickly low scrub by kind people trying hard not to be clumsy. I think there must have been some of our H.E. in the stores.

To the people on shore the attack seemed appallingly sudden: they could do nothing except watch helplessly as the ship burst into flames. But then, with immense courage (for they knew that the wreck was almost certain to blow up) Harold Caccia and Norman Johnstone rowed out in a small boat to rescue the wounded. The Assistant Naval Attaché had been severely injured in the legs, and although conscious could take no active part in the rest of the escape. Of the four men who had been on the bridge three, including Oliver Barstow, were never seen again. It was only by a miracle that the fourth, Mark Norman, was blown clean off the bridge and on to the deck below. Though badly wounded, he survived and recovered. Peter was wounded more seriously than his own narrative suggests: when Norman Johnstone found him he thought he was dead—a blackened bundle streaked from head to foot with blood. He must have been unconscious for several minutes, and he suffered three bomb-lacerations, in head, shoulder and thigh.

Within a few minutes of the attack the *Kalanthe* sank, a blazing wreck, taking with it almost everything that the survivors possessed. With wonderful courage and skill the women in the party did what they could for the wounded: there was only one trained nurse present—Joan Stavridi—but Nancy Caccia and Doreen Blunt had worked for the Red Cross in Athens, and somehow they managed without medical supplies of any kind. They had no drugs or disinfectant, and for bandages they had to tear their shirts into strips. Their most difficult casualty was the scalded Greek sailor who had lost most of his skin and moaned so persistently that they debated whether they should give him one of the knock-out drops, or suicide pills, which had been salvaged.

In a letter to her parents written ten days later Nancy gave a graphic account of the disaster from the shore-party's point of view. During the attack itself she crouched in the cave with the children. Then

I ran and ran, but my legs were wobbly like a dream. The boat was drifting and on fire, and the sea all round full of black wreckage. I could see Harold getting into a small boat and going out ... I went on down to the rocks to where the wounded were coming in and asked someone, I don't know who, if they had seen Ol. No. I was feeling sicker and sicker. Some badly burnt Greeks were brought ashore, blackened, with skin hanging in strips off their arms and hands ... Then Mark Norman was lifted out pitch black, covered in blood and sea water, but speaking lucidly. Peter appeared also pitch black and streaming with blood, but giving orders and sitting up, looking skinny and shivering.

Harold and Gilbert then came back from the boat where they had been and I asked them for the last time, and they shook their heads, so I went on with the wounded after that. We had nothing to even begin to clean them with, so I took off my blouse and ran to and fro sluicing sea water over them to wash the black out of the wounds and see what was what ... Peter had a wound in his leg, bleeding profusely, and another small one in his shoulder. We tied them up with various bits of underclothes and things. Actually neither was bad, though they looked unpleasant and he lost a lot of blood and suffered from shock. Later I found a two-inch gash in his head, but that was not as deep or serious as I feared. We got him to lie down and keep covered up with coats, with difficulty, whilst he kept reiterating: 'Is Mark getting the BEST ATTENTION?' as though I had not called in the best Harley Street man I should have ...

As the sun set a single small boat came across from Kimolos, and Graham Sebastian, who had been the Consul General in Athens, with great resource went back with its pilot and collected some more small craft, which ferried the survivors across to the larger island. There, providentially, was a new but unequipped hospital built of stone; and into this empty building the wounded were carried, up a steep hill. 'I shiver a good deal, probably from shock,' Peter wrote in his journal afterwards:

> My leg hurts a bit. Nance is fine. Try not to think about Ql. Reach Kimolos. Get shifted on to camp beds which are carried uphill under the first stars by gangs of kindly Greeks ... Lance-Corporal Turkhud gives me his pipe and the sergeant-major his tobacco and I eat a bit of bread and get half washed and my wounds dressed (head, shoulder, leg.). Sleep.

Somehow remembering that the telegraph lines to Crete were routed through the island of Siros, Graham Sebastian found to his amazement and relief that he could still get a message through. Thus news of the attack reached the British authorities in Crete, and on the next night but one a party including a military doctor was dispatched in a caique to the rescue.

Among the islanders of Kimolos morale fluctuated sharply. Rumours were rife—that the Germans were mopping up the islands one by one; that they would reach Kimolos at any moment; that they were about to bomb the pretty little white village flat. Not surprisingly, one faction of the castaways was in favour of trying to find a boat which would take them to Turkey and of risking internment there, rather than simply sit and wait to be captured; but Peter, characteristically, opposed this plan on the grounds that it amounted to running away, and Harold Caccia agreed that even for the civilians such a course could offer little chance of success. Hobbling about on a crutch cut for him by the sergeant-major from the branch of an olive tree, and wearing a pair of Oliver's shorts, Peter rallied the remains of the service personnel and insisted that they would all get out safely.

The relief expedition from Crete arrived on the second morning, but once again the party was pinned down by having only a very slow ship at its disposal. The master of the caique said that he would be able to reach

Crete in one night only if the south wind was not blowing; and the first time they set out, with the wounded jammed down among the boat's ribs, the south wind immediately arose and the skipper refused to go on. The casualties were carried painfully back up to the little hospital, but Captain Forrest-Hay, the army doctor, told the skipper that they must sail the next night, whatever the weather, as the wounded could not wait any longer for proper treatment.

The next evening they set off again, but once they were off the south coast of Milos the head-wind again sprang up and the master refused to proceed. His passengers then asked him if he could not turn half-left, across the wind, and make for the volcanic island of Santorini, where they could lie up for another day. The man refused, whereupon he was ordered, more or less at gun-point, to do as he was told. Only then did the wretched fellow admit the reason for his inability to go to Santorini: he had never been there, and did not know how to find the island.

While the argument proceeded, the ship had been sailing in a circle, and presently two R.N.V.R. officers, who had been picked up suffering from shell-shock in the Piraeus, volunteered to find Santorini on their own. They proposed to sail for two hours with the Pole Star dead astern and then to turn hard to port and see what happened. Since, short of turning back, there was virtually no alternative, Harold Caccia insisted that the plan be held to, and the voyage proceeded with the two officers in navigational control; in the middle of the night, however, Nancy, who was lying awake in the deck-house, heard the men arguing urgently with each other about which was north and which south, and she began to wonder whether they were not suffering from a worse degree of shock than had been apparent. In any case, it was too late to change the plan yet again, and, after some persuasion, on they went.

At last, to everyone's immense relief, they suddenly saw a spurt of fire in the lightening darkness dead ahead, and a moment later realized that it was the volcano of Santorini spouting flame. They reached the island just as dawn was breaking and sailed safely into the shelter of the towering cliffs, which offered the best possible protection from low-level air attacks.

In the anchorage they found a Greek coaster, and this took them on to Crete, together with a mass of Greek refugees. They completed the last leg of the voyage with no alarms, and from Crete the wounded, the women and the children went on to Alexandria aboard the destroyers *Havoc* and *Hotspur*, accompanied (though they did not know it) by the entire gold reserves of the Greek banks.

In Egypt the ill-fated Yak expedition was wound up. Norman Johnstone took the main party back to England, but Peter stayed on for a few weeks, first recuperating and then once again spending profitable time with A Force. He was pleased to find *The Flying Visit* prominently displayed in a Cairo bookshop, and he astonished officials of the Egyptian Government when he politely refused their request that he should write the life of King Farouk. He might, they repeatedly assured him, name any fee he liked, and they could not understand how anybody could be so indifferent to proffered riches.

Afterwards Peter was several times criticized for the part he had played in the débâcle: his commando force, it was insinuated, should never have taken its explosive and demolition equipment on board the *Kalanthe* in the first place (although it seems certain that the ship would have sunk almost as rapidly even if no explosive had been present). It was suggested, also, that there should not have been anybody on board at the time of the attack: if the whole party had been ashore, the ship would still have been sunk, but no lives would have been lost. But this argument ignored the fact that the Assistant Naval Attaché had—rightly— ordered steam to be kept up to give manœuvrability in the event of an attack, and that the Greek crew could hardly be left unprotected.

Criticism came easily from anybody who had not been involved; yet the fact was that at no stage of the expedition did Peter behave in anything but a sensible and courageous manner. To the other members of the Yak mission he was a perfect leader—calm, optimistic, funny, endowed with altogether extraordinary endurance, able to go for long periods without sleep, to drive huge distances, and to ignore all physical discomfort. It was sheer bad luck first that his original task proved an impossible one, and then that he should reach Greece when the situation was already hopeless; and yet, in spite of all the difficulties, the morale of the little unit had been sky-high throughout their operation.

It was a long time before Peter came to terms with Oliver's death and ceased to reproach himself for it. At the end of her letter home Nancy wrote:

> Peter is always telling me how tremendously Ol was enjoying his time in Greece, and how good he was at everything he had to do, calm, efficient, reliable, cautious, and very brave. Peter misses him terribly. They all loved him ... I am sure you couldn't find a happier group in the whole army.

Peter's physical wounds healed quickly, and when he arrived back in London he seemed unimpaired by the experience. To Joan Bright, who was running the Commander-in-Chief's Special Information Centre in the War Office, he appeared exactly the same as always. In her book *The Inner Circle* she wrote:

> He walked in as imperturbably as he had walked out of M.I. (R) for Namsos that evening many months ago. It was always good to see his square face with its wide smile and to straighten out one's own fevers and uncertainties against his calm acceptance of events and tolerance of human frailty. He was a four-square, basic, solitary sort of person, immune to luxury, to heat or to cold, with a rock-like quality that made him the most staunch of friends and a kindness which made him the least vindictive of enemies.

12

Strategic Deception

For the rest of 1941 Peter was again becalmed in London, running the School of Street Fighting in Battersea. In a gigantic heap of bomb-ruins he devised an excellent scenario for urban warfare; visiting officers were delighted by the precision with which his demonstration squad ferreted the supposed enemy out of their blasted strongholds, and by his own immaculate appearance. Also, by a typical stroke, he took the pigeon-shooting in Holland Park, where Holland House was still owned by Lord Ilchester, father of his friend John Fox-Strangways; and he and some brother-officers once shot over a hundred pigeons there in a day. Yet he was never happy while stationed in London: he would far rather be abroad, at close grips with the enemy.

His presence in London meant that he could once more take an interest in affairs at *The Times*, but there, too, events took a disagreeable turn when, in November 1941, Geoffrey Dawson was suddenly dismissed and replaced as Editor by Robin Barrington-Ward. Peter never got on nearly as well with B-W as he had with Dawson; neither properly understood the other—a failure of communication epitomized by an incident later in the war, when Peter suggested that it would be an excellent means of deceiving the Germans if *The Times* were to print false but carefully planned and contrived items of news. To B-W such an idea was unthinkable and downright dishonest: to Peter, B-W's refusal to try it was thoroughly unpatriotic.

It was Wavell who came to Peter's rescue. At the start of 1942 he was Commander-in-Chief of the Allied Forces in the South-West Pacific, and from his headquarters in Java, at the beginning of January, he sent an urgent request to the War Office for staff officers with knowledge of the Far East. On hearing that Peter was available, he sent a personal signal to the Chief of the Imperial General Staff: SHOULD BE GLAD OF PETER FLEMING AS EARLY AS POSSIBLE FOR APPOINTMENT MY STAFF. At once Peter began preparing to depart, but he fell victim to an infuriating series of delays and changes of plan, some of which — when he eventually did leave England six weeks later — he listed in his diary:

1. W.O. [War Office] signal to Wavell offering six officers with alleged Far East qualifications.
2. 8.1.42 A.W. [Wavell] replies 'Send P.F. quickly'.
3. W.O. wire back what appointment, and does he mean quickly or slowly?
4. A.W. says he means quickly and gives indication of job ...
5. Told I am leaving my Liberator on Jan 23.
6. Sent down to Farnborough for an oxygen test ...
7. Not Jan 23, Jan 26.
8. Not Jan 26; not before Jan 31.
9. Rumour that they have to train the Liberator crew in night-flying, for which the weather is unpropitious.
10. Further unmotivated postponements, until at last we troop down to Bournemouth on Feb. 8.
11. We are weighed, haphazardly fitted out with fur-lined clothes, helmets, masks, boots, silk gloves and gauntlets, Mae Wests, parachutes and flat things which you wet and put inside your boots to generate heat ... Typical security tycoons put on an unnecessary act and take away our identity cards. I get my secret papers sand-wiched between inflammable stuff that looks like flattened ginger-snaps ... Off to tea (the Last Supper, someone says) in a distant mess. I ring and just manage to get through and say 'I'm off' when they announce we are postponed twenty-four hours.

Back to the field, where the doctor shows us prosily over the plane, a bit of a black hole lined with mattresses. In the dusk out-side I and the two G-2s for Wavell are told to stand down: we are being replaced by tank spares ... So we go angrily back to a taxi-less London on a slow, late train.

Now we are booked on *Bangor*, a flying boat via West Africa, due to leave on the fourteenth, but soon postponed to the eighteenth. This means civilian clothes, changing back my passport from Officer to Government Official, and — even when one does start — endless possibilities of further delays before one even reaches Cairo, where there is probably another Priorities Board ... The whole thing had been like China:

'The camels will come tomorrow.'

'The camels will come next week.'

'The camels have no intention of coming. Their teeth are bad, they cannot march.'

'It is not true that their teeth are bad. They will come on the second of next month, after the wedding of the owner's daughter.' And so on.

It is a golden rule of travelling to make sure that whoever is in charge of your means of transportation is not less keen than you are on your reaching your destination.

Maddened by all these delays, he decided to go—as he had in 1941—by sea; and eventually, on February 13th, he really did leave. 'The last, I hope, of about fifteen farewells to Merrimoles, where my departures have become part of the routine of life,' he wrote in his diary:

A lovely morning sky: frozen snow crackling in the old road. England's fortunes feel, to her inhabitants, very low today ... Singapore is falling, we are still appealing against the light in Libya, and only an almost continuous series of undetected [he meant unsolved] murders keeps the British public in heart ... People lunching at Quaglino's were, however, keeping a stiff upper lip. A dreadful lot of shits—except, of course, at one's own table.

That same day Jonathan Cape published *A Story to Tell*, a collection of Peter's short stories. Several of them dated from the beginning of his literary career: written between 1930 and 1933, they reflected facets of his life and travels, and their backgrounds—Scottish shooting lodges, country-house theatricals, Central American revolutions—closely matched his own. There were also three pieces written in 1936, among them *A Tent in Tibet*. In a typically self-deprecating introduction he drew attention to their various faults, concluding: 'They amount, I am afraid, only to cheap melodrama; but perhaps even cheap melodrama will provide an acceptable distraction in these days of expensive tragedy.' Whatever its shortcomings, the book was at least a means of keeping his name before the public, and he was glad to hear it reported in brisk demand at Hatchard's bookshop in Piccadilly.

He took the train to Glasgow, and there joined the aircraft-carrier *Formidable*. On board he unexpectedly made a congenial new friend in the person of Admiral Sir James Somerville, who was taking passage to the Far East. Peter recorded in his journal the day he went on board: 'He gave me a drink and talked with ardour about Joan B [Bright], who has clearly made a big hit with him. He then talked most sensibly about deception, by means of which he claims to have got all his Mediterranean convoys, except one, three days' grace east of Gibraltar. A most charming and impressive man.'

The flight deck of the aircraft-carrier, with its bridge to one side and its angular smoke-stack, reminded Peter of a production he had seen at the Kamerny Theatre in Moscow in 1933. But he was greatly impressed by the efficiency with which the ship was run, and listed the differences between it and most units of the Home Forces:

1. Officers and men are all here all the time.

2. Instantaneous intercom throughout the organization by ship's wireless. No nonsense about 'He's gone to his dinner,' etc.

3. Apparently very little bumf.

4. Administration seems to be laid on & not to interfere with practically everything else.

5. Today is (I should think) the first day in the last four months during which I haven't heard anyone talk about either food or the price of drink; because the first is excellent & very well served & the second is dirt cheap ...

6. Security is first class.

The *Formidable* sailed before dawn on February 17th, and Peter was soon absorbed in the ship's routine. On the 20th he wrote in his diary a fine description of three Albacores (strike and reconnaissance aircraft) returning from a mission and landing on the wet, pitching deck through squalls of rain.

That same day (although he did not know it) the job towards which he was sailing almost disappeared. From his headquarters in Java, Wavell wrote to Joan Bright: 'We have lost the battle here by a month or six weeks, I think ... I fear Peter Fleming will reach me too late, but I am sure he will find a job in China or Burma.' Even if Peter had known how bad the situation in the Pacific had become, he could have done nothing to alter his own trajectory. As it was, he gladly accepted the routine of ship's life, spending much time on the bridge swapping yarns with Somerville. On February 24th he reported: 'Today the Admiral told me stories without stopping for ¾ of an hour. He is a born raconteur, not a professional one.' The Admiral was equally delighted to have a congenial companion: another of Joan Bright's regular correspondents, he wrote to her on February 25th:

Peter and I hold much converse on the bridge, which he inhabits to a large extent. I tell him stories and he tells me that I ought to write a book. Why should authors be so keen on other people writing books? I'd do my best to discourage them. He has some very interesting and amusing stories about his varied experiences, and is damn good company. There's no one else really bright on board.

One evening a rumour came round that a German tanker had left the Azores, and amid great excitement the whole convoy turned about to pursue it. This meant that they would reach Freetown, in Sierra Leone, later than Peter had been hoping, but somehow he did not seem to mind. 'I should be fuming and fretting,' he noted, 'but a wholly discreditable animal fatalism governs my blameless, negative, animal life.' Rather than worry, he enjoyed himself observing the members of the crew, not least a cook who, one evening before Action Stations, ran round and round the flight deck 'under derisive cheers from its more crowded points. He didn't run very fast or very well, but he is a man of great moral courage.'

Another day one of the aircraft slithered over the side of the carrier as it was taking off, and the pilot had to be rescued. As they were closing the splodge of bright green dye that marked his position, a sailor beside Peter cried: 'There's the bastard's fucking head!'—which made him reflect that 'if foul language is used as a kind of quaint and amiable patois, it loses all its force as invective: for if the wretched boy in the sea had been a German, the sailor could have said nothing more.' It was a measure of Peter's naivety that, at the age of thirty-four, he found such language remarkable. By no stretch of the imagination could he be said to have led a sheltered life, for in his travels he had repeatedly exposed himself to every sort of risk and associated with people from every level of society. Yet the fact remained that at home his upbringing and life had been essentially aristocratic: he had scarcely ever dealt with members of what was then still known as the working class, and he was quite unused to their vernacular. This state of affairs was by no means entirely to his liking: as he had confided to Mike Calvert in Kent, he often wished that he could cross social boundaries more easily; but his shyness, reinforced by a natural fastidiousness, denied him any such ease of communication.

The war had a slight but noticeable effect on his language. In peacetime he never resorted, either in speech or in writing, to even the mildest form of obscenity, but the relentless pressure of service vulgarity did occasionally induce him to use words like 'bloody' and 'bugger'. Yet not even in the army was he ever known to tell a dirty story: not because he was prudish or disapproved of salacity—simply because dirty stories did not interest him.

On the evening of February 27th he went down with a temperature of 105°, but it proved to be only a recurrence of the malarial fever to which he fell prey from time to time, and after a night sweating in the ship's sick-bay he fully recovered. Next day he went for a flight in an Albacore, which he thoroughly enjoyed. 'Landing,' he observed typically, 'you can't see what's happening, but I had no qualms.'

The *Formidable* reached Freetown in the early morning of March 1st, and he went ashore in search of an air-passage to Accra and Cairo. He was carrying a letter, signed by a Major-General at the War Office, which proclaimed that he was travelling at the personal request of General Sir Archibald Wavell for urgent duty, and that he should be allowed to 'proceed without let or hindrance by the speediest means'; and this had a beneficial effect on the local movements officer, who promised him a flight within two days. He was oddly touched by a little scene which took place that afternoon when he went out to bathe in a cove: a posse of small boys, though much frightened by an Alsatian that was with his party, washed his feet with sea-water out of bottles and tried to make him buy model canoes. When he refused several requests from one of them, the boy complained: 'Master, you let me down. All de time you let me down.'

On March 3rd Peter duly got a passage in a Douglas U.S. Army bomber—a troop-carrier which took him via Marshall Field in Liberia to Accra on the Gold Coast. 'The two long metal benches down the sides remind me of a cafeteria,' he wrote, 'by reason of the dish-like depressions designed to receive each piece of cannon fodder.' Staccato entries in his diary recorded the uncomfortable progress of the next few days:

4.3.42 A v. hot night coughing and dreaming. Strange dream of Archie Rose in the stables at Pitt House during an air raid warning ... Took off 0715 in (to our horror) a troop-carrier like yesterday's completely unventilated save for a blow-hole in the lavatory. So we fly at about 1000 feet and sweat like pigs. Landed Lagos 0900 & took off 1000. A quorum of disappointed passengers failed to displace us ... I *am* in luck, though the next three days are going to be bloody uncomfortable.

5.3.42 Wrong. It isn't too bad with only a few passengers. We flew up over the jungles and came down on scrubby desert at Kano, well remembered and adequately described in notes which are now at the bottom of the Aegean ... We have picked up two (South

African?) airmen, one of whom has a five-months old cheetah (as he believes) but possibly an ocelot serval I shd have said ... A very handsome and endearing little [creature], it clung to its master when the engines started up & hid its fierce head under his chin. Soon after that it unhappily began to shit at frequent intervals & was banished to the lavatory, which I judge it has long since rendered untenable.

6.3.42 Khartoum, then Wadi Seidona ... At supper an intelligent-looking Free Frenchman, who, when the talk turned to China & I said I had been in the N.W. in 1935, said: 'Ah, about the time Fleming and Maillart made their journey.' I turning out to be Fleming, the Americans became more respectful. Hook [another officer] and I gatecrashed the club and got a game of squash, which seems touch-wood to have killed my cough.

7.3.42 Took off [for Cairo] at 0800. I slept for 2½ hours. (What a tremendous difference it makes being able to lay on great chunks of oblivion in the air) ... Nineteen days since I sailed from Glasgow— exactly the same time as last year.

In Cairo he was grounded for a week, but again put the time to good use by burrowing through the files of A Force and learning all he could about the theory and practice of deception. The city, he found, appealed to him no more than it had a year ago:

Cairo still (and unavoidably) a pretty good disgrace. They nominally start work earlier in the afternoon, but the place remains idle, heart-less and unreal, *mouvementé* but not gay ... Noises as before: barrel organ plays Lambeth Walk at 0700 outside Shepheards [Hotel], kites scream mildly about the roofs, motor horns never stop.

On March 14th he flew on down the Persian Gulf. His destination now was Delhi, for Wavell, withdrawing from Java and the Pacific, had established his new headquarters in India. On the 16th Peter stayed in the fort at Sharjah and collected shells on the beach ('a forgotten but potent pleasure'). Next day in Karachi he noted that 'the end of a journey has always this advantage over its beginning: that periodicals, almost wherever found, are always readable and often absorbing.' A flying boat took him on to Gwalior, and he completed the last stage of the journey by train. After 'four hours of rigid self-control on the telephone' he got through to General Headquarters in Delhi to warn them that he was coming—with the result that, when he at last arrived very tired and dirty, he was met by a resplendent sergeant and by a note from Wavell inviting him to stay in his own house. His marathon trip thus ended agreeably in unexpected pomp and luxury.

Wavell himself was in Calcutta at the time, but he returned to Delhi a few days later and on March 26th wrote to Joan Bright:

> Peter Fleming is staying ... he is full of ideas, I don't quite know yet how I shall use him but next time I go to Burma, probably next Monday, I shall take him with me and leave him there to get on to Chungking and have a look round. I think he has a hankering to start something in some wide open spaces and also has some ideas on enemy deception worked from China. So he may go on a visit there but will come back here, I hope. He's an attractive person.

As in his relationship with Carton de Wiart, Peter discovered in Wavell a man whom he immediately liked and respected, and who, moreover, shared many of his own characteristics: deeply modest, diffident about his own abilities yet of great moral strength, widely read, taciturn to a degree that many people found disconcerting, Wavell spoke—when he did utter—in a very slow drawl, and was always wary of showing any sign of emotion. He and Peter were thus naturally tuned to each other's wavelength; they understood each other well, and, as a mutual friend remarked, found the long silences which punctuated their conversations intensely satisfying.

Their reconnaissance trip to Burma began on March 29th, when, in company with General Alexander, they flew to Dum Dum, outside Calcutta. There Peter was stuck for the rest of the day, waiting for another plane to arrive—'a hot, listless afternoon with the faint, faraway, quite unmistakable smell of defeat in the air.' The Generals continued on their own to Chittagong, Mandalay and finally Maymyo, the seat of the Burmese Government. Peter, following later in a Blenheim, was somehow reported to have been shot down, and when he finally drove up to Government House in Maymyo, Wavell 'gave an almost emotional grunt, which touched me'.

Government House, with its 'idle and ridiculous courtiers', struck Peter as exceptionally unpleasant. A far more stimulating meeting was with Orde Wingate, who within a year was to achieve legendary fame as the inventor and leader of the long-range columns which penetrated far behind the Japanese lines into enemy-held Burma. 'A rude, proud, good man,' Peter recorded, 'almost too well prepared to tell any general where he gets off. I should say no sense of humour. Immense self-confidence.'

Next day, April 4th, he set out alone for Chungking, still the seat of the Chinese Government, locked in its apparently endless war with Japan.

As he drove out to Lashio and took off at dusk in a Dakota, his mind slipped pleasantly back to the journey that he and Celia had made up the Burma Road in 1938, and then much further back into the mists of memory:

> The lights were out in the plane, and it felt soothing and romantic passing through the twilit border air. We kept only a few hundred feet above the passes in the mountains; we were not more and some-times less than level with the peaks. More than ever they looked like folded dragons' wings. The darker it got, the more you saw of bush or jungle fires, generally small broken circles of lively flames, the same sort of things, I suppose, as the gorse fires one watched on the Ridge at night from the dormitory windows at Durnford ... For some reason I felt extremely happy.

No record survives of his first wartime visit to Chungking, but it seems certain that he made fruitful contacts in the intelligence field, for he returned repeatedly to the Chinese capital during the next three years and carried out a vital liaison role there. Back in Delhi, meanwhile, his fertile mind dwelt more and more on deception, and within Wavell's head-quarters he took over the small section known as G.S.I. (d) whose role was to devise deception programmes and put them into practice.

After the war he defined the object of strategic deception as—

> to make your enemy take—or refrain from taking—a particular course of action; and thereby to improve your chances of defeating him. Merely to gull him—to implant in his mind a false picture of the true situation—is only half the battle: it is not enough, even, that he should 'do something about it'. He must do what you want him to do.

Peter's enemy was Japan, and for the next three years he applied himself with energy, humour and positively oriental guile to the problem of bending the strategy of Tokyo to the Allies' will. His main theatre of operations was Burma, through which the victorious Japanese advanced almost to the gates of India early in 1942, and from whose jungle-covered mountains they were not dislodged until the middle of 1945; but the tentacles of his intrigue reached out to many other countries in the Far East, including Malaya, Thailand, Vietnam and China.

From the start Wavell was a keen exponent of the value of deception as an extra weapon, and one evening after dinner he expatiated to Peter and to Bernard Fergusson (another formidable soldier who was to make his name as one of Wingate's Chindits) about the classic case of

Meinertzhagen's haversack. Colonel Richard Meinertzhagen was an intelligence officer on the staff of General Allenby in Palestine in 1917, and as part of the preparations for the third Battle of Gaza he had ridden slowly across the Turkish front at Beersheba. When some of the defenders opened fire on him, he slumped in his saddle, pretending to have been hit, wheeled his horse and galloped away. From his stricken figure there fell the celebrated haversack—in which, together with a large sum of money, was a collection of documents carefully contrived to suggest that Allenby's main assault was to be directed on Gaza, whereas he was in fact planning to attack Beersheba. The Turks swallowed the bait and in consequence were defeated.

Wavell's discussion of how he and Peter might repeat Meinertzhagen's ruse lasted until 1 a.m., and its direct outcome was Operation Error— the first live mission which Peter undertook in the Far East. The aim was to persuade the Japanese that Wavell himself had been involved, and injured, in the Allied retreat from Burma; and at the same time to slip them a whole batch of false information about Allied strengths and dispositions. The bait was to be a brief-case of Wavell's filled with apparently important secret documents and abandoned in the path of the advancing Japanese army. Peter's role was first to assemble the contents of the briefcase, inventing whatever seemed appropriate, and then to dump it at a point where it would have the best chance of being found.

He set about the task with enthusiasm and imagination, persuading Wavell to part not only with some private letters but also with a well-loved photograph of his daughter Pamela. To add further verisimilitude, Peter forged a letter ostensibly written by Joan Bright in the War Cabinet Office in London, to Wavell, skilfully weaving into its chatter a number of apparently indiscreet (but in fact fictitious) remarks about plans and movements of important people. So cunningly was this document contrived that Wavell later wrote to Joan disclaiming all responsibility for it. If Peter pretended that he (Wavell) had composed the letter, he wrote, 'the truth was not in him. It was his work entirely, except that I think I cut out some pomposities ... I am surprised he had the nerve to show it to you.'

Armed with his bundle of deception, Peter set off from Delhi for Burma at 6.30 in the morning of April 29th, accompanied by Wavell's A.D.C., Captain Sandy Reid-Scott of the 11th Hussars. They flew to Dum Dum, but had to sit about until next morning before going on to Shwebo. There Peter unfolded the plan to General Alexander: but he, though in principle approving, had too many urgent problems on his mind to take a close interest. The Allied retreat was proceeding so fast that it was already too late to use the setting originally projected for dumping the brief-case—the landing ground at Mandalay—so a new one was chosen at the Ava Bridge, which crossed the Irawaddy at Sagaing, some fifty miles south of Shwebo.

Allied troops were at that moment retreating across the bridge, but it was due to be blown up at 1900 hours that evening. Therefore Peter, whose aim was to drop the brief-case somewhere beyond it, had to reach it as soon as he could. Having enlisted the help of Mike Calvert, who happened to be in the area commanding a composite battalion, and having acquired a Ford Mercury, a jeep and a spare driver, he set out as fast as possible for the south, picking his way through a mass of Chinese motor transport coming the other way.

Arriving at the headquarters of 17 Division in Sagaing a few minutes before seven, he discovered that the Allied withdrawal across the bridge would be completed by 8 o'clock, and that the bridge would be blown by midnight, at the latest. As he had only an hour of daylight left, he drove straight on across the bridge and selected a suitable place to crash the Ford. 'The situation on the further bank appeared most favourable,' he later wrote in his official report—a document which, though couched mainly in military language, was frequently infiltrated by typical Fleming phrases:

> At approximately 19.30 hours, having made skidmarks to the best of our ability, we drove the car over a small but steep embankment on the right hand side of the road SAGAING–MANDALAY, some 400 yards from the bridgehead. The results were not spectacular. The car flounced down the embankment without overturning, crossed a cart track, and plunged into a small nullah, at the bottom of which it came to rest with its engine still ticking over self-righteously. We let the air out of one front tyre, punctured the other, and removed the ignition key. The car is, or was, clearly visible from the road and about thirty yards away from it. Being in good condition and the right way up, it
>
> (a) is more likely to attract the enemy than most of the wrecks he finds along the roads of Burma.
> (b) has the appearance of having been abandoned in a hurry.

In the boot, besides Wavell's brief-case, they left a service dress jacket-ribbons with the Commander-in-Chief's medal on the breast, a valise containing a blanket marked 'Captain A. Reid-Scott, 11th Hussars', one blanket and three novels from the Shwebo club library. They withdrew across the bridge at 20.00 hours and drove off in the jeep, whose driver supposed they had been setting booby traps.

Two spans of the bridge were successfully blown at about 11.30 that night, and at first light the next morning Peter returned to the west bank, to find enemy shells bursting between one and two miles away, but no sign of activity immediately beyond the river. This state of affairs led him to conclude that there was a good possibility that no casual passers-by had interfered, or would interfere, with the car until the Japanese found it. He flew back to Delhi satisfied that the mission had gone reasonably well, but feeling at the same time that it had all been 'rather tame'.

In a note scribbled on the end of Peter's report, Wavell fully supported his modest claim that Error had not been bungled. 'Good,' he wrote, 'very well carried out.' And Brigadier Walter (Bill) Cawthorn, the Director of Military Intelligence, to whom Peter was directly responsible, endorsed the Commander-in-Chief's verdict. Yet Error, like almost all deception operations, left tantalizingly unsettled the one question to which an answer would have been most welcome: *did it work*? Although Peter attached to his report an appendix devoted to an attempt at answering this question, he could reach no firm conclusions. It was, he argued, fairly certain that the Japanese had found the brief-case, and probable that its contents would have reached the Japanese intelligence service. A much more difficult question was whether or not the deception had worked. 'Did the enemy see through the documents?' Peter asked rhetorically:

> More than 80 per cent of the documents, personal and official, were genuine; the important minority of fakes were carefully concocted and, being mostly couched in allusive or otherwise slightly indefinite terms, were almost, if not quite, proof against definitive exposure. In other words the forgeries, though they included suggestions which may be disbelieved by the enemy, contained no statement of fact which he can disprove. In the circumstances it is considered that the documents were in themselves so persuasive that the enemy, though he may not accept all their implications in full, cannot afford to leave out of his calculations the general trend of the information thus conveyed to him.

In answer to the question: 'Did the enemy see through the ruse itself?' Peter wrote:

> Sherlock Holmes, had he been promptly on the spot, could without difficulty have deduced from the skidmarks and other indications

that there was something fishy about the supposed accident. But it is safe to assume that, long before his Japanese equivalent could have reached the Ava Bridge, large numbers of Dr Watsons had decisively prejudiced all chances of reconstructing the crime.

Summing up, Peter decided that

the worst thing we could come up against would be a German liaison officer at Japanese HQ in Burma who was familiar with the story of MEINERTZHAGEN's haversack. A great deal will depend on at what stage and on what level suspicions are first aroused.

Beneath this final paragraph Wavell added a note:

I always realized this danger, and after Fleming had gone thought I had made a bad mistake in including in the exhibits a paper which connected me with the writing of Allenby's life, but it was too late to recall it ... Any harm done if the Jap decides it was a plant? I don't think so.

All this cautious analysis gives an idea of the care and thoroughness which had gone into the making of the operation: for Error—although the crashing of the car sounds a rather *Boy's Own Paper* exploit—was in fact an important part of Wavell's general plan for saving India. The ingredient of tactical deception—the attempt to make the Japanese think that the Commander-in-Chief had been involved in the retreat from Burma—was relatively unimportant: the vital part of the plan was its strategic implication—the false information in the haversack which might persuade the enemy that Allied strength in India was far greater than in fact it was, and so might make the Japanese pause, giving Wavell the time which he badly needed to regroup and strengthen his forces. He himself made several attempts, both later in the war and after it, to discover how successful the ruse had been; and although he could obtain no proof, he did in 1944 get from Chinese intelligence sources a gratifying report that during the first Burma campaign the Japanese had captured important documents which indicated that India's defensive potential was greater than Tokyo had supposed.

In Delhi Peter established his office in a kind of black hole on the ground floor of one of Lutyens's great red sandstone government buildings. He lived in various places: having stayed with the Wavells for a few weeks, he perched in two other temporary lodgings before settling eventually in the bungalow inhabited by Colonel Jack Tweed, the commander of the Viceregal Bodyguard, and his wife Kath—and there he lived, whenever he was in Delhi, as their grateful guest for the remainder of the war. The routine which he established for himself made few concessions to the Indian climate: he would ride out very early almost every morning (thereby establishing a regular habit, for he had never been a very keen horseman before). At lunch-time, when everyone else retired for a siesta, he would take his sandwiches along to the swimming-pool in the grounds of the Viceroy's House and lie out in the blazing sun. He acquired a long-legged, curly-coated black mongrel named Blondie, which enjoyed giving chase to other riders on his early-morning excursions, and he was looked after by an Indian bearer who—other officers believed—gently but persistently cheated him. In the evenings he was always on the look-out for a game of squash, and whenever circumstances allowed he would go off duck-flighting, borrowing an impounded shotgun from the police, driving out of the city to some near-by *jeel*, and, if necessary, sleeping on the ground so as to catch the morning as well as the evening flight. Whenever he did this (according to a colleague) he would simply make two or three primeval circling movements, like a dog, and go straight to sleep, ignoring the substantial possibility of being bitten by a snake.

He spent much of the rest of the summer of 1942 extending his own knowledge and contacts. In the middle of May he slipped out through the North-West Frontier to Kabul, the capital of Afghanistan. There, in a setting nominally neutral but in fact alive with spies of every colour and description, he cultivated a most useful contact in the American Embassy —a man who had already established a channel of communication with the Japanese. Through him, and through the German Embassy in Kabul, much false information was passed—or in some cases sold—to Tokyo.

It was in China, however, that Peter played his most important role, for his previous experience enabled him to establish an excellent working relationship with General Cheng Kai-min, the Director of Military Intelligence in Chungking, and he became an unofficial but extremely useful liaison officer between the Allied powers and the Chinese Government—a role rendered all the more vital by the fact that the Americans were deeply suspicious of the Chinese and continuously liable to misinterpret their actions. Peter visited Chungking repeatedly and always enjoyed going to the Chinese wartime capital, since he never much cared for India. On one of his trips he recorded in his diary how, squatting under the wing of a Dakota in pouring rain on the airfield at Kunming, he 'shared a tremendous, absolutely foolish joke with the groundstaff coolies ... and realized again with pleasure how great a gulf there is between India and China.' After the war, describing in the *Spectator* how he used to fly from Calcutta to Chungking, he remembered:

> The streets of the two cities provided as vivid a comment as you can find in Asia. Garbage, corruption, poverty, crowds, noise and a steamy climate were common to both. But it was hard, almost, to believe that the Bengalis and the Chinese were members of the same race. The brown men dressed in white looked listless, sullen, foolish, ineffective, miserable; the yellow men dressed in blue, swarming up and down the tortuous, dark grey alleys clinging to the scarred bluffs above the Yangtse and the Kialang, looked exactly the opposite of all those epithets. You felt as if you had landed on another planet—more inconvenient, more expensive, if anything a slightly smellier planet than the one you had left that morning, but a planet (and this was what struck you more forcibly than anything) with a sense of humour.

Chungking provided Peter with the idea for another exercise in deception—Operation Purple Whales, which was inspired by a chance perusal of the minutes of the Joint Military Council. This body sat in Chungking; its proceedings, he wrote in his official report,

> were taken down verbatim, and their discursive, often inconsequent and generally allusive pages produced upon the reader the effect of an overheard conversation. This medium instantly recommended itself as a vehicle for high-grade forgery ... When allusion takes the place of assertion, the forger's victim can be shown (as it were) the intended picture without the opportunity of analysing its component parts; and if his own information or the march of events invalidates that picture, he can still not be *quite* sure what it was that he was meant to see.

Peter's plan was that he should compose a fake record of an imaginary meeting of the Joint Military Council and sell it, via the Chinese, to Japanese intelligence agents. He sent an outline of the project to London, and at the end of April was notified that the Chiefs of Staff had approved the scheme and had asked their Joint Planning staff to prepare an appreciation of what the Allies wanted the Japanese to believe their strategic intentions to be. On May 5th, he received the appreciation, whose five main points included the fact that Britain would be ready to invade the Continent with ten divisions any time after early July, and that the first air raids on Tokyo had been only experimental, so that the Japanese capital could expect far heavier attacks in the future.

This last line had already been adumbrated in the Error documents and was in any case, as Peter pointed out, more propaganda than deception. In an exchange of secret telegrams with London he therefore worked out a revision of the plan.

In the past few weeks communications with China had become difficult, so at the end of May he again went to Kabul, calmly chartering a taxi the whole way from Peshawar and back (a distance of some five hundred miles), to make another reconnaissance of the deception possibilities. These, he reported, were great, but not particularly suited to a document such as he was contemplating for Purple Whales, so he quickly returned to Delhi, having decided that Chungking would be the best place for staging this particular production.

In their final form the thirteen typed pages of the document resembled, as he himself put it, 'an unusually tedious and ill-constructed one-act play'. They purported to be the minutes not of a meeting in Chungking but of a session of the Inter-Allied Conference in Delhi, since this scenario made drafting easier. Yet the final version of the script was not achieved without a number of drastic last-minute changes: as Peter was fast discovering, the path of an international forger was beset by numbers of scarcely foreseeable difficulties and traps.

One serious mistake, which would have exposed the entire document as a fake, survived unnoticed until the penultimate draft. The fictitious conference was supposed to have been held in Delhi on May 31st, and the forged minutes referred both to the first British 1,000-bomber raid on Germany and to the German reprisal raid on Canterbury. The first reference was just all right, for the 1,000-bomber raid had taken place on the night of May 30th, and news of it might conceivably have reached Delhi the following morning; but the second was impossible, for the reprisal raid was launched on the night of May 31st—a few hours after the alleged conference was supposed to have ended. Luckily, an intelligence officer spotted what would have been a disastrous slip in time for the offending references to be removed; but there was, as Peter wrote in his report, no excuse for the mistake 'save that the forger who aims to hoodwink the Combined General Staffs of the Axis Powers needs to work in something more nearly resembling an ivory tower than the accommodation allotted to G.S.I. (d).'

On June 20th, taking the MOST SECRET document with him, Peter set out by train and air for Chungking, where he arrived after dark on the 22nd. Next day he handed the papers, together with a covering letter from Wavell, to General Ho, Chief of the Chinese General Staff, for him to pass them on to Marshal Chiang Kai-shek. But while he waited for a reaction yet another snag threatened the project. The Indian intelligence service intercepted a radio signal from the Japanese Minister in Kabul to Tokyo reporting that General Davidson—one of the leading actors in Peter's script—had been received by the Viceroy in Delhi on May 30th. This perfectly true bit of information had been gleaned from the Court Circular, which, for some inscrutable reason, was still published in the Indian capital, and Peter judged it necessary to advance the date of his theoretical conference from May 31st to May 30th.

The alteration meant that two pages of the script had to be amended and retyped in Delhi—for both paper and typewriter had obviously to be consistent throughout—and the replacements were flown to Chungking. Peter reported afterwards:

> The incident, though as things turned out it added only three or four days' delay, aptly illustrates the danger which the forger runs *as soon as he relates the imaginary to the real*. Purple Whales is thirteen pages long. Practically the only real things in it (apart from the paper on which it was typed ...) were (a) the names of the participants and (b) the date of the conference. Both, as has been shown, gave trouble, and (b) in particular proved almost disastrously intractable.

After a few more days' delay, Chiang Kai-shek personally gave the order that Purple Whales should be transmitted to the Japanese, and Peter heard later that Chinese agents had sold his one-act script to a high-ranking Japanese officer for ten thousand Chinese dollars. Once again, as with Error, it was impossible to gauge what the effect of the document had been; Peter, however, was pleased with the whole operation— first because Chiang Kai-shek had taken it seriously and appeared to understand the potential value of deception, and second because he himself had learned valuable lessons in the course of the project's development.

In a long and closely reasoned discussion of Purple Whales' chances of success, he argued that the Japanese were unlikely to realize that they had bought an expensive forgery:

> Sooner or later suspicion will probably be aroused [by the failure of Allied strategy to conform with the script's predictions]; but not before the gist of the document has had *some* impact on a high level. I do not think it will be easy for the Japanese Service Chiefs to begin to suspect. The idea of using (e.g.) the personality of the Deputy C-in-C in a forgery—a forgery which depicts us bickering with our Allies—is entirely alien to their mentality. We have a number of

senior officers on our side who would be virtually incapable of seeing the point of Purple Whales if it was explained to them; it is safe to assume that their counterparts exist in Tokyo.

This paragraph contains a hint of how well Peter already understood the Japanese mind. Although on the whole he despised it, he gauged its limitations perfectly, and as the months went by, became ever more expert at exploiting them. He consistently amazed his colleagues by the accuracy with which he predicted Japanese reactions.

His own mind ranged ceaselessly over this new form of warfare in which he had accidentally landed, and while he was in Chungking waiting for Chiang Kai-shek to put Purple Whales into action he completed a substantial secret paper entitled 'Total Intelligence'. In this he made out a strong case for creating in London some central organization in which all available intelligence could be pooled for use in time of war. Drawing attention to the large number of existing intelligence agencies, he proposed not that they should all be amalgamated but that there should be created a central pool, perhaps called 'Imperial Information', to which all the others would have access. The paper was perfectly serious in intent; all the same, it contained some typical asides—for example, when the author described what would happen under the existing system in the event of the British Government suddenly wanting to seize the Ruritanian port of San Adolfo. There would, Peter wrote, be an almost total dearth of local knowledge, and by the end of the first week of planning, contact would have been established with the following:

(a) Miss Pink, authoress of *Ruritanian Rampage*: six weeks in the country: anxious to help: easy to take out to lunch: quite useless.

(b) Mr White, archaeologist: spent five years in a marsh 490 miles north-west of San Adolfo: anxious to help: would like to go back to his marsh: might just as well do so.

(c) Professor Scarlett, sociologist, author of *Ruritania Irridenta, the White Guard in Zenda* (illustrated pamphlet dealing with atrocities), etc: many years in the country: took part in triumphal entry to San Adolfo in 1904: expelled from S.A. 1912, re-entered 1922, freedom of city 1925, burnt in effigy 1930, would like to go back there: has no recollection of town being on the railway: anxious to help, but would insist on serving with the Ruritanian forces: worse than useless.

What Peter was clearly hoping—although he did not say so in his text— was that Wavell would become the first post-war head of Imperial

Information. His paper travelled via Wavell's office to London, and there copies of it were printed, one of them finding its way into Room 39 at the Admiralty, where Ian was working as personal assistant to the Director of Naval Intelligence.

In Delhi the immediate result of Purple Whales was that G.S.I. (d) was strengthened and rehoused. The exercise had shown all too clearly that the staff of the section was too small to be safe: it was more by good luck than good planning that serious mistakes had been avoided, and more heads were obviously needed to maintain the increasingly complex intelligence surveillance which Peter's projects demanded. Some heed was also paid to his remarks about an ivory tower, and G.S.I. (d) was rehoused, in slightly less acute discomfort, on the first floor of the head-quarter building.

In August 1942 he began planning a trip to London. Whether he himself suggested it, or whether he was ordered to go by Wavell or by Briga-dier Cawthorn, is no longer clear; but in any case the object of the journey was to confer with the London Controlling Section—the unit which, under Colonel Johnny Bevan, was master-minding deception programmes all over the world. To Peter's chagrin a row broke out about what he was supposed to be doing, mainly because the right messages had failed to reach their destinations. 'But that's not how it will get round,' he wrote in a tense note in his diary on September 8th: 'It'll be "I hear the Chief [Wavell] caught P.F. trying to nip off to London." *Christ* I hate that sort of thing. I wish to God other people wouldn't involve one in these balls-ups. Still, it is something that the Chief sees the point.' His discomfort was greatly increased by a tele-gram from Celia telling him that Roger Pettiward had been killed in the Commando raid on Dieppe. Peter had never enjoyed anyone's company more than he had Roger's in Brazil, and now in his journal he made a fleeting, nostalgic return to the parody language of *Brazilian Adventure*:

> I never saw him since the war began ... always wanted to see him in uniform, knowing that he would look in some way eccentric. He *was* a good and funny chap. You can't write down his humour. Near Goyaz: 'We artists are a sensitive lot and something tells me we've got a flat tyre.' I think it was him, but it may have been me, who, when Neville Priestley kept on finding Spoor and Slots and Pug-marks round our camps in his bogus professional way, saw the trail of a snake in the sand and identified it as the pug-marks of a Raleigh all-steel bicycle.

Four days later, on September 12th, Peter took off on the first of the many hops to London. As he left, Wavell handed him an envelope saying: 'If you have time, I wonder if you'd mind looking through this: but only if you have time. I don't think it's any good.' 'It', Peter wrote in his diary,

> was three thousand words on 'What is Military Genius?' answering an article by Liddell Hart in the *Strand*. Bloody well done and most sensible. I asked if I was supposed to be a better judge of military genius than he was. 'No, but I'm no writer,' he said. He is one of the best and surest users of the English language now practising.

Peter's journey home was protracted by a series of hold-ups, not least in West Africa, where he headed one entry in his diary: *Lagos—The Home of Delay*. But his joy at arriving back in England after an eight-month absence was enhanced by the fact that his return coincided with the opening of the pheasant season, and he managed, between his military appointments, to fit in a few brief excursions into the Oxfordshire fields and woods.

On October 12th he dined in London with General Bernard Paget, Commander-in-Chief of the Home Forces, who sent an enormous car to ferry him to Hammersmith—a move, Peter reflected, 'which was kind though perhaps not good. Not much impressed by his rather Blimpish staff. They appear to have four principal and one subsidiary enemy— the Press, the House of Commons, the War Office, C.L.O. [? Illegible], and finally the Germans, with whom alone they are not in contact.' A week later he was asked to lunch at Chequers, the Prime Minister's country home:

> Winston, wearing a boiler suit, made plans for sending wood blocks up to London whenever cars went 'so that we could sometimes have a fire.' Smuts was there, talking in a high-pitched voice and looking like the wise, shrivelled head of a tribe. I liked his son Japie, who asked permission to go over Germany in a bomber and was instantly refused by Winston.

By the end of October Peter's official business was completed, and while he waited for a passage back to Delhi he snatched a morning's shooting at Turville, not far from Nettlebed. 'Lovely day with the leaf coming off,' he wrote in his diary, 'manœuvring successfully along a steep flank of the Chilterns, same sort of country as at Braziers. We drew for places at the beginning, quite a pre-war atmosphere, killed thirty-six pheasants and some hares before lunch, and when we got back to the house there was C [Celia] in her police uniform with a message that I am off this afternoon. This is the fifth time that I have gone overseas.'

He took off next morning in a Liberator, and spent the eight-hour haul to Gibraltar lying in a 'draughty and surrealist' coffin on top of the freight. He saw Gibraltar for the first time from the rear-gunner's hammock-like seat—'a smaller, whiter, more sudden place than I had imagined it.'

In Cairo he met General Alexander, back in triumph from the desert, where the great battle of El Alamein was in progress and the Germans under Rommel were at last on the run. Alex seemed to Peter 'like a small boy of great character—simple and direct and inquiring, with many curiosities and few inhibitions. I should say a great sense of proportion.' The news of victories in the desert prompted Peter to rehearse again his own feelings about what he was doing: for although he thoroughly enjoyed deception work on an intellectual level, it denied him any chance of joining in the actual fighting and so left him emotionally un-satisfied:

> It really is good news and I skipped away feeling like a million dollars. But it is high time I shot one of our opponents or at least put myself in a position to do so. Roger killed, Robin Gurdon killed, J. Fox [John Fox-Strangways] badly wounded—all sorts of chaps ... and me doing this ungentlemanly stuff far from the heat and dust, and not even getting any training.

Back in Delhi he resumed control of G.S.I. (d); but for him the high-light of that year's end was a tiger-shoot during his Christmas leave in Bastar State. Years later in the *Spectator* he described how, from a *machan* twenty feet up a tree, he shot the one and only tiger of his life:

> It was painfully exciting. The distant brouhaha of drums and horns and savage cries growing steadily louder as the beaters approached: a crash in the undergrowth, and then this monstrous, lovely cat with blazing eyes padding downhill towards me. An easy shot ... It was the beaters ... who ran all the risks and took all the exercise: and though they seemed thoroughly to enjoy the whole thing and were delighted with the result (for they ate the tiger), I felt vaguely Gunga-dinned [out-ployed].

Considering the head and skin of the animal, which he had mounted and which adorned the floor of his study at Merrimoles, he reflected:

Little is left of that splendid animal on which I drew a breathless bead twenty-two years ago. Still ... if I hadn't shot the tiger, nothing would be left of it at all.

The years 1943–45 were the heyday of Peter's career in deception. Under his direction G.S.I. (d) immensely extended its activities and influence and became a valuable weapon in the dogged struggle with the Japanese in the Far East. He was fortunate in securing the enthusiastic and regular support of three exceptional senior officers—first Wavell; then Cawthorn, an Australian who appreciated exactly what he was trying to achieve; and finally Lord Louis Mountbatten, who at the end of 1943 took over from Wavell as Supreme Allied Commander in South-East Asia, when Wavell became Viceroy of India. And yet, in spite of the help he got from the top, the success of the deception programme was largely due to Peter himself—to his imagination, his energy, his sense of humour and his unquenchable optimism. Deceiving the Japanese became an absolute passion. *Has it done any harm to the Japanese?* was the question constantly on his lips, and he imparted some of his own great relish for the job to everyone who worked with him.

In the course of the war his organization was twice reshaped and renamed. In March 1944 it was formally taken over by the headquarters of the Supreme Allied Commander, South-East Asia, and renamed 'D Division'; and in 1945, after Mountbatten had moved his headquarters south to Kandy in Ceylon, D Division was converted into a Command Unit so that it could remain in Delhi, and was rechristened Force 456. By then, however, the name D Division was so well established that it continued in use for the rest of the war. Peter himself remained head of the organization until the end of hostilities, and was in a pleasant position to exploit the independence and slight ambiguity of nomenclature that his unit enjoyed: with one hand, as the head of D Division, he would write an order for the commander of Force 456; and with the other hand, as the commander of Force 456, he would accept the order and go quietly off to do whatever he wanted. The Supreme Commander himself (who much liked him and admired his work) was frequently baffled by his unexplained disappearances.

In March 1943 D Division was greatly strengthened by the arrival of Peter Thorne, the youngest son of General Thorne, for whom Peter had worked in Kent during 1940. Peter Thorne's quick, incisive brain and ready sense of humour made him an ideal anchor-man, and it was he who ran the office whenever his commanding officer slipped off—as he frequently did—to China or some even less mentionable destination. Another invaluable member of the team was André Bicat, in civilian life an artist, who had been sent out to Delhi to take over the development of camouflage, but, realizing that the job was entirely futile, had persuaded Peter to take him on. His task was to create the physical evidence—mock battles, explosions, lights, dummy parachutists, and so on—which Peter's deception schemes demanded.

The secretarial work in the office was done by a team of girls drawn from the families of the headquarters staff, among them Wavell's daughter Joan. The girls found Peter immensely attractive and adored working for him, no matter how strange the requests he might make of them. He required one of them, for instance, to pose as a Wren and to write passionate love-letters to an imaginary boy-friend in Ceylon: it felt, as she afterwards remarked, distinctly odd to pour out her heart to someone who did not exist, to interlard the amorous passages with carefully prepared and apparently indiscreet revelations about military affairs in Delhi, and to know all the time that the letters thus produced would find their way—by a tortuous route which Peter himself had devised—into the hands of the Japanese intelligence service.

Perhaps his greatest asset was the sheer force of his own personality, which enabled him to make direct approaches to the most senior officers, from Wavell and Mountbatten downwards. Generals would stand up—quite instinctively—when he came into the room, and many sought his opinion on their problems as though he himself had been of equivalent rank. The ease with which he moved in the highest military circles naturally made him unpopular with some of the ambitious intelligence officers with whom Delhi was densely populated; but it also made him uniquely successful at getting what he wanted. Whenever a dispute broke out about the priorities which D Division was achieving, the Supreme Commander would back him up unreservedly.

D Division's main means of transmitting information to the Japanese was a small network of secret agents. Many of these were *double*-agents—that is, they had first been hired by the Japanese or by the Germans and were ostensibly still working for them, although in fact they had switched their allegiance to the Allies. Easily the best of Peter's double-agents was a man known as Silver—a Hindu called Bhagat Ram (or sometimes Kishan Chand) who appeared to be giving such devoted service to the Axis powers that he was awarded the Iron Cross—one of Germany's highest military decorations. Silver did indeed perform many services for the Germans and Japanese—among them to smuggle the revolutionary leader Subhas Chandra Bose out of India into Afghanistan, and thence to Europe. But Silver's main allegiance was to Russia, and he served the British only because they were allies of the Soviet Union. Kabul was his favourite hunting ground. He made regular trips there from Delhi, taking with him comprehensive intelligence reports which he pretended he had put together himself from his own network of agents, and which he handed over to the German or Italian legation in the Afghan capital. In fact almost all his information was supplied by D Division, who were able to monitor the radio traffic that went out from Kabul to Berlin and Tokyo and so could check how much of their own material was reaching the enemy headquarters. With care and stealth they gradually enhanced Silver's reputation by feeding him with information of higher and higher priority, and the Germans eventually judged him so valuable that they sent him an extra-powerful radio set so that he himself could transmit directly to the headquarters of the *Abwehr* (intelligence service) in Berlin. At one stage Silver appeared to be doomed, for an Afghan who knew him well spotted him in Delhi in the company of British service personnel. D Division suggested strongly that it would be wise for him not to return to Kabul, thinking that if he did he would certainly be liquidated; but he insisted on going back. Silence fell for nearly five months; then the British heard that Silver had indeed met the Afghan again, but that when the man asked him to dinner he had poisoned his host by slipping a dose of chopped-up tiger-whiskers into his curry.

Another double-agent—less notorious but perhaps more typical—was Owl, an Indian peasant in his late twenties called Adjudya Das. Captured by the Japanese in Singapore as a private in the Indian infantry, he had been perfunctorily trained and parachuted back into India with a Japanese radio set, on which he was to report troop movements, bomb damage and so on. No sooner had he landed, however, than he reported to the nearest police-station with his radio and asked what he could do. D Division took over control of his set and used him to play it back to the Japanese from Calcutta. Before long his own cautious reports began to whet the appetite of the Japanese, and they started asking him more detailed questions, to which Peter's team was only too happy to supply answers.

During 1943 D Division opened a tactical headquarters in Calcutta. At first this was run by an engineer called Colonel Tom Foulkes, but later it was taken over by Colonel Frank Wilson, an officer in the 19th Lancers whom Peter had met at a cocktail party. Besides speaking Urdu—and therefore being able to translate the messages which were sent out in English from Delhi for onward transmission to the Japanese—Wilson was also a caricaturist of considerable skill, and on Peter's instructions compiled a sketch-book in which he drew and described members of various regiments whose presence in Calcutta—generally fictitious— D Division wanted to establish. Like many of the other documents that Peter perpetrated, the sketch-book was eventually sold in Kabul for a handsome sum. In company with most of the other people in D Division, Wilson found his environment becoming ever more densely tenanted by phantom characters, among them the notorious 'Harry Singh' and 'the inebriated colonels'—an imaginary group of officers whose alleged enslavement to alcohol furnished the Japanese with a rich mixture of real and bogus information.

As the deception radio network expanded, so too did D Division's skill at producing material happenings for the Japanese to witness. Having started life in the bandsmen's quarters of the Viceroy's House, André Bicat's section eventually expanded into several factories, in which it produced a variety of ingenious devices. One of them, at least, Peter himself could claim to have invented: this was *Pintail*—a bomb with a spike on the nose which when dropped would root itself vertically in the earth and then, after a pre-arranged interval, start sending up Very lights. *Parafexes* simulated rifle and automatic fire and grenade explosions (they were really no more than specially developed fireworks), and *Aquaskits* and *Aquatails* provided various kinds of aquatic illumination. But perhaps the most successful items were the *Paragons*, or dummy paratroops. Because aircraft were relatively scarce over Burma, and because most observers had had little if any experience of parachute-dropping, a single medium bomber could release a whole company of miniature figures without anyone on the ground realizing that he was witnessing a physical impossibility. Indeed, by means of Bicat's various devices a single Liberator, in one sortie, could deploy the ingredients of an entire company battle which might last as long as six hours.

Nor was it only inexperienced observers who were deceived by what they saw. Whenever he could find a good enough excuse Peter would hold a demonstration outside Delhi, to which he would invite all the senior officers involved, including Mountbatten. The visitors always enjoyed themselves, even though they were often completely foxed: Peter would give them cards and ask them to write down exactly what they saw and heard—and the results showed that they were often substantially deceived.

In his search for means of deception Peter's inventiveness was endlessly fertile—and indeed, for his colleagues, one of the main pleasures of working in his office was the constant boiling-up of ideas. Many were absurd, and the air was constantly full of jokes; but beneath the high spirits the purpose was deadly serious, and even the most abstruse projects were seriously intended. One of Peter's more bizarre ideas was that he should organize the dropping into occupied Burma of a corpse—ostensibly that of a British-paid agent—equipped with codes and a radio set, which the Japanese would play back to D Division in Delhi. This scheme, it seems likely, was inspired by Operation Mincemeat, whereby, in April 1943, a body—floated ashore from the British submarine *Seraph* off the coast of Spain—successfully conveyed to the German intelligence service a great deal of misleading information about Allied plans for the Mediterranean, and decoyed substantial numbers of German troops away from Sicily before the Allied invasion. (The episode led in due course to Duff Cooper's short novel *Operation Heartbreak* and to Ewen Montagu's book and the film *The Man Who Never Was*.)

Peter's plan was in many ways similar to Operation Mincemeat, but its execution was not rendered any easier by the fact that a suitable body had to be procured in Calcutta at the height of the hot weather. Plenty of people were dying, for a major famine was in progress, but almost every corpse was far too emaciated to pass muster as that of a well-nourished secret agent. A further complication was that the dead man had to be a Moslem, for this was specified in the dossier already provided by the office in Delhi.

The man in charge of the operation was Gordon Rennie, a South African who had joined Peter's unit as a result of a recommendation from Bernard Fergusson. For four days Rennie and his colleagues searched Calcutta for a suitable corpse, being rewarded at last with the body of a man of about forty. Having backed a fifteen hundred-weight truck up to the General Military Hospital, they drove off to a private house which D Division had rented in the suburb of Tolligunj; there they shaved the dead man's face, cut his finger- and toe-nails, dressed him in uniform and united him with his codes, radio set and personal documents. Finally they strapped on his parachute which had been specially packed with its lines crossed. Then, wearing face-masks soaked in *eau de cologne* to protect themselves from the smell, they took off for Burma. On the first run over the dropping zone they released some Pintails, and, when these had started sending up Very lights, pushed out the body and the wireless.

All this preparation was ill rewarded, for the set never came on the air. The dispatchers never knew whether their man had been found by the Japanese, or whether the radio had been irreparably damaged in its descent. The failure may have been caused simply by the inability of the Japanese in the area to use the radio and the codes provided.

D Division's greatest problem was the incompetence of the Japanese intelligence staff. Although amazingly credulous, and willing to swallow (as Peter put it) the 'most outrageous and implausible fabrications', they were often so slow-witted that they failed to make even the most obvious deductions from the information which they had been fed. Nor were D Division's designs furthered by the fact that many local Japanese commanders apparently held their intelligence staff in the utmost contempt and paid little or no attention to their advice and warnings. The ignorance and folly that prevailed on the receiving end encouraged Peter to transmit, among his serious messages, a good deal of ribald abuse designed mainly to annoy. One of his agents called Brass, for instance, repeatedly told his Japanese contact that his commanding officer was living with a prostitute, and that the ruling family of Japan had short, furry tails, of which they were inordinately proud.

D Division's prospects were substantially improved in August 1943 by the arrival in Japan of the brilliant Indian revolutionary Subhas Chandra Bose. After a long but only lukewarm flirtation with the Germans in Europe, he was received in some state by the Japanese and promptly appointed himself Supreme Commander of the Indian National Army—the force which the Japanese had formed in Malaya from Indian prisoners captured in Singapore. Two months later Bose made himself Head of State, Prime Minister and Minister for War and Foreign Affairs in the 'Provisional Government of Free India'. It was his burning ambition that the I.N.A. should enter India, with himself at its head, in company with the victorious Japanese; and to this end he began attempting to build up the strength of his ragged force and to improve the quantity and quality of the intelligence reaching the Japanese High Command.

D Division were delighted by Bose's arrival in the Japanese camp. While he had been in Germany they had maintained regular contact with him (though he did not realize it), and now they hoped that his wide experience of clandestine activity would greatly increase the receptivity of the Japanese intelligence service: as Peter himself put it, they looked forward to dealing with a sophisticated adversary who could be relied on —as the Japanese could not—to see the point of the information they gave him.

Their hopes were partially fulfilled. Soon after Bose's arrival a new wave of agents landed in India, and in a very short time they had been rounded up, persuaded to work for the Allies, and sent into action playing their radio sets back to the headquarters of the Indian National Army. Yet not even Bose's presence could overcome the other major difficulty which hampered D Division's activities: the chronic uncertainty about Allied operations in the south-east Asian theatre. Time and again Mountbatten projected a major assault, only to have the promise of essential equipment (such as landing-craft) withdrawn at the last moment, so that all his plans had to be changed; and time and again Peter, with his uncanny knack of anticipating the future, had produced as his deceptive feint the very plan on which the Supreme Commander then had to fall back. As Peter remarked to one of his colleagues, it was impossible to tell a convincing lie unless he knew what the truth was going to be, and in the end the number of occasions on which he involuntarily foreshadowed the truth proved rather embarrassing.

This lack of long-term plans, combined with the inefficiency of the Japanese themselves, ensured that the deception practised in South-East Asia could never be anything like as sophisticated as that carried out from London or from Cairo. In the Middle East, and even more so in Europe, the efficiency and skill of the Axis intelligence staff meant that far more complicated and subtle ruses could be employed, with a very good chance that the enemy would make the deductions which the Allies wanted.

Deception by radio offered a good example of the disparity. Such was the skill and sophistication of the deception teams in England that—as part of the plans for the Normandy landings in 1944—they not only created an entire phantom corps by means of putting out wireless messages, but maintained for twenty-four hours a day the radio traffic that a corps would generate. In the Far East no such comprehensive deception was possible, for the Japanese had neither the physical means to monitor such a volume of traffic nor the intelligence to interpret constructively such messages as they did manage to intercept.

Even so, the results obtained from Delhi were far from negligible. Enemy documents captured at the end of 1943 showed that D Division's efforts to put over a dummy order of battle had been extraordinarily successful: the Japanese had a fantastically exaggerated idea of Allied strength in South-East Asia, believing that the Supreme Commander's resources extended to more than fifty divisions. For the rest of the war the Japanese High Command was persistently deceived about the S.E.A.C. order of battle, and was to some extent inhibited in its decisions by the belief that very powerful seaborne and airborne forces opposed it.

Although direct proof was always hard to come by, Peter did glean some evidence to show that several of his individual deception plans had been successful. Most were designed to decoy enemy forces away from areas on which attacks were planned, or into areas of no particular concern to the Allies; one that appeared to succeed was Plan Stultify, which exerted a strong threat, by sea and air, against the area of Moulmein. The object was to accelerate the withdrawal of the Japanese forces from the area of Rangoon, and this the plan seemed to achieve, for when the Allies reoccupied Rangoon from the sea in May 1945 they landed with virtually no opposition. Another success was Plan Sceptical, which intimated a major airborne assault on Bangkok, linked with an overland advance on the city down the Burma–Siam railway—a combined threat which drew strong Japanese reinforcements into the area. It was impossible to establish how far these notional threats against the Kra Isthmus and Siam influenced Japan's military plans; but by the time the Allied invasion of Malaya was due to be launched no Japanese field formations remained there, only a few second-line units.

On the tactical (that is, the more local) front, no scheme was more successful than Plan Cloak which, by means of dummy wireless traffic and a large air-drop of Paragons, Pintails and other devices, decoyed the enemy to the wrong section of the Irawaddy and so secured for 4 Corps almost total surprise for its crossing of the river and its attack on Meiktila in February 1945.

Besides devising and organizing such schemes, Peter himself was constantly on the move. In May 1943 he accompanied the D.M.I., Brigadier Cawthorn, to the Quadrant Conference in Quebec—a long and exhausting air journey which enabled him, as if in compensation for its rigours, to spend a night at home on the way. He found Merrimoles looking its loveliest, with the fields springing green and the wild cherries trailing their clouds of white blossom on the edges of the beech-woods. Nichol, then aged four, struck him as 'merry and friendly and rather nice-looking'. At the conference he and Cawthorn made an abortive attempt to take over control of strategic deception in the whole of the Pacific—the ultimate responsibility for which still rested with the Americans. When the conference was over Peter came across his brother Ian in Washington. Discovering that Joan Bright was also there, they proposed one evening that they should all go to New York together. This they did, but no sooner had they arrived than Ian typically disappeared on some business of his own, leaving Peter to take Joan to see Ethel Merman in *Something for the Boys*. Joan found the two brothers 'an attractive pair, amusing, good-looking, sure of themselves and devoted to each other.'

Peter's transatlantic trip was an exceptional one: his most frequent destination was Chungking, where he maintained vital contacts with the Chinese intelligence staff. On many of his visits he carried deception programmes in his brief-case, for personal delivery of this kind was by far the safest method of conveying secret material to the Chinese dispatchers. To his delight the Chinese embraced the theory and practice of deception enthusiastically: on one occasion he noted in his diary that Colonel T. T. Chen (a staff officer with whom he was often in contact) asked him '"should we encourage the Japs to attack the Russians?", which looks as though they have been flying fairly high.'

All this intrigue left Peter little time for literary activity; but in 1943 he did play a leading part in one attractive literary project—the publication of Wavell's anthology of poetry *Other Men's Flowers*. Had it not been for Peter's firm encouragement in the first place, and for Rupert Hart-Davis's tact in the later stages of the operation, this celebrated book would almost certainly have been still-born. After months of argument it came out in 1944, complete with notes which Wavell added at Rupert's suggestion, and with his own sonnet 'For the Madonna of the Cherries' which Rupert had also persuaded him to include. When Wavell got finished copies he gave one to Peter with a remark that even by the standards of the recipient was self-effacing: 'I suppose you'd better have this,' he drawled. 'I don't think it's much good, but you can always give it away.' His affectionate and grateful inscription was written not on the fly-leaf but on a sheet of paper clipped to it—in case, presumably, Peter really did decide to give away his copy. *Other Men's Flowers* was a Book Society choice, and has gone through one edition after another ever since.

Peter himself wrote nothing intended for publication during his time in India. Yet even in his official reports and cables he used English with extraordinary precision: members of his staff would watch fascinated as he composed reports in longhand, writing without apparent effort but with amazing fluency, never hesitating, scarcely ever making a correction, yet always producing a perfectly clear and economical statement of the facts. Even his long and frequent secret cables to the London Controlling Section were perfectly phrased: composing in telegraphese was a very great technical pleasure to him, and his passion for arranging words in the best possible order was one of the bases of his life.

Sometimes the absence of any normal outlet for his writing was reflected in his diary, which is studded with finely observed scenes and incidents—for instance on one trip to China when he was suffering from a boil in his nose:

9.9.43 Kunming at 1400 ... still slightly feverish and feel as if I had a lump of slightly poisonous dough at the back of my nose ... set off to see a French doctor ... he gave me a chit to Dr Tsin ... Tsin away but a quorum was found of a young and inept Chinese doctor and several nurses, mostly pretty. A most enjoyable discussion ensued in Chinese, French and English while the doctor poked periscopes into my nose, ears and throat. Finally he dug out a fountain-pen filler, opaque with dirt, and squirted a couple of shots of rat-poison into my nose amid tumultuous applause ... I went home feeling better mentally, if not physically, to find that 80 per cent of my September whisky ration had leaked into my clean shirts.

11.9.43 Up early, watched a young man having a fit on the other side of the muddy river, heard the rooks of Kunming making an English noise in the chill grey air ... People carrying dead rats swinging reverently like censers on the end of a string ... A man lying on his back dying, flapping his arms.

20.9.43 Kunming. Air raid. Hooter goes 0715. A few people running outside my window, but the family opposite stand fast. It has sounded all night as if someone is dying in the small dark hovel ... Shave and have breakfast while a long procession, carrying next to nothing, streams out of the city along the opposite bank of the river. The sky is full of the noise of fighters going up and transports evacuating ... Went up on roof. Others went to a trench. Servants, possibly fortified by *sang-froid Anglais*, took no action and watched the fleeing crowds with tolerant contempt ... Two evacuee sampans went past, one propelled by a woman with a baby on her back and a little girl of ten. To the fifteen passengers, including able-bodied men, it would have seemed as eccentric to help as it would seem to us to try and help a taxi-driver in similar circumstances.

His other main literary outlet was his letters home—to Celia, to Nichol and to his nephews at Merrimoles. His letters to the children were always warm and vivid—models of what such correspondence can be. To his four-year-old son he wrote in 1943:

Dear Little Nicholas,

Thank you very much for the letters you have sent me. I liked them very much. Please write some more. They come quite quickly in an aeroplane and it is very nice getting letters when I am such a long way away ... I am sorry I wasn't there for Christmas and your birthday, but when I come back everyone can have an extra birthday, which will mean getting one or perhaps two lovely presents and having whatever sort of treat you want. Of course it will be no good asking for a treat which I can't arrange, such as riding up to the village on an elephant. As long as it is a sensible sort of treat I will arrange it.

I have been having a lovely time living in the woods where we are having a battle with the Japanese ... Sometimes the Japanese came over to bomb us, but they were not much good and generally it was our aeroplanes going over to bomb them, which is very good for them as they are horrible people ... Then we had a lot of big guns, most cleverly hidden in the bushes so that you couldn't see them. They shot their shells a tremendous long way—further than from the farm to the village—and the shells went whistling over and all the Japanese had to run into their holes like rabbits, but often some of them got blown to bits. All the same they fought jolly well and were so brave and fierce that we weren't quite able to win the battle. When you go to a battle you don't get any bread to eat, only biscuits, but it is great fun and sometimes you get sausages out of a tin. We all slept in little trenches, and one morning it rained so that all the trenches were full of water with our blankets and clothes floating about in it, which was rather funny in a way.

I am awfully pleased to hear that you can spell your name, which is quite a long and difficult one, and I expect by now you can spell other things as well. If you are good at spelling and writing, and also a sensible sort of chap, it is rather a good thing, because when you grow up it makes it easier to do the things you want to do, and sometimes people will send you specially in an aeroplane to some lovely place to write things about it, and you can generally take Mummy with you, or one of your friends, and perhaps there will be tigers to shoot, or something equally nice. So if I were you I should see that you are good at writing and at all your lessons when you start them. Give my love to everyone at Merrimoles and to Copeland [the milkman] and Brown [the gamekeeper]. Mummy says you have been looking after her rather well and I am very glad you are doing this for me because it is a great help and she is so awfully nice that she really deserves to be looked after properly. Mind you give my love to everyone in a serious way. Write to me again soon.

Love from DADDY

In cheerfully describing the delights of battles in the jungle, Peter gave an unconscious hint of the main weakness of his entire career in deception: his predilection for making unofficial visits to the front. He knew perfectly well that in running D Division he was doing an important and worthwhile job; yet, stuck in Delhi or Kandy a long way from the fighting, he could not help feeling an unworthy base-wallah, and whenever he could he slipped off to see some action in Burma.

The episodes he described to Nichol took place during the Allied invasion of the Arakan peninsula in 1943. Following in the wake of the spear-head troops, he was one of the first to realize that the advance had been dangerously easy, and he accurately predicted the heavy Japanese counter-attacks which soon drove the Allies out of the peninsula again.

There was some military justification for his presence in this operation, just as there was for later trips which he made down the coast to visit deception units stationed behind the enemy lines; but there was none whatever for flying with Wingate's second major offensive into the heart of enemy-held territory—a trip which he took in March 1944 and from which he was lucky to escape with his life.

At the beginning of 1944 almost the whole of Burma was in Japanese hands; but except in the Hukawng Valley, where the American General Stilwell was struggling to extend the Ledo road, there was relatively little fighting: for 250 miles, in a line running roughly north-east to south-west, the River Chindwin formed the dividing line between the rival armies, and across it patrols from either side probed the other's defences. The general situation was one of deadlock, and it was in an attempt to break the stalemate that General Orde Wingate conceived his last major expedition. His original plan was to introduce his Special Force, consisting of three brigades, into the area of Indaw, the northern-most communications centre of any importance in Upper Burma, and there to form, deep in enemy territory, an enclave into which much stronger forces could be flown. In order to achieve the element of surprise essential to the airborne forces, 16 Brigade, under Bernard Fergusson, marched in covertly from Ledo—a slog of 400 miles through appalling country and weather which he described memorably in his book *The Wild Green Earth*. In a pleasant valley just north of Indaw he established the stronghold known as 'Aberdeen'—a well-defended Dakota strip which became invaluable as a staging-post. The second part of the Special Force—77 Brigade under Mike Calvert—was to be flown in by glider to two clearings in the jungle code-named 'Broadway' and

'Piccadilly', some twenty miles east of Aberdeen, and there to establish another stronghold called 'White City', astride the railway.

Somehow—perhaps by issuing himself with the necessary order—Peter got himself attached to the headquarters of 77 Brigade and prepared to fly in with its advance party. He certainly had no business to do so: apart from the fact that the excursion was of practically no value to his deception activities, his own head contained a dangerously large amount of high-grade information which, had he been captured, might have been extorted from him by the Japanese. His departure and subsequent absence were concealed from the Supreme Commander, who did not discover for several weeks where he had been; had Mountbatten known more quickly what Peter had done, he would have had no alternative but to court martial him.

In any case, Peter left Delhi for Burma on February 27th to join Calvert as he made his final preparations, and his diary lit up at the prospect of action. 'The last day in Delhi was a pleasant cross between the last day of term and the last day of the holidays,' he wrote. 'Wish I were fitter and that so many people didn't look askance. Still, it's always been like that.' Two days later he was in the jungle:

> *29.2.44.* Lovely camp in a little re-entrant with burn down the middle and friendly sort of jungle climbing up the sides. The sun is setting and the B.O.R.s [British other-ranks] are joyfully throwing 69 grenades into the bushes thirty yards away. Shades of street warfare in Battersea. The crows here make a noise rather like the Joyce Grove rooks ... Shot well with my Luger and Humfrey's .45 Colt, impressing B.O.R.s and dumbfounding myself ... Slept on the ground last night without a net, slightly bitten by rather effete mosquitoes. Feeling very cheerful and peaceful and optimistic.

The same day Peter collected a slight, rather serious twenty-year-old Chinese orderly whose proper name was Young Man Sun but who was always known as Automatic, on account of his orderly and methodical habits. Peter gave him his old Caucasian knife, which he had bought in London with Celia in 1934, to wear in his belt, and asked him to make a scabbard for the new American matchet which he had just acquired, whereupon Automatic

> produced a thing like a small umbrella-stand. He also cut a step for me to sit on outside my eyrie-like *basha*, a most romantic place looking over the tangled jungle into the moon. He seems devoted but doesn't yet know what he is in for.

Nor, for that matter, did his master. That evening he watched a long glider-rehearsal, of which he left a vivid description in his journal, observing characteristically that the gliders coming back to land in the dark 'seem to be travelling slowly and would be as easy to miss as a cock caper.' Next day he bought some candles, bootlaces and toothpaste and got his hair cut 'by an ill-disposed Asiatic' in the canteen at Sylhet. This completed his preparations for take-off on March 5th.

His glider was number 15P—the fifteenth in the run to Piccadilly. 'I am co-pilot to a charming and enthusiastic American,' he wrote in his diary: 'The thing not to do is to press the knob which casts us off. When landing I may in an emergency have to pull a lever called 'Spoilers', thus (they say) bringing us down faster. I dare say I shall manage.' With this hopeful forecast he closed his journal for the moment, leaving it behind in a brown envelope marked 'Lt. Col. R. P. Fleming: to await return.' As things turned out it was lucky he did so—and luckier still that he described the events which followed in a brilliantly written report—a document which uniquely combined strict military detail with Peter's inimitable observation and sense of humour.

The take-off of 77 Brigade's advance party was charged with excitement, because only a few minutes before the leading gliders were due to become airborne, a U.S. Airforce pilot arrived with some excellent photographs of Piccadilly taken three hours earlier which showed that the clearing had been liberally obstructed with tree-trunks and was crisscrossed by tracks. This meant that all the night's sorties had to be switched to Broadway; a new plan was swiftly worked out, and the first tugs and gliders went off only a few minutes late.

15P, as Peter himself remarked, never gave her passengers the impression of being a lucky aircraft. First her original pilot was put out of action by a jeep-crash; then, as she was being jacked up to receive Jean, a pony destined for the Brigade Commander, one of the supports slipped and the glider sustained damage that put her out of commission.

A new 15P was accordingly fed into the take-off line, but since this aircraft had no stall for the pony, Jean and her handler had to stand down, the man's place being taken by Automatic. This meant that the complement (besides the American pilot, Lieutenant Williams) consisted of six officers, seven British other ranks, one Indian other rank, and one Chinese. Each Dakota took up two gliders, and by 8 p.m. 15P had worked her way to the head of the queue as the short-tow glider on the port side, with her sister 14B on the long tow to starboard.

At 8.15 the pair took off without mishap, but trouble began almost at once. From this point Peter's report tells the story:

The pilot had asked for one man to be detailed to come forward if it proved necessary to trim her, and this man was ordered forward immediately after take-off. It soon, however, became apparent that the glider was not behaving satisfactorily, and at ominously frequent intervals the pilot called 'another man forward' until all the passengers were wedged in a sort of pâté immediately behind the pilot's and co-pilot's seats.

From a relatively enviable position in the latter, I (and nobody else) was able to see 14B, the long-tow glider on our starboard quarter. Or rather, I *had* been able to see her, for at an early stage in the flight I realized that she was no longer with us. At this point I made a serious error of judgment in not informing the pilot that 14B had cut, for if I had (he afterwards told me) he would have cut too— owing to the danger of 14B's loose tow-rope removing our starboard wing—and we should have landed on or near our base at Lallaghat.

My reasons for suppressing this information were (apart from ignorance of its full implications):

(a) The pilot appeared to have quite enough on his mind already.

(b) I considered it essential to take no action which might lessen the Brigade Commander's chances of getting at any rate part of his staff into Broadway that night ...

15P reached an altitude of 8000 ft and proceeded on her way with every sign of reluctance. It had become apparent that the controls ... were not working ... Spells of relatively smooth flying alternated with mild but disturbing aerobatics, during which the glider shuddered convulsively and the blue lights on the tug see-sawed up, down and sideways across our field of vision. [There was no radio communication between tug and glider]. F/O Williams afterwards told me that he was expecting the tail to come off, and I consider that he showed commendable determination in maintaining his objective in these circumstances ...

We crossed the Chindwin at 8000 feet approximately one hour after take-off. At about 2140 hrs 15P had a fit of recalcitrance which culminated in (according to the pilot) an attempt to loop the loop. She banked steeply, causing all loose objects in the cockpit and elsewhere to come adrift. The pilot struck the release mechanism above his head, and we found ourselves diving, fairly steeply and in comparative silence ...

For what must have been several minutes we spiralled unsteadily towards a point where a stream bed in a gully splayed out in an irregular patch of white sand. On this restricted and uneven space ...

F/O Williams put the glider down with extreme skill and a resounding bump which broke open the forepart of the cockpit. Impelled
partly by tactical considerations and partly by a sense of self-
preservation (for the pilot and I, at the bottom of a groaning and
blasphemous pile of soldiery, were now most unfavourably placed),
I ordered all ranks to deplane with their arms.

None of the party was seriously injured, and, having ordered six men to
form a perimeter fifty yards in radius, Peter burnt all the ciphers and
secret documents—a process which took some time and illuminated uncomfortably the wreck of the glider on the white sandbank. While the
bonfire still blazed a single aircraft suddenly materialized out of the night
and put in a short, sharp attack with cannon or machine-gun fire.

Clearly the party had to leave the area as soon as possible; and so,
having completed the cremation, and having used two dummy buffalo-
wallows made of hessian to form a prominent ground-to-air signal in the
shape of an arrow pointing south-west, Peter withdrew his men in a
northerly direction.

Before they left the clearing, he pointed out—in the first of several
exhortations that undoubtedly played a large part in the success of their
escape—the following factors:

(a) That if we behaved sensibly we had practically nothing to fear
from the Japanese, who were almost certainly in a greater state of
alarm and confusion than we were ourselves;

(b) that no one was to think of himself as a 'survivor' or an 'evacuee'
but rather as a member of an unusually well-found fighting patrol,
inserted in the enemy's rearward administrative areas and perfectly
capable of seeing-off the small parties from L. of C. [Lines of
Communication] units which were all we were likely to meet at this
stage;

(c) that we had been damned lucky so far.

The party then climbed a low escarpment and for three hours marched
briskly along a little-used path, with two men who had no nails in their
boots bringing up the rear. At about 1.30 a.m. they came within earshot,
though not within sight, of a village from which emerged 'loud and for
the most part petulant voices in Japanese as the local post turned itself
out', presumably on receipt of news of the glider's landing. Backing off,
they retraced their steps and then were forced to cross a boggy glen; this
they did backwards, 'leaving tracks so heavily down by the heel (owing
to the weight of packs) that they would not have deceived Lestrade, let

alone Sherlock Holmes.' Finally, when the moon set at 3.30, they halted for the night in the jungle.

Next day they lay up in a patch of elephant grass and sorted themselves out. They carried eight days' K rations, and Peter at once put the party on half-rations in case their stay in the jungle should be protracted. Every man was armed with a sub-machine-gun, a Sten gun, a ·303 rifle or a ·300 carbine, as well as with grenades, and the officers also carried pistols. There was plenty of ammunition, and a number of compasses. Peter had all non-essential possessions buried, and (as part of his campaign to maintain morale) ordered all the men to shave whenever the daily water ration allowed it. He then split the party into three—the headquarter and reconnaissance group, consisting of himself, one other officer and one British soldier, and two other sections. Whenever they moved, Peter and the Recce Group led, covered by the sections.

The worst of their predicament was that they were completely lost— a fact which might have dispirited other leaders, but one to which Peter reacted in a thoroughly characteristic way. In his report he wrote:

> Our position was on paper complicated, but in practice simplified, by the fact that we did not know where we were, and had no map of the area other than the escape maps ... Opinions differed as to our flying-time east of the Chindwin, and the pilot did not know the course on which we had been flying. It was, however, fairly clear that we were between thirty and fifty miles east of the Chindwin and almost certainly south of the Uyu river.

The only sensible course of action, Peter decided, was to walk back towards India. He considered striking east, to see if he could find White City on foot, and heading north-east, in an attempt to join Bernard Fergusson's 16 Brigade in Aberdeen. But both, he decided, were ruled out by the lack of maps and inadequacy of rations, and he announced to the party that they would march west towards the Chindwin, cross it, and rejoin the Allied forces.

During their first day they heard nothing, and at 1700 hrs Peter led the Recce Group off to have a look at the first stage of the night's march. After only half a mile he came cautiously to the edge of a large and apparently oblong space:

> While spying this through field-glasses I observed a Japanese in an elaborately camouflaged uniform (including a silly sort of hat and— as far as I could see—a mask) proceeding across my front at a range of approximately three hundred yards. His gait was one of exagge-

rated stealth and he was moving so slowly, with what appeared to be a machine carbine at the ready, that at first I assumed he was stalking a deer or buffalo ...

I then noticed, on the far side of the clearing, what appeared to be a camouflaged hide and near it the legs of a man whose body was concealed by a bush. I accordingly sent the remainder of the Recce Group back to the main body, who would by this time be moving up. Meanwhile I had lost the exponent of slow-motion eurhythmics, but on moving forward found him again up a tree, in a *machan*, the base of which appeared to be improvised from some form of metal plate, presumably with a view to protection from small arms fire. He was gazing intently towards the centre of the clearing, and his buttocks offered, at two hundred and fifty yards, a target which it required the strongest sense of duty to forego.

I withdrew, picked up the main body and made a short detour to the south-west. It appeared however that the clearing curved, and that we were on the inside of the curve, for very soon we bumped the edge of it again, at a point where another Japanese, in an attitude of exaggerated vigilance, was peering through a loophole in a kind of camouflaged stockade.

This necessitated another slight detour, but this too brought us back to the perimeter immediately behind another sentry crouching in a tunnel-like *basha* and sedulously watching his front. It was now nearly last light. We shifted off and halted for a few minutes. I took the opportunity of pointing out to the party that conditions locally were much more favourable to us than we had supposed. All the evidence available suggested that:

    (a) the local commander was in a state of flap;

    (b) his troops, who appeared to be thin on the ground, were committed to a static defensive role;

    (c) he was obviously expecting an airborne landing in the clearing and had made careful arrangements to ambush it;

    (d) there were bound to be other similar clearings in the area which he would have to watch;

    (e) he had misappreciated our role and probably exaggerated our strength;

    (f) we had the initiative.

By this time the Dakotas had begun to drone overhead on the Broadway run, lending colour to the local commander's (alleged) fears. I do not consider that the above appreciation was far wide of the mark, and it had a noticeable effect on the morale of all ranks (including my own), and the march continued in an atmosphere of discreet truculence.

After proceeding for perhaps a mile and a half and almost bumping a small group of tents in or near which ducks were quacking, we reached, recced and crossed a narrow neck of the clearing which at this point appeared to be unsuitable for glider landings and was watched either not at all or inefficiently.

Thus away, the crew and passengers of 15P marched through the jungle for three more hours, crossing several small clearings and trying without success to find water by digging in the dried-up hollows. At 2.30 a.m. they halted for the rest of the night, and next day pressed ahead through relatively open teak jungle. Their main worry was lack of water, and they were not at that stage much concerned about being captured: as Peter observed, even if an enemy patrol had made contact with them, it would have been an unenviable task for anybody to search them out among the noisy dead leaves of the teak.

During that day's advance they had a major slice of luck, in that an arbitrary alteration of course brought them straight to a large pond of sweet water which (they afterwards discovered) was one of the sources of the Nathan river. Down this 'admirable and deserted watercourse' they marched for the rest of that day, finding nothing more sinister than one set of naked footprints on a path that crossed their line of advance.

The following day (March 8th) they again kept to the stream but made less progress because of the increasing density of the jungle; and on the 9th the cover was so thick that the main body lost touch altogether with the Recce Group, which meant much counter-marching to previously-agreed rendezvous. In the evening they reached an area that seemed—from the sound of woodcutting and other domestic activities—unhealthily congested; so Peter ordered a few hours' sleep and then took the party on again in the dark, circumventing the dangerous area. In the middle of the night-march they halted by a pool, 'partly to drink and partly to restore any confidence which the party might have lost as a result of our recent encounters and evasions.'

Their seventh march, next morning, was a brief one, and brought them to the edge of a large open space, short of which they lay up. At 4 p.m. the one Indian member of the party, who was on guard, creditably spotted a patrol of fifteen Japanese marching very fast along a path that ran just inside the jungle on the far side of the clearing; but the fugitives kept still, and the enemy marched on unaware of their presence. At 7 p.m. Peter gave out that it was his intention to cross the Chindwin within the next forty-eight hours; they moved off again, and after only two hours' march through easy jungle found themselves at the top of a steep escarpment below which flowed the river.

After some preliminary scrambling down and up the escarpment they reached the bank at about nine the following morning and settled in a triangular patch of jungle. The river looked about 650 yards wide, and there was a disappointing absence of boats: believing that the far bank was dominated by enemy patrols, Peter considered it essential that his party should ferry all its stores and weapons across. He thus appeared to be in some difficulty, and later wrote:

There seemed nothing for it but to build a raft, and to this task all ranks addressed themselves with enthusiasm under the ingenious direction of Major Faulkner, the Brigade Medical Officer. Our scope as shipwrights was limited by the fact that we were working in or on the outskirts of a village and only a few yards from the main land line-of-communication in the area [a path along the river-bank], and cutting or hammering was therefore out of the question.

This in no way deterred Major Faulkner. All packs (fourteen British, one American) were emptied and repacked with empty water-bottles and K rations (which we believed incorrectly to be watertight) at the bottom, the remainder of the contents being stowed on top of this supposedly buoyant foundation. The packs were then divided into three lots of five, each of which was enclosed in a groundsheet ... The three floats thus formed were to be lashed together within a framework made of half a dozen lengths of dead bamboo ... Two paddles were improvised, and would each be wielded by a non-swimmer seated on the raft. The remainder of the party, sustained where necessary by Mae Wests, would hang on to the bamboo framework and propel the raft swimming ... The raft was far too heavy and fragile to be carried down the bank and would have to be assembled in the water after dark.

These novel and pleasantly absorbing tasks were interrupted throughout the day by various alarms, which grew frequent towards evening but were all caused by Burmese passing along the path behind us or along the foreshore immediately below us. (It is a measure of the good luck which had attended our stealthy progress that, after six days and nights in Burma, none of us had yet set eyes on a native of the country, and when one was sighted it was necessary to form a queue at the relevant O.P. [observation post] to avoid too conspicuous a display of curious faces ...).

At last light sentries were withdrawn. I gave out my orders and we moved down to the beach-head and took off our trousers and boots. All three floats were placed in the water; all three floated. Tremendous activity ensued among the shipwrights, accompanied by a good deal of splashing and the creaking of bamboos. In a surprisingly short time the raft was assembled, and the arms, clothing and equipment loaded on to it in that order.

At this point it was discovered

   (a) that the raft had been aground for some time,

   (b) that all the groundsheets were full of water and the packs were waterlogged.

I ordered the raft to be unloaded and dismantled.

Our situation at this stage appeared so unpromising as to be almost comic. Fifteen officers and men, in nothing but their shirts and by this time extremely cold, were engaged in dismantling, by the brilliant light of the moon, a contraption which had hitherto seemed their only hope of escape. For an hour and a half we had been making a good deal of noise in the immediate vicinity of a village, the whole foreshore was plastered with our tracks, our waterlogged packs were too heavy to be carried away, and we were dominated at less than a hundred yards by a steep bank carrying a track on which even an optimist had to admit the probability of patrols.

In spite of the difficulties nobody lost heart, and the men split into small groups for the crossing. The first to go were the four non-swimmers, wearing Mae Wests and escorted by Major Pringle, who in happier days had swum for the Royal Military Academy at Sandhurst. Some time after they had left, Peter and the others—still on the far bank—heard screams, and they learnt later that Signalman Angus had been drowned. He was an excellent man, Peter reported; he had shown himself very cool and resourceful, and his Mae West had been tested before he wore it—so there was no easy explanation of the tragedy. With him went the diary which Peter had carefully kept during the past few days—the second action-journal that he had lost. The first, which he had spent the whole day writing up, went down in the wreck of the *Kalanthe* in April 1941; and this second one he had given to Signalman Angus because he was the only man who had a waterproof tobacco-pouch.

The rest of the men crossed the river safely by 2300 hours, but during the night Major Pringle and another officer twice returned to the east bank to collect stores that had been left behind. These two officers thus swam the Chindwin five times in the course of a single night. On the west bank the survivors lit huge bonfires and sat over them till daylight, too cold to sleep and trying to dry their clothes.

In the morning they redistributed their remaining rations and prepared for another series of clandestine marches. After an unsuccessful search for Signalman Angus's body they set off at 10.30, but they had gone hardly a mile when they bumped into an observation post manned by the 9/12 Frontier Force Regiment, who, as Peter reported, treated them 'with some reserve, one sepoy up a tree removing the pin from a grenade.' The Indians told them that there were British units all along the west bank of the river to the south, so they set off again in that direction and in another two hours fell in with a patrol of the 1st Battalion of the Seaforth Highlanders, at whose headquarters they were regaled with a large meal. Jimmy Marks, the Seaforths' Mortar Officer, remembered the menu exactly: fried bully beef and tea, followed by the regiment's special pudding called Chindwin Duff, which was made of biscuits powdered and mixed with raisins and condensed milk. Marks also remembered Peter standing in a cleared patch among a tangle of sawn-down bamboo looking extraordinarily neat and collected, and worrying less about himself than about finding a comfortable place for his servant Automatic to sleep.

Summing up the experience in his report, Peter concluded that the main factor contributing to their escape had been consistently good luck. Apart from this, and 'a certain amount of tactical common sense', he believed that their best ally had been high morale:

> All ranks came out full of self-confidence and genuinely anxious to rejoin their brigade in the field, and there is no doubt that practically everybody keenly enjoyed a great many of their experiences after the somewhat alarming first night.
>
> I attribute the high level of morale ... to the doctrine laid down by Brigadier Calvert (Commander, 77 Independent Infantry Brigade) and inculcated by him in training. This doctrine consists in effect in maintaining a sense of proportion with regard to the Japanese, the jungle and other real or supposed hazards which beset a small, isolated detachment in enemy-occupied territory. The feeling of being hunted is an unpleasant one, and personnel who become oppressed by it are liable to act, should a crisis or irksome delay arise, in a foolish and unsoldierly manner. Though I never felt justified in attempting any offensive action, I think we managed to avoid this hunted feeling.

In the last paragraph of his report Peter generously praised the coolness of several of the officers and other ranks in the party. He did not, of course, mention his own, but several of his fellow-survivors did, and they made it clear that without his unshakeable courage and determination their chances of escape would have been infinitely smaller.

It was typical of him that, having just reached safety, he not only had himself flown at once to Bernard Fergusson's enclave Aberdeen and then to Mike Calvert's stronghold White City, but there insisted on driving a jeep out into the jungle so that he could mortar the surrounding Japanese. One of the most hazardous take-offs he ever made was in a light aircraft in which Bernard Fergusson had flown across from Aberdeen. When Fergusson reached White City the Japanese were attacking it, and he took out (besides Peter) two Gurkhas who had been wounded by the bombardment during the night. In his book *The Wild Green Earth* he recorded the unorthodox departure with a certain satisfaction:

> Now Peter Fleming was a big boy at school when I was a little one; I used to be frightened of him; but on this happy occasion, having put one (stretcher-case) Gurkha on the stretcher platform, and inserted another underneath it, I climbed up behind the pilot with my legs round his neck, and put Peter in the Black Hole in the bottom of the aircraft, where he couldn't see a thing, not even daylight. Thus, with our departure punctuated by an occasional mortar burst, we took off for Aberdeen; with Fleming, sometime Captain of the Oppidans, underneath, and with Fergusson definitely on top.

Never again did Peter manage to put himself in such a dangerous position; never again did he become so closely involved in the fighting. For the rest of the war—even though D Division's work became ever more sophisticated and successful—he was denied any chance to distinguish himself in action.

For months—and indeed for years—he had been in that frustrating state of being extremely busy and constantly rushing about without ever getting the chance of any concrete achievement. So uncertain was he about what he wanted to do when the war ended that in the summer of 1945, after the victory in Europe, he signed on for a further year in the army. Much of his frustration came out in a long letter which he wrote to Barrington-Ward at *The Times* from Delhi on June 30th, 1945—a time when there was still no end of the Japanese war in sight:

> Dear B-W ... One of your preoccupations at the moment must, I imagine, be staff-planning, and, though I don't suppose I am a major factor in any of your problems, I rather assume that *The Times* has, or imagines that it may have, some sort of use for me

after the war. So I feel I ought to let you know how things stand with me at this moment. In the first place, if you *do* want me, I'm going to be a very bad starter. I've deferred my release, which is due this autumn, for a year. From my own point of view this is a silly thing to have done, but for various reasons which I won't bother you with it really wouldn't have been fair to my superiors, my subordinates or the Japanese to walk out on the job at this stage, though I've had more than enough of it. This of course means that if I figure in your plans at all, it can only be in the long-term variety.

In the second place, though for the last five and a half years I've had little time or inclination to think about my personal destinies, I *have* made various discoveries about myself, among them the fact (at least I'm pretty sure it is a fact) that Nature never intended me to be a pillar of *The Times*: a flying buttress, perhaps, but not a pillar. I won't bore you with half a page of introspection on this subject; but you knew me well enough before the war not to reject out of hand the contention that I'm too much of an individualist, too much of an adventurer, and have too many blind spots to play an important part on *The Times*.

Even if this were not the case (in the third place) it would be unfair not to point out, what may not have occurred to you very forcibly, that four or five years of exile in the rather childish atmosphere of this sub-continent don't improve one's qualifications for helping to guide British public opinion through the sort of problems which will confront it when I return to civil life. You can't have an *important* member of your staff never quite managing to remember whether Dumbarton Oaks [an Allied conference held near Washington in 1943]

(a) has just been acquired by the National Trust or

(b) is run before the Kentucky Derby.

This is perhaps not a very vital point, but it does—from your staff-planning point of view—re-emphasize the fact of my being a bad starter.

In the fourth and I hope the last place, there is the question of what I shall *want* to do when I stop playing with the Japanese; and this question I'm afraid I simply can't begin to answer, except to say that I should hate to sever all connections with *The Times*. I've had a fairly busy war and during the last three and a half years I've literally hardly ever been continuously in the same place for more than two weeks at a time; and this, as you may imagine, has had an unsettling effect on my already restless character. So as far as my personal inclinations go, I shall simply have to wait and see what they are.

I'm sorry to inflict this long and not very constructive screed on you (and I apologize for not inflicting it earlier. I've been shockingly neglectful of my private and professional affairs) ... I badly need your guidance and advice.

I hope you and the family are well. Please give them my love and remember me to P.H.S. which it will be very nice to revisit, in spite of sad memories of Geoffrey [Dawson had died on 7 November 1944].

When he wrote this letter Peter was clearly expecting to stay out east for longer than in fact he did. Soon after the Japanese surrender in August he closed the offices of D Division (or Force 456, as it was by then officially known), and in a charming letter thanked all the girls who had worked for him, explaining how difficult it had been to think of a token present which would adequately express his gratitude for all the hard work they had done:

The only solution I have been able to think of is to offer everyone a copy of one of my books. Those who have read these works will realize that this is not much of an offer, but even my severest critics have never denied that an early Fleming (there are, perhaps fortunately, no late ones) will often make an acceptable Christmas present to an old governess or an unimportant aunt.

In October he travelled extensively in Burma, Malaya and Vietnam to assess the results of his deception schemes, and at the beginning of November he flew home from Saigon expressly to reach Nettlebed in time for the first pheasant shoot of the season—a day which he had arranged by remote control and which turned out successfully, with a bag of ninety-nine pheasants and fourteen partridges.

Friends who had not seen him since the war began were astonished to find that the only British decoration he had won was the O.B.E: with his pre-war record and character, they thought, he must have got a D.S.O. at least. They could not know—for he certainly would not tell them—that he had done as well as anyone possibly could have in the strange career into which fate had guided him. Mountbatten, writing to him in January 1946, thanked him handsomely for all his hard work and said that the only serious defect in Peter's organization had been that he himself 'was trying to do more than one man could possibly hope to achieve'. The Chinese, too, appreciated his efforts on their behalf, and awarded him the

Order of the Cloud and Banner. With this he was pleased, in a modest way; and of his O.B.E. he once said to a friend—with only the faintest trace of irony—that he was delighted to have the same decoration as his grandmother had won in 1918 for running the family house in Grosvenor Square as a hospital for wounded officers. But it was perhaps because of his own disappointment with what he had been able to achieve in the war that afterwards he wrote and talked so little about the many strange things that he had done.

One incident which he *was* happy to relate took place on the coast of the Arakan peninsula, where he was visiting deception units in the field accompanied by his naval adviser, Ran Antrim. Returning after a couple of hours' absence to their encampment, he found Antrim (who had absolutely nothing else to do) idly flicking through some girlie magazines, and appeared to be greatly shocked. Antrim, amused by his reaction, said 'Really, Peter, you sound almost like a bishop,' and Peter was delighted by the remark. If ever he wrote his autobiography, he said, that was what he would call it: *Almost a Bishop*.

13
Squire of Nettlebed

It seemed very odd to some of Peter's friends that after the war he did not, as they put it, *do* anything. In his letter to Barrington-Ward he had deliberately stepped off the ladder of succession at *The Times*; he was offered, and refused, the safe Conservative seat of Henley and South Oxfordshire which his father had once held; his war career in deception made him a natural candidate for high office in one of the secret intelligence departments in Whitehall, yet he made no move to continue with that kind of work.

Anybody who thought this strange failed to appreciate one fundamental fact about Peter: he had absolutely no conventional ambition. He did not *want* to edit *The Times*, and in no way craved the power that the editorship would have given him; he did not *want* to be a politician, for politics (particularly on the home front) bored him rigid, and he would have been nauseated by the cant and hypocrisy of Westminster; he did not *want* to be head of M.I.5.

What he did want—he discovered as he gradually settled down at home—was to go on writing and at the same time to manage his estate. He wanted, in short, to become a literary squire, and he cultivated this modest aim with marked success for the rest of his life. His sense of duty was private rather than public—to his family and his land, rather than to the State—and now at Nettlebed he sought to work it out.

Before the war he had never had much chance to take a close interest in the estate, but now for the first time he came to grips with the land that his uncle had given him. Of the 2,000 acres nearly half were woodland; but the majority of the woods were concentrated on the eastern side of the estate, where he had built Merrimoles, so that he owned two quite different types of country. The eastern half was heavily timbered, with large beech-woods and many ornamental trees planted in the fields; the western side was far more open and was known as 'the partridge ground' because of its clear, rolling fields. The farm land on both sides was of poor quality—typical Chiltern soil, thin, chalky and full of the flints that in earlier years had been used along with brick to give the area the distinctive texture of its buildings. Two of the farms were let, and only two—Bromsden and Howberry Wood—were in hand, so that the agricultural staff was relatively small. It was many years since two of the twenty-seven gardeners employed at Joyce Grove had gone out armed with besoms on the mornings of shooting days to sweep the gravel rides down which the guns would walk; but on the forestry side the estate still employed fourteen men, and a small saw-mill in the estate yard converted much of the home-grown timber into planks or fence- and gate-posts.

Like most of the rest of England in 1945, the place was thoroughly run down when Peter returned to it: a good deal of the timber had been compulsorily felled during the war, and on the farm there was very little machinery, cart-horses still being used for much of the work. In any case, quite apart from the depressing effects of the war, the place had drifted, without the galvanizing presence of an owner, since the death of old Robert in 1933, and Peter found he had inherited a tradition whereby the estate ran at a slight but persistent loss. Although profits from forestry more than made good the losses incurred on the farm, there was a further large burden in the form of the old-age pensioners, whose pensions were paid by the estate and who lived rent-free in cottages which the estate had expensively to maintain. Altogether—besides the land—Peter found himself the owner of some fifty cottages and houses in the village of Nettlebed, and even those that were let brought in only a token rent.

Fortunately for his tenants, he proved the least extortionate of landlords. He was happy to let past traditions run on, and he erred, if at all, on the side of generosity: when tenants defaulted on their rent he was always apologetic about pressing his demands, and he was as surprised as he was pleased if the estate ever made a profit. It was never his aim to squeeze huge amounts of money out of his land: he would far rather—as he had proclaimed in his original manifesto of February 1940—try to 'create, in this corner of Oxfordshire, a non-artificial, unsubsidized example of what we would all like England to be'. Luckily he had the means to carry out this modest social experiment: although his mother still had control of the money that his father had left, his own accumulated book royalties yielded enough income for him to live on and enabled him to view the estate's poor financial performance with equanimity. Celia, too, had earned herself handsome amounts of money on stage and screen: her pre-war reputation had been greatly enhanced by her unforgettable performances in the films *In Which We Serve* and *Brief Encounter*, for the second of which, in 1946, she won an Oscar as the best actress of the year.

For the first time since the house had been built, the family settled down together at Merrimoles. Except in good summers, when life could spill out agreeably on to the terrace, it did not prove a very comfortable home. The kitchen had been sited much too far from the dining-room; Peter had nowhere to write except a small and rather depressing study at one end of the ground floor; and the central heating was so inefficient that in winter the occupants generally abandoned the pleasant drawing-room and huddled round the fire in a much smaller room that had been designed as a nursery.

To Peter, however, these shortcomings were of minimal importance. What mattered to him was that the house stood on a lovely site, in the middle of his land—and here he created a small-scale replica of the kind of establishment that had given him so much security in childhood: a country house, a nanny, a cook, a gardener-cum-groom, horses to ride, dogs, and, all round, the family's own acres into which the children would be able to spread themselves as they grew up. Nichol, who was six when the war ended, was soon reinforced by Kate, born in 1946, and by Lucy, who followed a year later. Peter wanted them all to have a conventional upbringing: he put Nichol down for Eton as soon as he was born and sent him, when he was eight, to a near-by preparatory school. The girls were also entered for traditional boarding schools.

Peter himself remained in the army until the autumn of 1946, but for the last six months of his service he was virtually unemployed and had plenty of time to learn some rudiments of forestry and agriculture (of which he was until then largely ignorant) and to resume the threads of his literary career. He returned to *The Times* as just the sort of flying buttress that he had hoped he might become—a writer of Fourth Leaders, on a retainer of £250 a year (Barrington-Ward had offered him £500 but he, characteristically, had protested that this was far too much and had got the amount halved). Of these urbane, five-hundred-word trifles, these witty and epigrammatic comments on the more abstruse news items of the day, he became a master, and he contributed fourth leaders at an average rate of one a week for the next four years. Now that the *genre* is unhappily defunct, it is perhaps worth recalling one example of Peter's work:

SHAVING TIME

Some men, probably, can remember quite clearly the first time they shaved. It was an adventure in its way. The borrowed razor, cleaving tortuous rides in the jungle of lather, played havoc with our adolescent pimples: blood flowed freely, and was not very cleverly staunched. 'Signs of a struggle,' the police would probably have noted if they had had cause to enter the bathroom when we had finished; but though the experiment was attended by anxiety and suffering we emerged from it with a feeling of pride. A good deal of our face was down, as the farmers say, to sticking plaster; but the remainder, when we passed our hand over it in a mature and contemplative manner (which we did at least once every minute), no longer felt like the pelt of a half-grown dormouse afflicted with mange. Nobody, henceforth, could tell us that we should have to think about starting to shave soon. We had thought about it; we had started; we had shaved.

But the novelty did not long outlive the sticking-plaster. Shaving became a routine and like most routines engendered, at times, the wish to rebel against it. It is done, or anyhow it ought to be done, at an hour when both tempers and time are short. Our reserves of self-discipline have been heavily drawn upon in order to get ourselves out of bed at all, and we are in no mood to devote ten minutes of our valuable time to the otiose and Sisyphean task of scraping off our face a crop of stubble which will be back there again tomorrow morning. A sense of the futility of human endeavour overwhelms us as we look back down the years and tot up the man-hours devoted exclusively to depilation. Even if we only have to shave once a day and even if it only takes us ten minutes to do so, we have lost over three weeks—three whole weeks—in every ten years since we started to shave. If we began at sixteen and if we live till ninety-six, we shall have lost—squandered, written off, rendered null and void—something like six calendar months, counting the extra three hours and twenty minutes on account of leap years. The thought is really intolerable.

The trouble with shaving has hitherto been that you cannot combine it with any other form of activity. When a man takes up his razor he as it were puts himself into a trance, cuts himself off from the stream of human experience. He can, at his own risk, think about something else; but so he could if he had been buried alive. This morning a correspondent gives us all some hope that the iron curtain which daily bars off the shaver from the rewards and penalties of human existence may be on the point of lifting; he reports having seen, on a recent morning, a respectably-dressed individual walking down a street near Hyde Park and shaving himself, as he walked, with a patent machine.

Most of us would find this feat rather difficult at first. Unless at any time we had had the invaluable preparatory experience of playing the fife in a military band, a certain hesitation might be noticeable in our gait, a tendency to stumble, to zigzag, to pause for longish periods in front of shop windows. It may be some time before shaving, like smoking before it, is promoted from something done in private and generally at the halt to something done in public and if necessary on the move. Meanwhile the activities of the pioneers in this movement will be followed with admiration, curiosity, and plenty of cotton wool.

Like almost all contributions to *The Times* of those days, the Fourth Leaders were anonymous, and it became an agreeable pastime among Peter's friends to discern, from their inimitable style, those that were written by him.

He returned also to the *Spectator*, at first writing book and theatre reviews; but in August 1946 he embarked on an altogether new type of enterprise, creating an *alter ego* which was to survive for a quarter of a century. The journal carried a weekly column called 'Spectator's Notebook' written by the editor, Wilson Harris, and signed by him with the pseudonym 'Janus'. When Harris went on holiday Peter took the column over and for his own pseudonym selected 'Strix'—the Latin for 'screech-owl' (and also, as a good-natured critic once pointed out, for 'drain-pipe').

'Janus has left London for a well-earned holiday,' the first Strix column began,

and for the next three weeks these notes will come to you from an altogether lower level. The finger of his deputy can by no stretch of the imagination be said to be on the pulse of affairs. I am in the confidence neither of our rulers nor of their opponents, Ambassadors do not invite me to luncheon, and though I once knew a bishop he died, I am sorry to say, some years ago ... But it were otiose to dwell further upon disabilities which will speak all too plainly for themselves: the proof of the egg-powder is in the omelette.

Early Strix columns consisted of several independent paragraphs on different subjects, but Peter later adopted the practice of writing a single article, and he gradually established himself as an essayist of great elegance and individuality—the best, one literary friend claimed, since Hazlitt.

Though no less urbane and amusing than his Fourth Leaders, his Strix articles were much more idiosyncratic, for in the *Spectator* he was less closely circumscribed by narrow traditions and by the need to be strictly topical. Strix did frequently comment on affairs of the moment, but more often the column reflected its author's various preoccupations —with literature, with the theatre and above all with the country. 'Max Beerbohm in tweeds' was one comment on Strix's style, and the phrase— kindly intended—was perhaps not an unfair description of the new tenant of 99 Gower Street.

Peter's decision to live in the country was received with great scorn by Jonathan Cape, who assured him that if he settled at Merrimoles he would cut himself off from the pulse of literary London and so would blight his career. Cape quite failed to realize that Peter was essentially a country person, and that it irked him severely to live in a town; and yet, in spite of the alleged disadvantages, the new bumpkin continued to serve Cape handsomely as a literary adviser and spotter of talent. Among the new authors he brought to the firm was Fitzroy Maclean, whom he happened to meet at the very moment when the rival publishers Collins were dithering over a book which Maclean had just completed. Hearing something of the manuscript, Peter asked the author if he could see it, read it, immediately offered him a flat 20-per-cent royalty, and so secured for Cape a best-seller in the form of *Eastern Approaches*.

Another author whom Peter cultivated was Adrian Carton de Wiart. In July 1948, when Cape asked him to find out what was happening about the general's autobiography, he wrote back;

I see him fairly regularly and my impression is
(a) That the book is definitely not tied up with anyone.
(b) That none of it is written.
(c) That it probably never will be written.
(d) That it may not be a very good book if it is.

Of these forecasts only the third proved wrong. The general finished the book, but *Happy Odyssey*, which Cape published, proved rather a disappointment, due mainly to the author's excessive modesty (he nowhere mentioned that he had won the V.C.). Yet Peter remained fascinated by Carton de Wiart: he got him elected (along with Wavell and Bernard

Fergusson) to a small dining club in London, shot with him frequently and later tried to write a full-scale biography of this extraordinary warrior.

In his dealings with Cape Peter was far more forthright than most other people dared to be, and he would not suffer fools just because they happened to be in the firm's pay. When Jonathan sent him a copy of Alexander Baron's novel *From the City, From the Plough*, he returned a scathing assessment of the book's jacket:

Dear Jonathan,

Thank you very much for sending me that good war-book. I thought the dust-wrapper a particularly fine bit of work in its own *genre*. The vomit-coloured background, merging into a tasteful black, makes an instant appeal to the senses, and there is a masterly insouciance about the way in which those lacunae of stagnant glue are grouped round the central tea-mug. There is a splendid sort of *challenge* about the whole composition. It defies you to guess what it represents, it defies you to find in whatever it does represent any clue as to what the book is about, it defies you to look at it more than once, it defies you to buy the book. I think it does a swell job.

If its—and the title's—object was to conceal or gloss over the blurb's admission that 'this is a war novel,' they do it very well; but if they are meant to support, however indirectly, the idea that 'this is the novel you have been waiting for,' I do not think they are well-chosen.

If you were to insert a sub-title—'Being Some Account of the Salvage Drive in Lechlade Rural District'—the dust-wrapper would be a coherent whole. As it is—well, have another look at it yourself.

See you on Wednesday, I hope.

Your almost infallible adviser,

PETER

With his commitments to *The Times*, to the *Spectator* and to Cape, Peter had a good deal of work. Yet none of it fully extended him; he hankered to complete some more solid and enduring piece of writing, and early in 1947 he started a novel for which he chose a simple title—*The Sett*. Like all his fiction this drew closely on his own experience, its inspiration being the activities of the Auxiliary Units in Kent in 1940.

The manuscript begins promisingly with sketches of life in 303 Special Topographical Unit, which has established its underground head-quarters in an enlarged badger sett in a chalk-pit on the lip of the

Chilterns. Whether or not Peter had in mind an actual chalk-pit, it is impossible to say; but the one he described lay—even if only in his imagination—somewhere between Merrimoles and his childhood home Braziers. In this well-hidden and equipped den twelve men are living, commanded by Colonel George Tariot.

At the start of the story the German invasion has been an unqualified success; England's surrender has been announced by church bells, the Government has withdrawn to Canada, and Buckingham Palace has become the Nazi headquarters in England, known as 'the Brown House'. The thirty S.T.U.s scattered about England are in tenuous radio contact with the exiled Government in Ottawa, but soon their ciphers fall into the hands of the enemy, and they are unable to send any more messages.

For several chapters the author skilfully explores the possibilities of the situation, showing how claustrophobia threatens the mental stability of the men living under ground, how any small success they gain (such as an ambush of a party of officers) is cancelled out immediately by German reprisals, and how closely the men who have returned to the earth become involved with the life of the woods that protect them. He also introduces one or two agreeably rustic characters, among them Ted Harbottle, the old poacher whom the Germans have left at large: 'Coinciding as it did with the first weeks of the shooting season, the German invasion of England did not at first command a large measure of Harbottle's attention.'

The further Peter went, however, the greater became the difficulties in which he found himself. The narrative kept getting interrupted by long and largely irrelevant character-descriptions; close-up pictures of life in the sett alternated uncomfortably with discussions of global strategy; the characters—and the language in which they spoke—were distressingly wooden. Perhaps the book's greatest single fault was that it had no consistent focus, no one viewpoint which a reader might easily occupy.

Nobody saw the shortcomings of the manuscript more clearly than Peter himself, and a diary which he began to keep on his fortieth birthday (May 31st, 1947) shows not only what a strugle he was having with the book, but also how desultory and unfulfilled he felt in general:

31 May Saturday. Forty and lucky to be around, I suppose. Rode before breakfast on a Burmese morning, completed by two little doves which might have rectified the local colour anywhere in the tropics ... Cinders [his horse] full of grass and sluggish. Worked on *The Sett* all morning: fluentish but trite—I don't think it'll come to anything, but I must finish something. Nanny intervened to prevent Tink [the cat] torturing a nest of baby rabbits in the lavender; nothing will come of it in the end, but she is nice about animals.

1 June Picture postcard day. Went to arbitrate in a complicated landlord v. tenant dispute near Shiplake but found I was a week too early, so took C and the Hart-Davises to bathe at Shillingford ... Arthur Villiers came to tea ... he remembered Winston being pleased, when he had written it, about the last sentence in his obituary of Mokie; it is a very good sentence [see page 30]. Nanny has taken the five little rabbits into the nursery, which is simpler than shutting the cat up.

2 June Rode early. Same sort of day—temp. over ninety in parts. Two rabbits dead, but Nanny takes her casualties like a man ... Worked on and re-read *The Sett*. It is like slick scenery with no proper actors and no plot; at least, I can't think how the plot is going to work out. Butlers seem to keep on crossing the stage and rearranging the papers in a most impeccable way, but nothing actually happens ...

12 June Eric Linklater came down to lunch and said, persuasively, that I ought to write a book about the Heroic Spirit. I wish I could write a book about Mustard and Cress. Dictated letters to Judy [Frankie Wilson's wife, and Peter's secretary], rode, and that was all.

A week later his unsatisfactory existence was violently interrupted by an accident, which he later recorded in his journal:

19–29 June Not a very good interlude, and not over yet. Started out riding round after lunch. Going along the ride in West Leaze bank Cinders stumbled, came down, did a slow somersault and brought his vast quarters down on me. I had fallen clear and was spreadeagled on rock-hard ground and realized at once that I had had it in some way. I was only about 800 yards from the house but of course invisible unless someone came along the ride. I did not pass out, but when the bad stuff was over I found I couldn't move.

He lay there helpless for several hours until he was found by one of the expatriate Polish soldiers who were still living in a camp of Nissen huts near by, and when he eventually reached hospital in Reading it was discovered that his pelvis was broken. From this, the most serious injury he ever received, he took several months to recover. It was nearly eight weeks before he was strong enough to shoot again, and even then (he reported in his game-book) he 'sat in a chair like a rajah' as rabbits came out of corn that was being harvested, 'and the gun felt very heavy.' Even after another three weeks, when he chased the first partridges of the season on September 6th, he noted that he was 'still walking rather slowly'.

Although to most of his friends his eventual recovery seemed complete, there were people in London who felt that he was never quite the same again. Some of the spring had gone out of him, they thought, and his attitude to life seemed slightly to have changed: whereas in the past he had always been old-fashioned in a pleasant and amusing way, his ideas were now tinged by a reactionary and faintly tiresome intransigence. The change was very slight, but enough to provoke comment in Printing House Square.

His behaviour certainly tended to be old-fashioned. He favoured a few slightly antiquated words (such as 'bugger,' which he used instead of 'homosexual' or 'queer'), and bought a series of ancient cars, preferring above all a vintage Rolls-Royce shooting brake which, being hopelessly un-mechanical, he drove with an atrocious grinding of gears. He never dreamt of having his hair cut at any barber except Trumper's in Curzon Street, and although for most of his life he used the same brand of hair lotion from that establishment, it took him years to grasp the fact that the two separate and sharply defined liquids in the bottle (yellow over green) should be shaken together before he applied them to his head.

His good clothes, though well cut, had a faintly Edwardian air about them (before that again became fashionable), and in London he always looked smart rather than comfortable. He himself was well aware that he could never pass himself off as a man about town, and once in the *Spectator* he recorded how a man living in the country soon 'finds that any dandiacal impulses he may have had tend to atrophy' because his good clothes, rarely worn, outlast their fashionable life.

> His lapels are wrongly cut, the buttons on his sleeve are too many or too few, his trousers are too narrow or too wide. On my rare appearances in society there often comes into my head a sentence from some old, forgotten novel: 'Uncle Hector, too, was there, up from the country—a rubicund old fellow, dressed in the fashion of a bygone age.'

At home Peter's clothes, though never scruffy, were invariably casual. Unless he had to go to a meeting he would never wear a tie: open-necked shirts or roll-necked jerseys appealed to him most, and he almost always wore a tweed jacket made from a yellowish-brown cloth associated with, although not exclusive to, Black Mount. Every now and then he would embrace with enthusiasm the latest sartorial innovation, or create one of his own: soon after the war, for instance, he acquired a liking for blue jeans; later he became a passionate advocate of string vests, and later still one of thigh-length rubber waders, in which he floundered through the undergrowth on his solitary shooting expeditions, maintaining—in the teeth of all the evidence—that they were far more practical and comfortable than any other form of footwear.

His basically conservative nature came out strongly in the way he harked back to the army. Although anything but conceited about his achievements in the war, he used the title 'Colonel' for the rest of his life; on the estate he was known as 'the Colonel' and addressed simply as 'Colonel' by the men. Indeed, he ran the whole estate on para-military lines, and since many of the men had been in the army anyway, it seemed perfectly natural that he should. In his speech, too, he deliberately retained military overtones, using, for instance, the expression 'hot meal' for any form of repast. 'Got to help a friend give a hot meal to the Queen,' he said one night in the Garrick, to explain his appearance there in full evening dress. 'Wouldn't have him in the regiment,' he would say of anyone for whom he did not much care. He still cherished the memory of his father's valour, and soon after the war sent a copy of Winston Churchill's obituary notice to its author, asking if he would sign it. Churchill replied from his home at 28 Hyde Park Gate:

> My Dear Peter, (for that I must call you),
>
> I gladly sign the note I wrote about your dear father who served in my squadron of the Queen's Own Oxfordshire Hussars. It would be nice of you to send me a copy, if you have one, of the reprint, as I would like to keep it among my papers. It gave me pleasure in reading these lines to think of him again intently.
>
> Let me see you some time.
>
> > Yours very sincerely,
> >
> > WINSTON S. CHURCHILL

With time on his hands and his military inclinations still strong, it was natural that Peter should join the Territorial Army; and he carried on family traditions by enlisting in the Fourth Battalion of the Oxfordshire and Buckinghamshire Light Infantry. Waiving his true rank, he joined as a lieutenant, but quickly rose again to command the battalion. In Nettlebed he became Vice-President, and later, President of the local branch of the British Legion, and every year the Remembrance Day parade through the village.

To complete the recovery from his accident, early in 1948 he went for the first time to the West Indies. To him the appeal of sun and sand was strictly limited, and so, predictably enough, were the attractions of the Caribbean. His rather off-hand view of the place came out in a letter which he wrote on March 9th, from Guadeloupe to the author and traveller Freya Stark, with whom he had stayed in Barbados:

My Dear Freya,

What (and to be frank it is not very much) I like about this place is the contrast. It is probably pure bad luck that the supply of electricity failed, utterly, two nights ago and has not since recovered ... To nail up all the doors of the lavatories except one, on the other hand, strikes one as a wilful and almost too empirical experiment with the laws of supply and demand, especially at a time when there is no moon ...

I *did* enjoy staying with you ... I was very idle in Barbados, which I think was probably good for me and which I certainly wouldn't have been if you hadn't provided such an idyllic background ...

Late though the hour is, somebody has started to slaughter a pig in what we should call the Saloon Bar. Unless, of course, it's a *crime passionelle.*

Yours ever,

PETER

Even without the riding accident, it seems unlikely that he would ever have finished *The Sett.* He did take it up again from time to time, and made enough progress to create, by an odd fluke, a character called Moneypenny—the very name that his brother Ian, a few years later, was to bestow on James Bond's boss's secretary. But he was strangely feckless about the book—the loose foolscap sheets on which he wrote in long-hand were not even numbered—and after about 30,000 words he gave it up.

To nobody—not even to his closest friend Rupert, who since 1939 had been living at Bromsden Farm, on the estate—did he divulge that he had tried and failed. He simply forged ahead with his journalistic work and at the same time took an ever more active part in the affairs of South Oxfordshire.

On the estate he never did much physical work—not because he was lazy or disdained manual labour, but rather because he was clumsy with his hands and had a lethal effect on machinery. He did sometimes drive a tractor at hay-making and harvest, but apart from that his main contribution to domestic economy was to ignite, periodically, various heaps of old straw and manure which lay about the place, thereby nearly asphyxiating anyone who lived close at hand. The day-to-day running of the place was left to a bailiff, and Peter's role was, in the main, exhortatory. The same restlessness that before the war had driven him all over the world now drove him incessantly round the estate: if he was not walking or riding he cruised the private roads in one of his ancient *barouches*, always stopping to have a word with any of his men whom he met, but always—even though he might not have any urgent commitment—in a hurry to press on. 'Do you want to come round?' he would ask of anyone who happened to be with him, and the question became a routine method of indicating that a tour of the estate was about to begin. He could not bear sitting about, and he would often leave lunch with the meal scarcely finished—even if a guest was present—abruptly remarking that he had to see the cowman.

He directed operations from the estate-yard in Nettlebed, where, opposite the stumpy, conical chimney of an obsolete brick-kiln, he had a cold, draughty and exceedingly uncomfortable office. Its spartan interior was almost undecorated, except by large photographs of his father and grandfather, and by a notice proclaiming

EXPOSITION OFFICIELLE

DES

CHASSEURS DE SERPENTS

which a Strix fan had sent him after he had confessed in the *Spectator* that, as a means of deterring picnickers, he sometimes put up notices saying 'Beware of the Snakes' along his side of the Nettlebed–Reading road (it escaped the attention of the motorists that snakes appeared to frequent the south side of the road only).

His office, he knew quite well, was grotesquely inefficient (the telephone was all but inaudible, and to communicate with his secretary, up some stairs, round two corners, and in another room, was in itself a major undertaking); yet he grew very fond of it and once declared in the *Spectator* that if—as was perfectly possible—he could emerge from his place of work in the evening and see a woodcock roding overhead, he did not in the least covet the facilities of the most modern office in London. Indeed, the idea of routine work in a London office filled him with dismay, and he never ceased to be glad that he had abandoned his career in the City with such dispatch.

In the village he took an interest in community life which was dutiful rather than enthusiastic. He became President of the Working Men's

Club (whose excellent premises had been built by his grandfather), and President also of the Nettlebed Cricket Club, for which he often played. He was never much of a cricketer, being only a moderate batsman, a complete non-starter as a bowler, and—because of a weak right elbow which prevented him from throwing overarm—a very peculiar fielder; nevertheless, by sheer determination he sometimes managed to scrape up twenty or thirty runs, and was always a most welcome member of the side.

He also instituted the custom of bringing his own eleven to play the village on Whit Monday—although in doing so he made a social *faux pas* which caused a good deal of local irritation. The match began in the morning, and instead of taking the more democratic alternative of giving both teams lunch in a marquee on the ground, he always invited his own side back to Merrimoles, leaving the village to console themselves in the Sun Inn—a move which (though he never realized it) produced considerable resentment. Even after the war, in which he had been thrown into close contact with every kind of person, he still found it difficult to talk at any length to the ordinary people of the village, and as he toured the estate his conversations with the men were always stilted and banal. (This awkwardness, however, did not prevent him from getting to know his men well.)

It was shooting, more than any other activity, that brought him into close and affectionate contact with the stretch of country which he had inherited. Once in Calcutta during the war, when Frankie Wilson had asked him what he intended to do when he got home, he had replied: 'I'm going to shoot and shoot and shoot.' And shoot he did, with an enthusiasm that became almost obsessive.

He had no wish to achieve the monstrous bags of pre-war battues, in one of which 1,400 pheasants had been killed during a single day round Bromsden Farm. He did not like having half-tame pheasants about the place, and although he continued to employ old Harry Brown, the game-keeper, he would never allow him to rear: he much preferred to have relatively few wild birds, which flew far better than any artificially produced, and if the first time through yielded a bag of a hundred, he was more than content. He took great trouble organizing the three or four full-scale days which he held each season, and he ran them like military exercises: the guns were marched about between drives almost at the double, amid a good deal of banter, and Peter would issue orders with a mock severity that delighted his guests. He himself would rarely draw a number and stand in the line; he preferred to stand alone, behind the line, and shoot only those pheasants which came over really high, having beaten the guns in front.

His own excellence as a shot ensured that he received many invitations elsewhere. Although never very stylish—he was efficient, rather than graceful—he was generally reliable and sometimes brilliant, and for years shot regularly with the same groups of friends—with the Bowes-Lyons at St Paul's Walden, with the Mounts at Wasing, the Astors at Hever, and with Michael Dawson (Geoffrey's son) at Langcliffe, in Yorkshire. The 'Remarks' column of his game-book contained many asides, not all of them to do with the chase. 'Splendid day—all wild birds and mostly very good,' he wrote after seven guns, including King George VI, had killed 549 pheasants at St Paul's Walden on November 14th, 1947. 'H.M. very accurate indeed. Everyone in good form over Dalton's resignation' (Hugh Dalton had been the Labour Chancellor of the Exchequer). Five years later Peter commemorated the death of the King by noting: 'I think he was a very good, but probably not a great, shot. He absolutely loved shooting.'

Exactly the same verdict might have been passed on Peter himself. He did absolutely love shooting, and what he liked best of all were solitary expeditions, or those undertaken with only one other gun, on which some rather improbable feat was achieved. At home he was to some extent inhibited by the disapproval of Brown, the keeper, who did not like having his preserves constantly stirred up by the squire marching and counter-marching through them; the result was that he would frequent the extremities of the estate, among them Nettlebed Common, a wild tract of land behind the village, part of which had been scalloped into flooded pits by the extraction, years ago, of sand and clay for brick-making. These stagnant lagoons, surrounded and in some cases almost covered by dense undergrowth, occasionally harboured a mallard, a woodcock or what Peter called a 'web-footed' cock pheasant; and if he managed, against all odds, to secure one of these elusive fowl, his afternoon was made.

His shooting seasons gradually assumed a regular pattern. Towards the end of June he would begin remarking, with unusual animation: 'Only six weeks to the start of the shooting season!', or 'Extraordinary—there's only just over a month till shooting begins again!' Then, on about August 10th, he would drive north to Glenkiln, Tony Keswick's estate in Dumfriesshire, where he invariably spent the Twelfth. After two or three days' shooting there he would go on to Black Mount, joining a huge family party for about a week. On his way south again he would sometimes stop for a couple of days' grouse-driving with Michael Dawson. Back at Nettlebed he would salute the opening of the partridge season on September 1st by beating the estate's farthest bounds in a series of what he called 'death-marches'. In November and December he would shoot the coverts and take up his numerous outside invitations, and in January he would often take a week's wildfowling or snipe-shooting in Ireland or Scotland.

It was on one of these New Year expeditions that there occurred the celebrated incident of Barstow's Goose. In January 1948 Peter rented a shoot called Dippin, on the southern end of the Isle of Arran, and went there for a week with John Barstow (the elder brother of Oliver) and another friend, Ronnie Shaw-Kennedy. One morning, as they returned to breakfast from the morning flight, John announced that he had shot a goose (his first) but that it had fallen into the sea and he had been unable to retrieve it. Many ribald doubts were cast on the existence of this bird; but since the tide was coming in, and the wind was on-shore, Peter thought it worth returning to the scene—and there, sure enough was a sodden corpse. When they collected it, however, they found it was not a goose at all, but a merganser, which has a strong claim to the title of the fishiest and least edible duck in existence. As all kinds of meat were then still scarce because of post-war rationing, they carefully wrapped up the remains and posted them to Cyril Connolly at White's Club, in London, with a card saying 'With love from Lady Mary.'

Once Peter had established his annual sporting pattern, he scarcely varied it, although his own interests did shift from time to time. For example his enthusiasm for deer-stalking—never very strong—died out completely. In the first few years after the war he used the .275 Mauser which *The Times* had given him to shoot one or two of the fallow deer which had escaped from parks and were by then living wild in the woods round Nettlebed; and in 1948 he acquired a splendid elk-hound called Trigger who, partly by instinct and partly by training, chased any deer that he put up in a wide circle and brought it unerringly back to the rifle. After a couple of years, however, Peter's heart softened, and he often wrote in his game-book at the end of the season: 'Several fallow about, but I spare them.'

At Black Mount, too, he left the deer to others, shooting his last stag in 1953. There, as elsewhere, his chief delight became long, solitary expeditions to the highest and remotest parts of the forest, and he particularly liked going after ptarmigan, which inhabit only the high tops. 'Go up Beinn Doe [the mountain opposite the front of the lodge] and shoot a ptarmigan,' his Uncle Phil would say to him as soon as he arrived, and he was only too pleased to obey the order the moment he stepped out of his car. His 'stravaigs' and 'work-outs' featured strongly in the Black Mount game-books, where 'Peter his usual stravaig' became a common entry. Even on really abysmal days, which were signalled by the family phrase, 'Crowdies in the drawing-room' (meaning that everyone had stayed in and eaten crowdies, or scones, by the fire), he alone would brave the elements. Later on he himself created a phrase which instantly entered the family vernacular: one evening he wrote in the game-book: 'Having exhausted meteorological pejoratives, would describe weather as continuous cloudburst,' and thereafter the words 'meteorological pejoratives' were used as a kind of shorthand. Sometimes the filler-up of the game-book would write 'a really horrible day of the meteorological pejorative type,' but often the two words on their own were enough to indicate to connoisseurs that the weather had been of outstanding filthiness.

On all his solitary forays, whether in Scotland or at home, one of his chief pleasures was the company of his dogs. After some bizarre experiments (among them that of encouraging Trigger, the elk-hound, who was the size of a chunky Alsatian, to hunt rabbits and retrieve pheasants) he settled down to owning a succession of black Labradors. It was strange that—passionately keen as he was on dogs—he never became very good with them. His training methods were individualistic, to say the least: disliking violence, and hating to chastise puppies, he was always too gentle with them at the start and generally failed to establish the basic obedience essential for proper control. Instead of beating dogs when they disobeyed him, he would attempt to subdue them by various forms of mental pressure and hypnosis, glowering at them in disapproval or addressing them in a voice histrionically loaded with a mixture of anger, reproach and regret. The result was that most them were maddeningly wild: incurable chasers of hares and, until age steadied them, a menace to any organized shoot.

Occasionally, however, his unorthodox methods produced a winner. The best dog he ever owned, called Slipe, was by any standards exceptional. Peter got him as a puppy in 1949, and soon his game-book was full of the dog's praises: 'Slipe got one runner brilliantly ... Slipe particularly good ... Slipe is now a dog of recognized brilliance.' One incident that gave him enormous satisfaction was when Slipe—still not fully mature—began digging at a rabbit-hole during a hunt for a hen pheasant that had come down and run. One of the other guns said snootily: 'I see your dog still chases rabbits,' to which Peter replied: 'I don't *think* he does.' A moment later Slipe forced his wide head deeper into the hole and emerged with the pheasant which had, most unusually, gone to ground.

Peter became deeply attached to this marvellous shooting companion, and when Slipe was run over and killed—tragically enough, by a friend and colleague—his master was in great and (for once) visible distress. 'Slipe was run over on the main road just before midnight ...' he reported in his game-book:

> I had been out and forgotten to shut him in, and he had gone off after a bitch. He was alive when I got there. I took him down to the vet but his back was broken. The vet got his syringe and he died in my arms.
>
> He was a brilliant dog, and at four years old was just in his prime. He had great persistence as well as dash, would retrieve anything from a jack-snipe to a sparrow-hawk, and was wonderful in water. He was keen, gay, loyal and clever. His fault was a tendency to rove when off duty. His mother had it too, and it cost them both their lives.

Altogether, Peter's luck with dogs was wretched. Slipe's son Pistol also proved excellent, but when he was four he got cancer of the hock and had to have one hind leg amputated. One of his successors, Sealion, also died in Peter's arms, having picked up poison, and another, Sukie, was killed on the main road in exactly the same way as Slipe. Each of these losses was a heavy blow to Peter, for he loved the dogs dearly and enjoyed their uncomplicated society as much as, if not more than, that of most people. He found it simpler to establish satisfactory emotional relationships with dogs than with most humans: in returning unquestioningly his own loyalty and affection, the Labradors made easier company for him than someone who was liable to ask embarrassing questions.

There was in his nature some deep, elemental streak that gave him a great affinity not merely with dogs but with many kinds of wild creatures, and Merrimoles was intermittently occupied by a succession of semi-tame hawks, owls, magpies, ravens, badgers and foxes, to say nothing of a grey squirrel which, in the intervals of wrecking the drawing-room curtains, ate all Peter's ties and wove the chewed-up remains into a nest. His aim in harbouring these birds and animals seemed to be to gain their trust and to share their wildness: he did not want to keep them confined, but preferred that they should come and go as they wished. He admired hawks most, training a goshawk, a buzzard and several kestrels to come to his call and perch on his wrist; but he also had a special affinity with owls and liked nothing better than to be able to go outside as dusk was falling, have his whistle answered out of the beech-woods behind the house, and, a few moments later, see a large, blunt-headed, tawny shape come flitting silently down out of the darkening trees.

Some friends saw in Peter's endless shooting a form of escapism—

a retreat from the fact that his literary career was so stagnant; but this idea, though superficially plausible, was not in fact correct. It is perfectly true that in the late 1940s he was at a loss for a good subject for a book; yet even when he became immersed in a subject that stimulated him, and was in the middle of producing a book, he in no way curtailed his shooting activities.

There were two main reasons why he devoted so much time to the chase: first because he enjoyed it, and second because it gave him the daily exercise on which his well-being depended. There was scarcely a day in the winter on which he did not walk at least three or four miles—frequently much more—and even on Sundays he would often have someone drive him to a point five or six miles away, whence he would walk home.

In the winter of 1948 he arranged a brief but agreeable return to the pattern of his own pre-war existence. As the Communist revolution rolled across China, he sent a long memorandum to the Editor of *The Times* suggesting that the paper should once more send him to the Far East as its Special Correspondent. Typically enough, he volunteered to go any time after February 1st, the day on which the shooting season ended. In discussing his chances of being accepted as a bona fide correspondent he mentioned the fact that he had won the Order of the Cloud and Banner: 'Some play might usefully be made with the fact that the Chinese gave me a medal (I believe quite a good one; it is at least very large) for services in the last war against an enemy whom the Communists were also fighting.' He also raised—deferentially—the question of who was going to finance the trip, pointing out that: 'I must make it clear (with apologies) that, whereas fifteen years ago I could, and would, have mounted this expedition, if you can call it that, more or less single-handed, I now have commitments which preclude this.' In due course *The Times* agreed to send him out to China as its Special Correspondent 'to investigate and report on the new conditions there,' and the paper paid his outward air-fare and advanced him £500 on account. He set off in February, armed with a letter, couched in flowery terms on Printing House Square writing paper, which announced that the Editor had instructed him 'to visit—if conditions permit—the newly liberated areas of China with the object of describing the social and economic progress being made there.'

Conditions, unfortunately, permitted him hardly any useful manoeuvring: he never managed to penetrate the Communist areas, and was forced to observe the great political convulsion from the areas on the coast that were still in Nationalist hands. His *laissez-passer*, as he himself laconically noted later, 'didn't work'. As a result, he was unable to send any news or feature articles back from the field, and wrote nothing until he got home, when he produced two thoughtful but not very vivid turn-over articles. The whole trip was thus rather a failure; but he consoled himself by once again shooting with the Keswick brothers near Shanghai. 'Very jolly houseboat expedition,' he reported in his game-book. 'Pheasants and snipe unchanged after fifteen years.'

Back at home, he resumed the role of the literary squire—a role which he engagingly described in an article for *Leader* magazine's series 'One Man's Week' on May 28th, 1949:

Monday 7 a.m. Ride out to inspect alleged rabbit damage to ley above Upper Shaw. 'Alleged', it turns out, is putting it mildly. Retake, on outward journey, decision to get rid of Mukden, a huge, flea-bitten grey; rescind it on way home, when he goes beautifully. Lovely morning. Both dogs behave well …

9.30 a.m. Go to Estate Office. Letters from the ministries of Agriculture, Food, Works, Labour, Health, Town and Country Planning, and Fuel and Power. Visited, while dealing with them, by a civil servant. Charming man. Has come to collect evidence, additional to that already submitted in triplicate, which may or may not lead to the settlement of a claim, lodged two years ago, in respect of damage done to requisitioned property by a Service Department. Try to work out, when he leaves, how much he earned during the hour he spent in my office. Try to work out how much I should have earned by writing a brilliant article for an American magazine, if he had not come. Try to feel aggrieved. Fail, knowing that I should not have written an article, brilliant or otherwise, but would have gone to see a man about a young badger.

11 a.m. Go to see a man about a badger. No luck so far.

After lunch Go to London to be a dramatic critic. Maddened as usual (down, *hysterica passio*!) by hoardings extolling an airline which 'takes you there AND BRINGS YOU BACK!' What is there so extraordinary and so creditable about an airline which, having flown from A to B, flies back from B to A? Surely the public does not expect B.E.A. to sell its flying-machines like worn-out camels when at long last they reach their destination?

5 p.m. Meeting of the Council of the Royal Geographical Society …

7 p.m. At the Incognito Theatre. My programme has the title of the play and the name of the theatre on the outside, the list of *dramatis personae*, an embargo on smoking and a few advertisements on the inside, and nothing at all on the back. It must be worth something, but I do not think it is worth sixpence. Nor, to my way of thinking, is the play. What on earth am I to write about it?

Tuesday I write something about it. I also write something about the situation in Indonesia. I do not understand the situation in Indonesia, which is to my discredit; but neither on the other hand do I pretend to understand it, which I think in a negative sort of way is to my credit. When they ask if I will write something about Indonesia, I say: 'Certainly, if you want me to.' Then I write something. Quite possibly, it is a penetrating *aperçu*.

After lunch Walk to Charing Cross and take the tube to Blackfriars. This is the only section of our great Underground Railway System which I regard as, and indeed know from experience to be, negotiable. Full-time citizens of London may, and no doubt must, attempt more ambitious subterranean journeys; I always get lost if I do. Arrived at Blackfriars [*The Times*], I write a humorous essay, or to be more accurate an essay which long association and preconditioning will cause its readers, like Pavlov's dogs salivating when he rang a bell, to suppose humorous. This week it was (if I remember rightly) about a new Government regulation dealing with the control of jellied eels.

Wednesday Do some more writing. Telephone to various people who I think (mistakenly) may be able to produce a fast bowler to play against the village on Whit Monday. Attend meetings of the National Association of Charcoal Manufacturers and the Royal Literary Fund and return home in time for a Committee Meeting of the Working Men's Club and Institute. Less stormy than usual.

Thursday Woken early by the patter of tiny feet. Yaks, if stampeded, would make more noise, but not much more noise, than Kate (three) and Lucy (two), who constitute a knockabout turn known to our guests as the Reveille Girls. Wonder what Pavlov would have made of Toby and Trigger, who never budge from the bed in my dressing-room until I start brushing my hair. Have tried going downstairs without brushing my hair. Sticklers for protocol, they stayed where they were.

Out riding, meet Brown going round his traps, very pleased because he has got a hen sparrow-hawk with a drop of poison he put in a pigeon she killed yesterday evening. Long, deeply interesting conversation about the pheasant prospects.

Back to breakfast. Celia has a letter from Nicholas (*Dear Mummy and Daddy, I hope you are both well, I am*). Somebody has sent her a play in which the principal character is sixty years old in the first act, eighty in the second, and stone dead in the third. The author thinks this would be a splendid part for her.

Go to the Estate Office. Collins reports another bull calf, Kirkup reports that the Douglas fir transplants in Bix Larches are going brown, Sharpe reports grave trouble with a damp-course in one of the Catslipe cottages, and Mr Hall reports that a Ministry of Labour inspector is coming to see whether my saw bench complies with the Factories Act...

Friday C to London to try on clothes for her new film. Decide to devote whole day to literary composition.

9 a.m. Desk cleared for action. *9.10* See carrion crow in dead tree. Open window stealthily and engage crow with .22. Miss it. *9.15* Back at desk. *9.20* Nanny reports that the ponies have got out again. *10.30* Back at desk. *10.40* Mr Wells rings up from his farm six miles away to say that the fallow deer are on his clover again, and can I possibly come over? Say I am terribly sorry but I've got a lot of work to do. Is there a buck with them? Mr Wells says yes, big as a donkey, looks like the old white one that was there in the winter. Makes you fair wild to see them stuffing themselves with that young clover.

10.45 Depart for Mr Wells's farm with Trigger and the Mauser carbine, only to find that a collie has shifted the deer. Decide to waste no time looking for them. Waste an hour.

12.30 Back at desk. Total output for morning: 23 words, not particularly well chosen. Do a bit better in the afternoon. After tea play squash with a man I met in Saigon in 1945 ...

Afternoon Letters from Government Departments, of which nowadays one receives so many, are customarily either dull, minatory, irrelevant or incomprehensible, so it is a pleasure to get a courteous and faintly exotic one from the Colonial Office. 'Your name,' says the writer, 'has been given to me as a Chinese interpreter. If you are able to read a Chinese dialect and would be interested in the possibility of, say, six months in Malaya ...' Need hardly say that my command of Chinese (and command is emphatically not the *mot juste*) no more qualifies me to act as an interpreter in that language than it qualifies me to play cricket for England.

Feel slightly flattered, all the same.

Saturday One of Brown's sons has found a woodcock's nest in Offal Wood, the first that I ever remember being found on the place. No good for a photograph, because when sitting she is indistinguishable from the beech leaves ...

J comes over from Oxford for lunch. He recalls—while for some reason we are talking about Shakespearean criticism—Oscar Wilde's remark: 'The central problem in *Hamlet* is whether the critics are mad or only pretending to be mad.'

Cricket against the neighbouring village in the afternoon. After being dropped twice, make an extremely lucky five not out. Someone politely says that I am playing just as well as ever this year.

In the evening try for pigeons on some peas with the new decoys. Nothing doing, but the dogs kill a stoat, getting bitten on the nose in the process. Beaten at chess by C after dinner. Sit up late writing pontifical article about Formosa.

Sunday. Day of rest. Write humorous essay about blancmange, then go and see a man about a young badger. Still no luck.

This disarming chronicle contains many hints of the squire of Nettlebed's likes and dislikes, of his difficulties, and of his busy but not altogether satisfactory existence. One can discern (in chronological order) his hatred of bureaucracy, his anxiety to write something successful, his fondness for wild animals (the badger), his ignorance and dislike of foreign politics (Indonesia), his faintly bucolic attitude to London (the tube), his struggle to write Fourth Leaders (near Blackfriars), his fondness for his dogs, his passion for shooting (the pheasant prospects), his admiration for Celia's skill as an actress, the distractions of trying to write in the country (the crow and the deer), his love of China and of anything novel or bizarre (the first woodcock's nest).

'Still no luck,' the article ended—and that remained, for the moment, an apt summary of his attempts to write a book. Meanwhile he was busy with a number of minor projects—among them three charming fifteen-minute radio talks on his experiences with trains, which he gave in November 1949. He also edited several collections of Fourth Leaders for publication in book form, and contributed two profiles to the glossy magazine *The Sketch*—one of his friend Peter Cazalet, who had established himself as a leading trainer of race-horses, and one of Carton de Wiart. In 1950 he kept up for several months in the *Spectator* a regular weekly commentary on the Korean War which commanded considerable respect in military and political circles.

It was not until 1950 that he at last produced another book. 'Here are, at a guess some 40,000 words of an unfinished and well-nigh unfinishable non-thrilling thriller which might be called *The Sixth Column*,' he wrote on August 26th to Rupert Hart-Davis, who by then had established his own publishing firm. Peter went on to disparage his own manuscript:

> The dullest of critics would, I am sure you will agree, be justified in pointing out that
> (a) Nothing happens.
> (b) The characters scarcely exist.
> (c) Much time is wasted on reconstructing events which the reader already knows about.
> (d) It is neither, to put it mildly, the one thing nor the other ... I nevertheless mean to finish it.

Finish it he did, and *The Sixth Column* was published in the summer of 1951. If the author's own criticisms were unnecessarily severe, they did contain many grains of truth, for the book cannot with the best will in the world be described as a great success. It is the story of a Soviet attempt to bring Great Britain to her knees by the implementation of a document known as 'Plan D'. The aim is to undermine what is left of the national character—already weakened by the war and its aftermath—through a subtle propaganda campaign run by well-known public figures inside the country, and so to convert the English into a race of small-minded, mechanical bureaucrats who will cease to play any part in, or have any influence on, international affairs.

The central theme was one about which Peter cared deeply, for in the state of the country under the post-war Labour Governments he discerned the beginnings of just such a descent as he described: an obsession with bureaucratic detail, a humiliating lack of ambition, and a general retreat from the high ideals and courage that had made Britain victorious in war. Thus *The Sixth Column* was in a sense a call to arms; the trouble was that the author could not step far enough outside his own conventional environment to bring the story to life. One of the leading characters, for instance, is Sir Archibald Strume, a retired army officer with a weather-beaten face who lives in a substantial house on the Chilterns, looked after by an ancient nanny and surrounded by dogs. He rides before breakfast, shoots a great deal, and, as a profitable hobby, writes books. The other characters—among them a general in the Brigade of Guards who has become the Director of Military Intelligence, a Russian playwright posing as a defector, and the smooth young English broadcaster who is the villain—are no more lifelike than this cardboard copy of Peter himself; and the book as a whole—although it contains many amusing ideas and asides—is spoilt by clumsy development and lack of exciting action. Like *The Sett*, it suffered from having no consistent viewpoint, moving uncomfortably from the country to M.I.5 and other points in London, and from one character to another. It was greeted with respectful but unenthusiastic reviews, and its sales—compared with those of *Brazilian Adventure* or *News From Tartary*—were paltry.

Once again, however, by means of his strange gift of prophecy, Peter had managed inadvertently to weave into his book elements of the future. He dedicated it to his brother, Ian, in whose mind James Bond had not yet been born, but who was to produce *Casino Royale* only a year after *The Sixth Column* had appeared; and although Archie Strume had nothing physically in common with Ian, there was, in the literary success which Peter ascribed to him, a strong pre-echo of the success which Ian was to achieve with Bond.

Strume (as described by Peter) had made a great hit with his hero Colonel Hackforth, in thrillers whose 'violent and, to say the least of it, curious events' had 'far-reaching international implications'. Hackforth though deriving principally from romantic figures such as Rupert of Hentzau and Raffles, seems to have embodied many of the characteristics which later made Bond supreme, among them a tendency to operate at the very highest level as a kind of secret agent acting on behalf of Governments, and to commandeer aircraft or midget submarines as the need arose.

It may be that in describing Archie Strume's success Peter was allowing himself a small exercise in wishful thinking. But he seems to have sensed that he himself would never make a hit by writing fiction, and he never tried another novel. Whether he was aware of it or not, the emotional blight forecast more than fifteen years earlier by Harold Nicolson had finally set in: Peter had for so long made a practice of concealing and playing down his emotions that he was no longer able to give rein to them, even pseudonymously, or to open himself up enough to engage the attention of an ordinary reader of fiction.

After the completion of *The Sixth Column* his muse again deserted him, except as far as essay-writing was concerned. In May 1951 he begun contributing to the *Sunday Times* (which then was unconnected with *The Times*) a fortnightly signed column called 'Marching at Ease'. This was clearly designed by the paper to be a spirited commentary on public affairs, but Peter got it off to an unpropitious start by proclaiming that he did not 'see it having very much momentum or any easily discernible purpose', and that he himself was 'now completely out of touch with ideological circles'. Not surprisingly, in view of its author's lack of interest in politics, the column scarcely ever came to life: it carried paragraphs about far eastern politics, territorial army manœuvres,

London theatre productions, the author's dogs, and the minor events of country life, and it exuded quiet but sustained hostility to the Labour Government. It also contained one memorable phrase, when Peter described the Shakespeare Memorial Theatre at Stratford-on-Avon as 'a courageous and partially successful attempt to disguise a gasworks as a rackets court.' But an author who hit top gear only when extolling the delights of ptarmigan-shooting was obviously not ideal for the *Sunday Times*, and in January 1952 he gratefully surrendered the column to someone else.

At about the same time, as a means of keeping his name in the public eye, he and Rupert decided to publish the diary, long laid aside, of his trip through the Caucasus with the Gages in 1934. This appeared in 1952 under the title *A Forgotten Journey*, with the text in its original state apart from the addition of a few footnotes. Of these, some were useful but others childish and almost intolerably facetious: for instance, to the brief remark 'Lot of aeroplanes about' he appended the portentous comment: 'The diarist's powers of detailed observation are not here deployed to full advantage'; and of another occasion in Moscow, when he had written 'I helped T. Bazley, who is here, to buy an airmail stamp,' he added '"Who is here". The diarist at this point exhibits an attention to detail which will strike many as superfluous.' These additions were a sad contrast with the original material, most of which was splendidly robust and funny.

So short was he of ideas that in 1953 (and again in 1955) he accepted a purely commercial commission which in his heyday he would surely have rejected: in each year he wrote a series of twelve short anonymous essays (one for each month) to grace the Midland Bank's annual calendar. His motives were entirely financial: royalties from his books were dwindling, this job was well paid, and he needed the money. And yet, even when his own earning power seemed to have diminished rather drastically, he could still write to the new Editor of *The Times* (Sir William Haley) and claim that he was being overpaid for the work he was doing: 'I am worried (though not to distraction) by a circumstance of which you are possibly not aware ...'

To chronicle this low ebb in Peter's literary life is perhaps to make it sound as though he had become dull and ordinary. Nothing was further from the case. He was still a marvellously attractive person in every sense of the phrase. His name was still one to conjure with, and an aura of glamour surrounded him. On the estate he was loved as much as he was respected, and everyone who knew him got enormous pleasure from observing and then relating to others his mild eccentricities. With his close friends he was still splendidly amusing, and he always created, by his very presence, an atmosphere of suppressed excitement and anticipation. In his company, one felt, life was on its mettle to produce some bizarre or ridiculous incident, and almost always it did.

Another pleasant trait was his eagerness to encourage young men who wanted to write, to travel or to farm, and his readiness to give unobtrusive help to any friend who had fallen on hard days. When Frankie Wilson came out of the army without much money, Peter allowed him to live almost rent-free in the cottage on top of Windmill Hill, in Nettlebed; and in 1952, when Mike Calvert was court-martialled, Peter flew to Germany at his own expense in order to bear witness to the fine qualities in Calvert's character.

His loyalty, both to friends and to members of his family, was unfaltering, and even when his mother's behaviour became grotesque—as it did in 1951, when she announced she was going to marry the eighty-nine-year-old Marquess of Winchester—he never wavered in his support of her and never uttered a word of disapproval or complaint.

Altogether he greatly enjoyed the life of literary rusticity which he had chosen, and he was particularly glad, in 1952, to be elected High Sheriff of Oxfordshire. He welcomed this office (which his grandfather had also held) not because it enhanced his status, but because it gave him a chance to make some positive contribution to the well-being of the county which he loved. During his year of office he was still commanding the Fourth Battalion of the Oxfordshire and Buckinghamshire Light Infantry, and on one occasion he greatly enlivened the opening of a session of the county court by arranging a guard of honour to greet the judge.

His general satisfaction with life was evident in a short broadcast entitled 'This I Believe' and given in July 1953, in which—almost unprecedentedly—he revealed something of his innermost faith:

> If ever I write my autobiography (which is fairly unlikely) I shall not devote the opening chapter to emphasizing the fact that I am a biped: I would expect my readers to take it for granted. For much the same reasons I don't, in this short talk, propose to waste much time in saying that I believe in large, impeccable abstractions like truth or beauty or decency or justice, because I think that really everybody believes in them, at least everybody who knows what they are.
>
> I am one of those unlucky people who must, if they are honest, admit that to all intents and purposes they haven't got a religion. I

wish I had, but I haven't. I was conventionally brought up in the Church of England, and I'm not an atheist or even an agnostic. I occasionally go to Church. But I just seem not to be religious in the same way that I'm not musical. I do, on the other hand, believe very strongly in the Human Spirit, by which I mean man's capacity— whether he is a Christian or a Moslem or the most primitive kind of spirit worshipper—to rise above his internal or external difficulties, to make great sacrifices and do shining deeds, to be a hero or a saint. I believe it is by using this capacity, in however humble or restricted a sphere, that man can justify himself and by his achievements or his example play his part in the unending fight between good and evil. I don't think we shall ever win this fight, for evil is a very strong force and folly (which often has the same consequences as evil) is in some ways even stronger; but I should have thought it was quite possible to lose it, and that is why I rate so high the privilege of taking part in it. I know that mine is a rather sublunary point of view, but I don't feel justified in demanding for myself a purpose in life which is either higher or more clearly defined than that of trying, within the narrow limits of my power, to leave the world a better place than I found it—or anyhow no worse.

I don't believe that I shall have another life after I die, any more than my dog will. Perhaps we shall; but that sort of immortality, if it comes, will come as a pleasant surprise. My own guess is that only the Human Spirit, with its undying tradition of goodness and endeavour, is immortal, and that the individual's chance of immortality is comprised in the opportunity he has during his life-time of upholding and enlarging that tradition.

This personal faith, if you can call it that, has been formed during a life spent partly in travel in remote places, partly in war, and partly in the English countryside. I am very conscious that many will find it rough and bleak and rather pagan, and I am sure I would be a better man if I could see beyond God's works to God himself. But I can't; and it is no doubt because of his mercy that I find in my trivial, earth-bound ideals the basis for a confident serenity.

The more deeply he immersed himself in country pursuits, the rarer became his visits to London; and even when he did go to London, his appearance—with his tweed suit and weather-beaten complexion—was such as to make him seem out of place in the formal surroundings of Gower Street or Printing House Square. Yet never did he become the slightest bit of a bumpkin: he was far too intelligent for that, and it was part of his charm that inside his apparently rustic framework there lurked so original and endlessly inquisitive a mind.

Not that he was above using his rusticity as an excuse for refusing offers: in 1959 he politely declined an invitation to become a fellow of the Royal Society of Literature on the grounds that, living in the country, he would be unable to attend the Society's meetings; and in a private note to Freddie Birkenhead he added:

> I thought I ought to let you know that I am declining this honour on the grounds that, coming as I do very seldom to London (and, though I did not say this, being allergic to all forms of *conversazione*), I know that in practice I should never turn up.
>
> I do hope that nobody will be offended by this rather churlish response to a generous offer; and if you see a chance to soothe any ruffled feelings with a reference to my bucolic habits and general philistinism, please take it.

14

Amateur Historian

It was Celia's brother John Johnson, a literary agent, who at last opened up for Peter a new and profitable line of literary endeavour. In a letter dated July 29th, 1954, he cast a craftily-placed fly ov erthe calm pool of life at Merrimoles:

> In a few years' time the attempted German invasion (1940–41) is going to have a fascination and interest to people who were not old enough to know much about it ... They will want to know what it was like to be there, how nearly we were invaded, what the German plans were, our preparations, life at the time, etc. etc. It seems to me that here is a marvellous subject for a serious, authentic but pre-eminently readable book ...
>
> We have discussed the idea with one of the best publishers and they think it has great possibilities, but of course it depends on the writer. It would be a fairly long job to do properly, and, apart from anything else, ought to be done by someone with an *entrée* into military circles ... Thinking of your many friends, I wondered if you knew of anyone who you think could do it justice ... I hope you won't mind me bothering you with this but I think whoever did it might make quite a lot of money.

Peter rose to the bait, but did not swallow it immediately. On August 5th he replied:

> I think your idea sounds rather a good one and there is obviously a fascinating book to be written on those lines. It isn't easy to think of anybody who could do it. You want somebody like Trevor-Roper

for the German end of it, but it would be important to have a non-academic approach, based on some first-hand experience of what was going on at the time, and especially of the atmosphere prevailing, for the British end ...

Theoretically, I could probably do some of the British side of it, but you want someone who could tackle both, and I will go on thinking and let you know if I have any constructive ideas.

Such was the genesis of *Invasion 1940* which, in purely financial terms, proved easily the most successful book that Peter wrote. It did not take him long to decide that he himself could manage the entire project; he began collecting material almost at once, and he signed an agreement about terms with the agents on October 15th. Rupert Hart-Davis was to publish the book in England, and the American rights were sold to Simon & Schuster for an advance of 4,000 dollars.

It was not long before Peter's quest for the facts of 1940 led him deep into the bureaucratic jungle of Whitehall, where he waged a long and ultimately ridiculous battle with the custodians of the Government archives. At first—since he was quite unused to the sort of skirmishing in which he now found it necessary to indulge—his tactics were rather amateurish; but gradually he perfected a strategy based on patience and attrition which in the end gained him nearly everything that he wanted.

Whenever his request for a particular document was rejected, he would write a formal and elaborately polite letter to Sir Norman Brook, the Secretary to the Cabinet Office, asking if some special arrangement could be made for him to see what he wanted. After a decent interval—one of weeks or months, rather than of days—Brook would reply in equally courteous terms, almost always explaining why the request could not be granted. Peter would then wait to see if he could obtain what he needed by some other means. At first he tried to manipulate the old-boy network, appealing for help to friends in high places; but even this proved largely futile, and in the end he depended a great deal on luck.

In several cases he managed to obtain from the Pentagon in Washington copies of documents that had been denied him in London; but by far his greatest slice of good fortune occurred when he accidentally got a sight of a study by Ronald Wheatley called *Operation Sea Lion*. Wheatley was then a young member of the staff which, under the aegis of the Cabinet Office, had set out in 1948 to unravel the great hoard of military archives captured by the Allies at the end of the war. His study of the

German plan for the invasion of England had been compiled principally for the benefit of the authors of the official history of the war, and had not, originally, been intended for publication.

Peter heard of the existence of this document early in his own researches, asked to see it, and in due course was refused permission on the grounds that it was not going to be published. Months later he went into the Admiralty one day to try to clear up some obscure naval detail, and the pleasant but vague man in charge—apologizing for the fact that he had so little material on 1940—handed him a stout docket containing, among other papers, Wheatley's thesis.

As Peter later remarked in a letter to a friend:

A truly noble character would perhaps have exclaimed: 'Oh, but you mustn't let me see *this*!' But I had as near as a touch been given access to it officially and it was, I am afraid, without the slightest sense of guilt that I sat down and read very rapidly through it, making rough notes of the details that were new to me.

With typical honesty Peter told the Cabinet Office that he had seen the forbidden document, but the entire position had by then become somewhat unreal, as he later described in an article in the *Spectator*:

My next list of requests included one for a German map of the United Kingdom showing what they believed to be the dispositions of the Home Forces in September 1940. This had to be refused, as I could not have known of the map's existence if I had not read the forbidden thesis ... [he later obtained a copy of the map from the Pentagon].

But the height of absurdity came when my book was finished and I asked for official help in wording my acknowledgments to Mr Wheatley; brief though my glimpse of his work had been, I was in his debt for several details which were not available from other sources.

Whitehall, in the person of an irritable bureaucrat whom I did not know personally, pointed out over the telephone that Mr Wheatley's thesis was a restricted document, that I had seen it without authority, and that if I published any reference to it I might be involved in proceedings under the Official Secrets Act.

In spite of all this wrangling—which, after a good-humoured start, became at the end tiresomely acrimonious—Peter made excellent progress with the book. Not having much German, he used an expert linguist as a translator, and also got occasional help from a small research firm run by Joan Astley (formerly Bright) and Joan St George Saunders. On the whole, however, he preferred to do his own fact-hunting, for he could never be certain that another eye would pick out the details that would bring the narrative to life.

In April 1956 he sent the first sixteen chapters to John Johnson, who found them fascinating but a little stiff, and asked Peter if he could loosen up his style. At the end of June he sent a draft, complete save for one short chapter, to Rupert Hart-Davis, and another copy to the *Sunday Times*, where Ian was running the Atticus column. A month later the *Sunday Times* bought the serial rights for £5,000, and when the paper printed extracts for eight consecutive weeks in the autumn, its circulation went up spectacularly. Peter heard unofficially that the increase had been 40,000 copies, and although the paper would not confirm the figure, it did agree that the number had been 'very substantial.'

Just before the book went to press Peter heard that a decision had eventually been taken to publish Wheatley's thesis, and he managed to include a note about it at the end of his list of acknowledgments. In signalling his debt to Wheatley, he wrote, he could not 'help expressing a wistful envy of his readers, who will not need to digest the rich fruits of his research in a single afternoon with the shadow of the Official Secrets Act hanging over them'. And yet he was still not clear of the complications of that ill-starred document. For the American version of his book the publishers had chosen the title *Operation Sea Lion*; this was Wheatley's title too, and by the time the belated decision to publish Wheatley had been announced, it was too late for Simon & Schuster to make a change.

In the lull before publication of the book he made a quick trip to Canada, where he gave an exhausting but successful lecture tour arranged by the Commonwealth Relations Office. He sailed from England aboard the *Scythia* on January 19th, and returned by air, calling at New York and Washington on the way. The subject of his talks was the same as that of the book, for which he was able to create some useful advance publicity, and he found his audiences flatteringly enthusiastic.

In England *Invasion 1940* was published in April and was greeted with a chorus of praise and delight. Giving, as it did, an almost unparalleled excuse for reviewers to launch into personal reminiscence, it unleashed a spate of memories. 'To those of us who lived through it,' wrote John Connell in the *Evening News*, 'Mr Fleming's brilliant, scholarly, wise and witty account of that unique experience is bound to be as nostalgic as it is vivid and enthralling.' The *Spectator* declared that 'the charm of Peter Fleming's book is that it recalls five months in our national history when we all lived as never before, and many of us as never again ... a remarkable blend of Strix-like fancy and serious historical writing.'

The *Financial Times*, although admitting that it was 'a highly evocative account', produced the rather unconvincing idea that 'as there was no invasion of Britain in 1940, a book on the subject seems otiose.' *The Times*, however, felt that author and subject were uniquely matched: 'An experienced and enthusiastic soldier who was in the thick of it at the time would be worth hearing in his own right. But when, as here, he is also an artist with a keen eye alike for the heroic and for the ludicrous, 1940 has found its right man.' In an enormous leading review of more than 3,000 words the *Times Literary Supplement* praised his 'wicked eye for detail' and his 'historical sense of occasion', concluding that 'out of all this [material] Mr Fleming has fashioned a likeness of the British people in the summer of 1940 which, because of its inconsequence and its contrasts, is far more convincing than official versions.'

The Americans were no less enthusiastic. *Operation Sea Lion* was chosen as the Book of the Month Club's midsummer selection, with a guaranteed advance of 40,000 dollars, and when the book was published it was noticed in all the leading newspapers and periodicals. 'He carries us with him, enthralled and shattered, to the end,' said the *New Yorker*. 'Splendidly engrossing,' proclaimed *Newsweek*: 'A wonderfully interesting account of something that did not finally happen at all.'

Translation rights were soon sold in many countries, and within two years of its publication the book had earned almost £25,000, all of which Peter put into trusts for his children. Suddenly, with the first serious book he had ever written, he was back on—or near—the pinnacle of literary success which he had last scaled twenty years before with the publication of *News from Tartary*.

Now he was bombarded with suggestions for further books, all of which he rejected with the utmost courtesy and tact. Among the requests was one that he should write the history of the Grenadier Guards—a project which, for many obvious reasons, appealed to him considerably, but for which (as he said in a letter to the Regimental Adjutant) he did not think that he 'carried the necessary guns'. He was also pressed to write a history of Combined Operations, not least by Earl Mountbatten, who was then First Sea Lord. Peter found the idea attractive, and while he was hesitating he got a persuasive letter from Sir Geoffrey Blake, the Admiralty representative on the Advisory Panel for the Official War histories:

As you know, Winston and Dickie Mountbatten are most anxious that this great achievement should be put on record. Written in a similar manner to *Invasion*, it should have a great appeal to the imagination of the public both here and in America ... We are all agreed that you are the only author who can carry it out, and this, *The Final Count*, or call it what you wish, will be an odds-on double to your *Invasion* story.

In spite of these blandishments, Peter moved cautiously, for his experience of dealing with official sources in Whitehall had been insufferably tedious, and now he replied that he very much doubted if the authorities concerned would ever produce a set of conditions under which he would be prepared to work. 'But', he added, 'I am interested in the project ... and I can see no harm in pursuing it at least into the fringes of the bureaucratic jungle in which I suspect it may die a natural death.'

This, so far as he was concerned, was precisely what happened, and the history of Combined Operations was eventually written by Bernard Fergusson. Whether Peter was consciously aware of it or not, he preferred a smaller-scale subject in which there was more scope for studying the principal characters involved, and by the autumn of 1957 he had hit upon a historical episode that suited him perfectly—the Boxer Rebellion of 1900, in which the foreign legations in Peking were besieged by fanatical insurgents and saved from massacre only by the last-minute intervention of an international relief-force. His own knowledge of China, and of Peking in particular, gave him a flying start, and the ready-made combination of danger, farce, excitement and human eccentricity inspired him to produce a narrative which was even more vigorous and attractive than that of his first essay into history. His enthusiasm for the story was increased by the fact that one of the leading characters in the siege (and one of his leading sources) was the man who in 1900 had been the local correspondent of *The Times*—Dr G. E. Morrison, an adventurer who had travelled even more widely than Peter himself, walking not only right through China but also across Australia, and on one occasion being left for dead in New Guinea with two spears in his body. Peter was also fascinated by the character of the Empress Dowager, Tzu Hsi, who incited the Boxers to massacre the hated foreigners trapped in the legation quarter. This 'remarkable woman', as Peter described her, with a reputation not unlike that of Lady Macbeth, began her career as a third-grade concubine but intrigued so skilfully inside the Manchu Court that she maintained 'a position of great and often supreme power for nearly half a century'. 'From girlhood,' he wrote, the Empress Dowager had lived in a world whose outward un-realities are too many and too complex to describe, and whose inner realities elude the most adroit imagination. The high walls of the Forbidden City enclosed her, and were themselves enclosed by the higher walls of Peking ... Her public life was paved with ceremony and roofed with superstition. Of her private life we know little save that she was fond of amateur theatricals, water picnics, painting and pugs ... She preserved her early beauty with care and success ... The diplomatic ladies, each of whom was given a valuable ring before leaving the Presence, were enchanted with the Empress Dowager. It was no easier for them than it is for us to fathom the nature of a woman accustomed, since her twenties, to take a hand in the drafting of Edicts like the following, which dates from 1860:

As to Su Shun, his treasonable guilt far exceeds that of his accomplices [two of whom had been permitted to commit suicide, and two imprisoned for life] and he fully deserves the punishment of dismemberment and the slicing process. But we cannot make up our mind to impose this extreme penalty and therefore, in our clemency, we sentence him to immediate decapitation.

Of the siege incited by this amazing creature Peter reconstructed a vivid picture, weaving together the military and domestic threads with apparently effortless skill and lightening what might otherwise have been a gloomy tale by his relish for the absurdities of the situation ('Pony-meat and rice were the staple diet, washed down by champagne, of which there was a copious supply in the two stores.') He put the book together very fast, starting in the winter of 1957 and finishing it less than a year later. This time he was able to conduct almost all his research from Nettlebed, and he was once again helped by Joan Saunders. In writing his pre-war books he had always used a typewriter, but now he wrote in longhand with a fountain pen, always using nibs designed for left-handers, for which he had an inexplicable preference.

In October 1958, before the book was published, he became involved in an odd dispute with the *Sunday Times*. The paper offered £1,500 for the right to print four articles based on the book—either straight extracts or condensed accounts of parts of the story. Peter replied saying that he hoped they would not think it churlish of him to refuse the offer, but then wrote to Michael Berry, proprietor of the *Daily Telegraph*, telling him of the *Sunday Times*'s interest and offering *him* the serial rights. Soon afterwards Lord Kemsley (Michael Berry's uncle) raised the *Sunday Times*'s offer to £2,000, but this Peter also refused, explaining in a letter to Leonard Russell, the paper's literary editor:

The book tells in some detail the story of a curious and three-quarters forgotten incident in recent history, and to summarize the story in four magazine articles would be rather like giving away the plot of a thriller, and equally detrimental to the book's prospects. I cannot therefore, I am afraid, agree to any form of overall condensation (if you see what I mean by this loathsome expression) ... I feel that the book's chances of being widely read depend on its story retaining the qualities of surprise and 'forgottenness'.

In this letter Peter seems for once to have been acting disingenuously, for three days later he wrote again to Michael Berry, once more asking if the *Telegraph* would take the book. Whether he was after more money, or merely wanted to get away from the *Sunday Times*, is no longer clear; but whatever his motives, his tactics proved ill-judged, for in the end the book was serialized by nobody.

The Siege at Peking was published in April 1959, and like its predecessor attracted hundreds of column-inches of favourable reviews. In the *Manchester Guardian* Roger Fulford told his readers that they would be lucky to find 'a more enjoyable book than this' during 1959, and said that its importance lay 'in the window it opens into the mentality of the Chinese'. In the *Sunday Times* Raymond Mortimer's leading review declared that 'Mr Fleming's brilliant book helps us to understand the active loathing still excited in Asia by memories of colonialism.' Other accolades poured in from every side: 'Mr Fleming has a terrific story to tell. He tells it with method, brilliance, and a mature flowering of the delightful, clean humour that was apparent in his first book *Brazilian Adventure* (George Millar in the *Daily Express*); 'Lucid, vigorous and sardonic account ... [the author] knows a great deal about irregular warfare, has a remarkable style, at once fluent and incisive, understands China, and has a jolly G. A. Henty side. (Harold Nicolson in the *Observer*): 'Mr Fleming's writing has the brilliant intelligence of somebody who has really taken the trouble thoroughly to inform himself out of passionate interest in his subject matter ... one is enthralled from beginning to end ... It is in fact impossible for me to exaggerate the enormous pleasure that this account of the fifty-nine-years-old news from Peking has given me' (Elizabeth Jane Howard in *Queen*).

The tribute that gave Peter perhaps the most pleasure of all came from Paula von Rosthorn, a survivor of the siege whom he had tried in vain to locate. On November 24th, 1960, she wrote to him from Vienna:

As I am eighty-seven years of age I take it that I am one of the few survivors of the siege of Peking in 1900, and as such can really appreciate fully your book. Others will enjoy its many merits but few could possibly know how true it is in all its details.

The book was well received in America also, although its impact was less spectacular than that of *Invasion 1940*, and Harper's (to whom Peter had switched after falling out with Simon & Schuster) sold 10,000 copies in the first two months after publication. Once more the royalties were large enough for Peter to think it worth storing them up in trusts for the children. The book earned him one unexpected and not entirely welcome extra sum in the form of an out-of-court payment made in settlement of a threatened legal action. Soon after publication in England he got wind of the fact that the American producer Samuel Bronston and his associates were planning a film called *Fifty-Five Days at Peking*, and the more he heard of it, the more certain he became that parts of its action were based on material in his book. After considerable pressure from his solicitors, the Bronston organization admitted their error in not making contact with him and—on the day of the film's release—offered to pay his costs and £500 compensation.

Even before *The Siege at Peking* was published Peter had launched into a third historical study—an account of the British military expedition to Lhasa of 1904. Again he had found a splendidly esoteric subject set in a part of the world that he knew, and this time he produced a book that combined shrewd military analysis and character study with fine descriptions of wild country. If the story was less exciting than that of the Boxer Rebellion, it gained by the exotic remoteness of its setting and by its account of the extraordinary physical difficulties which attended the British invasion of Tibet.

The advance to Lhasa was conceived by Lord Curzon (then Viceroy of India) as a bold move in 'the Great Game'—the struggle for long-range control which Great Britain and Imperial Russia had waged for more than half a century in the highlands of Central Asia (and in which Peter himself had become marginally involved during his trek across Tartary). Tibet, Curzon believed in 1904, was in danger of succumbing to Russian influence, and he persuaded the British Government to dispatch to the Forbidden City of Lhasa a small expedition whose objective was to secure a treaty of friendship between Tibet and Great Britain. 'No military force', Peter wrote, 'before or since, has faced such vehement opposition from climate and terrain'; yet the mission, led with immense tenacity and resource by Colonel Francis Younghusband, accomplished its task, even though the spiritual ruler of Tibet, the Dalai Lama, fled eastwards before the news of the British approach and disappeared into the uplands of Sinkiang. For Younghusband, however, the whole expedition ended in disaster, since he not only fell out with the general who commanded his military escort but also became the victim of a political feud between Curzon and his former friend St John Brodrick, at the India Office in London. In the end, although he had brought off an extraordinary achievement, Younghusband was publicly censured.

Considering what a success Peter had already enjoyed with his earlier historical books, he was curiously self-deprecating when he began his research for *Bayonets to Lhasa*. 'I am trying to write a book ...' he said in several letters asking for information. 'Sorry to be a nuisance ... vaguely contemplating a study of the British expedition to Lhasa ... this rather improbable quest.' To Sir Alan Lascelles, an old and close friend, he wrote: 'This is a non-frivolous inquiry, so far as any inquiries coming from me can be regarded as non-frivolous.' He sought help also from Harold Nicolson, whose book *Curzon: the Last Phase* he drew on for material about the character of the Viceroy. Writing to Nicolson in July 1959 with a request for help, he went on to say:

> I brought myself up never to write to people who reviewed one's book, on the possibly mistaken grounds that to do so was slightly *deuxième*. But as I am writing to you anyhow, I must say how pleased and flattered I was by what you said about the Peking book in the *Sunday Times*. Undeserved, but highly gratifying; and beautifully done.

To which Nicolson replied:

> I am glad you enjoyed my review of your Peking book. The review did not, as you suggest, appear in the *Sunday Times*, but in the rival paper, the *Observer*, but we can let that pass ... I think I told you that Curzon once said to me that he had tried to sum up in two words the attitude adopted towards him by his old Oxford friend St John Brodrick. The two words were 'tortuous malignity'.

Diffident though his approach might be, Peter again worked fast, and he sent Nicolson a copy of the completed typescript in April 1960, only fifteen months after he had started on the project. On April 19th Nicolson replied:

> My Dear Peter,
> I was completely enthralled by your book. It is the sort of thing you do better than anybody else, combining the Henty touch with the stiff regimental upper lip behind it, and a very real human sympathy. I think you have caught Curzon exactly.

When *Bayonets to Lhasa* came out in January 1961 the reviewers shared Nicolson's opinion wholeheartedly, and the chorus of praise was no less extravagant than that which had greeted *The Siege at Peking*. One or two critics, among them Raymond Mortimer, felt that the author had not fully explored the complex character of Younghusband and had perhaps been excessively indulgent towards him; but apart from this there were no complaints. In the *Scotsman* Moray McLaren declared that this was 'the best book he has yet given us. His prose, always excellent, is here wielded with the technique of one who has acquired full mastery of his medium. He has exactly that manner of cool, ironic detachment masking deep and sensitive feeling which is the special gift of certain historians writing in English.' 'Colonel Fleming invests even the driest of departmental detail with the disturbing glow of great events,' said the *Guardian*, 'Meticulously documented and organized, witty, pointed, but—one is sure—scrupulously balanced, this book reads like an unputdownable thriller, taut with the poised drama of history.'

One newspaper—the *Financial Times*—urged Peter to continue his series of politico-military chronicles, suggesting the Red River Expedition and the Ashanti War as possible subjects; but these proposals missed the essential point that he liked writing only about those parts of the world that he knew, and in fact he had already chosen another subject that fulfilled all the necessary conditions—the Siberian Intervention of 1918.

His hero this time—a melancholy one—was Admiral Aleksandr Vassilievich Kolchak, the Commander-in-Chief of the Russian Black Sea Fleet who in November 1917 declared his allegiance to Great Britain because he felt compelled to honour his country's obligations to an ally whom the new Bolshevik Government, by withdrawing from the war against Germany, had shamefully deserted. Peter's interest in this strange and contradictory figure had first been roused during his own travels in Siberia and north-west China during the 1930s: White Russians, talking of the Civil War, had often mentioned Kolchak, generally with respect and admiration. Peter became curious to know what exactly he had done, and what had happened to him in the end; but not until 1960 did it occur to him to make serious inquiries. Then, by means of an announcement in the Agony Column of *The Times*, he made contact with the Admiral's son and gradually pieced together the extraordinary tale of how, after an Allied force had engineered a *coup d'état* in Omsk, Kolchak had been installed as Supreme Ruler of All the Russias, only to be defeated by the Red Army and forced to withdraw eastwards, in the depths of winter, along the Trans–Siberian Railway.

This time Peter's research took him far afield. He made several visits to Paris, in whose White Russian community he had discovered some survivors of the Siberian débâcle, and early in 1961 he travelled to Siberia for the first time since the 1930s. The main purpose of the journey was to visit Irkutsk (where Kolchak met his end) and go through the archives of the History Faculty in the University; but to defray the cost he approached the *Sunday Times* and managed to persuade the paper to pay his travelling expenses in return for two long articles which were published later under the heading 'Return to Siberia'.

In Moscow Peter wasted a good deal of time angling for a visa to visit Outer Mongolia, and it was not until his fourth day in the Soviet capital that he discovered the reason for the delay. Mistaking him for his brother Ian (he later wrote in the *Sunday Times*) 'the Mongols believed my connection with James Bond to be closer than in fact it is, and were not enthusiastic about a visit from the creator (as they supposed) of SMERSH.' When this misconception had been cleared up they granted him a visa; but by that time he and his passport were at the other end of Russia, and his excursion to Mongolia had to be postponed.

When he once again took the Trans–Siberian Railway to the east, the journey cast on him the same powerful spell as it had done thirty years before:

> Across the steppe the rusty grey curtain of the sky descends on an horizon which seems to be farther away than the horizons are at sea or in the desert; the forests, when they hem in the railway line, appear denser, less finite than the most daunting jungle. The eye seizes almost with avidity upon a horse and sleigh crawling across the middle distance, a single set of ski tracks disappearing under the trees.
>
> '*Vash khod*,' says one's opponent; 'it's your move.' As one reverts to the exigencies of a rearguard action on the chessboard, one is once more bounded in a nutshell, snug, sociable, secure. The sleigh-driver and the skier, outside, can count themselves lords of infinite space. How, one wonders, are they affected by the enveloping solitude, which even within the nutshell makes its impact on the traveller? But already the Peking Express, hooting with melancholy resolve, has left them far behind, almost beyond the reach of speculation; and one's queen, it is obvious, is doomed.

His stay in Irkutsk was a great success, for the University staff were generous with their help and the old partisans whom he met were anxious to relive their experiences of 1918. He returned to England with a rich store of information which he could have got from no other source, and carried on with his research at home.

His attempts to prize documents out of the Government archives were no less depressing than before; in June 1961 the Cabinet Office wrote answering his letter of five months earlier to say that he could not have access to the papers he wanted, and later, when the War Office did grant him permission to see some documents, he was allowed to peruse the papers on the paradoxical condition 'that you will not acknowledge in your book that access to the records has been permitted.'

Bureaucrats notwithstanding, he finished *The Fate of Admiral Kolchak* at the end of 1962, and the book was published the following April. The reviews, this time, were less unanimous; although several critics very much liked the book, some felt that, in spite of all his efforts, Peter had failed to bring Kolchak to life, and others that the story, besides being familiar in outline, was rather depressing. Sales certainly reflected these lukewarm opinions, for they fell well short of those of *Invasion 1940* and even of those of *The Siege at Peking*.

Nevertheless, by the spring of 1963 Peter had established himself as an amateur historian of originality and skill. In less than seven years between 1957 and 1963 he had published four solid and readable studies —a striking contrast with the nine lean years immediately after the war which had produced only one lightweight novel. Nor, during this fruitful period, did he in any way reduce his other activities: he continued to run the estate, to shoot, to ride, to write both for the *Spectator* and for *The Times* and also to travel widely.

At Nettlebed a succession of managers and bailiffs helped him run the estate; but none served him more loyally—or was more cruelly rewarded—than Geoffrey Webb, a professional land agent who arrived in 1956. Having worked at Nettlebed for three years, and impressed Peter more than any other agent he had employed, Webb was suddenly struck down by polio at the age of 32 and totally crippled for life, being left only with the ability to speak and with movement in one toe.

To this tragedy Peter reacted with characteristic generosity and perseverance. Not only did he keep the family going financially, paying for the two sons' education and allowing them and their mother to stay in their cottage as long as they needed; he also conducted a dogged campaign on Webb's behalf, drafting a letter from him to *The Times* and writing to the Minister of Health in an attempt to improve the lot of totally disabled patients. He was both astonished and deeply moved by the whole affair, for Webb confounded the doctors by living on far beyond the span they thought possible for him, by divorcing his first wife and marrying again, and in general by showing extraordinary courage. At one stage Peter tried to install him as tenant of a farm bordering the estate, but even when this plan failed he kept in touch with him and continued to visit him from time to time. After every such occasion he would come away saying what a remarkable person Geoffrey was: he never ceased to admire him.

Under Peter's genial supervision the estate ran smoothly on, still making a slight loss that gave no one any cause for concern. His love of the place grew year by year, and whenever he could he added more land to the acres that he already owned. In 1957, for instance, for the risible sum of £2,390 he bought seventy-seven acres of two contiguous coverts which had obtruded into the western side of the estate. A few months later he sent his brother Richard (who was running the family bank) a list of all the properties surrounding him, giving their acreages and the price that each might fetch in a sale. In an accompanying letter he wrote:

My own feeling is that, whatever ups and downs agriculture and forestry may undergo, all land in an undeveloped area within forty miles of London is bound to appreciate and to go on appreciating for ever. If I could, I would try to buy all the properties on this list as and when they come on the market, partly to make the estate more viable by increasing the rent roll, partly to avoid being encircled by developers, and partly (mainly, really) as a long-term investment for the children.

Within two years he had managed to snap up one of the places he mentioned—Bix Manor Farm, whose 122 acres made an extremely useful addition to his eastern flank—and the accuracy of his forecast was strikingly borne out by subsequent events. The price of farm land in his part of the country—about £100 an acre when he wrote the letter— appreciated tenfold within the next fifteen years.

There is no doubt that Peter wanted the estate to become a viable entity—and indeed it could have been one, had it been more efficiently run. Peter himself, however, was by no means the most businesslike of squires. The main trouble was that—in spite of his brief incarceration in Wall Street and the City—he had absolutely no conception of finance: until the very end of his life he never appreciated that the best way of making the estate pay would be to invest capital in modern machinery and buildings. Rather than buy the new tractor or combine for which his bailiff was agitating, he would always muddle on with the old ones as long as possible and seek to raise his income by means of some esoteric but fiddling sideline: thus at one stage charcoal-burning was to be the estate's salvation, and at another the breeding of ponies (both projects came to fairly ignominious ends). He once startled a man who had applied for the job of agent on the estate by asking him to examine the feasibility of a plan for stocking the swimming-pool with goldfish. The aim, Peter said, was both to make money by selling the fish and to rid the pool of algae. The man—not yet familiar with Peter's ideas—suspected that his leg was being pulled, and did not know whether or not to take the request seriously. Fortunately he did, and he later got the job. No less fortunately, the scheme for the fish was still-born.

Peter did, on the other hand, succeed most strikingly in his aim of preserving a corner of Oxfordshire as a pleasant place in which country people might live and work. Everyone on the estate loved working for him, and never during his lifetime did he allow the pressure of urbanization to encroach upon his preserve. Estates close by his were ruined by sporadic building, but he never sacrificed a single useful acre to developers, and he not only kept his land intact, but actually increased it.

His main pleasure, always, was his woods, and for years his prize exhibit was a plantation of Christmas trees at the end of the vista in front of Merrimoles. The two-and-a-half-acre patch of ground had always been a sour field, in which attempts to grow potatoes had regularly proved unsatisfactory, and it was mainly to avoid having to cultivate it any more that Peter got the foresters to plant it up. But the trees thrived prodigiously, and for season after season they yielded a handsome profit at Christmas time; writing in the *Spectator* in 1955, he reckoned that his net income by the end of that year would be at least three times the amount of his original investment, and that there were still some 25,000 trees to sell. What pleased him even more, however, was the astonishing amount of natural regeneration that had taken place: among the serried ranks of Norway spruce there had sprung up a mass of oak, ash, beech, cheery, sycamore, larch, Scots pine, Douglas fir and horn-beam; and in an unusually lyrical passage he allowed himself to speculate on the future of this fortuitous silvicultural triumph:

> I like all the woodlands that I am lucky enough to own; indeed, not to put too fine a point on it, I love them. If after death the soul is still fettered with curiosity, as a falcon is with jesses after she has been released, mine will hanker above all to see, after many decades, what has happened to those woodlands ... A century hence on this particular plot, a veteran handful of the original 43,500 Norway

spruce will, perhaps groggily, survive ... But the main crop will be oak, beech, cherry and sycamore growing slowly towards maturity; and although it would be hubristic to hope that eventually a descendant of mine will fell them and benefit thereby, I should like, at least, to feel that some old man will retail (and preferably dismiss as moonshine) the legend that this little wood, many years ago, was nothing but a mass of Christmas trees.

It seems strange that, dedicated as he was to forestry, he did very little to manage the woods for the benefit of his other passion—shooting. As the post-war plantations grew up, several of them became impenetrably choked with brambles and other undergrowth, but rather than have them promptly cleared he fatalistically allowed them to run riot. The result was that during the 1950s the shooting on the estate declined to its lowest level. Another cause of the decline was the increasing intransigence of the old keeper: Harry Brown was a splendid man; in his time he had been a first-class gamekeeper, and now he could hardly be blamed for occasionally falling out with his idiosyncratic employer.

'Easily the lowest bag of pheasants ever recorded here,' wrote Peter in his game-book at the end of 1953, whose entire season yielded only 112 pheasants. The next year was even worse, and he noted that 'an air of decay has come to hang over the game situation on the estate'; but the nadir was reached in 1955, when Peter scarcely shot at home at all, and the bag for the year amounted to eleven pheasants and seven hares. 'No comment is possible on this season,' he recorded. 'Except for one hopelessly unsuccessful day (cocks only) after Christmas, I did not shoot the coverts. Brown was retired at the end of the year; he was seventy-two, and should have gone before.'

This fiasco was almost entirely Peter's fault: he knew that he should have got rid of Brown sooner, but he was annoyed by his own failure to do so, and in the end could scarcely bring himself to speak to the old man. Goaded by the lack of opportunity at home, he sought out more rough shooting farther afield and was delighted, in 1954, to hit on Otmoor, a huge bowl of low-lying land just beyond the eastern outskirts of Oxford. Otmoor—then undrained—was being used by the R.A.F. as a bombing-range: a control-tower invigilated over the gloomy expanse of flooded fields, and in its centre stood a battered target made of corrugated iron in the shape of a cross. To this sodden wilderness, pockmarked by the impact of countless twenty-five-pound bombs, Peter would repair on winter afternoons, usually alone but sometimes with a friend, and for a couple of hours he would struggle about the over-

grown fields and ditches in search of snipe and an occasional pheasant.
Several times, during one of his forays, bombing began, whereupon
he would withdraw, at a dignified pace, towards the outer fringes of
the range. To be bombed while shooting snipe on the outskirts of
Oxford was a combination of events which he found exceptionally
pleasing.

The year after Brown had retired brought a renaissance on the estate.
Freed from the presence of an elderly and disapproving retainer, Peter
himself covered more of the ground than for many seasons past, often on
his own. The entries in his game-book took on a pioneering note—'The
first birds killed in the Trench since 1939,' 'First bird killed on this bit of
ground for years,'—and he also explored the sporting possibilities of
Kingwood Common, a tract of semi-jungle which lay about a mile clear
of his south-western boundary, but on which his family held the shooting
rights. At the end of the season he recorded: 'First season without a
keeper, but best results since 1953 ... I killed forty of the pheasants [out
of 154] on solitary afternoons, and a feature of the season was the
amount of exercise and good dog-work it provided.' For the next few
years he continued to do without a keeper, and although a new farm-
hand, Dennis Warren, successfully reared a number of pheasants, he
himself became more and more addicted to solitary expeditions. In 1958
he began the custom (which he maintained for the rest of his life) of
counting the cartridges fired on these one-man forays: he was careful to
make sure he counted right, and was scrupulous about not cheating (for
otherwise, as he remarked, the exercise would have been pointless). The
score for the first year was as follows:

Days out	Acreage available	Pheasants Cocks Hens		Woodcock	Pigeons	Hares	Rabbits
45	c. 3000	84	31	12	9	1	2

Total head: 139. Rounds fired: 275

He found that to 'break twos', as he put it, was about the best he could
do, and during the season he could tell at a glance how consistent his
form had been by the number he was over or under twos. As he grew
older his sight gradually lengthened, but although he used spectacles for
reading and writing, he never wore them for shooting.

Nothing stopped him shooting—not even the great cold in the winter
of 1962–3 which brought almost all other activity in the country to a
standstill. The iron weather set in on Boxing Day, and Peter's game-
book charted the icy progress of the next five weeks:

31 Dec Deep snow, v. cold ... *1 Jan* Snow slightly deeper ... *3 Jan* Snow iced over, pheasants tails frozen to the ice. Spared all save one ... *5 Jan* Frozen snow made operations almost impossible but provided some good, hard exercise ... *7 Jan* Still arctic ... I picked up a dead hen [pheasant] and the dogs a wounded one ... *9 Jan* Colder than ever. Pigeons have finished the kale ... *10 Jan* One hour, one shot. Almost impossible to walk through untrodden, frozen snow ... *11 Jan* Snow now so hard that one can often walk on it ... *12 Jan* Partridges too tame to shoot ... *14 Jan* Kingwood snowbound and blank ... *19 Jan* A three-hour trudge through the snow in an easterly gale. Sukie picked up the partridge which, though it could hardly fly, was quite plump. *21 Jan* No break in the bitter cold. Many pigeons dying, but other birds bearing up wonderfully ... *23 Jan* Over thirty degrees of frost last night in some places. A useful two-hour wade through snow ... *24 Jan* Dark, bitterly cold day. Long walk. *28 Jan* A slow thaw at last.

In an article called 'Snowscape' which appeared in the *Spectator* on February 1st, 1963, he drew an evocative picture on the estate under siege by the cruel weather, and in the course of it gave many hints on his affection for the creatures which he normally pursued with such diligence. To anybody who does not shoot it must seem baffling that a hunter such as Peter can be genuinely fond of his quarry; yet he had enormous respect and admiration for game-birds, particularly woodcock. His general knowledge of birds was enormous, and now he wrote with compassionate affection of the attempts made by partridges to find sustenance in the snow:

> Watching them at close range from my window, I am amazed at their endurance. Waddling—almost as clumsily as I do—through drifted snow, losing their balance and getting blown backwards by the wind across frozen patches, they struggle manfully on, doing their rounds of all the places where they have learnt to hope for food. When they find it they never quarrel over it, as small birds do, but peck busily and companionably away, a lesson to us all in adversity.

It was a disappointment to Peter that Nichol never shared his enthusiasm for the chase (once at Black Mount, when Nichol went off on his first attempt to shoot a grouse, Peter remarked that he looked like a Chinese general being led out to execution). But he was thrilled when Lucy, at the age of fourteen, proved a keen and talented shot, and at the end of 1961 his game-book reported:

She began by hitting a woodcock and a driven cock pheasant—never having handled a shotgun before—the first time I took her out, and went on to shoot consistently well. I suppose I enjoyed her prowess and her companionship as much as I have enjoyed anything in the way of shooting.

Four years earlier, in a letter to Basil Maine, who had taught him at Durnford, he had described his growing family in typical fashion:

Dear Maniac,

I was delighted to get your letter, and I hope you enjoy the partridges [which Peter had sent him] ... My children consist of:

Nicholas, 18, last half at Eton; no particular bent except for teasing schoolmasters.

Kate, 11, tall and rather beautiful.

Lucy, 10, looks like a North Korean, good horsewoman. They are all rather nice and very funny.

Just as Peter admired Celia's excellence on the stage, so he was immensely pleased when the girls, as they grew up, showed promise in particular skills or activities. He always liked them to do something well, and he was delighted when Lucy became an able rider. So keen was he for her to excel that he took her for immensely long hacks, and sometimes she became so exhausted that she had to drop her riding crop so as to cause an artificial halt and give herself time to recover her breath. Later, he was no less pleased when Kate learnt fluent Russian and ascended the hills at Black Mount as fast as anyone else, female or male.

Celia was never much of a country person: although she enjoyed walking about the estate, she did not shoot, ride or take any active part in farming or forestry, and she generally opted out of Peter's expeditions to Scotland, preferring to stay (for instance) with Alan and Lucy Moorehead in Italy. The one great interest which bound her and Peter together was the theatre: although he would on no account boast about anything that he himself had achieved, he enjoyed boasting mildly about *her* achievements. He admired her professional skill immensely, and followed every turn of her career with the utmost enthusiasm. Often he would remark to a friend how tremendously good she had been in a particular part, and in 1955, when she was playing the lead in William Douglas-Home's smash hit *The Reluctant Debutante*, he wrote to his former colleague in the O.U.D.S., Brewster Morgan:

Celia has been taking a well-earned holiday from *The Reluctant Debutante*, which is still playing to packed houses; but she rejoins the cast—luckily for them, since she really carries the whole thing on her shoulders—next week.

On the wider family front Peter's loyalty to the clan was never more apparent than when he stood resolutely by his mother as she plunged—to his intense embarrassment—into a legal battle with the Marchioness of Winchester. In 1951 Eve had announced her engagement to the Marquess, who was then eighty-eight and living, as she was, in the Bahamas; but a year later the old man had transferred his affections to Bapsy Pavry, the daughter of a Parsee high priest, and married her instead. Then in 1955, and again in 1956, the Marchioness issued writs against Eve alleging libel, loss of consortium and/or enticement. The age of the feuding parties alone made the affair grotesque—the Marquess was then ninety-three, Eve seventy-three and the Marchioness fifty-four—and the dignity of the proceedings was not enhanced by the plaintiff's habit of referring to Mrs Fleming in court as 'that viper'. For Peter, with his acute dislike of any form of emotional display, nothing could have been more disagreeable than to have to witness such a public exhibition of jealousy and spite; yet for day after day he or one of his brothers sat in court to give their mother moral support.

His loyalty was evident also in his relationship with Ian, to whom he was devoted. A rumour got about—perhaps because the two brothers did not see much of each other—that they could not stand each other's company; but nothing was further from the truth. Even if they could show it only in the most off-hand and public-school fashion, they loved each other deeply. Much has been made (notably by John Pearson in *The Life of Ian Fleming*) of the fact that at Eton Ian was overshadowed by the intellectual precocity of his elder brother, and that in order to assert himself he made ferocious physical exertions to become a brilliant athlete. This was true enough; yet it was also true that as a boy Peter stood in physical awe of his younger but much larger brother—so much so that when he came into his presence he would tremble with apprehension. Peter thus never had the faintest sense of being superior to Ian, in spite of his own great literary success before the war; and when Ian, after frittering away much of his life, suddenly at the age of forty-three hit on the idea of writing the James Bond thrillers, Peter's reaction was one of unqualified delight. Most authors would surely have been jealous at seeing their own fame and earnings so spectacularly outstripped by a late starter; but it never occurred to Peter to be envious. Instead, he was thrilled that Ian had at last achieved success. In private he would cheerfully admit that he thought the books were 'tosh'—but tosh of the highest order, fashioned with great professional skill; and he kept them all together, flanking a photograph of their author, on top of a small bookcase in his study—a little secular shrine. He also put at the disposal of James Bond's creator the services of Dr Knittpik (another of his *alter egos*)—a bibliophile and savant who lurked somewhere on the Chilterns and corrected, free of charge, not only Ian's manuscripts but also those of Anthony Powell and several lesser authors.

The friendship between Peter and Ian was not the sort that needed to be kept warm by frequent contact: it remained strong even though the brothers rarely met. Ian, cordially disliking field sports, always shirked the family gatherings at Black Mount; nor did he often come to Merrimoles, for the relationship with Peter that he wanted to preserve was his bachelor relationship, and when they did meet it was generally at Ian's club (Boodle's) or Peter's (the Garrick), where they could exchange gossip and jokes without the inhibitions of female company. And joke they did: for much of the time they were alone together they were incapacitated by laughter.

There were plenty of jokes at Merrimoles, too, and family life there was enhanced by the shooting and showing of a number of home-made films. Nichol became adept at handling the camera that recorded these epics, and the entire household took part, including any guests who happened to be staying. In the first—a silent film—Peter was drowned in the swimming-pool. In the second—an epic called *Cucumber* which involved a feverish search for buried treasure—Celia played the part of an Interpol policewoman; and for another, *Invasion 1957*, Peter procured some smoke-bombs from his friends in the Territorial Army, while Nichol, by means of trick photography, converted a circular biscuit tin into a convincing spacecraft from another planet.

The amenities of Merrimoles had been considerably increased, in 1951, by the construction of the swimming-pool on the terrace and, a couple of years later, by the addition of two new rooms on top of what had been a single-storey garage at one end of the house. The timber for the extension came from the estate, and it was built by Peter's own workmen, their names being carved on an oak shield which he mounted on the wall. Of the two new rooms the smaller became another bedroom, but the larger was designed as Peter's study: it was big enough to house a billiard table in the centre and, under the windows at the southern end, his desk, so that at last he had a commanding, eyrie-like position in which to write. This was what he had wanted when he originally sited the house: in front of him, as he sat working, the field fell gently away, flanked by woods on either side, and gave on to a wide glade known as Waterloo, which carried the eye on between more woods to further fields and the tops of beech-trees in the distance. On the window-sill in front of his desk stood a pair of old but powerful binoculars with which he could scrutinize any novel event or creature that manifested itself, and he often had at hand a .22 rifle with which to snipe at crows on the blasted ash tree a hundred and fifty yards down the field.

Loving this view, Peter several times had it painted—once in a straightforward picture by Peter Garrard, and once by Lawrence Toynbee, who designed a kind of animated frieze round the upper walls and ceiling of the loggia, his panorama including a bird's-eye view of the house and grounds among various scenes from Peter's travels and from local life.

At his desk in the new room Peter wrote not only his books but also a great many articles for the *Spectator*, besides a lesser number for *The Times*. As Strix he created for readers of the *Spectator* the image of an erudite and mildly eccentric country gentleman, with military experience and a keen interest in the theatre, living with his dogs and ever-changing menagerie of wild creatures in the depths of South Loamshire. Although he ranged over a wide variety of subjects, he was generally at his best when gently mocking his own peculiarities—as in a nostalgic essay about G.F. 7500 (his favourite Rolls-Royce shooting brake) which made the most of his mechanical ignorance:

> She was—nay (I hope) is—a splendid vehicle. I had her for five years, and what I notice chiefly now is that motoring *sounds* quite different. The Rolls had a body like a low-slung hearse, and as we sped ponderously along the roads, the whistling of the wind and the creak of timber gave one the illusion of being on board an old-fashioned sailing ship—a ship which, as the stresses of time wrought their will on the superstructure, seemed to be carrying, battened somewhere below hatches, an increasingly articulate cargo of voles and pipits.

On another occasion he described how, returning from an Irish snipe-bog with his shoes full of 'mulled ice', he suddenly remembered that there was a pint of hot coffee in the car:

> I found the thermos, took a swig, poured the rest of the coffee into my shoes and went on my way, warmed by the sort of glow which suffuses the feckless when they unexpectedly do something practical.

Often his weekly essays concerned shooting, and many were about animals, not least Nutto, the tame grey squirrel, and the two foxes Sophie and Satan, which were brought to him as cubs by the keeper's son. Strix composed one piece with the cubs in the pocket of his jacket (a ploy which, he clearly felt, not many of his readers would be able to emulate); and in a later piece he described how Satan had had one front leg amputated by the vet after being caught in a trap but nevertheless had established a reign of terror at Merrimoles:

> It is no good pretending that having a fox about the house makes the house any easier to run. The elderly visitor, left in the drawing-room while I fetch sherry, is found on my return to be in a state of agitation. 'Do you know,' he says in the tones of one who fears that his reason may be tottering, 'just for a moment I could have sworn a *fox* came into the room when you were gone.'
>
> Then there is the problem of the daily woman, a rather stern, imperious character. 'Mrs Wiles', the cook (a staunch alopecophil) ruefully informed me the other day, '*Tiene mucho miedo del zorro.*' I shall not be thanked, I know, if Mrs Wiles's fear of Satan causes her to leave our service; and meanwhile all breakages are attributed, if not to the fox himself, then to the nasty turn he gave her.
>
> Aloof, handsome, insolent and sly, leading a double life between the beech-woods and the drawing-room sofa, Satan is clearly storing up trouble for himself; but when you consider the hazards he has survived so far—two gin-traps, the loss of one leg and all his teeth—it is difficult not to conclude that he bears a charmed life: or at least that he has the luck of the devil.

In due course Strix and life in South Loamshire became so well established a feature of the *Spectator* that Peter and Rupert decided it would be worth publishing a collection of essays as a book. The result was *My Aunt's Rhinoceros* which came out in 1956 and took its title from the rhino from Joyce Grove which had lately come to roost in the garage at Merrimoles. A second assembly of distilled Strixiana, *The Gower Street Poltergeist*, was published in 1958, and, between these two, Rupert brought out a third collection of Peter's miscellaneous writings, mainly non-Strixian, under the title *With the Guards to Mexico!* This last title—surely incomprehensible to anyone except connoisseurs of the *genre*—was inspired by a seriously-intended but inadvertently hilarious study in French called *Peter Fleming: Sa Place dans la Littérature Anglaise*; its author, a count, had somehow won a prize with it; but now, with great good humour, he was deservedly sent up. In 1961 there appeared

Goodbye to the Bombay Bowler, described by its blurb as 'the last salvo from Strix ... who goes down with all his guns firing.'

In fact the Gower Street poltergeist's career was by no means over; but Strix, coming out in all these different editions, enlisted a small army of fans, and soon other writers began to parody him. Of the various counter-Strixes by far the most skilful was Trix, who in 1958 published a brilliantly-sustained take-off entitled *Plus Ça Change, Plus C'est la Memsahib* in the *National and English Review*. In an essay as densely stuffed with cryptic jokes as a Christmas pudding is with currants, Trix aired his life-long ambition to discover the identity of Strix, and worked his way craftily to the conclusion that since the Latin *strix, strigis* is a feminine noun, the writer behind the pseudonym must be Miss Frieda Lemming, the intrepid traveller with whom he, Trix, had spent a week snowbound on the Sino–Siberian frontier in 1931.

Peter was enchanted with this *pastiche*, and, discovering that Trix was his old friend John Verney, wrote to him enthusiastically:

> It really is the most delightfully labyrinthine *jeu d'esprit*, every twist in which—as far as I am concerned—comes off 100 per cent. I laughed out loud, several times, and am saddened only by the thought that nobody except I (and you) can see *all* the points which you make so cunningly and yet so humanely. Thank you for doing me so much honour and giving me so much pleasure.

Like Verney, a good many readers of the *Spectator* knew Strix's identity, and the disguise became still flimsier when *The Times*, reviewing *The Gower Street Poltergeist*, revealed that 'Strix is, of course, the off-handedly-amazing Mr Peter Fleming.' Even so, Peter continued to use the pseudonym, and when a later editor of the *Spectator*, Nigel Lawson, asked him to contribute regularly under his own name, he replied:

> I will gladly have a shot at the essay ... I would, however, much prefer to masquerade as Strix. There are various reasons for this ... Strix has, down the years, become a minor, idiosyncratic appendage of the *Spectator*: a sort of gargoyle ... From *my* point of view Strix has several advantages:
>
> 1. The leathers are the right length, if you see what I mean.
> 2. Pseudonymity is a great help in writing about almost anything I am likely to write about. I know it is a flimsy convention, but it does (for instance) allow one to write about one's own land, or one's own experiences, without appearing to boast—or to grumble—in an unbecoming way.

Although he maintained an astonishingly high standard, Peter often had difficulty in finding subjects about which to write, and he was always hoping that some minor accident would befall him. Thus when he set fire to himself with his pipe one evening while flighting duck, the incident was a godsend, and he fashioned from it a quintessentially Strixian description of his own impracticality and foolishness.

Another source of ideas was his circle of close friends such as Tim Nugent, Peter Cazalet and Tony Keswick, with whom he never ceased to exchange ridiculous jokes, either in person or by post. Once, when a tooth fell out, he sent it to Tony Keswick, and Tony had this repulsive outcast—long, thin, brown and crooked—mounted with maximum vulgarity by a jeweller in Hong Kong: surrounded by cheap pearls, it was enshrined on a pink base above the inscription: THIS TOOTH FELL FROM THE MOUTH OF MY FRIEND PETER FLEMING SHORTLY BEFORE 1957.

Peter, in turn, was delighted when Tony sent him a 'small, well-made luggage-label' with 'a craftsmanlike, rather obsolete appearance', on which was written: 'This coupon permits the licencee to export one moose. It must be attached to the moose and cancelled by the agent at the point of shipment.' This prompted a charming essay—which discussed Harold Nicolson, Lear, Beachcomber and Lewis Carroll, among others—on the importance of maintaining a flow of nonsense.

New books offered a more regular source of inspiration, and often he would enrich a straightforward review by weaving into it elements of his own experience. Almost always his judgments were sound, but once (as he himself readily admitted later) he was comprehensively deceived. The book in question was *The Long Walk*, which purported to describe how its Polish author Slavomir Rawicz had escaped from a Siberian prison camp in 1941 and walked some three thousand miles southwards into India. The book was to be published by Constable, and before it came out Ralph Arnold, one of the firm's directors, sent Peter a copy to see whether or not he thought the story genuine. Having enjoyed the book immensely, Peter replied:

The only ingredient which got my eyebrows slightly raised was the glimpse of the Abominable Snowman, which I cannot help feeling the ghost writer may have gone out of his way to conjure up. But otherwise everything seems, from my knowledge of conditions in the area, completely authentic, and I don't see how the cleverest impostor could have made it up.

Later, when *The Long Walk* was published (and immediately became a success) he enlarged this enthusiastic appraisal in the *Spectator*, declaring that, apart from the incident of the Snowman, 'the narrative bears the unmistakable stamp of truth.' Three months later, however, he completely changed his mind, mainly as a result of meeting Rawicz himself and discussing his wanderings with him and four other critics on a B.B.C. radio programme called 'The Travellers'. Devoting a second column to the saga, Strix recalled his earlier verdict on the book's veracity and went on: 'It is only when you read it a second or a third time, with an atlas open beside you, that strange omissions and daunting improbabilities begin to appear.' Among the topographical features which Rawicz must, by his own account, have crossed, but which he had not noticed, were the main road, lined by telegraph poles, from Lanchou to Urumchi, and a 20,000-foot mountain barrier. In allegedly traversing the entire width of Tibet he had never seen a lama or a lamasery, and had never encountered the staple food of the country, *tsamba*. By these and many other inexplicable anomalies, Peter was 'regretfully forced to the conclusion that the whole of this excellent book is moonshine.'

In almost everything he wrote—even if it was only an answer to an income-tax demand—Peter's sense of humour bubbled out. Probably no member of Universal Aunts realized that legs were gently being pulled when, in reply to an inquiry about whether or not he considered Mrs Valentine Fleming a suitable employer for a lady's maid, he wrote: 'Gentlemen: I can give Mrs Valentine Fleming, whom I have known from the moment of my birth, a very favourable reference.' But what, one longs to know, was the reaction of the person who had asked him for a reference for Chips Keswick (one of Tony's sons) and got the following answer: 'I have known Mr Chippendale Keswick since he was a small boy. I can best sum up my opinion of his character and qualities by saying that, if I were in charge of a large organization (other, perhaps, than an orchestra or a *corps de ballet*), I would spare no effort to induce him to join it.'

Even a serious letter to his solicitor would almost always be enlivened by some felicitous and unexpected phrase, and in 1965, when he took on a new secretary, Ann Horsfall, he welcomed her with a characteristic note:

> I hope you'll be happy here and like the job. I don't see why you shouldn't—the suicide-rate among your predecessors has been relatively low ... I think it might be sensible for you to have a hand in choosing any new furniture that the estate needs to buy, or you

might find your mind preyed on by a pouffe, if you know what I mean.

During Strix's heyday—the 1950s and early 1960s—Peter continued to write for *The Times*, but his relations with the Thunderer were far less happy than in earlier years. Many of his friends were still working in Printing House Square, among them Pat Ryan, Iverach McDonald and Oliver Woods; but he conceived a deep dislike for the editor, Sir William Haley, and gradually came to believe—quite without foundation—both that his dislike was reciprocated and that it led to a sustained campaign against him. It is perfectly clear, in retrospect, that no such campaign was ever contemplated, let alone put into action; yet at the same time it is easy enough to see how a series of incidents, each trivial in itself, made Peter feel himself the victim of a petty feud.

The ill-feeling began in 1954, when Peter heard in confidence that the Sultan of Muscat's armed forces were about to take the field against the dissident followers of the Imam of Oman, a persistent trouble-maker who had the backing of Saudi Arabia. The Foreign Office (Peter gathered) felt that it would be an excellent idea if an objective and reputable eye-witness accompanied the expedition, so he proposed to Haley that *The Times* should send him as its Special Correspondent. Haley, however, rejected his suggestion in a letter which said, in effect, that *The Times* could not afford the return air fare to Bahrain—about £400.

Peter then largely forgot about the project until, meeting Harold Macmillan at a shoot in the autumn, he asked what had happened about the Muscat campaign. Macmillan told him that the expedition had been postponed, but that it was due to be launched in December, and that he thought Peter should certainly accompany it. He promised to make what arrangements he could.

Very soon afterwards Peter got a message from *The Times* asking him to call on Haley as a matter of urgency, and a few days later he was in the leading Land-Rover of the Muscat and Oman Field Force as it closed in on the Imam's stronghold in the foothills of the Djebel Akbar. The campaign proved brief, bloodless and successful; but since it was outlandish and came as a surprise to almost everybody, *The Times* obtained a distinguished exclusive story. Peter was not much impressed to learn, on returning to England, that the event which had provoked his prompt dispatch had been an approach to the Editor by a senior member of the Foreign Office.

Two years later, in the summer of 1957, he again went abroad on *The Times*'s behalf, pioneering the road to Moscow and the Crimea which the Russians had just opened to tourists for the first time. Although the trip was straightforward (to reach Yalta, as he remarked, one merely had to proceed to Moscow and turn right), he took with him a young godson to help drive and look after the car. It was just as well that a second person was present, for in Smolensk Peter was smitten, and prostrated, by severe pains in the stomach. Having repelled, with some difficulty, an attempt to remove his appendix—on the grounds that it had already been taken out forty years before—he succumbed to a series of injections administered by a gigantic female doctor, and by the time he reached Moscow was more or less comatose. There, however, after a bout of his recurrent malarial fever, he fully recovered, and the drive to the south went smoothly enough.

Restless as ever, he constantly pushed on and was loath to linger anywhere longer than was absolutely necessary; but one place at which he did seem happy to dawdle was Yasnaya Polyana, the home and estate of that greatest of literary squires, Tolstoy. To suggest that Peter saw himself as even a minor Tolstoy would be a ridiculous exaggeration; yet clearly he felt a strong affinity with the great writer who had devoted himself to the active management of his land, and he walked for some time behind the pleasant white house in the woods that the novelist had planted.

On the journey as a whole, room for manœuvre was strictly limited, first by the obligatory presence in the car of an interpreter, and second by the fact that only the one great road, lancing southwards through the rolling wheatlands of the Ukraine, was open to tourists. Even so Peter did, in the Crimea, make one characteristic attempt to brush aside the restrictions. He was keen to visit Sevastopol and Balaclava, mainly out of historical curiosity but partly also out of journalistic inquisitiveness, for Sevastopol was the base of the Black Sea Fleet and might yield some interesting information. And so, having established that the coast road from Yalta was closed 'because of an avalanche', he and his young companion set off for Bakhchisarai, a legitimate tourist goal in the middle of the Crimea which lay on the road that approached Sevastopol from the north. His plan—which he had taken care to discuss only on the sea-front, away from hidden microphones—was to drive to Bakhchisarai and to carry on past it towards Sevastopol, in the hope that the interpreter—a singularly clueless man—might not realize until too late what was happening.

All went well until they left Simferopol, the last town before Bakhchisarai. Then they noticed that they were being discreetly tailed by a policeman on a motor-cycle. Peter ordered his companion to increase speed, and soon they were doing seventy miles an hour on a rough gravel road, with their wheels sending up such an enormous pall of dust that they could not see whether their escort was still with them or not. When they reached the village of Bakhchisarai they shot through its wide high-street in a moment with (as they had hoped) the interpreter pinned down in the back seat of the open car by the slipstream; but a few seconds later the policeman roared past them, covered in dust and doing eighty miles an hour, to disappear over the hill ahead. After a mile or two they came on him again: he had parked his motor-cycle across the road and was flagging them down. They got out and Peter, grinning hugely, congratulated him in his faltering Russian on the Crimean weather and the speed of his machine; the policeman, grinning no less broadly, returned the compliments. But when, after a few more pleasantries, Peter asked if he might proceed, the man replied that, greatly as he regretted it, the road was closed. There was nothing for the tourists to do except go and make dutiful admiration of the Tartar palace of Bakhchisarai and of its celebrated fountain, which had inspired Pushkin to his epic poem.

No mention of this episode ever appeared in *The Times*, but throughout the rest of the journey Peter either telephoned or posted dispatches to Printing House Square. Several of his photographs were prominently displayed in the paper, and when he returned home in August he wrote three turnover articles about the trip. After all this it was a pity that a tiresome dispute should break out about how much he was to be paid: *The Times* kept offering him what he took to be paltry amounts, and he became so disgruntled that he threatened to leave the service of the paper altogether—whereupon Haley sent him a placatory note:

> Quite frankly, we value your contributions so much when you do feel like writing that I do not want to do anything which might seem like losing the connection ... Once again, I would like you to know how much I value the feeling that I hope will continue to exist of *The Times* as a natural home for your work when you feel moved to write.

Irritated though he was by the paper's stinginess, Peter continued to offer Printing House Square ideas and suggestions, and in April 1959 he produced a magnificently Buchanish plan for making contact with the Dalai Lama, who was then still in Tibet but gravely threatened by the Chinese invasion. Peter's proposal—which he submitted first to friends in M.I.5 and in the Cabinet Office—was that he should be sent to Tibet to meet the Dalai Lama, ostensibly as a correspondent of *The Times* but also as a representative of the British Government. The prospects of making such an unofficial contact, he suggested, appeared to depend on two basic requirements:

a. Authority for a private Dakota-type aircraft with an endurance of 1000–1500 miles to use an airfield in Nepal or Upper Burma.

b. The insertion of a series of short, cryptic messages, probably in English, in one or more wireless broadcasting programmes known to be receivable in Tibet.

The purpose of the broadcast messages would be to convey to the Dalai Lama an invitation to fix (if he so desires) a rendezvous at which a plane could land on an improvised air-strip.

The chances of attracting the Dalai Lama's attention to, and establishing the bona fides of, the broadcast messages lie in the fact that in 1949, when he was about thirteen, he was taught English by Heinrich Harrer, an Austrian who during the war escaped to Tibet from an internment camp in India ... With help from Harrer it should be possible to devise something in the nature of a call-sign which, since its meaning would be apparent only to the Dalai Lama and his ex-tutor, would convince the former that the messages came from a friendly and reliable source.

This splendid project was, as Peter himself noted, 'overtaken by events' —the flight of the Dalai Lama into India. But he continued to offer *The Times* ideas, and in the autumn of 1959 he returned to the fold as, once again, a writer of Fourth Leaders. Strix happened at that time to have reached a low ebb, and although he continued from time to time to appear in the *Spectator*, Peter was glad of the stimulus provided by contact with another office.

In 1961 he planned a return to China and suggested a possible itinerary to Iverach McDonald; but the project was killed in infancy by the Chinese, who rejected Peter's application for a visa in a letter from the Embassy in Portland Place:

Dear Sir,

Your letter of September 29th has been received. In view of the fact that you are a vice-president of the Tibet Society in Britain which supports the reactionary upper strata of Tibetan slave-owners in their rebellious and traitorous activities against the Central Government of the People's Republic of China, interferes in the internal affairs of China and puts out scandalous and hostile publications against the Chinese people, we are afraid that we cannot conform with your request for a visa to visit China.

Yours faithfully,

CHOU HSAING-PU
Second Secretary

o which Peter replied:

Dear Sir,

Thank you for your letter conveying, in picturesque language, the Embassy's decision to reject my application for a visa.

As a lifelong friend of your country, I cannot help regretting that her representatives should find themselves obliged to adopt so illiberal an attitude; but I realize that you have your duty to do.

Yours faithfully,

PETER FLEMING

This letter was opened by the Chinese, date-stamped, and returned to Nettlebed, whereupon Peter got his secretary to send it in again, only to have it returned once more.

Obviously *The Times* was in no way to blame for the collapse of this plan; but soon Peter became involved in another dispute with the paper, this time over the payment for an article of fifteen hundred words on the 150th anniversary of Pop, the Eton Society. For this piece, which had needed a good deal of research and was written at a time when he was no longer paid a retainer, Peter was sent a cheque for £14. He returned it with a note saying that he would have earned more if he had been paid for his time at the basic rate for agricultural workers, and at this mild protest the fee was raised to £20—still a derisory figure for someone of his reputation.

A year later another small incident occurred which reinforced his belief in Haley's malignancy towards him: his name was dropped without warning from the Court Page note 'Today's Birthdays'. Had he made any effort to discover the reason, he would have found that the change had been made, on her own initiative, by a lady who had recently taken over responsibility for the birthday column: dismayed by the number of names she was supposed to include, she had conceived the idea that her subjects would be quite happy to appear biennially. As soon as her aberration was discovered, the full number of names was restored; but Peter, never knowing this, supposed that Haley had been responsible for this minor but irritating slight.

Later, when Peter's mother died, Haley declined to publish a short memoir of her written some years before by Lord Esher, on the grounds that the author was dead; and later still he rejected a letter which Peter wrote dissociating the family from a paperback life of Ian called *The Man With the Golden Pen*—this last at a time when the paper's correspondence columns were full of a controversy about the extent to which a biographer could ignore the wishes and feelings of his subject's family. Both these incidents inevitably reinforced Peter's sense of grievance. Typically, he did not share his annoyance with anyone; had he done so, some of it might have evaporated; but instead he bottled it up in a long memorandum which he laid down in the Estate Office. It seems very sad that his long association with Printing House Square should have been brought—largely through misunderstanding—to so low a pass.

In the autumn of 1962 Peter noticed a lump growing slowly on his neck. During the shooting season he naturally refused to do anything about it, but when on January 31st he went into a local nursing-home and had it removed, he discovered that it was cancerous. The swelling contained a highly malignant tumour, and the specialist, diagnosing this as a secondary growth, believed that he must have a primary source of cancer somewhere else in his body. Peter was sent, accordingly, to the Royal Marsden Hospital in Fulham, but a week of rigorous tests failed to reveal the expected primary source, and in the end the specialist changed his mind, deciding that the tumour in Peter's neck had been the only manifestation of the disease.

This second opinion proved correct, and Peter was delighted, in due course, to discover that he was almost unique—the one patient in thousands who recovers after only minor surgery. Even so, the episode gave him a severe shock, and it was years before he could be certain that he was safe. Until 1968 he went to a specialist every three months for an examination, and although no new manifestation of cancer was ever revealed, he found it impossible to banish altogether the spectre of the disease.

Even on him, unshakeable as he normally was, the first impact of the discovery was considerable: he, who was never ill, had fallen victim to a disease that might easily have proved fatal. Galvanized by the realization of his human frailty, he drafted an article called 'Mumbo Jumbo' in which he deplored the secrecy and dread surrounding cancer; it had, he wrote, been a shock to find that his own doctor, whom he knew well, had seriously considered concealing the real nature of his disease from him.

He did not publish this article immediately, for he did not wish to alarm people on the estate (the piece came out several years later in the *Spectator*, when he used it to support Richard Dimbleby, the broadcaster, who led a personal crusade against the attitude towards cancer that Peter so disliked). News of his own illness emerged gradually, and he did everything he could to minimize alarm—by carrying on exactly as he always had, by making jokes about the uniqueness of his case, and by constantly emphasizing the fact that his luck seemed to have been extraordinary.

Even so, he thought it only prudent to take what steps he could against the possibility of the disease returning, and he set about forming a charitable trust into which he could transfer many of the non-agricultural properties on the estate, thus (he hoped) reducing the eventual burden of death duties on his family. He also drafted six or seven pages of autobiography under the title *In Those Days*, from which the passages at the beginning of this book are taken. It was the world's loss that he never had the resolution to continue the story of his life beyond the age of nine.

15
Starts and Stops

There now set in another period of literary drought, and in the last eight years of his life Peter produced no further book. It seemed that the flow of inspiration which had brought the four historical studies into being so quickly had suddenly been dammed by the onset of cancer, and it never got going again. The factors that inhibited Peter were extremely complex: cancer, and the lingering anxiety which it inevitably created, was undoubtedly the most immediate. Another depressant was the death of his mother, closely followed by that of Ian; and a third debilitating influence was the great shift that took place in England during the 1960s towards literary permissiveness. Peter was always essentially a reserved and fastidious writer, and he could not bring himself to adopt the kind of strident, four-letter tone that became more and more popular—a circumstance which (needlessly) made him feel old-fashioned and out of touch. The effect of these various influences was to induce a crisis of confidence: although as Strix he sometimes still hit top form, his writing was all too often crippled by its diffidence. Almost every sentence seemed to be weighed down by asides, qualifications and withdrawals, so that his articles as a whole became static, lifeless and lacking in conviction.

Not that any of this was apparent in his family life, for he continued to pack his existence with a tremendous variety of occupations. It is not easy, in retrospect, to convey the fullness of his days: to say that he never wasted a moment is merely to hint at the rich variety of activities that he crammed into every twenty-four hours.

He was always up early and in his office by nine o'clock, by which hour he had read *The Times* from end to end. He would then deal with his post, and by ten o'clock would have dictated enough letters to his secretary to keep her going for the rest of the morning. He would then tour the estate, taking the closest possible interest in every problem that arose—and the greatest possible pleasure in any success achieved. After that he would return to the office to sign letters and deal with visitors. Lunch was an occasion for refuelling rather than for rest, and by about twenty to two he was outside again, either to go shooting or to play tennis. After a couple of hours' exercise he would return to the office once more to sign the remaining letters and to deal with any problems that had arisen since lunch. Then he would go home, have a bath, and retire to his study to write, or—if Celia had a first night—he would drive to London. And after he had been to the theatre, no matter how late it was or how tired he might be, he would always drive home.

Into the close-knit fabric of his existence at Nettlebed he wove an immense amount of work on behalf of local organizations, becoming more and more active in country and county affairs. He was President of the Oxford Branch of the Country Landowners' Association, and represented Oxford on the body's national council. (He also acted as President of the C.L.A.'s annual Game Fair when it was held at Shotover Park near Oxford in 1965.) He was an active member of the Thame Agricultural Association and of the Oxfordshire Agricultural Society, both of which held important annual shows in the area. In 1967 he became Chairman of the Management Committee of the Warburg Nature Reserve, which was created that year on land behind Nettlebed. A founder-member of the Timber Growers' Organization, he was active both in the T.G.O. and in the local branch of the Royal Forestry Society. But perhaps his most important role was that of the first Chairman of the Game Conservancy, which was formed in 1968 after a merger between the Game Research Association and the Eley Game Advisory Service. The union of these two bodies was not easily effected, and it was largely through Peter's firm yet courteous handling of the negotiations that the feathers of various ruffled parties were smoothed down enough to make the merger possible.

Another establishment in whose affairs he took a close interest was Reading University. He had been a member of its Council since soon after the war; in 1968 he deposited most of the early records of the estate in the Library, and later agreed to serve on the University's standing committee—although he did not live long enough to put this good intention into practice.

His involvement with all these organizations took up a good deal of his time; yet there is no doubt that, had he really been fired by an idea for a book, he would have forged ahead and written it in spite of all his other commitments. As it was, he was persistently frustrated—and not always (as will emerge) by his own diffidence.

The first subject he took up was a life of Adrian Carton de Wiart—a task to which his friend Pug Ismay had for some time urged him. At first Peter had resisted Ismay's blandishments, replying to one of his letters: 'For a number of reasons with which I won't bore you now, I don't think I am the man to do the book about Adrian.' Yet Carton de Wiart remained one of his heroes; he had already written an obituary notice for *The Times*, and this was published when the General died in June 1963. Then, more than ever, Ismay and Lady Carton de Wiart besought him to write the life, and at last, in January 1964, he yielded to their pressure, agreeing 'to have a shot at it'. He began to make contact with Carton de Wiart's daughters in Belgium and France, but a note of caution marked his requests for help: 'I am trying to write a life ...' he would begin his letters, as though aware that the task might finally prove impossible.

In April he stopped work for a pleasantly outlandish diversion, flying out to join Bernard Fergusson, then Governor-General of New Zealand, who was about to make a Vice-Regal tour of the Pacific Islands as the personal representative of the Queen. In less than four weeks H.M.N.Z.S. *Royalist* visited seventeen islands, and Peter thoroughly enjoyed the contrasts provided by the pomp of the Governor-General's progress superimposed on the islands' simplicity. He described the journey admirably in an article for *Holiday* magazine, showing particular enthusiasm for the strange contraptions in which the party was sometimes hoisted ashore. On Raoul, for instance, the largest of the Kermadecs, which was uninhabited except by a nine-man team of New Zealand meteorologists, the visitors were prevented from going alongside in their whaler by the strength of the sea; so

the grinning meteorologists, by means of a primitive diesel-operated crane, lowered into the thwarts a capacious laundry-basket in which, three at a time, we were hauled aloft and swung inshore, briefly tasting the delights of ballooning ...

When it was time to leave we said goodbye to them with regret, and they gave us a pig. Though hardly what might be called a keen student of Imperial protocol, I felt, as I shared an airborne laundry-basket with the headless carcass of the pig and Laura Fergusson's lady-in-waiting, that I was breaking fresh ground in this specialized field.

On Western Samoa he climbed the hill on which Robert Louis Stevenson lies buried and noticed that in the inscription on the grave the penultimate line of the author's own poem 'Requiem' had been misquoted. Into the line

> Home is the sailor, home from sea,

a second 'the' had intruded, and Peter enjoyed pointing out the mistake to the rest of the party. The sight of Stevenson's tomb seems to have left a strong impression on him, for he later wrote for his own headstone a poem that echoed, in its conception if not in its words, 'Under the wide and starry sky.'

On Tonga they were regally entertained by Queen Salote to what Peter off-handedly described to a friend as 'quarter of a mile of sucking-pig', and in May he flew home to continue wrestling with his jigsaw of the life of Carton de Wiart.

The autumn of that year was the gloomiest he had ever suffered, for his mother died on July 20th, and Ian, who was only fifty-six, on August 12th. Both deaths moved him deeply: when he came into the room where Amaryllis was nursing their mother *in extremis*, his face, normally so mask-like, crumpled into tears; and after her funeral he wrote to Rupert, 'She was a splendid person, and I reckon she did jolly well by the four intransigent brats of whom she was left in sole charge when she was just over thirty and I was under ten.'

Ian's sudden death from a heart-attack distressed him no less severely. He was at Glenkiln, with the Keswicks, when it happened; and when a telephone call came for him after breakfast on August 12th, bringing the bad news, he went out of the house without a word. After a few minutes walk he returned; but, not wishing to spoil the day's shooting, he said nothing until the evening. Only then did he briefly announce the news and set off for the south.

A few days later he wrote to Rupert:

> It was terribly rough about poor old Ian, but there was really nothing ahead of him, so I suppose one must feel that it was, in a repulsive phrase, 'for the best'. He could never have done anything again and, apart from the physical activity which it irked him acutely to miss, he was finding it almost impossible to do things like correcting proofs. He told me that he had finished with Bond and I suggested that he should auction the copyright in the character at Sotheby's, with a clause in the contract forbidding exploitation for, say, five years. He liked the idea and discussed it with Jock

Campbell (of Booker's) but I don't know if in fact it was feasible. I shall miss him very much indeed, and so will a diverse lot of other people.

Thereafter Peter defended Ian's family and memory to the best of his ability, first by becoming a director of Glidrose, the company which Ian had formed to manage the Bond income, and second by attacking anybody who maligned Ian's memory. Hardly ever did Peter really lash out in print, but in June 1965, when the *Observer* published a disparaging piece about Ian by Malcolm Muggeridge, he let fly a withering broadside in a letter to the Editor:

Sir—The curiously unpleasant article about my brother to which you gave such prominence last week was a rewrite of a similar piece which Mr Muggeridge contributed to the American magazine *Esquire* several months ago. I assume you did not see the original version. If you had, there are various grounds on which you might have thought twice about publishing the stuff.

(a) *Literary*. Mr Muggeridge's admission, in *Esquire*, that he had read only one of my brother's books and had no intention of reading any more might or might not have deterred you from 'inviting Malcolm Muggeridge, who has strong views on the subject, to comment on ... the whole Bond cult': but you would, I think, almost certainly have noticed that Mr Muggeridge's style is becoming less taut. 'I bet a wreath was laid on his grave marked "C" for "M"' (*Esquire*) appeared in the *Observer* as 'I shouldn't mind betting that among the wreaths at his funeral there was one from "C" to "M". There ought to have been, anyway'.

(b) *Accuracy*. In *Esquire* Mr Muggeridge attended a Secret Service reunion dinner 'two or three years running'; there were twelve or fifteen guests. In the *Observer* he attended only one of these functions: the guests numbered 'about twenty-five in all'.

(c) *Personal abuse*. To credit my brother with 'squalid aspirations' (the *Observer*) is possibly less offensive than to call him (*Esquire*) 'a Peter Pan of the bordellos', whatever that means. The fact that Ian's schoolboy son was certain to read the *Observer* article restores the balance.

These are all small things: there is one significant aspect in which the two versions of the diatribe differed, and which might have jeopardized Mr Muggeridge's chances of promotion from the back pages of *Esquire* to the front page of the *Observer* Weekend Review. To an American public Mr Muggeridge was prepared, and indeed appeared anxious, to reveal that he knew my brother well, was a great friend of his wife's and had frequently enjoyed their hospitality; from British readers, who sometimes have finicky views about what is decent and what is not, he shrewdly concealed these facts.

To vilify publicly, within a few months of his death, a friend from whom he had received nothing but kindness is not the sort of thing that it would occur to many of us to do; nor would a reputable literary critic pontificate at length about a writer with whose work he was almost totally unacquainted. But Mr Muggeridge's standards of conduct have always been idiosyncratic, and for him, I imagine, the only abnormal feature of this shoddy transaction is that it has— thanks to the *Observer*—brought him two handsome fees instead of one.

To this biting attack neither the author of the article nor his Editor returned any effective answer, and in a private note to the Editor Peter declared that he would never contribute to the paper again.

As a director of Glidrose [the firm formed by Ian] he was equally solicitous on his brother's behalf; he needed to be, for numerous disputes broke out about how best to reap the multifarious harvest that Ian's imagination had sown. A year before his death, when short of capital, Ian had sold a 51 per cent interest in the Bond royalties to Booker McConnell, the sugar firm run by his friend Jock Campbell, for £100,000; and in his will he left £289,000, but these sums included only a fraction of the money that Bond had earned or was about to earn, and it became the job of the Glidrose directors to secure the maximum benefit for Ian's widow Annie and their son Caspar.

One of their most pressing problems was to curb the various authors who were attempting to use Bond's name without permission, among them a Japanese writer who had translated Ian's books and by then had started one of his own called 'oo7—With Love from Hell'. A potentially more serious menace was the Bulgarian Andrei Gulyiashki, who had fashioned a confrontation between Bond and his own master spy Avakoum Zahov in a thriller which Cassell were proposing to publish in England. By the end of 1965 at least five other pirates were known to be at work in various parts of the world.

The only effective way of suppressing these plagiarists, the Glidrose board decided, would be to produce a 'Continuation Bond' book of their own and so to saturate the market with a form of authorized sequel. Among the possible authors suggested was Kingsley Amis. Annie was violently against the idea, and at first Peter also opposed it; but then he came to appreciate its merits, and it was his advocacy that eventually won her round. In a letter dated March 15th, 1966, he wrote:

> The Bulgarian, against whom Glidrose are taking all possible preventative measures, is not himself an important phenomenon. What is important is the alacrity with which publishers have jumped at the chance of cashing in on a piracy ... This brings out the importance of Glidrose either publishing, or at least having up its sleeve, a Continuation Bond, the existence of which would deter a respectable publisher like Cassell from taking (as they do) a keen interest in such a long-priced outsider as Gulyiashki.
>
> As you know, I was originally less than lukewarm towards the idea of a Continuation Bond; but, having seen more of the ramifications and repercussions of this extraordinary market, I now feel strongly that the right thing to do is to tell Kingsley Amis to go ahead.

In due course Peter's advice was accepted: the Bulgarian was suppressed, and Kingsley Amis was commissioned to write the book that finally emerged as *Colonel Sun*. At the same time, however, Glidrose were forced to commission a second Continuation Bond—*Per Fine Ounce* by Geoffrey Jenkins, who claimed in a letter to the board that his would be the only true continuation, because he had written the outline of the plot (set in South Africa) at Ian's request, and Ian had seen it and 'indeed was most enthusiastic about it'. Having several times pressed the Glidrose board to give him permission, Jenkins ended one letter: 'Unless, therefore, formal consent is forthcoming in the very near future, I shall write the novel whether or not it is granted.' Glidrose told him to go ahead, but on this book—as on Amis's—they retained the right of suppression; and when they saw *Per Fine Ounce* they exercised their right, for they considered the book unpublishable. *Colonel Sun*, on the other hand, struck them as a workmanlike job, and they decided that it should come out. Annie still strongly disliked the whole project, and Peter (as he remarked in a note to the Glidrose chairman) had some difficulty in 'getting her under starter's orders,' but eventually she too agreed. There was a brief dispute about the pseudonym which Amis would employ: 'George Glidrose' was suggested, but was opposed by Jonathan Cape, the publishers, on the grounds that 'this is not a name likely to have any selling or publicity power,' and in the end 'Robert Markham' was chosen.

In all these dealings the amount of money at stake was phenomenal. In 1963 Ian's royalties had amounted to £102,000, and in 1964 they more than doubled, to £230,000; but the *annus mirabilis* for the whole Bond business was 1965, when twenty-nine million copies of the books were sold all over the world, and Glidrose's profit before tax—swollen by the success of the film of *Goldfinger* and by the publicity surrounding the filming of *Thunderball*—rose to £353,000. By 1968 the financial problems of administering the estate had reached such proportions that Peter could do no more than clutch at what seemed to him a few fundamentals. 'All the problems are virtually beyond a layman's grasp,' he wrote to Glidrose's solicitors:

> As you know, I am a child in these matters, but I should have thought that the Trustees could (so to speak) spend quite a lot of money for him [Caspar]. Could they not, for instance, buy him essentials like cars, cartridges etc., pay the fee for a life membership of the London Library and undertake other forms of 'capital' expenditure without the money affecting his tax liability? I expect I am talking through my hat.

While Peter battled with Ian's affairs, he was struggling also with his book on Carton de Wiart. An announcement in *The Times* during March 1965 had brought in a considerable number of letters and reminiscences, but by September of that year he had begun referring in his letters to the fact that he was making 'minimal progress', and although he drafted three opening chapters during 1966, in October 1967 he wrote to one of the people who had helped him that the book 'is, and has been for some time, in a state of suspended animation'. Eventually he lost heart altogether and sent out a general letter to all his correspondents shelving the project indefinitely:

> I have given up—at any rate for the time being—the idea of writing this book. Its subject was a perfectionist, who set a great store on privacy and who in *Happy Odyssey* told the world all he felt the world needed to know about his life. The further my researches took me, the more doubtful I became of my (or anybody else's) ability to produce the sort of book that measured up to Adrian's standards; and so I have put the project on one side.

Enclosing a copy of this note, he expanded on it a little in a covering letter to Carton de Wiart's widow:

> The more I went into his astonishing career, the more convinced I became that I couldn't really do him justice ... I feel that perhaps I am being rather wet about the whole thing, and I know that Pug Ismay would have been disappointed by my decision [he had died in

1965]; but I suppose that it is just possible that one day I may have another shot at the book.

A few weeks later he wrote to her again: 'I had a lot of nice letters from people I wrote to, thanking them for their help over Adrian. Perhaps if I break a leg or something I may resume the task.'

This failure was so uncharacteristic of Peter that one is tempted to search for some deeper reason beyond the rather feeble excuses which he produced. No doubt he was inhibited by discovering that the General's love life had been far more diversified than he had at first supposed; but the main difficulty was that, after extensive research, he had been unable to discover the identity of Carton de Wiart's mother, and his discussion of the subject in his draft opening chapters greatly upset the surviving members of the family.

It was his lack of self-confidence, more than anything else, that stopped Peter writing his autobiography—a task which Rupert repeatedly urged him to undertake. Always he would deflect the requests with the same sort of flippant half-promises as he had used in writing to Joan Carton de Wiart: 'I might if I break my leg,' he would say, or: 'I might if you wrote yours first.' Nor would he seriously consider the other idea which Rupert often put to him—that of writing, or at least editing, a book about shooting. Much as he might admire the hunting sketches of Turgenev or the diaries of Colonel Peter Hawker, he could never abandon himself to the full-blooded enthusiasm of either of these authors; his attitude to shooting was somehow too intellectual, as he once hinted in an article he wrote for, but had rejected by, an American magazine:

> Dawns and dusks, lakes and hills and woods, the shadows of clouds chasing each other across the valley below, vast silences broken by small, sometimes significant sounds—the surroundings in which the hunter plays his part cannot alter the fact that his purpose is primitive and cruel; but they lend, as they have always lent, a redeeming touch of the aesthetic to a basically barbarous activity.

Never did Peter sign an article on shooting with his own name—and indeed, considering his own enthusiasm for the chase, he wrote extraordinarily little about it in any guise. Now and then Strix would discuss some shooting topic, and as 'Pudding' (his schoolboy nick-name) Peter contributed occasional articles to the *Field*. The depth of knowledge shown in these makes one wish that he could more often have overcome his aversion to writing directly about his own experience: for instance, in a piece about woodcock—'this charming, mysterious bird whose appearance is too often greeted with an unbecoming demonstration of fire-power'—he recorded how he had learnt to tell not merely when there was a woodcock about, but also when one had been in the area lately, and he advanced the theory that most dogs do not like the scent of this particular quarry: 'When my Labrador works the line of a woodcock, one can tell at once what she is at ... My own three-year-old bitch, like several of her predecessors, still wears when bringing a woodcock to hand the faintly peeved expression of a debutante who has chosen a chocolate with the wrong kind of centre.'

In another piece Pudding declared his admiration for the second Earl of Malmesbury, who calculated that in a lifetime devoted to shooting he had walked 36,200 miles—'very nearly once and a half times the circumference of the globe.' 'In spite,' wrote Peter, 'or, in my view, more probably because of these exertions, he had not been confined to his bed for a single day in "the whole of this, to us mortals, great space of time."'

If he could have collected scraps like this, and blended them together with episodes of his own shooting experience, the result must have been an admirable book. Yet the older he became, the less he was able to give out on any subject and to expose himself, either in writing or in conversation; the protective armour in which he had deliberately encased himself all his life became in the end so thick that practically no emotional communication was possible through it, either from within or from without.

Peter's withdrawal into himself was a process so slow and so gradual that it was almost imperceptible to the family: they noticed only that he became more taciturn, especially in the evenings, and that there were periods when he seemed to be sunk in gloom; but to friends who had not seen him for some years the change was marked and depressing. Visitors to Merrimoles could not help noticing how the house appeared to be inhabited by a collection of total strangers who scarcely spoke to each other. At meals, particularly, an electric silence would descend, for the air was charged by the tension that Peter's presence always generated, and many guests found themselves chattering involuntarily in an attempt to fill the vacuum.

No sign of this intellectual sterility, however, was apparent on the estate, in whose welfare Peter took a keener interest than ever before. As he walked the woods or cruised the roads (now in a Citroën shooting-brake, for he had long-since abandoned vintage cars), with his pipe clamped between his teeth, he seemed exactly the same as ever. The set of his head, with jaw jutting, reminded people of the figurehead of a ship: he was always forging ahead.

He was still as keen as ever to travel, and in the summer of 1966 he returned to one of his favourite stretches of country—the Caucasus which he had not seen since his wild shooting trip of 1934. For this visit he drove all the way, taking with him Kate, whose Russian proved thoroughly useful, and Peregrine Fairfax, who had once spent a year on the Nettlebed estate learning how to farm.

Apart from covering several thousand miles, the tourists did not achieve a great deal, but after the trip Peter wrote three pleasant articles for *The Times*. These were the last contribution of any size that he made to the paper: although from time to time he wrote a letter for the correspondence columns, and, when the Printing House Square diary opened, he would often ring up to suggest possible paragraphs, he did not seem to want to take any overt part in the paper's affairs. When his old friend Pat Ryan handed over the diary to much younger men, Peter's contact with the paper became almost surreptitious: he was still a frequent contributor of ideas for the column, but when Ion Trewin, a later editor, once sent him a cheque in payment for a tip, Peter tore it up in considerable indignation.

At home he made several attempts to embellish the estate, for instance by digging the bowl for a lake in the hollow at the end of the field below the house. His plan was to introduce a new feature—for the estate as a whole lacked standing water, except for a few overgrown dew-ponds—and at the same time to attract duck. Both aims, however, were frustrated; although the site appeared to be ideal, and although he tried various methods of sealing the bottom of the scooped-out bowl, no lake formed, some mysteriously efficient form of natural drainage persistently removing all water from it.

Another plan which did not quite come off was to erect a huge equestrian statue in Waterloo gap—the vista in front of the house. Hearing by chance that a statue of Lord Strathnairn (who had originally been Sir Hugh Rose, and who he believed might be an ancestor of his mother) was up for sale, he made inquiries of the Westminster City Council and discovered that the bronze equestrian figure—thirty feet high, including its plinth, and weighing some fifty tons—had stood until 1931 at the junction of Knightsbridge and Brompton Road. He inspected it in the council's wharf at Ebury Bridge, took an immediate fancy to it, and set about arranging its transport to Nettlebed, at the same time writing to the editor of *Debrett* in an attempt to ascertain Lord Strathnairn's ancestry. In this he was only moderately successful for although

Debrett's staff could trace the Scottish Roses back to 1592, they could not positively establish a connection with the Roses of Buckinghamshire—although, as the editor, Patrick Montague-Smith wrote in a letter, 'As both families have water bougets in their coats of arms, it suggests that they had a common source of origin.' Peter's attempts to acquire the statue eventually foundered, partly because of a higher bid from a rival fancier, and partly because, if it had been moved to Nettlebed, he would have had to arrange public access to it.

The lake and the statue were—or would have been—extravagances. But now at last Peter made serious efforts to render the estate more efficient, and in 1967 he launched the biggest and most revolutionary experiment that the place had ever known. Early that year Dennis Warren, who had risen from the ranks to become Estate Manager, was awarded a Churchill Fellowship (largely through Peter's advocacy) and went to America to study dairy farming; he returned with plans for an immense dairy unit in which five hundred cows would be milked, living on concrete under the zero-grazing system, never going out but having all their food brought to them. Peter, having the greatest confidence in Warren, embraced his ideas enthusiastically, and in less than sixteen months after he first sought planning permission, cows were being milked in what came to be known either, by its American name, as 'the cow-tel', or, in English, as 'the Unit'. To bring the enterprise into production in so short a time was a prodigious feat; and although Peter afterwards paid generous tribute to the leaders of his team—Dennis Warren, Leslie Kingswood (the farm foreman) and Ann Horsfall (the estate secretary), it was really the sheer force of his own resolve that drove a path through the mass of planning regulations and other bureaucratic barriers in the way.

The construction of the cow-tel was an enormous task, as it entailed not only the building of the milking parlour and the laying-down of the four-acre concrete apron on which the cows would live, but also the digging of a complex system of slurry-pits which drained into a three-acre lagoon, besides the creation of an entirely new water-supply. Indeed, it seems to have been the aquatic demands of the new enterprise that drew Peter most keenly to it: pressure in the public system was so low that he had already once asked for (and been refused) permission to install his own water-supply, and now the building of the cow-tel made a private supply essential. He apparently felt that even if the dairy enterprise should fail, the estate would at least be left with as much water as it could possibly need.

In any case, he hired a water-diviner, got a sharp reaction at an almost ideal spot, sank a bore-hole four hundred feet into the chalk, and was rewarded by the discovery of enough water to service most of the estate as well as the new cow palace. On June 30th, 1969, when bore-hole water was first drawn from a tap at Merrimoles, Peter ceremonially drank a glass of it and pronounced it finer than whisky.

During the construction of the cow-tel he further consolidated his position by selling the old estate-yard in Nettlebed for building. Not without a pang of nostalgia, he closed his draughty old office and moved into a converted cottage that looked out over the tennis court, less than half a mile from Merrimoles. The new building was much more comfortable and suffered only from the thinness of its inside walls, which made it almost impossible for either Peter or his secretary, in adjacent rooms, to have a private conversation.

The aim of building the dairy unit was to transform the estate's finances: by making a large capital investment, Peter hoped to raise the income of the place from virtually nothing to at least £25,000 a year. But it seemed an amazing decision on his part to have opted suddenly for this highly intensive and artificial form of farming. In general he greatly disliked anything artificial—yet nothing could have been less natural than the cow-tel which, apart from being a considerable eyesore and producing unprecedented amounts of liquid manure (as well as an unprecedented smell), had the severe disadvantage in his eyes of being inimical to game: by condemning all the land round it to more or less perpetual grass, it banished at a stroke the arable crops on which pheasants and partridges thrive.

There must, it seemed, be some overriding reason why Peter thought the cow-tel necessary—and indeed there was. In 1968, when the dairy unit, by reason of its exceptional size and modernity, was attracting visitors from all over the world, he wrote a short leaflet explaining the origins and purpose of the scheme, and one paragraph of his synopsis was particularly significant:

> The main object of the exercise is to make the estate into a going concern, capable (with luck) of facing the hazards of the future and in particular the impact of death duties. The Dairy Unit and the land which services it are let by the estate to a partnership comprising myself and my three children; the modest rent of £5 an acre can be increased as circumstances require and the land, not being in hand, will attract death duties at a lower rate.

To any casual observer Peter seemed, at the age of sixty, to be in the most robust of health. He took an immense amount of exercise, could walk most if not all of his contemporaries off their feet, and never spent a day in bed. Longevity was a family tradition: his grandfather had lived until eighty-nine and his uncle Phil was still in fine fettle at seventy-eight. There seemed every chance that Peter would go on leading very much the sort of life to which he was accustomed for another fifteen years at least. And yet in retrospect it is clear that in 1967 he was by no means confident about his health. Not only did he sanction the cow-tel and write the paragraph above about death duties: he also composed instructions for his own funeral and began sending to Rupert batches of material which he did not want to be forgotten. Always these consignments came with a flippant note—'Another load of rubbish for the archives'—but they surely would not have been dispatched at all unless Peter had had some kind of foreboding. The cause may simply have been residual anxiety about cancer, for although none of his regular check-ups had revealed anything sinister (and although in 1968 he was delighted to hear that his case was considered unusual enough to have featured in the *Lancet*), he could never be absolutely certain that the disease would not strike again. It also seems possible, however, that at about this time he had a mild heart attack, or at any rate was warned by his doctor that he might have one; for he knew that cancer, if it returned fatally, would kill him slowly, whereas some of the arrangements he made seemed to anticipate the possibility of sudden death.

Whatever the trouble, Peter told no one about it, not even Celia; nor did he in any way reduce his physical exertions. In the winter he walked the estate as tirelessly as ever, without a hat even in pouring rain; and in summer he developed a late-flowering enthusiasm for tennis, which he played in a manner that can be described only as unique. His loose right elbow made him weak on the forehand, and as a result he took almost every ball backhand, whether that was physically possible or not. Inevitably he missed or mis-hit a great number of shots, but, whenever he did connect, he hit the ball with a terrific slice, thus imparting to it a most ferocious spin. He sought to make up for his lack of skill by covering the back of the court at great speed, uttering, as he made one boss-shot after another, a stream of imprecations. '*Wet!*' he would cry, in the strangled voice he normally reserved for reprimanding his dogs, '*Curses!*' '*Hell fire!*', '*Worst shot of the day!*' and—in moments of extreme crisis '*God's boots!*' Although he would play doubles with good grace, he much preferred singles because they gave him harder exercise: on hot days he would take off his shirt and play until his whole torso was running with sweat—whereupon he would go home and plunge into the unheated swimming-pool.

There was never a moment during the day when he was not actively engaged on some task. He might only be driving round the estate, but he never did nothing. It was unthinkable, for example, that he might ever take a nap after lunch: he just could not slow down. Nor, to other people, did there seem any reason why he should, for he seemed in excellent shape.

Whatever he knew, or thought, was wrong with his heart, he certainly did not expect to die in the immediate future, for early in 1968, scenting at last an ideal subject for a book, he attempted to launch himself on a project which he knew would take two or three years. But 'attempted', unfortunately, was the operative word, for once again he fell victim to the bureaucratic obstruction of Whitehall that had so badly hampered him when he was writing about the German plans for invading England. This time, however, the lack of co-operation which he encountered was even more crippling; in the first case his letters to the Secretary to the Cabinet had all been answered, even if each reply had been preceded by a delay of several weeks; this time, many of his letters were not answered at all.

In April 1968 it became known within a limited circle that the authorities were considering the compilation of a history of strategic deception in the Second World War; and it was felt by those who had been principally concerned with this abstruse branch of warfare that Peter was uniquely qualified by experience, both military and literary, to write such a history. In June 1968 he sent to a friend in M.I.5 a short memorandum in which he volunteered to undertake the task, emphasizing his view that no decision about publication should be taken until the typescript had been completed; this, he estimated, should be by the end of 1970, at the latest. On June 19th his contact in M.I.5 wrote to say that he had sent the memorandum on to the Secretary to the Cabinet and hoped for a decision on it 'in the near future'.

Four months later Peter heard that the Chiefs of Staff had ordered a study to be made of the relevant archives, and that this was expected to take three months. This proved a highly optimistic estimate: in June 1969, having heard nothing further, he wrote for the first time, and in deferential terms, to the Secretary to the Cabinet, Sir Burke Trend, ending his letter by saying that 'from a purely personal point of view it would—as I am sure you can understand—be a great help to know whether I should continue to hold myself *en disponibilité* and if so for how long.' On July 3rd he received a courteous and sympathetic reply, in which Sir Burke referred to 'all sorts of rather complicated administrative questions' which he hoped were being sorted out.

There were no further developments for another three months, but in October 1969 Peter's friend in M.I.5 told him that he was expecting a decision in the very near future. A month later the friend reported that the project had been more or less given clearance by the Government, who had referred it to the Opposition.

On January 6th, 1970, Peter wrote a short note to Sir Burke recalling his correspondence of the previous summer and asking whether there had been any developments. Receiving no reply, and the mails being in chaos after the introduction of the two-tier postal charges, after five weeks he sent a copy of the note to Sir Burke's secretary in case the original had gone astray. This elicited, a month later, a courteous note from Sir Burke in which he held out hopes of a meeting 'some time after Easter'.

Two months later, in May 1970, Peter wrote again to Sir Burke's secretary explaining that the officers concerned with strategic deception in the last war would be holding their annual dinner on June 10th, and wondering—since this would be 'a particularly convenient occasion to arrange contacts with a number of important witnesses, before the Grim Reaper removes any more of them' (one important witness had just died)—whether there was any chance of a decision being taken before June 10th. This letter was not answered.

It was, by then, more than two years since he had first volunteered to compile a history of deception under conditions which would have left control of the whole project in the hands of the Government; throughout the two years he had been encouraged, at fairly regular intervals, to believe that a decision was about to be taken on his offer, and that probably it would be favourable. On August 26th he wrote again to Sir Burke, reminding him that in March he had held out hopes of a meeting 'some time after Easter' and asking whether it would be possible to make contact with some official who could outline to him the conditions of service under which—if he should eventually be asked to write the history—he would be required to work. This letter was not answered.

On October 8th—with some reluctance, for he disliked pulling strings —he solicited the help of his friend Alec Douglas-Home, the Foreign Secretary, who replied in sympathetic terms. But still Whitehall made no move, and on December 16th Peter wrote yet again to Sir Burke Trend, referring to his letter of August 26th and asking for definite rejection or acceptance of his request for an interview with someone

in a letter to a friend that this action might well have cooked his goose, but that he felt that after three years he 'had had about enough'.

While he waited for Whitehall to make up its mind, he forged steadily ahead with his great project at Nettlebed. The gradual build-up of the herd in the cow-tel (the second largest in England) attracted the interest of the entire farming community, and the stream of visitors became so large as to be a considerable nuisance. But Peter found that he much enjoyed the unfamiliar role of agricultural pioneer; and although the first financial returns from the cow-tel were considerably below those predicted, he watched the enterprise grow with a quiet optimism that inspired tremendous confidence in all those working for him. Few aspects of the venture gave him greater satisfaction than the arrival on the drainage lagoon of some duck; and when he shot a mallard there one evening he felt that, whatever might come of the dairy unit itself, the assets of the estate had been substantially enhanced.

Another source of satisfaction was the success of all three children, now grown up. Nichol, after trying for some time to find a *métier*, had begun to write and had had three thrillers published with modest success. Kate had reinforced her command of Russian by becoming a skilled researcher, and was devilling for Martin Gilbert, who had inherited from Randolph Churchill the immense task of completing the official life of Sir Winston. Lucy, taking after her mother, had already made a strong impression as an actress in several stage and television productions, and Peter watched her—as he watched Celia—with the keenest pleasure and devotion.

During 1969 his blind family loyalty involved him in a curious incident which—for once—he handled with a considerable lack of finesse. Hearing suddenly that Ian's son Caspar was about to be expelled from Eton for having a loaded revolver in his room, and discovering also that Caspar possessed not just this one unregistered weapon but a whole collection, Peter volunteered to take charge of the illicit arsenal. This he did; but although he locked four automatic pistols and nineteen live rounds of assorted pistol, rifle and cannon ammunition into a cupboard, he was foolish enough to drop Caspar's prize firearm—a Browning automatic rifle—down the well by the barn in front of the house, whence it was soon recovered by an officer of the Flying Squad armed with a powerful electro-magnet.

Peter's aim, obviously, was to draw the police's fire from Caspar to himself; but why he told the detectives where the automatic rifle was, he never made clear. In due course he was summoned to appear at the magistrates' court in Henley on three separate charges of possessing firearms and ammunition illegally, and in the course of a rather unconvincing defence claimed that he had thrown the Browning down the well only to make sure that it was in a safe place. He could, he pointed out, have disposed of it in any of a number of far less conspicuous wells than the one he had chosen:

> There is, on the face of it, something furtive about the act of dropping a firearm into an underground tank, and the court may feel that, despite the fact that the police would not have known of the Browning's existence if I had not told them about it, I did at one stage have the intention of 'losing' the weapon altogether by hiding it in a place where it would never be found. If I *had* had that intention, it would have been an easy matter to get rid of it in one of the outlying, abandoned water-tanks, if necessary under cover of darkness; it is almost inconceivable that I would have disposed of it—in the presence, incidentally, of my gardener—in the only tank where I could be reasonably certain that it would sooner or later come to light.

Whatever view the court took of this specious argument, it fined him only £10 on each of the charges, and in the end the incident caused him more amusement than embarrassment.

A year later there began a sequence of far stranger events connected with Ian which Peter was never able to explain. It started in October 1970, when he was approached by a man whom he described (in an article published later in the *Sunday Times*) as 'Mr A'—a retired bank-officer of seventy-three who lived in Hertfordshire. In a short, type-written letter Mr A told Peter that he had some 'unusual and I believe very pleasurable news concerning your late brother Ian' [who had been dead six years], and asked if he might come and have a talk. Peter, agreeing rather reluctantly, arranged a meeting for the following Sunday.

When Mr A came he brought with him his middle-aged daughter Vera and a 60,000-word typescript on the cover of which was inscribed, *Take Over: A James Bond Thriller*. This, he explained, had been dictated by Ian to Mrs A (Vera's mother), who had died some three years earlier; Mrs A had transmitted its text from the spirit world to Vera, who had taken it down in longhand. Ian, he went on, was one of a group of authors who were anxious to carry on writing in the spirit world and so to prove to people on earth that life goes on 'very pleasurably' (as one of them put it) after death. The other authors were Conan Doyle, H. G.

Wells, Edgar Wallace, Ruby M. Ayres and Somerset Maugham; but when Miss Ayres later dropped out of the syndicate on her promotion to a 'Higher Plane', her place was promptly taken by Bernard Shaw.

Communication had first been established, Mr A explained, in December 1969, when Vera had been recovering from an illness. As she sat with a writing pad in front of her, her eye fell on a framed photograph of her mother on the piano, and she thought, 'I wish I could talk to you, Mum.' Immediately the pen in her hand started to write, and with difficulty spelt out the message: 'I love you, Vera.'

In the correspondence which followed, the process of automatic writing grew steadily more fluent, and the strangest thing about it was that the *handwriting became that of the mother*. Vera's own writing had always been rounded, loopy and backward-sloping; at school she had repeatedly been told that such backward-sloping words were a sign of bad character, and had been urged to tilt them the other way. But this she had never been able to manage—until suddenly, as she took down her mother's messages, she found herself writing in a sharp, pointed, italic hand that sloped steeply forwards.

It would be hard to imagine anybody harder-headed than Peter in matters of this kind, or anybody less easily impressed; and indeed, as he read some pages of *Take Over*, his scepticism built up rapidly, for he saw that although the book made use of the traditional Bond apparatus—M, Universal Export, Miss Moneypenny and so on—its style and execution were nothing whatever like Ian's. The scene that followed is best described by Peter himself:

When opportunity offered I said mildly that it did not *sound* very like Ian; he would not, for instance, have described a room in a private house, however villainous its occupants, as a 'lounge'. Vera, who was sitting with a pad on her knee, almost immediately wrote, in her mother's handwriting, 'Mr Fleming says Peter is perfectly correct in saying I do not use the word lounge.'

Impressed by the prompt establishment of what seemed to be some sort of *rapport*, I asked if Ian had a message for me. 'Mr Fleming says he is very pleased to be here with his brother and sends greetings.'

I had not, before Mr A arrived twenty minutes earlier, been prepared for a dialogue with the Spirit World, but my first impulse was to check the *bona fides* of my extra-terrestrial correspondent, about which, as I thumbed through more and more pages of *Take Over*, I became increasingly sceptical. I asked five more questions:

What was his second Christian name? *Lancaster*.

What was his son's second Christian name? *Robert* ... [both correct].

What were his house-colours at Eton? *Blue and yellow. No. Blue and red. No. I can't do it*. (The right answer was cerise and grey.)

Does he remember the name of the boy who broke his nose? *Yes*. Pause. *Bertram* (It was Henry Douglas-Home, a brother of Sir Alec.)

Does he remember the Russian for 'Yes' ('Da')? Pause. Two squiggles. *Scap. Please forgive me I cannot get this over*.

By this time I had read what was claimed to be one of the most exciting chapters in *Take Over*, and I told Mr A that with the best will in the world I could not recognize my brother's style. Vera at once wrote: 'He realizes the book is not his style but hopes to be able eventually to get this over correctly, although it may take time.'

He is pleased he is interested and willing to listen . Robert

Blue and yellow no blue and red no I cant do it Yes Bertram ∼ ∼ *Scap . Please forgive me I cannot get this over.*

blue and yellow no blue and red no I cant do it Yes Bertram Please forgive me I cannot get this over.

So, after a few more questions, this first meeting ended and the visitors departed. Peter was electrified. Sceptical though he might be, he was also tremendously fascinated and excited, and he drove over to the house of a friend on the estate, where he described what had happened with (for him) extraordinary animation, striding up and down the lawn as he talked.

Although he could not account for what was happening, he soon decided that Ian was in no way involved. Not only did the sheer incompetence of *Take Over* make it clear that Ian had had no part in the book's composition: it quickly became obvious that his alleged spirit was impossibly ignorant about basic family matters (it could not, for instance, give accurately the number, sex and names of Peter's children). It was soon apparent, in fact, that the only accurate answers that the automatic writing could give were those embodied in John Pearson's *The Life of Ian Fleming*.

At the beginning of November 1970 the spirit authors began to transmit 'Tales of Mystery and Imagination': in the next two months Edgar Wallace wrote five, H. G. Wells and Ian two each, Conan Doyle and Somerset Maugham one each: a total of 30,000 words. Later, Maugham began sending a full-length novel. All this work was, as Peter put it, 'tosh'—crude, devoid of literary merit, and all almost exactly the same. In November, after asking Peter's permission, Mr A submitted *Take Over* to Jonathan Cape, who not surprisingly rejected it.

In spite of its disappointing features, Peter continued to be absorbed by the whole affair. Having seen Mr A three times, and Vera twice, he ruled out any question of chicanery, being certain that they were 'both persons of complete integrity'. There was an undeniable and uncanny fascination about watching Vera sit quietly, pen poised, waiting for a message to come through: her hand, after a period of stillness, would gradually begin to twitch. 'They're trying to say something,' she would report—and off would go the neat italic writing.

But the most striking fact, as Peter pointed out, was that in a period of scarcely nine months 'some form of intelligence' had caused Vera to copy out, in her mother's handwriting, a 60,000-word book, some 30,000 words of short stories, and thousands more words of 'service traffic'. As anyone who has tried to produce a book will know, the sheer energy needed to put 100,000 words on paper is enormous, and it was very hard, in this case, to discern whence the momentum could have emanated. Had Vera been otherwise unoccupied, the feat—for someone with no literary background or inclinations—would have been remarkable enough; as it was, she had a full-time job, a house to run and an ailing husband (who died in February 1971) to look after.

Peter could find no convincing explanation of the affair; but in re-marking that neither Vera nor her father had any literary leanings or was

Dear Rupert.

Seeing that this is almost certainly the last letter, I shall ever write, it is a pity that I shall inevitably forget to post it.

Have you ever been marooned? I know you've had your adenoids out and all that, but have you ever really been marooned? It's quite a different thing. You know when your favourite novelist talks about "Death or worse than Death"? Well, this is one of the 'worse than death' things: the

1. The foregoing dossier has not been compiled to ventilate a grievance but to draw attention to the inadequacy of the administrative machinery for handling matters of this kind.

2. In this instance HMG were dealing (or failing to deal) with an individual who does not rely on his pen for a living, who has many non-literary interests & who possesses an equable temperament. To make a put that together he of plausibly charge them with stirring such talents as he has for three years; they have involved him in a great deal of time-wasting correspondence, much of it disappointingly unilateral; & that an ordinary commercial publisher so treating his authors with a comparable lack of consideration would quickly go out of business.

Peter's writing at 18 (top) and 64

'qualified by intellect or education to produce even the inferior fiction for which they have acted as a channel of transmission,' he denied himself the one explanation that struck other people as possible. The slushy fiction allegedly transmitted by Ian, Somerset Maugham and the others seemed exactly the kind of thing that a man like Mr A might produce. The language was precisely the kind that a man of his background might use when attempting a literary style (the frequent appearance of the word 'pleasurable' by itself suggested a connection—witness Mr A's opening letter to Peter); and, as Mr A readily admitted, he had read *The Life of Ian Fleming* with avidity. It seemed by no means inconceivable that Mr A was transmitting *all* the material, telepathically and sub-consciously, to his daughter. Yet even if he was, the reappearance of the mother's writing seemed inexplicable.

In any case, the affair of the ghost Bond greatly enlivened Peter's winter, and in the spring of 1971 he wrote an article about it. This he offered to the *Sunday Times*, which accepted it by return of post, paid £500 for the first British serial rights, and later used it as the main feature of the week.

Especially when revived by an episode like that of the automatic writing, Peter seemed very much his old self—intensely interested in anything new and always looking for the ridiculous aspect of everything he came across. But during 1970 his secretary Ann Horsfall several times sensed that he was not as well as he made out. Once, about a year earlier, he had told her that he thought he had cancer again, because he was losing weight; but the specialist's regular examination proved this fear to be groundless, and after that he never made any more remarks about his health. It was more from his moods and from tiny variations in his behaviour that she suspected all might not be well. In the mornings, for instance, she noticed that (although he always rose at dawn) he was very slow to get going, and sometimes his face would take on an ominous grey colour beneath its perpetual tan. On several occasions he gently urged Leslie Kingswood to press on with the task of making his coffin from wood grown on the estate; and before he left home for his annual trip to Scotland in the autumn of 1970 he put all his correspondence into such meticulous order as to suggest, almost, that he thought he might never return.

But return he did, and after he had left Black Mount he wrote a letter full of gratitude to his hostess there, Uncle Phil's wife Joan:

This must be the umptieth rather than the umpteenth time that I have written to thank you for having me to stay at Black Mount; but my gratitude is as deep as ever. I loved being there, as I always do. You and Phil have, without any apparent effort, made it a wonderful base, or rallying-point, or whatever you like to call it, for a far-flung and steadily-expanding clan. I don't suppose you pause to consider the scale of the intangible benefits which you go on, year after year, conferring on generation after generation of the family; but I do, and they are very great.

That winter Peter enjoyed his shooting as much as ever, and he kept a minutely detailed record of it in his game-book. This, to his great pleasure, had been given a new lease of life. For the past few seasons, because the pages were running out, he had made his entries in microscopic writing; but in the summer of 1970 Higgs, a firm of printers and stationers in Henley, had enlisted the help of a retired book-binder and had inserted into the back of the book a thick sheaf of new pages prepared to exactly the same specification as the old. On these new sheets Peter entered his reports with scrupulous exactitude, even recording an 'illicit recce' made against the partridges on August 31st, the day before the season officially opened.

His away-days were as varied as ever, and on December 14th, after shooting with the Mounts at Wasing, he remarked, 'Shot messily, but can now claim to have wiped, on two consecutive days, the eyes of the Provost and Vice-Provost of Eton. Possibly a record?'

At home the season proved the best since the war, with a record bag for the estate of 617 pheasants. Peter was particularly pleased with the performance of the Japanese pheasants which, with the help of Tony Keswick, he had introduced in 1969, when twenty-eight eggs had been flown half-way round the world and delivered by a Rolls-Royce belonging to the Japanese Prime Minister's daughter. The Japanese birds, he noted, 'are handsome and succulent and much more evasive and aloof than "European" reared birds.' His personal bag was also a record: he kept up an intensive solo pursuit of cock pheasants and woodcock, and instituted the custom of entering his average to date at the bottom of each page—fifty-four head for ninety-seven shots, and so on. His final average was 275 head for 531 shots, or nineteen under twos. How strange and how fitting it was that in this, his last winter, he should have surpassed his own high standards.

At the end of April 1971 the security dam in Whitehall suddenly gave way and, to his huge relief and delight, he was at last authorized to pro-

ceed with the task of writing the Official History of Strategic Deception.
Whether his long memorandum had contributed to the breakthrough, he
had no means of telling; but in any case he went eagerly to work. One of
his first tasks was to obtain security clearance; for this he needed two
referees, and his sudden return to ebullience was clearly apparent in the
letters he sent to Harold Caccia and Tim Nugent:

> I am required to complete Form 53924 Dd. 17860 12/65 SC.s which
> as you know very well is a Security Questionnaire ... and I have
> made so bold as to put forward your name as one of the two
> character referees.
>
> I hope you don't mind. It might be as well, if you are interrogated,
> to conceal the fact that I am a Jehovah's Witness and to gloss over
> my Trotskyist leanings; and there is no *real* need to reveal that Ron
> Obote-Foulkes, author of *With Tariq Ali to Buckingham Palace!* is
> one of my *noms de plume*. Otherwise you can be frankness itself.

From Tim Nugent this brought a reply which glowed with the warmth
of a lifetime's affection:

> Well! Well! I do find myself in awkward situations at times, but to
> vouch for your character is about the stickiest I have ever ex-
> perienced. But I will do my best, and thank you for the hints you
> have given me as to what to keep dark in your rather murky past. As
> a matter of fact I have just given a reference for a clergyman ...
> which elicited warm thanks from the Bishop. I shall therefore use the
> same sort of language when I am asked about you. 'Intones the
> Responses clearly', 'Is thoroughly reliable with the Collection',
> 'Goes easy with the Communion wine', etc. etc. Of course, my dear
> Peter, I will gladly do anything I can, and I feel very honoured to be
> your chosen referee in conjunction with the Provost of Eton ...
> Best love to all at Merrimoles, and I look forward to seeing you
> soon.

Having obtained the necessary clearance for himself and his secretary
Ann, he also engaged the services of a research assistant inside the
Cabinet Office, got a pass for parking his car on Horse Guards Parade,
and undertook to acquire a safe in which to incarcerate any secret
documents he might bring home with him. Once loosed into the archives
so long denied him, he began reading avidly, not least through the end-
of-term report which he himself had compiled about D Division's
activities in South-East Asia. He also began writing to all the survivors

of the deception teams he could find: his plan was to tell as much as possible of the history through the characters who had shaped its course. That he had been held up so long was a tragedy—both for himself and for the official history. His enthusiasm and aptitude for the subject were unparalleled; and the book—had he written it—would surely have been the crowning achievement of his post-war literary career.

On the Spring Bank Holiday he held his usual cricket match against Nettlebed. Although he no longer played for the village, and although his own contemporaries had long since ceased actively to support him, he still took the field as captain, batting last and fielding mid-off. As usual, his declared aim was to lose by one run off the last ball of the day, or, failing that, to win by a small margin; but on this occasion he succeeded in neither plan, as his side for once gave the village a sound thrashing. He himself did not have to bat, but he astonished everybody on the field, not least himself, by taking a superb catch at deep mid-off. As the ball rose towards him the disloyal young men in the slips offered high odds against him holding it, but hold it he did, with an incredulous grin on his face, and the applause that broke out contained at least as much genuine pleasure as irony.

The highlight of that summer on the estate was Lucy's wedding at the beginning of August. Peter had been delighted when she had announced her engagement to Joe Laycock, son of the late Major-General Sir Robert Laycock, who had been an old friend; then he had gone through a period of anxiety when the couple proposed not to have a traditional wedding; but finally, when they decided to get married in St Bartholomew's Church in Nettlebed, he was once again full of benevolent enthusiasm.

The day of the wedding was brilliantly fine, and at the reception, which spread out over the terrace at Merrimoles, Peter moved happily among many of his closest friends. The one feature which depressed him was the sight of his Uncle Phil, who at last was failing and was being wheeled about in an invalid chair. That, said Peter (as he had often said before), was the one fate which he hoped at all costs to avoid: 'Anything but a bath chair.'

Looking back, some of his friends remembered that he had been looking thin and perhaps a little drawn; but otherwise they saw no cause for apprehension on that lovely afternoon as the foundations of another generation of the family were laid.

16

Sudden Exit

On August 9th, 1971, Peter set off by road on his usual autumn trip to Scotland. He was in excellent spirits, looking ahead both to the immediate prospect of shooting and, in the longer term, to a winter of work on his book. He took with him his latest Labrador, Chort, who, although only three, had already shown exceptional promise and steadiness.

His first call was on Roger Fleetwood Hesketh, near Southport in Lancashire. To him he seemed in fine fettle, and the two men had a useful and enjoyable discussion about strategic deception, for Hesketh had worked in the London Controlling Section and had already written a book about it. This had been suppressed by Whitehall, but in the course of his research Peter had discovered that large parts of its text had been copied—without permission—by another author into a popular book which was about to appear in America.

Having stayed the night in Lancashire, he drove on next day to Marske-in-Swaledale, where he had lunch with Rupert and was in sparkling form. In the afternoon he went on again to Glenkiln, where he enjoyed the society of the Keswick family as wholeheartedly as ever. The ingredients of his stay were exactly the same as in other years: pigeon-flighting, long and arduous pursuits of grouse, and, in the evenings, jokes and games round the fire.

The twelfth was a fine day, although it produced a disappointing bag of only twenty-five grouse, and Peter was pleased by Chort, who behaved admirably. On the 13th an inch of rain fell and the party made what Peter described as a 'masochistic sortie' up the glen. On the 14th there was more cold rain, but Chips Keswick and Peter went out together, got lost in the mist and wet through, and shot eight grouse, a snipe and a woodcock. 'A sporting walk,' Peter recorded: 'Great fun.' What he did not record was that when they returned to the car at about 3 p.m., and Chips suggested that they should try for snipe in a bog that was right at hand, he took the unprecedented step of declining the offer. 'I've never in my life refused that kind of suggestion,' he remarked, 'but I just don't think I can go on.' Since he appeared to be tired, rather than ill, Chips merely thought that he had at last begun to feel his age, and reflected that all the Keswicks had been expecting him to do so for the past ten years.

On the following day Peter again drove northwards, stopping for lunch with the Fergussons at Ballantrae. Once more he was in cracking form, and after he had left, Bernard's sixteen-year-old son Geordie, who was Peter's godson, declared that he was the nicest man he knew.

At Black Mount he was absorbed as usual into a large family party, and on August 16th he joined a small army of guns who shot sixty-three grouse between the main Glencoe road and Loch Laidon. On the 17th—a beautiful day—he behaved in absolutely characteristic fashion, starting out with the main party but breaking away on his own, taking Henderson, the head stalker, with him, to look for a bird that had been hit during the morning. For some reason he never entered that day's operations in his game-book.

The 18th of August was another perfect day—cloudless and hot, with a gentle breeze. The party of eight guns left the lodge at eleven and set off in Land-Rovers up the stony track to Black Rock, one of the most distant beats, which Peter had frequently tramped on solitary forays. Because of the heat he was wearing jeans, rather than plus-fours, and a bush shirt; as they drove up into the brilliant morning he seemed unusually loquacious, recalling unprovoked some of the service that his shirt had seen in Burma during the war.

They left the vehicles at about 11.20 and formed up into a line, the stalkers and ghillies alternating with the guns. Peter's cousin Robin asked him to be the right-hand gun, the lowest in the line, because on that face the grouse were inclined to fly downhill and to present the most difficult shots to the guns at the bottom. Peter was delighted, having always been at the top of the line on earlier occasions, and said: 'That would be *great* fun.'

The line strung out up the hill above him, and they all set off along its flank, climbing gently with the sun already hot on their backs. Ahead of them was the smooth dome of Creag Dhubh—the Black Rock— and in the distance behind it the 3,000-foot mass of Buachaille Etive, the towering rampart that guards the southern entrance to the Pass of Glencoe.

They had been going only ten minutes when a good covey of grouse got up in front of Peter and he killed a right and left. Chort retrieved both birds, and Ian McRae, the stalker on Peter's left, came down to collect them. As Peter handed them over he made some remark about how encouraging it was to see so strong a covey early in the day.

McRae turned uphill again to regain his place in the line, but he had gone only a few steps when he heard a groan behind him. Turning, he saw that Peter had gone down on his face. For a second he thought that he might be drinking from a burn, but then he realized something was wrong. He shouted 'Colonel Peter's down!' and ran to him; but in the few seconds that it took him to cover the ground, Peter had died. He never spoke or moved again, and a doctor who examined his body afterwards concluded that he could have known absolutely nothing about what had happened: the heart-attack which killed him was so sudden that he was dead even before he hit the ground.

They carried his body across the hollows and laid it beside a chunky, flat-topped rock that stood alone in the grass and heather, while another of the stalkers, Donald Cameron, ran to telephone for help from the near-by chair-lift. Had Peter chosen them himself, he could hardly have found finer circumstances: to the north and east there were magnificent views far into the high corries of Corrour, which the family had once taken, and out over the great bleak expanse of Rannoch Moor, which he had stalked as a boy. His life had been extinguished suddenly, without pain, after a moment of intense satisfaction in pursuit of the sport he loved best.

After considerable discussion, half the party decided to go on shooting, for they believed—and surely they were right—that this was what Peter would have wanted. His body was taken back on a stretcher to the end of the road, and thence by Land-Rover to the lodge. Thus, for the last time, the hunter came home from the hill.

In the south the news hit Nettlebed with a stunning impact. The family was widely scattered—Celia cruising in the Aegean, Lucy and Joe on their honeymoon in Turkey—and Nichol immediately began trying to recall them. Among the estate staff there was a feeling first of disbelief: Peter had seemed so rock-like, so imperishable, that it was impossible for the men to believe they would never see him again. His presence was everywhere, extraordinarily strong. In the estate office Ann Horsfall took from the safe the envelope which, on his instructions, she had deposited there four years before. Inside it was a single sheet of instructions, whose characteristic humour, now overpoweringly combined with sadness, reduced everyone present to a helpless mixture of laughter and tears:

R.P.F.: FUNERAL ARRANGEMENTS

1. Unless lost at sea or for other reasons unavailable I would like to be buried in the churchyard of St Bartholomew's Nettlebed.
2. The funeral service should be as short as possible. Although it is unsuitable to the occasion, I would like the hymn *The day thou gavest, Lord, is ended*, to be sung.
3. I would like my coffin to be made, or improvised, from beech or oak grown on the Estate. It does not matter if the timber is green, or how rough a job it looks. The lighter the coffin is, the better.
4. I would like the coffin (with me inside it, naturally) to be taken by tractor and trailer—or by whatever form of estate transport may then be in use—to the churchyard through Joyce Grove. Damage to the turf between the Kitchen Garden and the Orchard must be made good; the cost will not be large, and is, I believe, recoverable under Funeral Expenses.
5. I have never been keen on Flowers.
6. I would like the attached epitaph to be put on my headstone; this may require a 'Faculty', and involve a skirmish with ecclesiastical bureaucracy.
7. The question of a Memorial Service I leave to my family ... [In a later note he had added: 'If there is a memorial service, I would like it to be at the Guards Chapel; the parking facilities are unrivalled.']
8. I would like arrangements to be made for any estate workers who help with or attend my funeral to be given a good, strong drink when it is over.
9. I would like my dog, unless it is a young one and difficult to control, to be in attendance. This cannot do any harm; there are respectable precedents (including, I think, Edward VII); and by giving people a distraction and something to talk about, the dog will help to make a tiresome event less tiresome.
10. No mourning.

All these instructions were faithfully carried out. The estate staff felt, as one, that they owed Peter a debt which they could never repay, but they were comforted by discharging some small part of it in carrying out his last wishes as well as they possibly could. Leslie Kingswood, the farm foreman, who was by training a carpenter, was at first distraught that he had never made the coffin which Peter had for years been urging him to construct; but now he laboured at it day and night, and produced a beautifully plain and neat piece of work out of wood from a beech tree that had grown close behind Merrimoles.

The funeral was held in Nettlebed exactly as Peter had instructed. The only mistake he made was in asking that his dog should be present. Chort came into the church; but instead of providing a welcome distraction, the sight of him standing there, uncomprehending yet wretched, was almost intolerably sad. Later, a memorial service was held in the Guards Chapel, made splendid by drums and trumpets from the band of the Grenadier Guards, and by a moving address from Tim Nugent.

The epitaph which Peter had left was engraved on his tombstone, with his initials (as he had asked) carved very small at the bottom. Perhaps it was inspired by Stevenson's 'Requiem'; certainly it was the only serious poem he ever wrote:

> He travelled widely in far places:
> Wrote, and was widely read.
> Soldiered, saw some of danger's faces,
> Came home to Nettlebed.
>
> The squire lies here, his journeys ended—
> Dust, and a name on a stone—
> Content, amid the lands he tended,
> To keep this rendezvous alone.
>
> R.P.F.

Sources and Acknowledgments

Peter's own published books are listed at the front. In addition to these, in 1935 he contributed to an essay on the Elizabethan explorer Sir Humphrey Gilbert to *The Great Tudors*, edited by Katharine Garvin (Ivor Nicholson & Watson); in 1955 he translated André Migot's *Tibetan Marches* from the French (the book was published in England by Rupert Hart-Davis), and in 1956 he expanded an article called 'Posh Lingo' which had first appeared in the *Spectator* for inclusion in Nancy Mitford's *Noblesse Oblige* (Hamish Hamilton, 1956). He wrote forewords for Clifford Johnson's *Pirate Junk* (Jonathan Cape, 1934), Michael Calvert's *Prisoners of Hope* (Jonathan Cape, 1952), *Seven Years in Tibet* by Heinrich Harrer (Rupert Hart-Davis, 1953), James Morris's *Sultan in Oman* (Faber, 1957), *The Amazon* by Robin Furneaux (Hamish Hamilton, 1969), and a new edition of Henry Walter Bates's *The Naturalist on The River Amazons* (Dent, 1969).

Besides these published works, he left a considerable archive of papers, among them several short stories, one unfinished novel – *The Sett*, written in 1949 – and three chapters on a life of Adrian Carton de Wiart. For a man of such verbal precision, he was curiously careless with his records: he never stuck a single one of his hundreds of press-cuttings into a scrapbook, but left everything in ill-sorted files and bundles. He was not, in any case, a great preserver, saving almost no family papers and little of his own early correspondence. For much of his life, however, he did keep meticulous records of his shooting, and his game-book proved a fascinating source of information.

For my account of his life at Nettlebed I relied largely on my own memory and on conversations with local people. As Peter's godson, his constant shooting-companion and the tenant of one of his farmhouses, I shared his great love of the Estate and, from the moment I was old enough to carry a gun, repeatedly tramped its fields and woods in his company.

Without the help of the Fleming family it would have been impossible to write this book, and main debt was to Celia, who first entrusted me with the task of trying to recreate Peter's life, and then answered my questions with unfailing patience and good humour. Peter's brother Richard was another indispensable source of information and encouragement, as was his cousin Robin. From Amaryllis (of whom Peter was particularly fond) I gained many insights into the character of their mother. Peter's children – Nichol, Kate and Lucy – all contributed invaluable memories.

Flemings apart, my principal assistant was my father Rupert. As Peter's longest-standing and closest friend, he should perhaps have written the biography himself; had he done so, the result would have been a much more scholarly book. But in his generosity he handed the opportunity to me, giving me not only all his material about Peter but also the benefit of his own life-long experience of publishing, editing and writing. He kept an eye on my work in all its stages, excising errors – and clichés – with the ruthless precision of a surgeon. I cannot thank him enough.

I am indebted to the editors of *The Times*, the *Spectator* and the *Sunday Times* for their permission to use quotations from Peter's articles first published in those newspapers; and to Leo Cooper, who first published Peter's report on the crash of glider 15P as an appendix to a new edition of Michael Calvert's *Prisoners of Hope*, and who kindly allowed me to print substantial extracts from it.

I am grateful to the following publishers for their permisson to use extracts from the books for which they hold the copyright: Chatto & Windus, for *The Precarious Crust* by Laurence Irving; Faber & Faber, for *Journey to a War* by W. H. Auden and Christopher Isherwood; Heinemann, for *Forbidden Journey* by Ella Maillart; Hutchinson, for *The Inner Circle* by Joan Bright; Methuen, for *Boys in the Making* by T. Pellatt; John Murray, for *With an Eye to the Future* by Osbert Lancaster.

Miss Mary Hodgson and her staff at the BBC Written Archives Centre provided the most prompt and professional service an author could wish for.

Finally, I should like to thank Jill da Silva and Charlotte Hofton, who typed indefatigably on my behalf.

DUFF HART-DAVIS

Index

Index

Index

OXFORD

MORE OXFORD PAPERBACKS

Details of a selection of other books follow. A complete list of Oxford Paperbacks, including The World's Classics, Twentieth-Century Classics, OPUS, Past Masters, Oxford Authors, Oxford Shakespeare, and Oxford Paperback Reference, is available in the UK from the General Publicity Department, Oxford University Press (JH), Walton Street, Oxford OX2 6DP.

In the USA, complete lists are available from the Paperbacks Marketing Manager, Oxford University Press, 200 Madison Avenue, New York, NY 10016.

Oxford Paperbacks are available from all good bookshops. In case of difficulty, customers in the UK can order direct from Oxford University Press Bookshop, 116 High Street, Oxford, Freepost, OX1 4BR, enclosing full payment. Please add 10 per cent of published price for postage and packing.

STRINDBERG

A Biography

Michael Meyer

This outstanding biography of Strindberg reveals previously unknown details about his three tempestuous marriages, his dabblings in the occult, his recurrent bouts with madness, and his friendships with Gauguin, Munch and Delius, that were the touchstones of his tormented life.

'This will remain the standard life in English for many years.' *Spectator*

'Meyer assembles all the evidence brilliantly in his monumental new life of the Swedish dramatist.' *Sunday Times*

Oxford Lives

THOMAS HARDY

A Biography

Michael Millgate

'the standard biography, indispensable to all who covet the particulars of Hardy's life' *Times Higher Education Supplement*

'a superb work of scholarship' *Listener*

Oxford Lives

T. S. ELIOT

A Study in Character and Style

Ronald Bush

In this major study Ronald Bush explores the complex relationship between the life and work of T. S. Eliot, and argues that
Eliot's character was torn by the same conflict that charged
his greatest poetry: an almost unbearable tension between
romantic yearning and intellectual detachment. Skilfully com-
bining biography and literary analysis, Bush examines Eliot's
development from 'Prufrock' and *The Waste Land* to *Four
Quartets*, and demonstrates how Eliot's struggle for personal
and artistic honesty set a standard for twentieth-century writing.

'To read [this] book is to admire it—for its commitment,
personal and impersonal in the right ways; for its range of
materials adduced and of consideration prompted; and for its
combination of profound respect for Eliot with dedication to
strong discriminations and unflinching admissions . . . unremit-
tingly alive with and to argument.' *New York Times*

MALCOLM LOWRY

A Biography

Douglas Day

The extraordinary novel *Under the Volcano* is regarded by
many as one of the half-dozen literary masterpieces of our
century. Until this biography was published little was known
of its author.

A man who wrote about what he knew, Lowry's chaotic
life gave him experience of the personal hells he created in his
novels. Alternately hilarious and heartbreaking, Douglas Day's
biography tells of the alcoholism that shadowed Lowry's adult
life, his wanderings through Europe and America, his two
tempestuous marriages, and his constant struggle to write. With
a wealth of anecdotes—many of them Lowry's own witty
embroideries of his adventures—Day paints a revealing portrait
of this brilliant, clumsy, shy, prodigal, and outrageous genius.

'a brilliant, sympathetic, necessarily sad book, Lowry's first
biography and a milestone' *The Times*

ELIZABETH GASKELL

Winifred Gérin

Winifred Gérin was the first biographer to make full use of the mass of material that became available with the publication of Elizabeth Gaskell's *Letters* in 1966. She reveals her as an admirable mother to her four daughters, a graceful and accomplished hostess, a dedicated social worker, a great traveller, and a delightful correspondent with a wide range of friends among the great political and literary figures of her day. The book won the Whitbread Literary Award in 1976.

'This biography of an enchanting woman who produced three wholly different literary masterpieces gives one all the available facts, interpreted with sympathy and intelligence' *Daily Telegraph*

EMILY BRONTË
A Biography
Winifred Gérin

Emily was perhaps the least accessible of the Brontë sisters, and Winifred Gérin goes a long way towards explaining her personality, without becoming so dazzled by her strangeness that she does not also see her as human. She gives us a sharp impression of the sensitive Emily, tracing her development from unhappy schooldays, her love of the moors, the writing of *Gondal*, *Wuthering Heights*, the French essays, and her poems, to her death.

'a biographical landmark' *Observer*

'one of the monuments scholarly, literary, intuitive, of our time' *Financial Times*

MORE LETTERS OF OSCAR WILDE

Edited by Rupert Hart-Davis

Sir Rupert Hart-Davis's edition of *The Letters of Oscar Wilde* received great acclaim when it was first published a quarter of a century ago. Since then, many new letters have come to light. Full of splendid Wildeisms, they are now presented for the first time in paperback.

'Almost every page contains something amusing or picturesque.'
John Gross, *Observer*

Oxford Letters

JONATHAN SWIFT

A Hypocrite Reversed

David Nokes

Winner of the James Tait Black Memorial Prize for Biography. Dr Nokes presents a gripping and authoritative portrait of Swift in his multifarious roles as satirist, politician, churchman, and friend. He puts into perspective the legends of madness, and the mysteries surrounding Swift's romantic attachments to Stella and Vanessa, that have so often distorted our picture of the writer.

'should remain the standard one-volume life for years to come'
New York Times

Oxford Lives

JOURNALS OF DOROTHY WORDSWORTH

Edited by Mary Moorman

The cherished companion of two great poets, William Wordsworth and Samuel Taylor Coleridge, Dorothy Wordsworth is herself a poet in prose. Her *Journals* combine an intense and minute observation of nature with a genuine poetic imagination.

Oxford Letters and Memoirs

THE DIARY OF A COUNTRY PARSON, 1758–1802

James Woodforde

Edited by John Beresford

James Woodforde was parson at Weston Longeville, Norfolk, from 1774 till his death in 1803. His life was obscure and tranquil, his character uncomplicated; he loved his country, sport, good food, and established institutions, and was warm-hearted and generous. His diary covers nearly every single day in his life from 1758 to 1802. What makes it a classic as well as a remarkable document of social history is Parson Wood-forde's rare ability to bring vividly to life the rural England of two centuries ago.

'compulsive reading' *The Times*

LETTERS OF JOHN KEATS

Edited by Robert Gittings

Written in a fraction over four years, 1816 to 1820, the large body of Keats's letters forms the most complete portrait we have of any English poet. With extraordinary candour and self-knowledge Keats gives us his experience of almost everything that can happen to a young man between the ages of twenty-one and twenty-five; an all but day-to-day account of the working processes of a poet; and finally, as Robert Gittings says, 'some of the most profound comments on art, philosophy, and the human condition that any single person has produced.'

Robert Gittings has selected 170 letters, each elucidated by explanatory notes. He has also provided a Preface, and Introduction, and an Appendix.

LEAVES OF THE TULIP TREE:

Autobiography

Juliette Huxley

It was as a governess at Garsington, Lady Ottoline Morrell's mansion outside Oxford, that Juliette Huxley met the glittering Bloomsbury set, and among them her future husband Julian Huxley. She recalls the excitement and occasional chaotic moments of their courtship, and their later life together in London. She also describes with affectionate humour friendships with D. H. Lawrence and Frieda von Richthofen, Aldous and Maria Huxley, and H. G. Wells.

'This is the story of a real-life Jane Eyre, her romantic courtship and stormy marriage to a brilliant masterful and ruthless Mr Rochester.' *Observer*

'Against a background of two World Wars and enormous social change, Juliette Huxley's autobiography has a fascinating and at times sad immediacy.' *Times Educational Supplement*

Oxford Letters and Memoirs

THE LIFE OF KATHERINE MANSFIELD

Antony Alpers

Until recently it has not been possible to deal freely and frankly with all the events of Katherine Mansfield's life. Conventional mores, respect for the privacy of her lovers, family, and friends, and the lack of some crucial material, have all prevented it. Little was known, for example, of her disastrous one-day marriage, her elopement with her childhood friend, Garnett Trowell, and her subsequent affair with Ida Baker. Now, drawing on newly opened manuscript collections, private papers, and personal contacts to which he has had exclusive access, Antony Alpers has been able to expand his 1953 biography in a new, award-winning interpretation of this volatile and vulnerable genius.

'This is in the way of being a definitive biography, and as such utterly engrossing, simply because Katherine Mansfield herself is always engrossing.' Kay Dick, *The Times*.

FANNY BURNEY

Selected Letters and Journals

Edited by Joyce Hemlow

Novelist Fanny Burney's life was notably colourful and adventurous; happily it was also one which she recorded in detail in journals and numerous letters which show her to be an acute and frequent humorous observer of men and manners. Presented chronologically, this selection forms a continuous narrative of a remarkable life.

'enthralling' Malcolm Muggeridge

VIRGINIA WOOLF

A Writer's Life

Lyndall Gordon

Winner of the 1985 James Tait Black Memorial Prize for biography.

A new perspective on Virginia Woolf is opened up by this biography, which traces the private life that ran parallel with but distinct from the well-known facts of her public career.

'Lyndall Gordon must be one of the most accomplished literary biographers of this generation . . . outstanding and stimulating . . . [an] excellent treatment of the woman and her art.' *British Book News*

'At last the most filigree of artists is given the substance that several decades of anecdotage and gossip have trivialised.' *Punch*

'a masterpiece of the kind of intuitive biography in which Virginia Woolf herself believed' *Times Higher Education Supplement*

EDWARD THOMAS

A Portrait

R. George Thomas

Some years before her death, Edward Thomas's widow gave George Thomas open access to her husband's correspondence—some eighteen hundred letters rich in significance and quality. It is these letters that lie at the heart of this superb biography, which reveals so much about Thomas both as a writer and as a loving husband and father.

'an absorbing book [which] provides an indispensable aid for any future study of the poet and his work' *Guardian*

'takes its place as the standard work' *Times Literary Supplement*

Oxford Lives

GISSING

A Life in Books

John Halperin

Writers' lives are rarely as interesting as their books. The life of George Gissing is an exception. Expelled from college at the age of nineteen for stealing money in order to support his mistress, an alcoholic prostitute, Gissing went to America, where he almost starved to death in 1876, returning to England to lead a life as fascinating in its tragic grandeur as any of his novels. In this absorbing biography, John Halperin constructs a portrait of a man entrenched in his time, solidly Victorian, yet a precursor of much that was to preoccupy the twentieth century.

'from now on this is obviously the book to which anyone interested in Gissing's life ought to turn first' *Observer*

ALONG WITH YOUTH

Hemingway, The Early Years

Peter Griffin

Foreword by Jack Hemingway

Peter Griffin has drawn upon much previously unpublished material—including numerous letters and five early short stories—to trace the formative years of one of America's most celebrated writers. His compelling biography is the first part of a three-volume life which promises to become the definitive Hemingway biography for this generation.

'This book has shown me insights into my own father's character and behaviour I would not have thought possible.'
Jack Hemingway

'brings to sparkling life the Hemingway legend' *Financial Times*

'the first critical biography to appear for sixteen years . . . abounds in fresh material . . . highly readable and well-researched' *Irish Times*

'surpasses all previous work on the subject . . . adds a great wealth of detail' *Scotsman*

M. R. JAMES
An Informal Portrait
Michael Cox

To many readers M. R. James is best known as a former Provost of both Eton and King's College, Cambridge, who was also the author of 'arguably the finest ghost stories in the English language'. For scholars his name is associated with outstanding work in the fields of biblical scholarship, medieval studies, bibliography, and paleography. Michael Cox has drawn on previously unpublished sources to present a sympathetic portrait of this erudite, humorous, and genuinely lovable man.

'It says much for Mr Cox that his biography of this . . . figure, as insubstantial as many of his spectres, holds the attention throughout.' Bernard Levin

JAMES JOYCE
Richard Ellmann

Winner of the James Tait Black and the Duff Cooper Memorial Prizes

Professor Ellmann has thoroughly revised and expanded his classic biography to incorporate the considerable amount of new information tht has come to light in the twenty-two years since it was first published. The new material deals with most aspects of Joyce's life: his literary aims, a failed love affair, domestic problems, and his political views.

'The greatest literary biography of the century.' Anthony Burgess

'Richard Ellmann's superb biography . . . [is] a great feat of twentieth-century literary scholarship.' Christopher Ricks

'A superlatively good biography of Joyce.' Frank Kermode, *Spectator*